Strategic Performance Management

Effective performance management is core to successful organizations. The new edition continues to look at performance management as an interdisciplinary field of study and practice and draws upon a wide set of business disciplines, including strategic management, organizational behaviour, organizational theory, and management accounting.

The book provides a contemporary examination of theories, issues, and practices related to performance management with an original performance management framework, grounded in concrete organizational phenomena, therefore making it more accessible and meaningful to practitioners, scholars, and students. The updated edition also examines organizations' evolving use of digital business transformation and the effect on performance management design.

With updated cases, the latest edition will help readers to gain insights into the fields of strategic management, organizational behaviour, organizational theory, and management accounting and how they contribute to the study and practice of performance management.

Ralph W. Adler is Professor of Accounting at the University of Otago, New Zealand. He has taught graduate and undergraduate students in the USA and New Zealand for more than 35 years. Ralph is the Director of Otago's Centre for Organisational Performance Measurement and Management and serves as the Chairman of the Performance Measurement Association of Australasia. He qualified as a Certified Public Accountant (USA) in 1984 and was made a Fellow Chartered Accountant of Chartered Accountants Australia and New Zealand in 2016. Ralph is a past holder of the Coopers and Lybrand Peter Barr Fellowship and the American Chamber of Commerce Business Education Fellowship. He is a graduate of Colgate University, NY (BA), Duke University, NC (MBA), and State University of New York Albany (PhD).

"An important aspect of corporate culture is a strong performance culture that recognises and rewards the right behaviour beyond achieving short-term financial goals. This must be underpinned by an effective performance measurement system. The focus on ESG and digitalisation of businesses also challenge the performance management systems of many companies. The new edition of Ralph W. Adler's book provides a useful framework for approaching the design of a performance measurement system and is a timely reminder of the importance of an effective performance measurement system for a high-performing and ethical organisation."

Mak Yuen Teen, *PhD, FCPA (Aus),*
Professor (Practice) of Accounting, National University of Singapore

"I love when a book not only contains all the relevant information but is written in a way that can be understood by many, not just elite academics. This is one such book. From what I have read, I would recommend this book for those studying, teaching, or working in the area of management accounting – with an emphasis on performance management. By critiquing and comparing respective early frameworks and providing a clear history of performance management, Adler has cleverly derived a new and original performance management framework. This conceptual model then informs the remainder of the new edition with the addition of ethical behaviours and digital business transformation. Providing detailed knowledge of prior research is essential to informing these new and improved ways of organizational structure and ensuring the capture of 21st-century innovations."

Robyn Pilcher, *PhD (USyd), MCom, BBus, FCPA, FIPA, CMA,*
Adjunct Associate Professor, Curtin University, Australia

"This textbook does an excellent job of condensing and presenting in a manner understandable to students the multifarious field of performance management (management control). The framework developed and used throughout the textbook captures the various elements of performance management in a manner that can be readily applied in practice."

Ralph Kober, *Associate Professor of Accounting, Monash University, Australia*

Strategic Performance Management

Accounting for Organizational Control

Second Edition

Ralph W. Adler

Routledge
Taylor & Francis Group

LONDON AND NEW YORK

Cover image: © Getty Images

Second edition published 2023
by Routledge
4 Park Square, Milton Park, Abingdon, Oxon, OX14 4RN

and by Routledge
605 Third Avenue, New York, NY 10158

Routledge is an imprint of the Taylor & Francis Group, an informa business

© 2023 Ralph W. Adler

The right of Ralph W. Adler to be identified as author of this work has been asserted in accordance with sections 77 and 78 of the Copyright, Designs and Patents Act 1988.

First edition published by Routledge 2018

British Library Cataloguing-in-Publication Data
A catalogue record for this book is available from the British Library

Library of Congress Cataloging-in-Publication Data
Names: Adler, Ralph William, author.
Title: Strategic performance management: accounting for
organizational control / Ralph W. Adler.
Description: 2nd edition. | Abingdon, Oxon; New York, NY: Routledge, 2023. |
Includes bibliographical references and index. |
Identifiers: LCCN 2022025546 (print) | LCCN 2022025547 (ebook) |
ISBN 9781032211893 (hardback) | ISBN 9781032211886 (paperback) |
ISBN 9781003267195 (ebook) | ISBN 9781032383163 (ebook other)
Subjects: LCSH: Organizational effectiveness. | Performance. | Organizational
behavior. | Strategic planning. | Managerial accounting. | Management audit.
Classification: LCC HD58.9 .A35 2023 (print) |
LCC HD58.9 (ebook) | DDC 658.4—dc23/eng/20220601
LC record available at https://lccn.loc.gov/2022025546
LC ebook record available at https://lccn.loc.gov/2022025547

ISBN: 9781032211893 (hbk)
ISBN: 9781032211886 (pbk)
ISBN: 9781003267195 (ebk)
ISBN: 9781032383163 (eBook+)

DOI: 10.4324/9781003267195

Typeset in Bembo Std
by codeMantra

Access the Support Material: www.routledge.com/9781032211886

For my father, John, and in loving memory of my mother Anita and son Peter.

Contents

Figures

Tables

Preface

This book is the culmination of over 30 years of researching and teaching about performance management. In writing the book, my intention is to offer insights into the successful practice and study of performance management.

Senior management is invested with the responsibility of ensuring their respective organizations' effective practice of performance management, a responsibility that is one of senior management's most, if not the most, important challenges. As this book reveals, performance management comprises an interdisciplinary field of study and practice that draws upon a broad array of business disciplines, including strategic management, organizational behaviour, organizational theory, and management accounting.

The book is easy to distinguish from other books on performance management. First, and unlike all other books, the discussion of performance management is conducted using a genuinely interdisciplinary approach. Second, the book has been designed to be every bit as accessible and meaningful to practitioners as it is for students and scholars of performance management. Third, the book contributes to bridging the divides between the research, practice, and study of performance management. The divide between research and practice is the most often mentioned one (Bromwich and Scapens, 2016; Chalmers and Wright, 2011; Marshall et al., 2010; McCarthy, 2012; Parker et al., 2011). Readers will quickly see that this book's pages liberally cite evidence from scholarly journals, practitioner journals, and company/industry publications, thereby helping to address the research-practice gap. It will be further recognized that the book's interweaving of the scholarly and practitioner literatures not only helps to reduce the gulf between the theory and practice of performance management but also helps to address what Burke and Rau (2010) and Burke-Smalley et al. (2017) see as the divides existing between research and education and practice and education. The very fact that the book's target audience consists of students, practitioners, and scholars wanting to develop their knowledge of performance management means the book is naturally serving an educational need. As such, the book's dual theory and practice approach further contribute to bridging the practice-education and research-education divides.

Writing a book on performance management that synthesizes research and practice from the fields of strategic management, organizational behaviour, organizational theory, and management accounting poses significant challenges. As the book's author, my background is uniquely suited to the task. I possess an undergraduate degree in psychology. My MBA included a concentration in accounting. And my PhD was in organizational studies, a course of study that itself featured multidisciplinary, if not always interdisciplinary, teaching and learnings in psychology, management, and sociology. I have also worked in industry for a number of years, where I had first-hand experience in performance management practice, and was the managing and founding partner of a consulting firm that specialized in issues of performance management.

In sum, I have devoted a large proportion of my working life to studying, researching, and teaching performance management theory and practice. This book represents my latest attempt to advance the field, while at the same time offering practitioners useful and directly applicable insights and advice into their performance management practices.

Ralph W. Adler

Dunedin, New Zealand

March 2022

REFERENCES

Bromwich, M., and Scapens, R. W. (2016) Management accounting research: 25 years on. *Management Accounting Research*, Vol. 31, pp. 1–9.

Burke, L. A., and Rau, B. (2010) The research-teaching gap in management. *Academy of Management Learning & Education*, Vol. 9, No. 1, pp. 132–143.

Burke-Smalley, L. A., Rau, B. L., Neely, A. R., and Evans, W. R. (2017) Factors perpetuating the research-teaching gap in management: a review and propositions. *The International Journal of Management Education*, Vol. 15, No. 3, pp. 501–512.

Chalmers, K., and Wright, S. (2011) Bridging accounting research and practice: a value adding endeavour. In E. Evans, R. Burritt, and J. Guthrie (Eds.), *Bridging the Gap between Academic Accounting Research and Professional Practice*, 1st ed., pp. 59–68.

McCarthy, W. E. (2012) Accounting craftspeople versus accounting seers: exploring the relevance and innovation gaps in academic accounting research. *Accounting Horizons*, Vol. 26, No. 4, pp. 833–843.

Marshall, P. D., Dombrowski, R. F., Garner, R. M., and Smith, K. J. (2010) The accounting education gap. *The CPA Journal*, Vol. 80, No. 6, pp. 6–10.

Parker, L. D., Guthrie, J., and Linacre, S. (2011) The relationship between academic accounting research and professional practice. *Accounting, Auditing & Accountability Journal*, Vol. 24, No. 1, pp. 5–14.

CHAPTER 1

Performance management

An introduction

CHAPTER OBJECTIVES

- Show how the study and practice of performance management is an interdisciplinary as opposed to a multidisciplinary endeavour.
- Identify and discuss the four disciplines that contribute to the study of performance management.
- Describe the plan of the book.

PERFORMANCE MANAGEMENT AS AN INTERDISCIPLINARY FIELD OF STUDY AND PRACTICE

Performance management is often considered to be, or certainly such is the case for accountants, a subfield of management accounting. Although it is certainly the case that the major advancements in the field of performance management have been driven by management accountants, it is fairer and more accurate to view performance management as an interdisciplinary field of study involving the disciplines of strategic management, organizational behaviour, organizational theory, and management accounting. Performance management, which is broadly about how organizations design their organizational structures, systems, and cultures to encourage employees' implementation of their respective organizations' strategies, is informed and enriched by practitioners and scholars working across these four broad disciplines. Contributions to this interdisciplinary field of study have been ongoing for the past 50-plus years.

The description of performance management as an interdisciplinary science should not be confused with the word multidisciplinary. The latter term refers to studying a particular topic from various fields of speciality, while all the time remaining inside one's speciality. In other words, an organizational behaviourist would study performance management with a purely

DOI: 10.4324/9781003267195-1

Review Question 1.1: What four business disciplines contribute to the study and practice of performance management?

Answer: Please see the Answer section starting on page 283

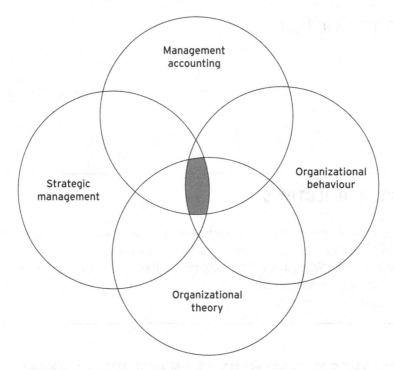

FIGURE 1.1 Multidisciplinary and interdisciplinary perspectives.

Review Question 1.2: What is the difference between multidisciplinary and interdisciplinary approaches?

Answer: Please see the Answer section starting on page 283

organizational behaviour lens. This researcher or practitioner would not employ other lenses (e.g., organizational theory, management accounting, or strategic management), and most certainly would not adopt a unified lens that draws together the contributing business disciplines. In contrast, interdisciplinary research and practice require scholars and practitioners to situate themselves at the intersection of the multiple contributing disciplines and employ a single, integrated lens.

Figure 1.1 illustrates the multidisciplinary and interdisciplinary nature of performance management. Each of the diagram's four circles represents a disciplinary perspective; and the intersection of the four circles, which appears as the shaded region, represents performance management's interdisciplinary perspective.

PERFORMANCE MANAGEMENT'S FOUR CONTRIBUTING ACADEMIC DISCIPLINES

Let's look at how each of the four separate disciplines contributes to practitioners' and managers' uses of performance management. Management accounting is a field of study and practice that involves the collection, analysis, and communication of information for internal decision-making. The ultimate aim of management accounting is to produce better decision-making and, in the process, generate better organizational performance. As performance management practitioners and scholars, our particular interest in management accounting lies in its ability to direct employee attention. Management accounting's construction of budgets is a classic example. Budgets serve multiple purposes that are relevant from a performance management perspective. First, they serve to allocate resources. This allocation informs employees of the strategic priorities of the company. Organizations that allocate substantial parts of their budgets to research and development initiatives are communicating something very different from organizations that allocate small sums to their research and development efforts. Budgets can also reinforce organizational lines of authority and responsibility. Managers are typically assigned the task of overseeing a particular part of the organization. The budget communicates what this part is (including the employees and other assets that come under a manager's control) and provides a general outline of what is expected (by virtue of the line items that constitute the budget). Furthermore, budgets serve to influence what employees do, and this influence can be further supported by attaching rewards and/or penalties to employee achievements. In particular, the targets management accountants help set when formulating budgets are highly likely to impact employee behaviour.

Strategic management comprises the formulation, implementation, and control of the unique set of activities an organization will undertake to achieve its major goals and initiatives. An organization's senior managers, who are invariably tasked with this responsibility, will systematically seek to grow and leverage their respective organization's core competencies to achieve a sustainable competitive advantage. While strategy formulation is not explicitly a part of performance management, the process of strategy implementation certainly is. Accordingly, strategic management is a central part of performance management.

Organizational behaviour (OB) involves the study of how people, as individuals and as part of a larger group, structure and perform their work. OB is essentially social psychology applied to work settings. It examines human behaviour in a work environment and assesses how task structure, motivation, leadership, and communication affect organizational performance. OB practitioners and scholars aim to understand and predict worker behaviour in their similar quests to create more efficient and effective organizations.

Organizational theory (OT) comprises the study of entire organizational systems, as well as the groups of people and subparts that constitute these organizations. It is particularly concerned with how to best design and structure organizations. Part of the OT process involves matching the organization's design and structure with key internal and external factors. The former includes influential managers and technocrats within an organization, and the latter includes competitors, regulators, and lobbyists. OT practitioners and scholars are interested in ensuring appropriate organizational and environmental alignment.

> *Review Question 1.3:* What are some examples of the insights each of the four business disciplines provides to the study and practice of performance management?
> *Answer:* Please see the Answer section starting on page 283

As the preceding paragraphs reveal, strategy formulation, and in particular the design of winning strategies, is a necessary part of an organization's attainment of superior performance. However, on its own, strategy formulation is insufficient. As Merchant and Van der Stede (2007:8) note, "It is people in the organisation who make things happen." Senior managers' role must therefore include ensuring its people are doing what is needed, which is implementing the organization's strategy. In fact, in its simplest and most basic form, this senior manager mandate constitutes the definition of performance management.

Parallels can be drawn between an organization's formulation and implementation of its strategy and a sports team's development and implementation of a game plan. In particular, no matter how masterful a sports team's game plan may be, it will have no effect and no relevance unless the players execute the plan. In a similar fashion, an organization's strategy may look good on paper, but unless and until it is implemented it will be of no help or consequence. This idea of irrelevance is well captured by the Japanese proverb: "Strategy without action is a daydream."

Ensuring the organization's strategy is being implemented, and, some practitioners and scholars would further add, the strategy being amended as the situation may warrant is the essence of performance management. How an organization goes about ensuring that employees implement its strategy is the focus of this book. This task, which is the responsibility of senior management, is highly challenging but eminently attainable. As this book reveals, senior managers need to possess a clear understanding of their employees' motivation if they, the senior managers, are to be successful practitioners of performance management.

The motivation of employees requires more than simply energizing them. It also requires directing employee energy. In fact, examples where organizational employees were energized but not effectively directed abound. As an example, a 2017 UK news story reported that train drivers in Great Britain were driving through stations they were scheduled to stop at. It was found that this behaviour was the result of how Great Britain's regulator measured on-time train arrival. Knowing that the regulator's measure was based on a comparison of the time a train arrived at its final destination against its scheduled arrival time, train drivers who found themselves behind schedule would skip train stations to ensure they reached their final station as scheduled. Such a decision may have enabled the driver and its train to arrive on-time at its destination, but it meant commuters' schedules at the bypassed stations were completely upended.

Another example of misdirecting employee energy involves the UK's Department for Social Development (DSW). A manager responsible for the various offices' operations became highly concerned by one of the office's persistently long lines that regularly stretched out of the office's front door and around the block. The manager instructed the employees of this office to address the problem. The employees responded by moving the reception area deeper inside the building and erected extensive client queuing barriers to organize the clients into a maze of many channels. While the employees were certainly energized into action, the solutions

> *Review Question 1.4:* Why must senior managers be capable of both energizing and directing employee behaviour?
>
> *Answer:* Please see the Answer section starting on page 283

they enacted essentially changed nothing about the situation. The amount of time clients spent standing in line did not change, for the employees failed to address the underlying reasons for the long lines.

As one final story of misdirected employee energy, when Carly Fiorina was CEO of Hewlett-Packard, she instituted an employee bonus system that offered $100 for any novel idea that a fellow employee signed off on. This bonus system coincided with the early 2000s when Hewlett-Packard was moving away from building business software and towards building customer hardware. Hewlett-Packard's new strategy led to a lot of bored software engineers with little to do. According to *Wall Street Journal* reporter Robert McMillan,

> One former HP employee, Peter Hagelund, told the [*Wall Street*] *Journal* that his division spent months in 2002 doing nothing but signing off on hundreds of one another's wacky ideas – including a design for chopsticks that also dispense soy sauce. Those employees ended up pooling their $100 earnings and splitting them evenly. Hagelund said that with his proceeds, he was able to buy a red Jeep Liberty.
>
> (Weinberger, 2015)

The task of energizing employee enthusiasm draws on principles of leadership. Meanwhile, the task of directing employees' energy so that it is congruent with the organization's ambitions relies on developing organizational structures, systems, and cultures that encourage desirable employee behaviours and discourage undesirable ones. The remainder of the book examines the performance management practices organizational managers draw upon to ensure high levels of employee motivation, loyalty, and commitment to implementing the organization's strategy.

PLAN OF THE BOOK

The book is divided into four main parts. The first part, "Performance management beginnings," consisting of three chapters, explores the history and beginnings of performance management. Chapter 2 defines performance management and discusses how performance management is practised, including who is involved and their various roles and responsibilities. Chapter 3 discusses the rise of performance management, and in particular the influential historical milestones that enabled its emergence. This chapter also introduces a novel conceptual model that portrays the key elements of performance management and serves as a roadmap for the book's subsequent chapters. Chapter 4 discusses the five main theories that underpin the study of performance management: contingency theory, agency theory, goal-setting theory, resource-based theory, and stakeholder theory. These theories derive from the academic disciplines of organizational sociology, organizational psychology, economics, and organizational strategy.

Part II, "Organizational strategy," presents and discusses organizational strategy. Since the purpose of performance management is to ensure employees are implementing their respective organizations' strategies, an understanding of the composition and operation of organizational strategy is essential to the study of performance management. Chapter 5 discusses how organizations determine their purposes and, in the process, develop enduring goals and objectives that are meant to motivate and guide employee behaviour. This chapter is followed by a new Chapter 6, which discusses the relationship between business ethics and performance management. After putting forward the argument that strategy has an implicit long-term orientation, the chapter proceeds to show that unethical behaviour will always be antithetical to strategy achievement. The next two chapters discuss the different paths organizations can follow when pursuing their respective goals and objectives. Chapter 7 defines organizational strategy and discusses its importance to an organization's success. It then proceeds to identify two types of organizational strategy: corporate-level and business-unit-level. Chapter 8 examines the concept of business-unit-level strategy, or what is commonly referred to as competitive strategy. It includes a discussion and critique of the competitive strategy taxonomies of Miles and Snow, Porter, Cooper, and Kim and Mauborgne. The chapter concludes by discussing some basic associations between competitive strategy and performance management system design. Chapter 9, the book's second new chapter, discusses the connections between organizations' evolving use of digital business transformation (DBT), competitive strategy, and the effect on performance management design and practice.

Part III, "Levers of employee influence," discusses the three main levers of performance management: organizational structure; organizational systems, processes, and procedures; and organizational culture. Chapter 10 identifies the defining dimensions of organizational structure as complexity, formalization, and centralization. Following a discussion about the need for these dimensions to complement one another, the chapter proceeds to discuss the four main types of responsibility centres and how senior managers decide which one of them is best to use. Chapter 11 examines how an organization uses organizational systems, processes, and procedures to influence employees' implementation of the organization's strategy. The chapter explores organizations' use of performance measurement systems, employee incentive systems, and human resource systems to exercise employee influence. Chapter 12 covers organizational culture. The chapter identifies the six dimensions of organizational culture. It further discusses how senior managers can identify gaps between their actual and ideal organizational cultures, as well as what an organization's leaders can do to create better alignment between their organization's culture and the organizational strategy it pursues.

The final part of the book, Part IV, "Contingent factors," identifies and discusses important internal and external contingent factors that must be considered when designing performance management systems. These contingent factors must be incorporated into the construction and operation of the three main levers of performance management if the organization is to achieve good performance management fit. Chapter 13 examines internal contingent factors, while Chapter 14 considers external contingent factors.

Chapter 15 presents the book's conclusion. This chapter revisits the conceptual model of performance management introduced in Chapter 3. Drawing on the work of Ferreira and Otley (2009) and Malmi and Brown (2008), the chapter discusses the need for senior managers to view their performance management systems as holistic. In particular, the chapter champions the need to ensure that all the elements comprising an organization's performance management system work in harmony to motivate and focus employee behaviour on the implementation of the organization's strategy. The chapter concludes by offering advice on research opportunities in the field of performance management.

REFERENCES

Ferreira, A. and Otley, D. (2009) The design and use of performance management systems: an extended framework for analysis, *Management Accounting Research*, Vol. 20, No. 4, pp. 263–282.

Malmi, T. and Brown, D.A. (2008) Management control systems as a package – opportunities, challenges and research directions, *Management Accounting Research*, Vol. 19, No. 4, pp. 287–300.

Merchant, K. and Van der Stede, W.A. (2007) *Management Control Systems* (2nd ed.), Harlow, Essex: Prentice Hall, Pearson Education Limited.

Weinberger, M. (2015) HP has a soy sauce delivery system for chop sticks, *Wall Street Journal*, Retrieved from https://www.businessinsider.in/under-carly-fiorina-hp-employees-used-soy-sauce-dispensing-chopsticks-to-game-the-system/articleshow/49265304.cms on 29 November 2021.

Performance management beginnings

1

Performance management beginnings

CHAPTER 2

What is performance management?

CHAPTER OBJECTIVES

- Define performance management.
- Discuss how performance management is practised, including who is involved and their various roles and responsibilities.

INTRODUCTION

This chapter discusses the origins of the term "performance management" and David Otley's adoption of this term from the field of applied psychology. The chapter describes how the management accounting discipline used to refer to this field of study as "management control." The chapter traces performance management's roots back to these earlier management control days to help the reader appreciate the concept's modern-day definition and application. Following the specification of the book's definition of performance management, a discussion of the various parties involved in the implementation and practice of performance management is provided.

PERFORMANCE MANAGEMENT'S ORIGINS

The first use of the term performance management can be traced to Dr Aubrey Daniels. Dr Daniels used performance management to refer to an organization's need for ensuring its goals are being consistently achieved in an effective and efficient manner. This organizational imperative, as will be discussed more fully below, has been traditionally viewed, since the mid-1950s, as the central task and responsibility of practitioners and scholars who design, operate, and study management control systems.

While Dr Daniels and his co-author Theodore Rosen (1983) were the first to make a formal reference to the term performance management, the term's initial use was largely confined to applied psychology and management journals. It was only in 1999 that David Otley brought

DOI: 10.4324/9781003267195-3

the term into the accounting literature with the publication of his *Management Accounting Research* article. Prior to this, the term "management control" was exclusively used.

David Otley, a professor at the University of Lancaster (UK), recounted in a personal conversation his motivation for introducing the term performance management into the accounting literature. He described how his student enrolments for a Master of Business Administration course he taught in the 1990s had been falling for a number of years. He was convinced that the title of the course – Management Control – was discouraging student enrolment. As he tells the story, the word "control" had become unfashionable. All around the world, and especially in Eastern Europe, control economies were in a state of decline and were commonly viewed as failed experiments in planned economies by the majority of the world's scholars and policymakers (Biersteker, 1990). The fall of the Berlin Wall and the disintegration of the Union of Soviet Socialist Republics were commonly pointed to as proof that control economies are not simply inefficient, but they are destined to fail.

Professor Otley, showing that he was not only a very accomplished management accounting scholar but an astute marketer as well, decided that a rebranding of the course title could lift enrolments. Accordingly, he decided to rename his course "performance management." This name change alone, for there were no changes in the course's content, produced a dramatic increase in student enrolment. The outcome proved to be a happy ending for both Professor Otley and his students, the latter of whom would have otherwise missed out on the opportunity to study this all-important management topic.

Although Professor Otley and his students attached a very positive perception to the term performance management, it is worth noting that the term does not resonate the same way for everyone. In New Zealand, for example, the term has a very negative meaning. It is a commonly used term by the human resources function to indicate that an employee is failing to meet an organization's required level or standard of performance and needs to be closely monitored. Should an organization deem the employee's lack of performance to be serious enough, the organization would begin to performance manage the employee. This process involves the organization offering the employee assistance and support to improve his/her performance, and usually involves the implementation of a performance improvement plan. Formal disciplinary action may also occur, such as writing the employee formal letters of warning and removing certain employee privileges and freedoms. If the employee's performance returns to a satisfactory level, then the employee will retain his/her job. If not, then further and more frequent monitoring will occur until the employee either demonstrates sustained job competence or is fired from the job.

In spite of instances where the term performance management conjures up anxiety and fear, the term has largely been perceived as neutral or better. As a result, and with a little bit of Professor Otley's magic, performance management successfully showcased itself as an invigorated field of study born out of its former name of management control. Accordingly, to understand the meaning of performance management, it is best to trace the concept back to its origin and start at that point.

Review Question 2.1: What is the origin of the term performance management?
Answer: Please see the Answer section starting on page 283

MANAGEMENT CONTROL

Professor Robert Anthony was the first to write about management control. He defined it as "the process of assuring that the organization does what management wants done" (1956: 268). Management control occurred as the result of the organization's design and operation of a management control system.

"Management," "control," and "system" are three relatively easy words to define and understand on their own. The combination of these three words, however, does not, at least at first glance, appear to convey Professor Anthony's idea of "assuring the organization does what management wants done." Consider, for example, the term "inventory control system." A typical definition of an inventory control system would comprise something like: a set of methods, procedures, and routines that a company uses to ensure adequate stocks of raw materials, work-in-process, and finished goods inventories are on hand for production and sales purposes at any given point in time. In essence, a very succinct definition, notwithstanding the limitations of its reliance on the very words it is attempting to define, can be achieved by reversing the order of the words appearing in the term "inventory control system" to produce: a system that controls inventory.

If an inventory control system is meant to control inventories, then one might logically assume that a management control system is meant to control management. But such a definition would appear to be at odds with Professor Anthony's definition, for he describes management control as a tool that is wielded by management as opposed to a tool that is imposed on management. To understand what appears to be a significant logical disconnection between the organizational process Professor Anthony was describing and the term that was originally chosen to convey this meaning, it is necessary to read the fuller set of Professor Anthony's work. Such a reading will show that he did in fact see management control as a process for controlling management. However, while we may associate the word "management" with an organization's senior-level decision-makers, Professor Anthony was using the word to refer to an organization's middle-level managers. In other words, management control systems were used as a tool by senior executives to ensure that middle-level managers were working efficiently and effectively in accomplishing the organization's goals and objectives, as determined by its senior managers. Accordingly, the term management control system was very much in harmony with the set of processes and outcomes Professor Anthony was trying to convey. It is perhaps unfortunate that the word "management," as opposed to the words "middle-level management," was used.

To appreciate more fully Professor Anthony's choice of management-level focus, it is important to understand the nature of the organizational structures that predominated at the time. In the mid-1950s, when the field of management control was being founded, bureaucracies and their hierarchal structures prevailed. In both the banking and manufacturing industries, with these two industries easily comprising the majority of any major stock exchange's market capitalization at the time, middle-level managers abounded. Alfred Sloan, the then CEO at General Motors (which at this time was the world's largest company), was a main catalyst behind the drive to professionalize managers. General Motors, and the many other companies that tried to emulate the success of General Motors by adopting its various management philosophies, contributed to the extensive growth of middle-level management. With so many middle-level managers working in the organizations of the 1950s and 1960s, it is not surprising that Professor Anthony, along with such other eminent scholars as Professors Anthony Hopwood (1974), David Otley (1983), Kenneth Merchant (1985), and William Ouchi (1979), chose to research and write about the critical need to ensure these managers are efficiently and effectively working to achieve their organizations' goals and objectives.

Today's organizations are quite different from those operating in the 1950s, or even those operating in the 1960s, 1970s, and much of the 1980s. Although hierarchies were a salient and ubiquitous feature of these organizations, a wave of new management practices calling for flatter organizational structures were introduced in the mid-1980s. The move away from tall organizational structures to flatter ones was largely a result of the total quality management (TQM) movement. TQM preached the importance of full employee responsibility. Instead of waiting for orders to come from line managers (who comprised the ranks of middle-level managers), TQM called on all employees, including and especially front-line workers, to take charge of process improvement, quality improvement, and even product innovation. The idea behind empowering employees was to make organizations more responsive to both their operational and strategic environments.

Toyota's production control system, which other companies from around the world began to copy in the mid- to late 1980s under the title just-in-time (JIT) manufacturing, had a further, highly influential impact on organizational designs and the prevalence of middle-level managers. JIT promotes continuous improvement through its constant attempts to reduce inventories. Its ideal goal of batch and inventory sizes of one unit is intended to energize people and reorient the way they think about how products are made and services rendered. Similar to TQM, employee empowerment is a central platform of JIT. In particular, employees at all levels of the organization, and, once again, especially those on the shop floor, are meant to take responsibility for how the work is ordered and processed.

With the advent of TQM and JIT came self-managing teams, autonomous work groups, and self-organizing systems. In such settings, not only is it the case that there is less need for middle-level managers, but it is actually desirable to have fewer middle-level managers. Since the intention of these work settings is to accelerate decision-making and organizational agility, it is preferable if the organizational layers between these empowered workers and senior managers are kept to a minimum. This is why Adler (2011) reports that at a major US retail bank, the bank's corporate policy was to have no more than three layers between its groups of empowered employees and the bank's president.

As a result of the delayering of organizations, and in the process the removal of many middle-level manager positions, senior management's task of "assuring the organization does what management wants done" (Anthony, 1956: 268) has come to include, and is increasingly directed at, the newly-empowered front-line workers. With their empowered status comes the responsibility to plan and manage the various organizational systems, processes, and procedures that will assist the organization's achievement of its goals and objectives. Accordingly, the idea that management control should focus on the middle-management level became less accurate, less relevant, and ultimately outdated. Professor Otley's introduction of performance management as the revised term to capture this indispensable organizational activity was therefore timely and necessary.

Review Question 2.2: How have the roles of middle-level managers changed over time and what are the reasons for this change?

Answer: Please see the Answer section starting on page 283

WORKING DEFINITION OF PERFORMANCE MANAGEMENT

Whether the term performance management should be the preferred alternative to management control is debatable. Although the former has the advantage of breaking free of specifying a particular segment of the organization, its singular reference to performance is unfortunate. As will be seen in later chapters, a major aim of performance management is to motivate and influence employee behaviour. In other words, the antecedents to performance, and in particular workers' motivation and how this motivation can be sustained at high levels, are an essential focus of performance management.

At this stage, we might do well to heed the words of Shakespeare's Juliet, when she says to Romeo:

> What's in a name? that which we call a rose
>
> By any other name would smell as sweet.
>
> (*Romeo and Juliet*, Act II. Scene II, ll. 47–48)

Just as Juliet proceeds to pronounce that Romeo's perfection would be undiminished without the name Romeo, so too might it be said that the practice of performance management would still retain its organizational importance even if another name were assigned to it. In sum, although the term performance management may be an imperfect descriptor of what the practice comprises, the term on its own should not interfere with our ability to offer recommendations for its use or study its impact.

There are instances, however, where performance management has been used in a way that only partially captures its fuller essence. For example, Melnyk *et al.* (2014: 175) state:

> The performance management system encompasses the process (or processes) of assessing the differences between actual and desired outcomes, identifying and flagging those differences that are critical (thereby warranting management intervention), understanding if and why the deficiencies have taken place, and, when necessary, introducing (and monitoring) corrective actions aimed at closing significant performance gaps.

Essentially Melnyk *et al.* are referring to performance management as if it were limited to simply performance evaluation. As later discussions in this book will make clear, performance evaluation is merely one part of performance management.

Such a definition as the one Melnyk *et al.* presents falls well short of not only what Professor Otley sought to capture, but also what Anthony (1956) was writing about when he first introduced the concept as management control. Additionally, the Melnyk *et al.* definition

---

Review Question 2.3: How does performance management compare to management control?
Answer: Please see the Answer section starting on page 283

fails to mention any of the notable ambitions Radnor and Barnes (2007: 392) associate with performance management when they write:

> A performance management system is one which provides information on the matters of importance (communication), promotes appropriate behaviour (motivation), provides a mechanism for accountability and control (control), and creates a mechanism for intervention and learning (improvement).

It is extremely unfortunate that such confusion about what comprises the performance management concept can prevail among today's scholars. Readers are advised to be vigilant for similar misconceptions they may encounter when undertaking readings beyond the present book.

In this book, the term performance management will be used to describe the field of practice and study involving senior management's attempts to ensure organizational employees are doing what they are supposed to do. Although the term performance management will supersede the term management control, the former term will encompass the history, theory, and practice of the latter term. The following working definition of performance management is adopted in this book:

> Performance management is the process by which senior managers of an organization influence employees throughout the organization to implement the organization's strategy and, when needed, the process informs the initiation of changes to the strategy.

This definition is consistent with Zimmerman's (1997, 2001) idea that control systems that focus on supporting organizational decision-making without monitoring the goal congruence and behaviour of subordinate managers, and employees more generally, are examples of decision-support or information systems, rather than performance management systems. For example, control systems that provide information on when to reorder inventory or when to undertake maintenance on plant and equipment are good illustrations of decision-support systems. Malmi and Brown (2008) suggest that these types of systems should be called management accounting or accounting information systems.

To qualify as performance management, the controls that management put in place must be capable of influencing and directing employee behaviour. Two broad types of control can be distinguished: formal controls and informal controls. Formal controls are written codes of practice or superior to subordinate spoken directives that guide and govern employee action. Typical examples of formal controls are employee handbooks, manuals of standard operating procedures, budgets, and written and spoken directives given by superiors to subordinates. Informal controls, which arise alongside formal controls via social relations and interactions (Kober *et al.*, 2003; Tucker, 2019), comprise the invisible, non-hierarchically derived set of organizational rules,

---

Review Question 2.4: Who is responsible for overseeing an organization's performance management system?

Answer: Please see the Answer section starting on page 283

prescriptions, and prohibitions that command and drive employee behaviour. These controls are shaped generically by the culture of a business (Langfield-Smith, 1997) rather than by any purposive, predetermined, or deliberate design (Tucker, 2019: 239). An organization's shared values, norms, and beliefs are some of the most potent examples of informal controls (Ahrens and Mollona, 2007; Cui *et al.*, 2016). Baraldi (1998) and Tucker and Thorne (2013) additionally include informal communications and unstructured peer group interactions as further examples of informal controls.

To appreciate the difference between management accounting or accounting information systems controls and the controls/influence that features in performance management, assume an organization has the goal of increasing automation in its production processes and it chose to allocate its plant's overhead costs to production departments based on direct labour hours. Although some scholars and practitioners might object to the chosen cost driver, arguing that it fails to honour the causal relationship between a cost's occurrence and its allocation, the use of a direct hour labour cost driver would likely aid the organization's adoption of automation and therefore it would constitute a form of performance management. In particular, the chosen cost driver would motivate departmental managers to reduce their department's number of production employees as a way to reduce the amount of costs they are allocated. To replace the lost production associated with the reduced headcount, the departmental managers would need to invest in automated production processes; and this outcome is exactly what senior managers desire. In a similar manner, if an organization establishes lower thresholds for salespeople's spending on travel and accommodation expenses before higher authority approval is required, then this new organizational policy will influence employee behaviour and would therefore also qualify as performance management.

In addition to its recognition that performance management must be related to influencing employee behaviour, this book's definition is consistent with classical definitions of performance management, such as the one proposed by Robert Anthony and John Dearden. They defined performance management as "the process by which management assures that the organization carries out its strategies effectively and efficiently" (Anthony and Dearden, 1980: 7). This earlier definition by Anthony and Dearden remains largely unchanged in the twelfth and most recent edition of their book which Anthony has co-authored with Vijay Govindarajan (2007), and is therefore referred to here as the classical performance management definition.

Classical definitions of performance management view organizational strategy as already determined and senior management's role under performance management becomes solely focused on ensuring the strategy is implemented (Kaplan and Norton, 1993, 1996). This view of performance management has been challenged by such scholars as Bourne *et al.* (2000)

Review Question 2.5: How does the concept of performance management fit into the
    role of an accountant?
Answer: Please see the Answer section starting on page 283
Review Question 2.6: What are the differences between management accounting systems,
accounting information systems, and performance management systems?
Answer: Please see the Answer section starting on page 283

> *Review Question 2.7:* How do strategy formulation, implementation, and control relate to performance management?
> *Answer:* Please see the Answer section starting on page 283

and Neely *et al.* (2000), who argue that performance management informs and challenges an organization's strategy formulation. A more recent definition of performance management, as proposed by Ferreira and Otley (2009), views the development of strategy and its plans as part of the performance management process. Accordingly, the definition used in this book, which proposes that strategy formulation, and in particular its reformulation, is informed by the performance management process, moves beyond the traditional approach of Anthony and Dearden but stops short of Ferreira and Otley's preference for subsuming strategy formulation under performance management.

Far from trying to steer a middle-of-the-road course between Anthony and Dearden's classical definition and Ferreira and Otley's more contemporary views, the working definition for this book is highly purposeful. To say that strategy is always a fixed input to the performance management process neglects the ancillary usefulness that information which is collected in the natural course of ensuring the organization is implementing its strategy can have on later conversations about changes to and tweaking of the organization's strategy. To say, however, that strategy formulation is directly under the purview of performance management makes the boundaries of performance management almost limitless. Extending its boundaries in this manner runs the risk that performance management will become a catch-all phrase for the management of everything. As Merchant and Otley (2007: 785) argue, these expansive definitions of performance management mean that "almost everything in the organisation is included as part of the overall control system." This outcome is neither helpful to scholars working in the field nor managers wishing to apply its practices.

CONCLUSION

The term performance management was first introduced into the applied psychology and management literatures in the early 1980s by Dr Aubrey Daniels and his co-author Theodore Rosen. Professor David Otley, in the late 1990s, adopted the term into the management accounting literature. While Professor Otley's actions were largely a rebranding effort, the fact is that more people are benefiting from its use than might otherwise have been the case.

This chapter lays out its working definition of performance management, defining it as "the process by which senior managers of an organization influence employees throughout the organization to implement the organization's strategy and, when needed, the process informs the initiation of changes to the strategy." This definition continues the tradition of viewing the need to influence employee behaviour as the mainstay of performance management, while additionally recognizing the importance of performance management in informing and influencing the set of interconnected, but separate, organizational processes related to strategy formulation and control.

REFERENCES

Adler, R.W. (2011) Performance management and organizational strategy: how to design systems that meet the needs of confrontation strategy firms, *The British Accounting Review*, Vol. 43, No. 4, pp. 251–263.

Anthony, R. (1956) *Management Accounting: Text and Cases*, Homewood, IL: Irwin.

Anthony, R. and Dearden, J. (1980) *Management Control Systems* (4th Edition), Homewood, IL: Irwin.

Anthony, R. and Govindarajan, V. (2007) *Management Control Systems* (12th Edition), New York: McGraw-Hill-Irwin.

Biersteker, T.J. (1990) Reducing the role of the state in the economy: a conceptual exploration of IMF and World Bank prescriptions, *International Studies Quarterly*, Vol. 34, No. 4, pp. 477–492.

Bourne, M.C.S., Mills, J.F., Wilcox, M., Neely, A.D. and Platts, K.W. (2000) Designing, implementing and updating performance measurement systems, *International Journal of Operations and Production Management*, Vol. 20, No. 7, pp. 754–771.

Cui, J., Jo, H. and Velasquez, M.G. (2016) Community religion, employees, and the social license to operate, *Journal of Business Ethics*, Vol. 136, No. 4, pp. 775–807.

Daniels, A.C. and Rosen, T. (1983) *Performance Management: Improving Quality and Productivity Through Positive Reinforcement*, Tucker, GA: Performance Management Publications.

Ferreira, A. and Otley, D. (2009) The design and use of performance management systems: an extended framework for analysis, *Management Accounting Research*, Vol. 20, No. 4, pp. 263–282.

Hopwood, A.G. (1974) *Accounting and Human Behaviour*, London: Prentice Hall.

Kaplan, R.S. and Norton, D.P. (1993) Putting the balanced scorecard to work, *Harvard Business Review*, Vol. 71, No. 5, pp. 134–147.

Kaplan, R.S. and Norton, D.P. (1996) Using the balanced scorecard as a strategy management system, *Harvard Business Review*, Vol. 74, No. 1, pp. 75–85.

Kober, R., Ng, J. and Paul, B. (2003) Change in strategy and MCS: a match over time?, *Advances in Accounting*, Vol. 20, pp. 199–232.

Langfield-Smith, K. (1997) Management control systems and strategy: a critical review, *Accounting, Organizations and Society*, Vol. 22, No. 2, pp. 207–232.

Malmi, T. and Brown, D.A. (2008) Management control systems as a package – opportunities, challenges and research directions, *Management Accounting Research*, Vol. 19, No. 4, pp. 287–300.

Melnyk, S.A., Bititci, U., Platts, K., Tobias, J. and Andersen, B. (2014) Is performance measurement and management fit for the future?, *Management Accounting Research*, Vol. 25, No. 2, pp. 173–186.

Merchant, K.A. (1985) *Control in Business Organizations*, Boston, MA: Pitman.

Merchant, K.A. and Otley, D.T. (2007) A review of the literature on control and accountability. In C.S. Chapman, A.G. Hopwood, and M.D. Shields (Eds), *Handbook of Management Accounting Research*, Vol. 2, Amsterdam: Elsevier, pp. 785–802.

Neely, A.D., Mills, J.F., Platts, K.W., Richards, A.H., Gregory, M.J., Bourne, M.C.S. and Kennerley, M.P. (2000) Performance measurement system design: developing and testing a process based approach, *International Journal of Operations and Production Management*, Vol. 20, No. 9, pp. 1119–1145.

Otley, D. (1983) Concepts of control: the contribution of cybernetics and systems theory to management control. In T. Lowe and J.L.J. Machin (Eds), *New Perspectives in Management Control*, London: Palgrave Macmillan, pp. 59–87.

Otley, D. (1999) Performance management: a framework for management control systems research, *Management Accounting Research*, Vol. 10, No. 4, pp. 363–382.

Ouchi, W.G. (1979) A conceptual framework for the design of organizational control mechanisms, *Management Science*, Vol. 25, No. 9, pp. 833–848.

Radnor, Z.J. and Barnes, D. (2007) Historical analysis of performance measurement and management in operations management, *International Journal of Productivity and Performance Management*, Vol. 56, No. 5/6, pp. 384–396.

Tucker, B. and Thorne, H. (2013) Performance on the right hand side: organizational performance as an antecedent to management control, *Qualitative Research in Accounting & Management*, Vol. 10, No. 3/4, pp. 316–346.

Tucker, B.P. (2019) Heard It through the grapevine: conceptualizing informal control through the lens of social network theory, *Journal of Management Accounting Research*, Vol. 31, No. 1, pp. 219–245.

Zimmerman, J.L. (1997) *Accounting for Decision-Making and Control* (2nd Edition), Chicago, IL: McGraw-Hill.

Zimmerman, J.L. (2001) Conjectures regarding empirical managerial accounting research, *Journal of Accounting and Economics*, Vol. 32, No. 1, pp. 411–427.

CHAPTER 3

The rise of performance management

CHAPTER OBJECTIVES

- Trace the history of the field of performance management, connecting its emergence and development with significant events occurring in allied business disciplines.
- Identify key milestones in performance management thinking.
- Compare and critique various leading scholars' attempts to develop performance management frameworks.
- Provide a conceptual model of performance management that communicates its key elements and serves as a roadmap for the book's chapters.

INTRODUCTION

This chapter traces the history of performance management and identifies key milestones in the evolution of performance management thinking. Special attention is paid to the contributions made by prominent scholars to the field of performance management and, in particular, these leading scholars' respective developments of performance management frameworks. These frameworks are compared, critiqued, and used as the basis for developing a unified performance management framework. This unified framework is subsequently used to motivate and focus on later chapters.

THE EARLY BEGINNINGS OF PERFORMANCE MANAGEMENT

Performance management describes a field of study devoted to helping managers keep pace with and, when necessary, make successful adaptations to changing external organizational environments. Performance management emerged as a dedicated field of study in the mid-1950s. Robert Anthony's 1956 book, *Management Accounting: Text and Cases*, provided the initial meaning and impetus to what largely constitutes the field of performance management, even in its

DOI: 10.4324/9781003267195-4

contemporary evolved state. As a testament to the enduring impact Anthony has had on the field of performance management, his 1956 book, albeit having undergone numerous updates in the form of new editions, retains its currency as one of today's leading and authoritative texts on the design and practice of performance management.

Prior to the mid-1950s, accounting inquiry and research largely focused on technical accounting issues. Generally, the focus was the determination of optimal input/output ratios. Typical examples included determining optimal product mixes, modelling the effect of depreciation on costs and selling prices, assessing the economic implications of leasing versus owning assets and calculating efficient audit samples. Essentially, the research agenda in the accounting field was largely captured by the dominant management paradigm of the time: Taylor's scientific management.

Scientific management is based on the concept that there is a single best way to organize, structure, and manage business activities. Proponents of scientific management view machines and humans as extensions of one another. The mandate of managers is to ensure the most compatible and economical fit between the two.

Time-and-motion studies became the classic tool whereby managers sought to ensure the most efficient workflow. Worker movements that did not conform to the one best way were deemed wasteful and became the focus of identification and elimination. An ultimate consequence of time-and-motion studies was the promotion of standardization of work and the division of labour into highly specialized tasks.

Interestingly, scientific management viewed the man-to-machine extension as not purely a physical relationship but a psychological one as well. The following quotation from Taylor's book, *The Principles of Scientific Management*, well captures this idea:

> Now one of the very first requirements for a man who is fit to handle pig iron as a regular occupation is that he shall be so stupid and so phlegmatic that he more nearly resembles in his mental make-up the ox than any other type. The man who is mentally alert and intelligent is for this very reason entirely unsuited to what would, for him, be the grinding monotony of work of this character. Therefore the workman who is best suited to handling pig iron is unable to understand the real science of doing this class of work.
>
> (Taylor, 1911: 59)

Ironically, the eventual demise of scientific management was largely self-inflicted. In the mid-1920s, Western Electric, a US manufacturer of telephones and telephone equipment, conducted a series of controlled experiments on a cohort of its workers to determine the effect of changes to the working environment on worker performance. Consistent with the goal of scientific management, the object was to determine the one/single best, the optimal level at which to set the working conditions.

One of the factors studied was workplace lighting. Initially, the lighting was increased, and the experimenters observed an increase in worker productivity. Successive increments in the workplace lighting led to corresponding increases in worker productivity. The experimenters then reduced the workplace lighting, expecting to observe a decrease in worker productivity. Instead, worker productivity increased again. According to some accounts of the Western Electric studies, after a series of reductions, the lighting became so poor that the workers were practically bumping into each other.

These experiments, far from supporting the idea of a single best way, indicated quite the opposite. There appeared to be no best way. Elton Mayo, a professor at what is now called the Harvard Business School, was invited to Western Electric to observe and help explain the unexpected worker behaviour.

Mayo's observations led him to surmise that the experiments had energized the workers into a cohesive, integrated social unit. Furthermore, he surmised these workers greatly enjoyed all the attention given them. In particular, the workers appreciated and felt a sense of pride, and even elitism, in being "selected" to work in a separate, isolated area from the rest of the workforce. On top of all this, there were men in white lab coats, even professors from Harvard, who would keenly observe the workers and take copious notes of their nearly every move. Accordingly, what Mayo concluded was that the worker productivity improvements had little to do with scientific management theory's preoccupation with aspects of the technical or physical environment but everything to do with the human and social environment. More specifically, he believed that the fuss being made over the workers changed their views about themselves and their relationships with their jobs and co-workers. Mayo contended that the workers felt a sense of liberation, a sense of being less the subject of constant outside supervision and, in its place, given the implicit freedom to enact shared, group control. This feeling led the workers to experience greater ownership of their work and, in turn, led to increased productivity.

Many scholars have objected to Mayo's interpretation of the Western Electric events. They believe the changes in worker productivity were merely the result of a type of experimenter bias, what Henry Landsberger termed the Hawthorne effect. The Hawthorne effect (the term derives from the name of the Western Electric plant where the studies on workplace lighting occurred) describes the situation where an observed significant positive effect results from workers knowing they are being observed and, as a consequence, behaving differently. Almost invariably, because the workers want to impress the observers, the workers perform to a higher standard, and therefore the observed effect is positive. A Hawthorne effect is further characterized by its spurious nature (i.e., there is no theoretical justification for the relationship between the cause and effect factors) and its momentariness (i.e., once the novelty of being observed wears off, workers' behaviour returns to its baseline level).

While it is true that Mayo's interpretation of the Western Electric studies has been vigorously disputed and challenged, this does not detract from the fact that those studies played a key role in ushering in a new management paradigm. This new paradigm became known as the human relations school and is based on the idea that any understanding of and improvement in worker motivation and performance requires an understanding of the human relationships and social dynamics of the people performing the work.

In sum, the emergence of the human relations school was the catalyst for the advent of performance management. More specifically, the human relations school provided the impetus for accounting scholars to move beyond seeing organizations in a purely mechanistic fashion. Instead of viewing workers as passive inputs to processes requiring management's scientific, optimization-oriented interventions, workers came to be seen as being dynamic, active, and socializing. Consequently, managers began to see that any attempt to curb costs, minimize waste, and/or maximize the effective use and operation of resources would require a fuller appreciation of the worker as a socially complex, rather than simply mechanistically complex, organizational contributor.

Review Question 3.1: What is scientific management theory?
Answer: Please see the Answer section starting on page 283
Review Question 3.2: What theory challenged scientific management theory, and why did this occur?
Answer: Please see the Answer section starting on page 283

THE EVOLUTION OF PERFORMANCE MANAGEMENT THINKING

Professor Anthony, writing 60 years ago, described management control, what the field now refers to as performance management, as "the process of assuring that the organization does what management wants done" (1956: 268). This definition would appear to encompass much more than what Horngren *et al.* proposed when they wrote, "A management control system is a means of gathering data to aid and co-ordinate the process of making planning and control decisions throughout the organization" (1994: 466). In fact, most accounting scholars would argue that the definition of management control/performance management extends well beyond Horngren *et al.*'s rather static and highly mechanistic definition. As Hopwood long ago pointed out, "The purposes, processes, and techniques of accounting, its human, organizational, and social roles, and the way in which the resulting information is used have never been static" (1976: 1).

In fairness to Horngren *et al.*, later editions of their textbook append to their earlier definition of the dependent clause "and to guide the behaviour of its managers and other employees" (2006: 470). This updated definition hints at the larger role that Emmanuel et al. (1990) have long associated with performance management. According to Sizer (1979: 244), "the management control process consists, in part, of inducing people in organizations to do certain things and to refrain from doing others." This idea of simultaneously promoting and restraining is similarly captured by Simons, who describes the necessity of the performance management system to both "inspire and constrain" (1995: 136).

Exactly what people are supposed to do and refrain from doing is further elaborated upon by Merchant. Absent an ideal world, that is, one in which "... all employees could always be relied on to do what is best for the organisation," some form of employee influence is needed (Merchant and Van der Stede, 2017: 11). More specifically, performance management systems will be required, and their fitness for purpose will be characterized by their ability to ensure an "... organization's strategies and plans are carried out, or, if conditions warrant, that they are modified" (1998: xi).

Merchant's idea that the successful implementation of the organization's strategy serves as the focal point of a performance management system is echoed in the writings of Anthony and Govindarajan (2007: 17) who state, "Management control is the process by which managers influence other members of the organization to implement the organization's strategy."

Together, these definitions of performance management provide two important insights. First, the ultimate goal of performance management is to aid in the successful implementation of the organization's strategy. Second, performance management seeks to achieve its goal by influencing employee behaviour. This influence is achieved through the sanctioning and promoting of desirable behaviour, and the discouraging and penalizing of undesirable behaviour.

PERFORMANCE MANAGEMENT TAXONOMIES

Taxonomies provide the visual ordering of things, such as places, objects, concepts, principles, etc. Physical scientists, including biologists or chemists, use taxonomies to create order and meaning among relevant animate and inanimate objects, respectively. Biologists, as an example, use the biological classification of kingdom, phylum, class, order, family, genus, and species to classify living organisms. Chemists use the periodic table to classify chemical elements.

In the social sciences, to which accounting belongs, taxonomies have similarly proven to be useful mechanisms for creating order and logic. More frequently, especially in a field like accounting, concepts and principles become the focus of establishing a taxonomy rather than objects. Two classic examples of well-known accounting taxonomies are the Financial Accounting Standards Board's classification of the elements of financial statements into assets, liabilities, equity, investment by owners, distribution to owners, comprehensive income, revenues, expenses, gains, and losses and management accountants' seminal classification of costs into the categories of fixed, variable, and mixed.

Performance management scholars have likewise relied upon taxonomies to order and present their ideas. Four main performance management taxonomies dominate the literature, namely the taxonomies of Anthony (1956), Ouchi (1979), Hopwood (1974), and Merchant (1985). While all four taxonomies seek to explain the sources or types of influence managers can exert on employee behaviour, each scholar's attempt appears to offer unique descriptions of this influence on behaviour. Anthony, for example, dichotomizes the sources or types of managerial influences on employee behaviour into formal and informal controls. Ouchi uses the categories of market, bureaucracy, and clan controls. Hopwood describes the choices as administrative versus social controls; while Merchant offers a trichotomy of results, action, and personnel controls.

A close inspection of these taxonomies reveals several common overlaps, with each overlap offering discernible connections to a set of well-recognized organizational techniques and practices. For instance, standardized systems and procedures feature prominently in Anthony's formal controls, Hopwood's administrative controls, Merchant's action controls, and Ouchi's bureaucratic controls. Organizational budgets, which form a subset of an organization's standardized systems and procedures, are examples of Anthony's formal controls, Hopwood's administrative controls, Merchant's results controls, and Ouchi's market controls. Organizational culture, meanwhile, is a dominant characteristic of Anthony's informal controls, Hopwood's social controls, Merchant's personnel controls, and Ouchi's clan controls. And finally, the control

---

Review Question 3.3: What is a taxonomy and why is it important to the study of accounting in general and performance management in particular?

Answer: Please see the Answer section starting on page 283

exerted through organizational structure is present in Anthony's formal controls, Hopwood's administrative controls, Merchant's action controls, and Ouchi's bureaucratic controls.

The similar strands running between Anthony's, Hopwood's, Merchant's, and Ouchi's taxonomies provide the opportunity for presenting a unified framework. Such a framework is offered in Figure 3.1.

There are two distinct advantages to this new framework. First, because the framework is grounded in concrete organizational phenomena, it is likely to resonate more fully with practising managers than previous taxonomies, which have been steeped in abstraction. In particular, Ouchi's market control or Hopwood's administrative control categories are concluded to have less relevancy for managers than terms like organizational systems, processes, and procedures; organizational structure; and organizational culture. This chapter's newly-proposed framework incorporates a more familiar practitioner language to describe the three main levers of performance management upon which managers can rely. As a second advantage, similar to

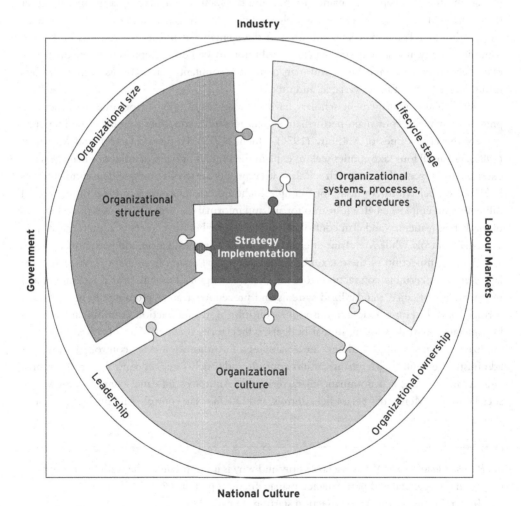

FIGURE 3.1 A revised framework of performance management.

what Emmanuel and his colleagues have argued, and which has been previously mentioned above, each of these three main levers of control comprises mechanisms for exerting control on employee behaviour that can on the one hand serve as a green light and encourage certain employee actions and on the other hand act as a red light and discourage other forms of employee conduct. This idea of constraining/coercing and enabling/empowering employee behaviour is more fully discussed below.

At the centre of the framework is strategy implementation. Consistent with the working definition of performance management adopted in this book (see Chapter 2), the ultimate goal of performance management is the implementation of an organization's strategy. It must be remembered that because employees are involved in the implementation of an organization's strategy, the success of any performance management system is a direct function of its ability to encourage/discourage the types of employee behaviour that will enable employees to individually and collectively implement the organization's strategy effectively and efficiently.

As noted, there are three main approaches or levers that can be used to affect performance management. The first – organizational systems, processes, and procedures – includes an organization's use of financial and non-financial measurement systems, reward and incentive systems, and human resource systems. Each of these systems offers senior managers the opportunity to influence employees' implementation of the organization's strategy. Budgets, a near-ubiquitous organizational feature, offer a prime illustration of this performance management lever. On the one hand, budgets communicate the types of actions employees should undertake and serve to energize and direct their actions. Budgets accomplish this objective by virtue of the financial authority they bestow on specific organizational members. Assuming the budget incorporates a difficult but achievable goal, then goal-setting theory posits that budgets will produce enhanced employee motivation. On the other hand, budgets routinely serve to constrain employee action. Organizational resources are scarce and limited, and budgets are created as a way to communicate how these scarce and limited resources will be utilized. In other words, budgets dictate the means within which employees and their subunits must operate. As a consequence, some employee-initiated plans may receive partial or even no support.

The second lever managers may use to influence employees' implementation of their organizations' strategies is organizational structure. This lever influences the way members of an organization interact with each other. An organization's structure is commonly communicated through organizational charts. These charts, which feature reporting boxes and reporting lines, specify employees' roles and relative relationships. Any given reporting box will have associated with it specific devolved powers. In other words, the devolution of power sanctions particular behaviours. Meanwhile, the reporting lines running between these boxes indicate employee accountabilities. This specification of superior/subordinate relationships ensures employee behaviour is constrained within predetermined, acceptable boundaries.

The final way an organization can influence its employees' implementation of its strategy is through its organizational culture, which comprises the values, symbols, routines, and rituals that characterize an organization's shared social programming. Although some scholars view organizational culture as a contextual variable (see, for example, Ferreira and Otley, 2009), Adler (2011) and Akroyd et al. (2019) argue that it is more appropriate to regard it as an integral and interdependent part of an organization's overall control system. Shared values, norms, and beliefs define an organization's culture, and these in turn play a powerful role in influencing or sanctioning allowable employee behaviour. Although some organizations' recruitment and selection processes ensure a good immediate fit between the organization's and a new member's belief systems, such immediate harmony is not always achieved. It is on these occasions that the organization's culture, which may itself be supplemented by targeted employee training and employee development, will standardize members' behaviour and bring it in line with the organization's accepted norms.

Depending upon the organizational setting, managers will configure and employ the three performance management levers in different ways. Some of the factors that affect the organizational setting are organizational size, lifecycle stage, organizational ownership, and leadership. These internal organizational factors, which will be separately examined and discussed in Chapter 13, are depicted in Figure 3.1 as orbiting around the three main levers of performance management. Framing the overall performance management process are the four external factors of industry, national culture, government, and labour markets. These factors serve to constrain an organization's performance management design and will be fully examined in Chapter 14.

It is important to understand that the three performance management levers must act in coordination. They must be viewed as part of what Malmi and Brown (2008) and Grabner and Moers (2013) call the "package" of control systems. When constructing the package, senior managers must strive to ensure the performance management levers possess strong interconnections that are capable of complementing each other as opposed to connections that may be either weakly supportive or, even worse, acting in opposition. An organizational culture that is characterized by innovation and entrepreneurialism would benefit from being paired with an organizational structure that is decentralized and promotes decision-making among all employees, even and especially those lower down in the organization. Furthermore, budgets in such a scenario might be used more for coordinating employee action than for evaluating employee performance and distributing rewards and incentives.

To visualize an example of a poorly constructed set of interconnections, consider an organization that has an organizational culture that is exemplified by conservatism and frugality. Such an organizational culture would exhibit poor pairing with a decentralized structure, participative decision-making, and loose budgetary control. Subsequent chapters will have much more to say about the design of and the linkages among the three performance management levers, as well as how these levers should be designed in light of various contingent factors that feature as part of an organization's internal and external environments.

It is also important to note that just as there can be too little control in an organization, so too can there be too much control. The dangers from a lack of control are obvious. Without a

---

Review Question 3.4: When comparing this book's PM taxonomy with other scholars' taxonomies, what are some of the similarities and differences?

Answer: Please see the Answer section starting on page 283

Review Question 3.5: Performance management is meant to constrain/coerce as well as enable/empower employee behaviour. What examples can you provide of this dual performance management influence?

Answer: Please see the Answer section starting on page 283

system of control, an organization's senior managers have no way of ensuring the organization is doing what it is meant to do. Some control is needed; and this will mean that at least one of the performance management levers will need to be used.

Managers must, however, especially those with micromanaging tendencies, restrict their urge to design too much control. A typical sign that there is too much control/performance management is when multiple controls/performance levers serve to merely duplicate one another. While some redundancy can serve to enhance an organization's resiliency and prevent unwanted behaviour (such as fraudulent behaviour), a performance management system that exhibits an "in triplicate" mentality will likely serve to slow down and interfere with employees' undertaking of important and vital organizational tasks. This danger is an especially serious problem for organizations that rely on innovation as a key success factor. The last thing an organization that pursues a strategy of innovation in its product/service offerings wants to do is to hinder or stifle its employees' creativity. More will be said about this issue in subsequent chapters.

The amount of control should be only what is sufficient to ensure the organization is on track for doing what it needs to do, which includes guarding against fraudulent and unethical employee behaviour. In other words, the Goldilocks principle applies here. Neither too little nor too much performance management is wanted. Instead there is a "just right" amount. While Figure 3.2 portrays this idea of optimizing performance through the right amount of performance management, later chapters of this book discuss the science and art of ensuring the "just right" balance of performance management.

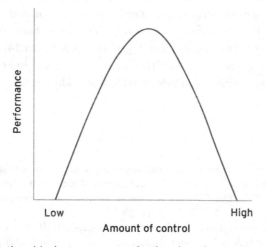

FIGURE 3.2 The relationship between organizational performance and the right amount of control.

Review Question 3.6: Can an organization have too much performance management? Discuss why.

Answer: Please see the Answer section starting on page 283

CONCLUSION

Performance management is a relatively new field of accounting/management study. It has only been around for about 60 years. Performance management's appearance in 1956 was made possible by the emergence of the management field's human relations school. This school of thinking moved beyond the mechanistic approach of Frederick Taylor's scientific management school and explicitly recognized the important influence of work-group dynamics and worker psychology on job performance. In other words, the human relations school's promotion of the social-psychological aspects of work was, and continues to be, the basis for performance management's focus on how managers influence their particular organization's members to implement the organization's strategy.

In addition to tracing the historical roots of performance management, this chapter showcased the evolution in performance management thinking. In particular, it identified and discussed significant milestones in the field of performance management. In the process, the noteworthy contributions of the field's leading performance management scholars were highlighted and placed in context.

The chapter concluded with the presentation of a unified performance management framework. This original framework has the advantages of being presented in the concrete language of practising managers and providing a richer description of performance management's dual role of simultaneously encouraging desirable employee behaviour and constraining undesirable behaviour. This framework forms the backbone of this book. Following this book's discussion of strategy (see Chapters 5–9), Chapters 10–12 will examine each of the three main levers of control: organizational structure; organizational systems, processes, and procedures; and organizational culture. This discussion will then be followed by an examination of internal contingent factors (Chapter 13) and external contingent factors (Chapter 14). For, as this book will show, performance management systems, if they are to be successful, must be specially designed and tailored to each organization's individual, and probably idiosyncratic, needs.

REFERENCES

Adler, R.W. (2011) Performance management and organization strategy: how to design systems that meet the needs of confrontation strategy firms, *British Accounting Review*, Vol. 43, No. 4, pp. 251–263.

Akroyd, C., Kober, R. and Li, D. (2019) The emergence of management controls in an entrepreneurial company, *Accounting & Finance*, Vol. 59, No. 3, pp. 1805–1833.

Anthony, R. (1956) *Management Accounting: Text and Cases*, Homewood, IL: Irwin.

Anthony, R. and Govindarajan, V. (2007) *Management Control Systems* (12th Edition), New York: McGraw-Hill-Irwin.

Emmanuel, C.R., Otley, D.T. and Merchant, K.A. (1990) *Accounting for Management Control* (2nd Edition), London: Chapman and Hall.

Ferreira, A. and Otley, D. (2009) The design and use of performance management systems: an extended framework for analysis, *Management Accounting Research*, Vol. 20, No. 4, pp. 263–282.

Grabner, I. and Moers, F. (2013) Management control as a system or a package? Conceptual and empirical issues, *Accounting, Organizations and Society*, Vol. 38, No. 6–7, pp. 407–419.

Hopwood, A.G. (1974) *Accounting and Human Behaviour*, London: Prentice Hall.

Hopwood, A.G. (1976) The path ahead, *Accounting, Organizations and Society*, Vol. 1 No. 1, pp. 1–4.

Horngren, C.T., Datar, M.D. and Foster, G. (2006) *Cost Accounting: A Managerial Emphasis* (12th Edition), Upper Saddle River, NJ: Prentice Hall.

Horngren, C.T., Foster, G. and Datar, M.D. (1994) *Cost Accounting: A Managerial Emphasis* (8th Edition), Englewood Cliffs, NJ: Prentice Hall.

Malmi, T. and Brown, D.A. (2008) Management control systems as a package – opportunities, challenges and research directions, *Management Accounting Research*, Vol. 19, No. 4, pp. 287–300.

Merchant, K.A. (1985) *Control in Business Organizations*, Boston, MA: Pitman.

Merchant, K.A. (1998) *Modern Management Control Systems*, Upper Saddle River, NJ: Prentice Hall.

Merchant, K.A. and Van de Stede, W.A. (2017) *Management Control Systems*, Harlow: Pearson Education Limited.

Ouchi, W.G. (1979) A conceptual framework for the design of organizational control mechanisms, *Management Science*, Vol. 25, No. 9, pp. 833–848.

Simons, R. (1995) *Levers of Control: How Managers Use Innovative Control Systems to Drive Strategic Renewal*, Boston, MA: Harvard Business School Press.

Sizer, J. (1979) *An Insight into Management Accounting*, London: Pitman.

Taylor, F.W. (1911) *The Principles of Scientific Management*, New York: Harper & Row.

CHAPTER 4

Theory and performance management

CHAPTER OBJECTIVES

- Discuss the necessity for theory to ground performance management practice and illuminate its further development.
- Discuss how contingency theory, agency theory, goal-setting theory, stakeholder theory, and resource-based theory contribute to practitioners' and scholars' understandings of employee behaviour and ultimately performance management success.
- Compare and contrast the different organizational theories' underlying assumptions about human behaviour and how these views impact the design, implementation, and practice of performance management.

INTRODUCTION

This chapter discusses five of the most prominent theories used to guide the research and practice of performance management. Each of these theories is separately described, discussed, and critiqued. The discussion of each theory includes illustrations relating the theory to performance management practice and research. This chapter concludes with the presentation of a table that associates each theory with specific elements of performance management. This table explicitly reveals the breadth of performance management issues covered by each theory. As will be seen, contingency theory and stakeholder theory are particularly useful theories for explaining performance management practice and guiding the field's research.

WHY THEORY IS IMPORTANT TO THE STUDY OF PERFORMANCE MANAGEMENT

Theory is an essential part of any business discipline's acceptance and future development. Without theory, a business discipline will at best be informed by trial and error. In such situations,

DOI: 10.4324/9781003267195-5

Review Question 4.1: What theories help to explain performance management practice?
Answer: Please see the Answer section starting on page 283
Review Question 4.2: Why is theory essential to the practice of business disciplines like
    performance management?
Answer: Please see the Answer section starting on page 283

managers will implement some sort of action and subsequently observe the outcome. Action associated with good outcomes will be retained, and action that led to poor outcomes will be jettisoned. As one might imagine, such a strategy is likely to be a very slow and inefficient way to promote organizational learning and the adoption of best practice.

Of course, an organization could do worse than trial and error. It could view the world as completely random or controlled by an omnipotent external agent. In either case, the organization would likely resort to intuition or mysticism. And before one dismisses these two possibilities as being too fanciful, it should be remembered that the Institute for Management Development's (IMD's) Annual World Competitiveness ratings show many countries' managers have limited business education and training. Without an understanding of the *science* of management and business on which to base decisions, greater use of informal approaches and personal schemas – including prevailing intuitions and even superstitions – are likely to feature.

A strong component of active theory development and refinement is essential to any business discipline's claim to current and future legitimacy. Theory helps to explain why events occur as they do, why the presence of specific factors creates particular outcomes, and why predictions can be legitimately made. In other words, theory helps focus thinking and, in the process, allows a more rapid movement to more efficient and effective states than an atheoretical approach.

Five theories can be used to help illuminate the study of performance management: contingency theory, agency theory, goal-setting theory, stakeholder theory, and resource-based theory. Each of these theories and their application to the study of performance management are discussed in the following sections.

CONTINGENCY THEORY

Contingency theory posits that there is no one, single best way to organize and manage an organization. The theory was developed in response to scholars' disenchantment with Max Weber's theory of bureaucracy and Frederick Taylor's scientific management. Starting in the late 1950s, a set of scholars, including Joan Woodward (1965), Paul Lawrence and Jay Lorsch (1967), and James Thompson (1967), argued that Weber's and Taylor's ideas failed to explain such key organizational factors as management style and organizational structure. As an example, this group of emerging contingency theorists contended that bureaucratic structures may work best on some occasions, but for the majority of cases, other forms of organizational structure offer a better choice. The best organizational structure for a given situation could be matrix, flat, or even boundaryless. The key to deciding which management styles or organizational structures to use, they argued, depended upon the set of internal and external factors existing in an organization's environment. These factors, which contingency theorists termed contingency factors, were neglected in Weber's and Taylor's conceptions of organizational influence and practice.

According to contingency theorists, no universally accepted model explains the diversity of organizational design, and therefore there can be no "one best" form of leadership or organizational design (Lawrence and Lorsch, 1967; Woodward, 1965). Instead, the preferred leadership style or organizational design will depend on the contingent factors that define an organization's environment. These contingent factors are sometimes referred to as situational and contextual factors (Chapman, 1997; Otley, 1980).

Some people have incorrectly viewed this axiom of "it all depends" as implying that because no one right way exists, all ways are equally meritorious and management choice therefore is irrelevant. Such thinking is profoundly wrong. According to contingency theory, because there are no generic, one-fits-all laws of business, the study and practice of management become even more demanding and challenging.

Whether it is selecting the type of responsibility centre to use, the most motivating compensation and reward system to design, or the most effective leadership styles to exhibit, the choices a manager makes are dependent on the internal and external contingent factors that characterize an organization's setting. The task of managers becomes not one of identifying the best option for any generic decision (e.g., what responsibility centre should be adopted?) but finding the best fit between the multitude of factors that define an organization's internal and external environments. Unlike population ecology theory, whereby organizations are argued to operate largely – if not exclusively – at the mercy of their environments, contingency theory places the weight of responsibility and accountability on management cognition, creativity, and capacity to create change.

Reference to an experiment in chicken breeding can help showcase the additional complexities and challenges contingency theory typically mandates. In this particular poultry experiment, a study was undertaken of the effects on egg production of using two different methods for populating cages containing multiple hens. The first method, termed individual selection, relied on identifying and placing in the same cage the most productive hens. Next, these hens were allowed to breed, and the most productive offspring were identified and placed together in the same common cage. This breeding and selection process continued for six generations. In the second condition, termed group selection, the most productive group of hens was identified and this entire group of hens was allowed to breed. Each sire family, that is, the mother hen and all her daughters, was housed as a group in a common cage. The best producing cage was identified and again allowed to reproduce. This process was repeated for a total of six generations.

Since it is the individual hen that lays eggs, it was expected that the individual selection method would be associated with the highest overall egg production. However, quite contrary to this expectation, it was the group selection method that led to the highest total egg production. The researchers observed that highly productive individual hens often achieved their high productivity at the expense of the other hens living in their communal cage. In contrast, the group selection method produced a harmonious community of hens that was accompanied by a dramatic drop in hen mortality from 68% to 9% and an equally dramatic 160% increase in egg production.

The point of recounting this experiment with egg production is to illustrate the contingency effects that exist even in a system as relatively simple and straightforward as an egg factory's egg production. Although egg production, at least on the surface, appears to be largely a function of a hen's fertility, other factors affect this egg production. And these other factors are not a simple function of diet (e.g., protein intake) or physical environment factors (e.g., amount of light). Instead, social factors interact with these other factors to determine ultimate egg production.

A classic example of contingency theory is Lawrence and Lorsch's (1967) study of organizational structuring and effectiveness. These researchers observed that there was no one best way to structure an organization. Rather, the decision about what organizational structure to adopt is best viewed as contingent upon the type of environment in which an organization operates. Complex, unpredictable, and fast-moving environments are best suited to decentralized organizational structures. Meanwhile, relatively simple, predictable, and slower-moving environments are best suited to centralized structures.

The applications of contingency theory to performance management are manifold. Contingency theory views the quest for organizational effectiveness as a kaleidoscopic jigsaw puzzle (see, for example, Malmi and Brown, 2008). In particular, changes to any one of the myriad of factors (with each of these factors being likened to a piece of the jigsaw puzzle) that are likely to impact on an organization's performance and success must be evaluated in light of the full set of factors. Before implementing organizational action, decision-makers must first examine how a contemplated change in any one factor may precipitate a change in other factors. When making this examination, practitioners may find they need to adjust various organizational factors to either compensate for or to take full advantage of the initial change(s) they make.

As an example, a change in leader, say the organization's chief executive officer (CEO), is likely to produce a different style of organizational leadership. There may be a change from perhaps a command-and-control leadership style to an interactive leadership style. The former leadership style is best associated with top-down, formal communication flows and the use of compensation systems that focus on an individual's ability to meet financial performance targets. Interactive leadership mandates very different communication flows and compensation system designs. As Adler and his colleagues note, interactive leadership calls for the use of participative and reciprocal communication flows and the use of compensation systems that are community-based and place a high reliance on intrinsic motivation (Adler *et al.*, 2017).

Not surprisingly, the adjustments to an organization's communication flows and compensation systems will likely prompt changes to the design of the organization's structure and have flow-on effects on the organization's culture. In other words, there will be a cascading of changes throughout the figurative jigsaw puzzle that represents the organization, with all these changes necessitated by the overarching need to ensure the best overall fit is achieved between the organization and its environment.

Various scholars have expressed reservations about contingency theory. In particular, it has been criticized for what is perceived as its failure to adequately conceptualize, define, and measure key variables of the theory (e.g., subunit interdependency, environmental uncertainty, organizational complexity). Scholars have also criticized the usefulness of research that has relied on contingency theory, claiming that many of these studies involve small sample sizes, often yield inconsistent results, and frequently fail to incorporate the wider context of organizations. Although these criticisms may have been valid in relation to research conducted in the 1980s and 1990s, they appear less relevant to more recent studies.

AGENCY THEORY

Agency theory seeks to explain the delegation of decision-making authority by a principal (often the owner) to an agent (often an employee). This theory recognizes that the typical organizational reality, whereby ownership is separated from day-to-day operations, presents significant challenges with respect to ensuring goal congruence among the various contracting parties. These challenges arise because the agents, whom the owners/principals have hired to run the business, may not share the same goals as the owners (Bertelli and Smith, 2010; Brown et al., 2010; Calabrò and Torchia, 2011; Jensen and Meckling, 1976). For example, agents may not share the same work ethic or possess the same risk utility function as the owners. Some of the recent corporate failures stand as poignant testaments to the latter case, if not also the former.

Agency theory posits that principals and agents are acting with complete rationality for the singular purpose of maximizing their own self-interest. The theory further posits that principals' and agents' pursuits of their respective self-interests will produce outcomes whereby the principals' interests are short-changed by the agents' actions (Gordon, 1998; Macintosh, 1994). As such, the theory is anchored by such key concepts as self-interest, adverse selection, and moral hazard.

According to Jensen and Meckling (1976), a principal can reduce an agent's dysfunctional behaviour by incurring auditing, accounting, and monitoring costs. In other words, a principal can use surveillance systems to stop and guard against unwanted agent behaviour. The principal can also seek to curb an agent's undesired behaviour by designing appropriate incentive schemes. Here the objective is to align the agent's self-interest/greed with the principal's self-interest/greed, as the reward an agent will be given is directly tied to his/her performance. A classic example of this reward-performance pairing is a piece-rate system, whereby an employee is paid a set amount for each defect-free unit of product made or each *bona fide* unit of product sold. This employee remuneration approach is related to agency theory's use of such concepts as signalling, incentives, and contracts (Macintosh, 1994).

It is important to note that the issue of self-interest would not be a problem if full and complete information was held by both parties. Under situations where the principals and agents possess perfect information, issues of goal conflict do not arise. When perfect information exists, the principals can clearly see how hard and effectively the agents are working, and the agents can see the effort taken and the magnitude of risks assumed by the principals. As such, agency theory incorporates the further concept of information asymmetry (Macintosh, 1994).

Just as principals benefit from perfect information, so too will agents. Perfect information ensures all pertinent job information is visible to the agent, whether this information relates to health and safety aspects of the job or the political machinations of the principals. The former type of information is undoubtedly important to someone working in a dangerous environment like a coal mine, but is also arguably quite important to a white-collar employee who may suffer adverse health effects from what is a highly sedentary job that often has high levels of work stress. Meanwhile, political machinations may manifest in such circumstances as hiring an agent who will subsequently be used as a scapegoat for some existing impropriety of which only the principal is aware or encouraging employees to undertake a merger with another company and then firing the same employees who are now seen as surplus to the company's requirements.

It is interesting to note that the agency theory literature largely views the agent as the one who restricts information flow. In particular, the agent is ascribed with possessing more information than the principal, and the agent uses this information asymmetry for his/her own personal gain. The agency literature even goes so far as to suggest that the agents can sometimes use misinformation or the fabrication of information as a further means to enhance their personal advantages.

Invariably agency theory paints a dark image of human behaviour. As Ghoshal (2005) notes, the gloomy views espoused by agency theory specify that employees cannot be trusted and that tight monitoring and control of employees must be undertaken. Failure to monitor employees and keep their greed in check will precipitate undesirable, opportunistic behaviour that will cost the organization. However, as Ghoshal observes, agency theory's pessimistic view of the world is not consistently supported by either empirical evidence or common sense.

Ghoshal labels agency theory as an example of a "bad management theory," whose impact has had much more to do with conditioning employee behaviour and producing self-fulfilling prophecies than explaining or predicting employee behaviour. In particular, Ghoshal argues business schools' 30-plus years of teaching these ideologically laden, pessimistic management theories has indoctrinated a generation of managers to not only view others as greed-fuelled, heartless, win-at-any-cost, back-stabbing schemers but also encourage all and sundry to adopt such an approach themselves lest they be swindled and taken advantage of first.

Putting aside the issue of whether agency theory represents a "bad management theory," the theory has been used to explain how, under conditions of information asymmetry, employment contracts should be written to promote principal and agent goal harmony. Quite often these contracts involve the specification of compensation. For example, salespeople, whose efforts are difficult to observe, typically have a large portion of their pay based on sales commissions. Meanwhile, factory workers may be paid piece rates, waitstaff may earn the majority of their wages through customer tips, and senior managers of for-profit, publicly listed companies may have substantial parts of their salaries determined by share options. In sum, agency theory has had a powerful effect on defining performance, and in particular an individual's (as opposed to a group's) performance. The focus of agency theory is almost invariably placed on controlling individual performance, whereby it is used to justify the type and amount of rewards bestowed on employees.

GOAL-SETTING THEORY

Edwin Locke developed goal-setting theory in the 1960s. Locke (1968) proposed this theory to explain motivation. In its most simple terms, the theory posits that when goals are set, motivation is enhanced. They do so by directing attention, energizing effort, increasing persistence, and unlocking and leveraging task-relevant knowledge and strategies (Locke and Latham, 2002). It is interesting to note that who sets the goals, that is whether it be a participative approach involving the affected employees or a top-down approach decided by a superior, is not nearly as important as ensuring that goals exist.

An early study by Latham and Baldes (1975) looked at the motivational, and in particular the performance, impact of management assigning goals to the drivers of logging trucks. The drivers worked for an Oklahoma, US logging company. As one of their job responsibilities, the drivers were responsible for loading logs onto their trucks. Management observed that many of the trucks were carrying loads that were significantly below the maximum legal net weight limit. In an attempt to boost productivity, management assigned the drivers a goal of ensuring loads of at least 94% of the maximum legal net weight. The drivers were told this management directive was part of an experimental programme. No rewards would be offered or any punitive action taken for either attaining or missing the goal. No special training of any kind was provided. In fact, other than verbal praise being given for improving performance, no other changes occurred.

The implementation of this goal-setting programme led to an improvement from an average load of 60% of the maximum legal net weight to close to 95%. This increase in productivity occurred within four months of commencing the programme and was largely maintained over the succeeding five months of the programme's operation. The success of the goal-setting intervention was reported to have saved the company from making an investment of $250,000 in the additional trucks that would have otherwise been needed to deliver the same quantity of logs to the mills.

When setting goals, it is important that the goals be difficult but attainable, a characteristic that Locke and Latham (2002) term "high goals." Goals that are too easy or viewed as impossible have low motivating potential. In fact, goal-setting practitioners have developed the acronym SMART for specifying what are seen as the ideal features of goals. The "S" stands for "specific." Goals must be clear, unambiguous, and well defined. A goal such as "being among the top 20% of all performers" would meet this definition, whereas stating a goal like "doing one's best" would not. The "M" stands for "measureable." Goals must be quantifiable. A goal of "being the best foreman in the world" would not satisfy this criterion because it is not measureable. How would "best" be determined? Would it be based on subordinate popularity, department productivity, or some other measure? And even if one particular measure or even a weighting of all the identified measures could be agreed upon, how would it be possible to collect performance data on all the world's foremen? Suffice it to say, such a goal does not meet the characteristic of measurability.

The "A" in the SMART acronym stands for "ambitious." Goals should be difficult and require employees to work at a high level of effort and ability to achieve the goals. To avoid pushing employees beyond their breaking point, the acronym's "R" stands for "reasonable." Impossible goals do not motivate; instead, they only serve to demoralize.

Discovering the borderline between motivating and demoralizing goals is not a simple matter. In fact, great debate exists in the literature about the usefulness of what practitioners and scholars refer to in varying names as "tiptoe," "stretch," and "BHAGs" (big hairy audacious goals). Examples of these extremely difficult goals are Toyota's goal of a 100% increase in fuel efficiency, which led to its development of the Prius, and the Singapore Port Authority's goal of moving from handling zero container boxes in overseas ports to handling 10 million container boxes within ten years. While Denning (2012) champions the use of stretch goals, saying "let's celebrate stretch goals. Let's set awesome goals for ourselves that uplift the human spirit, goals that inspire those doing work and delight those for whom work is done," Markovitz (2012: 34) warns against their use, advising "Let's dispense, once and for all, with the managerial absurdity known as 'stretch goals.'"

An enduring challenge for senior managers is to create goals that exert a maximum motivating effect on employee behaviour. Although the literature is quite clear on the need for goals and targets to be neither too easy nor too difficult, exactly what constitutes being "too difficult" is still the subject of debate. Generally speaking, it can be understood that a Goldilocks region exists between the non-motivating zones of "too easy" and "too difficult." The threshold between goals that are too easy and this Goldilocks region is evidenced when goals reach the point that they require employees to exhibit strong, and not just average, exertion, commitment, and innovation. Meanwhile, the tipping point between the Goldilocks region and goals that are too difficult occurs when employees begin displaying signs of demoralization, learning avoidance, and/or cheating to attain the goal.

The final letter of the SMART acronym is "T." This stands for "time-targeted." In particular, goals must have a due date or date of completion. For example, it is not sufficient to state a goal as "to have the highest customer satisfaction rates in our industry." The goal must be time-bounded and include an additional descriptor such as "for the year 2013" or "for the industry's most current five-year running average."

In sum, the use of goals, and in particular goals that conform to the SMART acronym, motivate employee behaviour. The management literature has shown a consistent and strongly positive correlation between motivation and performance. In other words, superiors who can better motivate their subordinates will reap the benefits of better employee performance.

STAKEHOLDER THEORY

Stakeholder theory is based on the idea that an organization's goals, objectives, and even the various work procedures and organizational activities it adopts are a product of the multiple groups of people who seek to exert their influence on the organization. The groups can be internal or external to the organization. The former consists of shareholders and employees, with these groups being responsible – either directly or indirectly through their delegated appointees – for planning, designing, implementing, and delivering their respective organizations' products/services to their customers. The latter group comprises customers, suppliers, unions, regulators, industry associations, lobbyists, and various governmental agencies (health and safety, environmental protection, taxation, etc.), who together collectively define the set of external expectations held for the organization.

Different stakeholder groups are likely to have different levels of power/influence. For one particular organization, employees may wield the most influence, while at another organization regulators may exert the greatest influence on the organization's activities. Additionally, the influence of any one group is far from static. Rather, it can, and is likely to, change over time.

Stakeholder theory can be easily contrasted with shareholder theory. Whereas the former theory suggests an organization must satisfy a wide array of groups that express an interest in the organization's activities, the latter theory argues that only the organization's shareholders matter. In shareholder theory's extreme form, management is only and solely responsible to the organization's shareholders.

Shareholder theory was proposed in the 1960s and is closely associated with Milton Friedman's work. The essence of shareholder theory is well captured by Friedman's (1962: 133) assertion: "There is one and only one social responsibility of business – to use its resources and engage in activities designed to increase its profits so long as it … engages in open and free competition, without deception or fraud." Stakeholder theory posits that managers have a duty to be the agents of *all* stakeholders. Managers assume two main responsibilities: they must ensure the ethical rights of all stakeholders are maintained and they must assert their power in a way that ensures proper recognition of the legitimate interests of all stakeholders, whether these stakeholders are shareholders, employees, customers, suppliers, governmental bodies, or the local community. In executing their role, and in sharp contrast to the shareholder perspective, managers are meant to trade off firm profitability for overall stakeholder well-being. In other words, while shareholder theory takes a rather narrow view of managers' mandate, stakeholder theory adopts a more utilitarian perspective. Furthermore, while shareholder theory sees all non-shareholder groups as a means to an end, and in particular requires recognition solely for the impact they have on maximizing the wealth of its shareholders, stakeholder theory views all stakeholder groups as an important end in and of themselves.

Stakeholder theory helps to explain organizations' formulation of strategy. For example, it can be used to understand how the power exerted by different stakeholder groupings influences an organization's determination of its goals and objectives. These goals and objectives become embodied in such key strategic documents as an organization's mission and vision statements.

RESOURCE-BASED THEORY

Under the resource-based theory, organizations are viewed as collections of resources that have the potential to endow an organization with a competitive advantage, which is defined as the ability to stay ahead of present or potential competition (Porter, 1985). An organization's resources are comprised of physical assets (e.g., machines, property, capital), intangible assets (e.g., patents, brand names, technological knowhow), and operational capabilities (e.g., routines or processes like total quality, just-in-time, lean manufacturing). When trying to understand the distinctions between these three types of organizational resources, physical and intangible assets can be viewed as resources that are tradable and non-specific to an organization. In contrast, capabilities are organization-specific and are deployed and bundled together by an organization to improve the productivity of its physical and tangible assets. In fact, this idea of building and leveraging capabilities is the essence of competitive strategy, which is discussed in Chapter 8.

It is senior management's responsibility to ensure their respective organizations grow their resources and unlock the potential advantages they offer. This task can be accomplished by developing an organization's resources internally or by obtaining them from external parties through acquisitions. Irrespective of which route, or both routes, an organization takes, it is crucial that an organization's senior managers commit to the current and future investments needed to develop/acquire the resources that will provide the organization's competitive advantage.

According to Collis and Montgomery (1995), resources are valuable (i.e., they enable competitive advantage and not simply short-run benefits) when they possess:

1 Inimitability
2 Durability
3 Appropriability
4 Substitutability
5 Competitive superiority.

Inimitability refers to how readily an organization's resource(s) can be copied by a competitor. A resource will be characterized as being more valuable when it possesses high inimitability, which means it is rare and has a low chance of being duplicated or imitated. Durability describes a resource's susceptibility to depreciation or obsolescence. Resources with low durability have to be replaced, augmented, and upgraded more frequently; and therefore these resources are characterized as less valuable.

Appropriability signifies which party or parties capture the value a resource creates. The parties include the company, customers, distributors, suppliers, and employees. Valuable resources confer appropriability with the company/organization being assessed. Substitutability refers to whether an organization has a resource that can be replaced by another competitor's resource. Low substitutability is associated with more valuable resources. The final characteristic of underlying value relates to a resource's extent of competitive superiority. When a resource is genuinely better than its competitors, it will be more valuable.

Organizations will find that they must remain vigilant to modifying and developing their resources if they are to stay ahead of their present and potential competitors. To attain this objective, organizations must be conscious of the changes occurring in their industry and the wider macro-environment. This understanding will likely require organizations to grow and refine their resources relative to their competitors and market forces more generally. When undertaking this task, senior managers may find Porter's (1985) Five Forces Model a useful tool. In other words, The resource-based theory integrates an internal emphasis focused on enhancing an organization's core competencies with an external emphasis on understanding, influencing, and leveraging the particular industry in which an organization operates.

Resource-based theory scholars typically view the development of internal resources as more important than the selection of the industry in which to compete. Organizations are encouraged to look inward for sources of competitive advantage (by developing core competencies) rather than outward (by evaluating industry attractiveness). Various studies have found that about 30–40% of an organization's superior performance can be explained by an organization's core competencies, while about 20% can be explained by the industry (Rothaermel, 2012).

Various criticisms have been levelled against resource-based theory (Priem and Butler, 2001a, 2001b). Some scholars consider it to be less of a theory than a tautology. In particular, since resource-based theory calls for organizations to build networks of valuable resources and then proceeds to define competitive advantage as the creation of a strategy that is based on an organization's development and configuration of a set of valuable resources, a circular argument exists. Critics also contend that resource-based theory lacks compelling empirical data to support its implied causality. They argue that many explanations beyond an organization's ability to hold valuable resources can be given for why it might achieve a competitive advantage. As a further criticism, the assumption that an organization's possession of valuable resources will be sufficient to maintain its profitability even when faced with a highly competitive market has been questioned. This issue of highly competitive industries is discussed further in Chapter 8.

In spite of these criticisms, resource-based theory continues to attract a strong following. Advocates note that resource-based theory, at a minimum, provides a good way for senior managers to manage their resource base. It is further noted that practitioners are frequently less concerned with a tool's theoretical soundness than its practical application. Resource-based theory, or so these proponents state, offers especially helpful advice for firms that operate in highly dynamic environments; for it helps them to understand how to marshal their assets and capabilities to enable firm survival (Ludwig and Pemberton, 2011).

HOW THEORIES CONTRIBUTE TO PERFORMANCE MANAGEMENT UNDERSTANDING

Table 4.1 depicts how each of the five theories just discussed helps to explain specific elements of performance management. This table relies on the framework by Ferreira and Otley (2009) for the listing of the performance management elements. Beyond being widely cited, this framework offers one of the most detailed compilations of performance management elements, which makes it a logical candidate for its inclusion here.

As Table 4.1 shows, resource-based theory is especially useful for studying such aspects of performance management as an organization's vision and mission, its success factors, its strategy and plans, and its key performance measures. The theory is also useful for understanding organizational change. As should be far from a surprise, resource-based theory's main contribution derives from its key implications for strategy formulation, implementation, and control. For example, resource-based theory contends that:

1 Organizational resources comprise the bedrock of an organization's strategy.
2 Senior managers must constantly strive to improve and upgrade their organizations' resources.
3 Organizations must be committed to ongoing investment in their resources.
4 Senior management must continually evaluate the fit between their organizations' resources and the environment/industry in which they operate.

TABLE 4.1 Organizational theories and elements of performance management addressed

	Contingency theory	Agency theory	Goal-setting theory	Stakeholder theory	Resource-based theory
Vision and mission				✓	✓
Success factors				✓	✓
Organizational structure	✓				
Strategies and plans					✓
Key performance measures	✓			✓	✓
Targets	✓	✓	✓	✓	
Performance evaluation	✓	✓	✓	✓	
Rewards	✓	✓	✓		
Information flows	✓	✓	✓	✓	
Information use	✓	✓	✓	✓	
Organization change	✓				✓
Strength of linkages	✓				

> *Review Question 4.3:* Are some theories better at explaining parts of performance management? If so, which theories better explain which parts?
>
> *Answer:* Please see the Answer section starting on page 283
>
> *Review Question 4.4:* What theory or theories do you believe are best suited to the field of performance management?
>
> *Answer:* Please see the Answer section starting on page 283
>
> *Review Question 4.5:* What are the implications of goal-setting theory on performance management design?
>
> *Answer:* Please see the Answer section starting on page 283

Agency theory and goal-setting theory are particularly useful in explaining an organization's target setting, its performance evaluation systems and processes, the performance rewards it offers, and the design and use of its information flows. While both theories address this similar set of performance management topics, they do so with highly contrasting ambitions. Goal-setting theory attempts to encourage employee action. Meanwhile, agency theory's focus is more on curbing and controlling employee behaviour than encouraging it.

Both stakeholder theory and contingency theory address a large proportion of the elements of performance management. Stakeholder theory helps explain the organizational goals and objectives that become enshrined in any particular organization's mission and vision statements. It also provides understanding of the success factors and targets an organization uses, as well as the performance evaluation systems and information flows it operates. Meanwhile, with the exception of failing to address the formulation of an organization's strategy (i.e., mission and vision, success factors, and strategies and plans), contingency theory helps shed light on all the other performance management elements in Table 4.1. It is for this reason that contingency theory features in so much of the research conducted on performance management. In addition, as Table 4.1 shows, only contingency theory provides understandings about the linkages between the several elements that comprise performance management. It is not surprising therefore that the set of articles appearing in Malmi and Brown's (2008) guest-edited special issue in *Management Accounting Research*, which examined the integrated nature of performance management's elements, featured a contingency theory approach.

CONCLUSION

The purpose of this chapter was to identify and discuss the theories commonly relied upon to understand and explain performance management practice. Five theories were examined, namely, contingency theory, agency theory, goal-setting theory, stakeholder theory, and resource-based theory. Each of these theories is capable of addressing multiple parts of performance management practice. Using Ferreira and Otley's popular performance management framework, it was shown that contingency theory and stakeholder theory prove particularly useful in guiding the field's research and explaining performance management practice.

REFERENCES

Adler, R.W., Hiromoto, T. and Suzuki, H. (2017) Amoeba management and organizational ambidexterity: similarities, differences, and implications for organizational fit and success, *British Academy of Management Conference*, 5–7 September.

Bertelli, A.M. and Smith, C.R. (2010) Relational contracting and network management, *Journal of Public Administration Research and Theory*, Vol. 20, Suppl. 1, pp. 21–40.

Brown, T.L., Potoski, M. and Van Slyke, D.M. (2010) Contracting for complex products, *Journal of Public Administration Research and Theory*, Vol. 20, Suppl. 1, pp. 41–58.

Calabrò, A. and Torchia, M. (2011) Conflicts of interest and governance mechanisms in Italian local public utilities, *International Journal of Public Administration*, Vol. 34, No. 7, pp. 447–460.

Chapman, C.S. (1997) Reflections on a contingent view of accounting, *Accounting, Organizations and Society*, Vol. 22, No. 2, pp. 189–205.

Collis, D.J. and Montgomery, C.A. (1995) Competing on resources: strategy in the 1990s, *Harvard Business Review*, Vol. 73, No. 4, pp. 118–128.

Denning, S. (2012) In praise of stretch goals, *Forbes*, 23 April. Retrieved from www.forbes.com/sites/stevedenning/2012/04/23/in-praise-of-stretch-goals/#121ef0987c04.

Ferreira, A. and Otley, D. (2009) The design and use of performance management systems: an extended framework for analysis, *Management Accounting Research*, Vol. 20, No. 4, pp. 263–282.

Friedman, M. (1962) *Capitalism and Freedom*, Chicago, IL: University of Chicago Press.

Ghoshal, S. (2005) Bad management theories are destroying good management practices, *Academy of Management Learning & Education*, Vol. 4, No. 1, pp. 75–91.

Gordon, L.A. (1998) *Managerial Accounting – Concepts and Empirical Evidence*, New York: McGraw-Hill.

Jensen, M. and Meckling, W.H. (1976) Theory of the firm: managerial behaviour, agency costs and ownership structure, *Journal of Financial Economics*, Vol. 3, No. 4, pp. 305–360.

Latham, G.P. and Baldes, J.L. (1975) The practical significance of Locke's theory of goal setting, *Journal of Applied Psychology*, Vol. 60, No. 1, pp. 122–124.

Lawrence, P.R. and Lorsch, J. (1967) *Organization and Environment*. Boston, MA: Harvard Business School, Division of Research.

Locke, E.A. (1968) Toward a theory of task motivation and incentives, *Organizational Behavior and Human Performance*, Vol. 3, No. 2, pp. 157–189.

Locke, E.A. and Latham, G.P. (2002) Building a practically useful theory of goal setting and task motivation. A 35-year odyssey, *American Psychologist*, Vol. 57, No. 9, pp. 705–717.

Ludwig, G. and Pemberton, J. (2011) A managerial perspective of dynamic capabilities in emerging markets: the case of the Russian steel industry, *Journal of East European Management Studies*, Vol. 16, No. 3, pp. 215–236.

Macintosh, N.B. (1994) *Management Accounting and Control Systems: An Organizational and Behavioral Approach*, Chichester: John Wiley and Sons.

Malmi, T. and Brown, D.A. (2008) Management control systems as a package – opportunities, challenges and research directions, *Management Accounting Research*, Vol. 19, No. 4, pp. 287–300.

Markovitz, D. (2012) The folly of stretch goals, *Harvard Business Review*, Vol. 56, No. 4, pp. 34–35.

Otley, D. (1980) The contingency theory of management accounting: achievement and prognosis, *Accounting, Organizations and Society*, Vol. 5, No. 4, pp. 413–428.

Porter, M.E. (1985) *Competitive Advantage: Creating and Sustaining Superior Performance*, New York: Free Press.

Priem, R.L. and Butler, J.E. (2001a) Is the resource-based "view" a useful perspective for strategic management research?, *Academy of Management Review*, Vol. 26, No. 1, pp. 22–40.

Priem, R.L. and Butler, J.E. (2001b) Tautology in the resource-based view and implications of externally determined resource value: further comments, *Academy of Management Review*, Vol. 26, No. 1, pp. 57–66.

Rothaermel, F.T. (2012) *Strategic Management: Concepts and Cases*, McGraw-Hill/Irwin.

Thompson, J. (1967) *Organizations in Action: Social Science Bases of Administrative Theory*, New York: McGraw-Hill.

Woodward, J. (1965) *Industrial Organization – Theory and Practice*, London: Oxford University Press.

PART **2**

Organizational strategy

Organizational goals and objectives

INTRODUCTION

The organizational studies literature describes organizations as collections of people who come together for some mutually agreed purpose. These people are typically called stakeholders. These stakeholders, either singly or in combination with other stakeholders, try to influence the operation and functioning of a given organization.

The word "stakeholder" is commonly used in the organizational accountability literature (Rasche and Esser, 2006). When defining stakeholders, this literature often ascribes a wide and encompassing view of who qualifies as a stakeholder. According to some scholars who study organizational accountability, a stakeholder is any party, whether it is an individual or a collection of individuals, who possesses an interest in the operations of a given organization. While this definition of a stakeholder will include an organization's employees, investors, and customers, it can also include parties who neither contribute to nor are affected by the organization's operations. For example, a teacher may have an interest in creating a learning activity that involves Singapore Airlines. This teacher therefore has an interest in the organization. Should this interest require Singapore Airlines to be accountable to the teacher?

The 2015 San Bernardino, California mass shooting, where a husband and wife killed 14 workmates at a Christmas party, provides another example of the complexities associated with determining who is a stakeholder. The US federal police force (the FBI) claimed Apple

DOI: 10.4324/9781003267195-7

> *Review Question 5.1:* What are stakeholders?
>
> *Answer:* Please see the Answer section starting on page 283

Computers had a duty to help with the FBI's investigation into the killings. In particular, the FBI demanded that Apple help the FBI hack into the deceased couple's iPhone. Although it can be argued, and the FBI initially tried to do this when it initiated legal proceedings to force Apple's compliance, that the FBI has an interest in Apple's products, does this qualify the FBI as an Apple stakeholder and therefore a party to whom Apple is now accountable?

The concept of stakeholder is often applied to an organization's construction of its goals and objectives. Unlike the way in which the concept is used for accountability purposes, it has a more targeted meaning when it is applied to an organizational goal and objective setting. In particular, stakeholders are not merely parties with an interest in an organization's activities. Instead, stakeholders must have a legitimate interest in the organization's activities. This legitimate interest manifests itself when an individual or party materially contributes to and/or is materially impacted by the organization's activities. In other words, under this definition, the teacher would not qualify as a stakeholder, whereas the FBI's status would be uncertain.

Due to the FBI's uncertain status as an Apple stakeholder, and because of the diametrically opposed views Apple and the FBI held about this status, the FBI lodged a court case against Apple in an attempt to force it to help. The Federal Court of California was asked to decide whether Apple's activities, and in particular its iPhone's secure mailbox, had: a) material impact on the FBI's investigation, and b), if (a) was proven, whether Apple had a duty to assist the FBI with hacking into the iPhone of the deceased couple. No court opinion was ever delivered as the FBI withdrew its case partway through the court proceedings. Therefore, on this particular occasion, we do not know whether, at least from a legal perspective, the FBI qualified as an Apple stakeholder (which was essentially part (a) of the court action). There are, however, a multitude of instances where the government, or a piece of it, could legitimately be seen to be materially impacted by organizations' activities. These instances could involve food safety, aviation safety, anti-competitive practices, and more. In fact, since nearly all organizations are required to pay taxes or are provided with an exemption from paying taxes (having been offered tax-exempt status), it is frequently the case that the government features as a stakeholder for most organizations.

The remainder of this chapter discusses how the stakeholder concept can be applied to understanding organizations' development of goals and objectives. This understanding is an important preliminary step to any organization's formulation and implementation of its strategy, both the corporate-level one it adopts and the business-unit-level or competitive one it pursues.

STAKEHOLDER EFFECTS ON ORGANIZATIONAL GOALS AND OBJECTIVES

As this chapter proceeds to discuss, an organization's goals and objectives are a product of its stakeholders' demands. Predominant organizational stakeholders are employees, shareholders, customers, suppliers, and government. For most organizations, these five groups comprise their set of stakeholders. As an example, imagine a software company that designs computer games. At the time of starting the company, the company's owners/shareholders would have requested permission from a government to establish the company. Following its incorporation, the company would hire employees and work with outside suppliers and contractors to develop its games. If successful, the company would seek to market its games to customers.

Obviously, not every organization has all of or just these five stakeholder groupings. For example, a city-based fire department does not have customers *per se*. It certainly does not market its core service (the extinguishing of fires) to specific people or organizations, nor would it be a usual practice to bill the victim of a fire. It is also the case that fire departments do not have shareholders. Instead, they are government-funded, typically at either a local or a national level.

In contrast to a fire department, mining companies will typically have additional stakeholders beyond the five mentioned. For example, international environmental activist groups such as Greenpeace are likely to feature as a stakeholder, as would other more locally-organized non-governmental organizations. These latter groups could span everything from river-care groups to indigenous people's action groups.

The important point to understand about these stakeholders is their respective desires to advance their own group's goals and objectives. On many occasions, these goals may be conflicting. Employees will want safe working conditions and what they feel is adequate compensation for their efforts. These goals may conflict with shareholders' goals to maximize the returns on their invested capital. While the potential for conflict will likely be greatest when shareholders possess a short-term investing horizon, even when a long-term perspective is taken the possibility of conflict between the interests of shareholders and employees is likely to exist.

In a similar fashion, conflicts can exist between the other stakeholders. Governments will want companies and their employees to obey all laws and generally act as good citizens. While companies and their employees will not necessarily seek to violate laws and/or behave without a social conscience, they could very well apply advantageous treatments to grey-area issues. For example, companies may seek to minimize their tax liabilities by avoiding certain types of transactions and activities (e.g., delaying the sale of an asset or changing the terms of the asset's sale so that it does not trigger a taxable event). Employees may be similarly motivated to engage in tax minimization (or worse) when their pay is connected to company profitability. Meanwhile, suppliers will, all other things being equal, want to maximize the prices they charge for their products and services, and customers will want to maximize their respective utilities by paying as little as possible without sacrificing any diminution in quantity or quality.

Figure 5.1 visually presents the typical collection of an organization's stakeholder groups. Each ellipse is meant to represent the set of goals and objectives of a specific group. As the diagram shows, there are overlaps between various groups. Some overlaps are substantial and others are more modest. The shaded region of the diagram represents the total area of overlap for all stakeholder groups. This area can be understood as a visual representation of the set of goals and objectives that are common to all stakeholder groups. If this set is sufficiently encompassing, to the point that it is able to capture each stakeholder group's most essential and non-negotiable goals and objectives, then the collective participation of all stakeholders can be achieved.

Some scholars believe that an organization's set of goals and objectives is the product of give-and-take negotiations between stakeholders, all of whom exhibit high levels of purpose and rationality. These scholars further believe that once this set of goals and objectives is well-articulated and fully shared among employees, shareholders, customers, suppliers, and other key stakeholders, then they become enduring precursors to the organization's long-term planning and the actions it undertakes.

Other scholars regard an organization's purpose as a function of perpetually-shifting competitions between various stakeholder groups and/or coalitions of stakeholder groups. These scholars view the stakeholders as rational in a political, but not necessarily economic, sense. As a result, an organization's goals are temporally-bound and subject to the whims of whichever stakeholder group or coalition can claim dominance. Hickson's (1987: 166) description of the kaleidoscopic nature of these ever-evolving coalitions is vividly portrayed when he writes:

> Those on the other side of the Atlantic see it [the defining of organizational purpose] as a sort of riotous American football! It is seen as a game of powerful groups in which some teams are much bigger and have thicker protective padding and harder helmets. Boundaries are elastic, the field is bumpy, and the number of teams in play fluctuates. They disagree as to where the ends of the field are, but eventually one team or coalition of teams pushes its way through holding the ball to where it says the end is.

In many organizations, Hickson's description of the genesis of an organization's purpose is probably much more accurate than rational theorists would care to admit. Certainly, we can readily think of organizations that display the free-for-all approach that Hickson describes. A nation/country's government would be a prime case in point. For example, political parties that campaign during an election may commit to certain political platforms and make various promises. But these platforms can, and usually do, change over time. In fact, they have even been known to change over the course of an election itself or at the conclusion of an election when

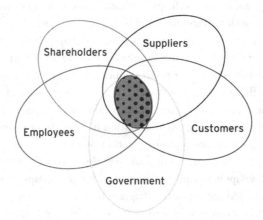

FIGURE 5.1 Organizational goals as the constrained product of key stakeholders' goals.

Review Question 5.2: Why are stakeholders important to organizations?
Answer: Please see the Answer section starting on page 283

Review Question 5.3: How are organizational goals determined?
Answer: Please see the Answer section starting on page 283

no single party can claim a majority and multiple parties therefore seek to form a ruling coalition. Sometimes it is the case that political parties that once decreed they would or would not cooperate with others contradict these earlier promises.

Of course, governments are not the only organizations that may feature Hickson's riotous football approach to establishing organizational purpose. Universities, hospitals, and many other usually public sector organizations, especially ones that are commonly seen to have multiple, distinct, and separate outlets for their products/services, often portray Hickson's approach to goal and objective setting. In a university, it is often the case that competing stakeholder groups will champion different purposes. Some groups will favour teaching, while others will prioritize research. Still others might emphasize their university's need to serve a wider social/political role (e.g., act as the social conscience of society). These groups, and perhaps others, are in a constant state of challenge and competition. At any given point in time, one group or set of groups usually holds supremacy and it is this group or set of groups whose goals and objectives are adopted by the organization. At other points in time, another group or set of groups may seize power and it is this new group or set of groups that determines the organization's goals and objectives.

MISSION STATEMENT

Irrespective of whether an organization's goals and objectives are the product of highly rational individuals, who seek to maximize their respective self-interests, or more closely resemble Hickson's portrait of organizational subgroup manoeuvrings and machinations, organizations will develop mission statements that are meant to communicate their goals and objectives. A mission statement comprises a succinct (usually one paragraph), factual description of the nature, focus, and scope of activities a given organization engages in, the unique set of resources it commands to enable its successful undertaking of the activities, and the key stakeholders it relies on when undertaking these activities. Mission statement descriptions should emphasize the present to near future. In other words, they should highlight what the organization is presently committed to doing. These mission statement characteristics can be summed up in the following list:

1   Succinct (usually one paragraph)
2   Clearly described
3   Factually based
4   Focused on the present to near future
5   Include reference to:
   a   relevant stakeholders
   b   segments of competition
   c   means of competition
   d   organization's objectives
   e   values.

Applying the above criteria, mission statements can be found as fit or unfit for purpose. For example, the following generic mission statement is unfit for purpose:

> Our mission is to exceed the expectations of our customers, inspire and reward our employees, and provide superior financial results to our investors.

This mission statement includes some but not all of the necessary ingredients that define a mission statement. It lists the main stakeholders (i.e., customers, employees, and investors), and at one sentence in length it certainly meets the definition of being succinct. The above mission statement, however, provides no description of what the organization does. The reader gleans nothing about the type of product/service provided, to whom or what part of the market the product/service is directed, nor what special advantage(s) (i.e., resources and capabilities) the organization possesses. In fact, there is not even any mention of what industry the company operates in. As a result, the above mission statement is unhelpful and unfit for purpose.

An example of a significantly better mission statement, one that possesses more of the essential criteria, is Apple Computers' mission statement:

> Apple designs Macs, the best personal computers in the world, along with OS X, iLife, iWork and professional software. Apple leads the digital music revolution with its iPods and iTunes online store. Apple has reinvented the mobile phone with its revolutionary iPhone and App Store, and is defining the future of mobile media and computing devices with iPad.

This mission statement does a good job describing what Apple does. It offers a very good description of its major business activities, especially the products it sells and the market leadership positions it has attained. The description also possesses succinctness. Missing from its statement, however, is any enunciation of the unique set of resources or the key stakeholder networks that enable Apple's delivery of what it proclaims to be "best," "leading," and "revolutionary." As such, Apple's mission statement is not fit for purpose. Incidentally, this idea of uniqueness features prominently in Chapter 8, where the concept of competitive strategy is fully presented and discussed. For now, it is sufficient to understand that an expression of the organization's uniqueness must be contained in the mission statement if the mission statement is to be deemed fit for purpose.

It is important to note that organizations need not disclose competitive secrets or commercially-sensitive information to meet the required mission statement threshold. For example, if an organization's production process supports the ability to deliver a mass-produced, customized product, the organization need not (and in fact should not) divulge specific details about its production process beyond what might already be public knowledge. Instead, the organization can simply state that it relies upon a proprietary production process to produce products that are tailored to customers' individual specifications without any sacrifice to cost efficiency. As another example, another organization might describe in its mission statement how it maintains and manages a network of supply chain partnerships that provide the basis for achieving lower production input costs than its competitors, without divulging the particular suppliers it has or the inward logistical processes it uses. An organization must not, however, fabricate or embellish descriptions of the resources or capabilities that create its unique value proposition. An essential component of a mission statement is its factualness.

Below is the mission statement for a university-based, student-run consulting business called Ignite Consulting Group:

> Ignite partners with organisations who work to enhance our communities. Our win–win model connects organisations with passionate and talented students, creating opportunities and nurturing socially-minded leadership. We help clients to overcome obstacles and achieve their aspirations through harnessing students' fresh perspectives. Students enrich their University experience and gain unique insights into community-oriented organisations. Together, we facilitate social change.

This mission statement meets all the essential criteria discussed above. It is succinct, factual, focuses on the present to near future, and describes its organization's objectives, the relevant stakeholder groups involved, the market segment it competes in, the tactics that enable it to compete, and the values it holds.

VISION STATEMENTS AND COMPANY SLOGANS

Many companies will create vision statements and/or company slogans. Similar to an organization's mission statement, vision statements and company slogans are meant to capture and communicate the essence of an organization's *raison d'être* and serve to motivate and even inspire the key stakeholders connected with the organization.

Vision statements should be:

1 Highly succinct (typically one sentence)
2 Clear
3 Timeless (i.e., communicating a vision that stands for now and the future)
4 Aspirational/inspirational.

An example of a good vision statement is Omron Corporation's. This company is an electronics company based in Kyoto, Japan. Its vision statement reads:

> To improve lives and contribute to a better society.

This vision statement contains all the expected criteria. It is a single sentence, or to be more precise the major part of a sentence that is missing its subject and main verb (i.e., "Omron seeks"). Omron's use of the infinitive verb structure (to make) conveys both the present and future. Furthermore, by stating its intention to contribute to the advancement of humankind, it possesses the hallmark of being aspirational (it contains ambition) and inspirational (its stated ambition has the potential to motivate others).

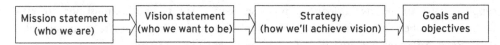

FIGURE 5.2 Connections between an organization's mission statement, vision statement, strategy, and goals and objectives.

Review Question 5.4: What are mission statements, vision statements, and company slogans? What are the essential characteristics of these statements and slogans?

Answer: Please see the Answer section starting on page 283

Kyocera Corporation, which is a very large and highly successful Japanese multi-national, provides a further example of a very good vision statement, in spite of the fact that it often incorrectly refers to this vision statement as its mission statement. Kyocera states:

> To provide opportunities for the material and intellectual growth of all employees, and through our joint effort, contribute to the advancement of society and mankind.

A final example of a good vision statement is Microsoft's, which reads:

> Empower people through great software anytime, anyplace, and on any device.

Company slogans represent a further distillation of their companies' mission and vision statements into a phrase that is meant to stay true to the spirit of the company's purpose and ambition while additionally showcasing the attributes of catchiness, a peculiarity that borders on mysteriousness, and the ultimate in brevity so that it can be displayed on a T-shirt. Apple's slogan, "Think different," is a perfect example. This slogan of two words captures the ethos of a company that seeks to disrupt its industry by offering products that lead, reinvent, and redefine (refer to Apple's mission statement above). The incorrect use of the adjective "different," which from a strictly grammatical point of view should be replaced with the adverb "differently," further helps Apple achieve an effective slogan. Omron's "Sensing tomorrow" is another example of a well-crafted company slogan.

Figure 5.2 shows the connections between an organization's mission statement, vision statement, strategy, and goals and objectives.

CONNECTING ORGANIZATIONAL GOALS AND OBJECTIVES WITH ORGANIZATIONAL STRATEGY

Organizational goals and objectives serve to guide organizations. Effective organizational mission statements will include reference to their respective organizations' goals and objectives. Often, organizations will refer to the same set of desired outcomes. Being "prosperous," "responsive to its customers' needs," "respectful of its employees," and "a good citizen in its community" are some of the more common phrases that populate mission statements. The fact that mission statements extol similar sets of goals and objectives should be interpreted neither as an example of superficiality nor as a source of surprise. Mission statements need not project organization goals and objectives that are unique to be fit for purpose. Instead, and assuming the other mission statement criteria have been met, the goals and objectives simply need to be clearly described and factually based.

The fact that similar organizational goals and objectives are shared by organizations hailing from a wide range of industries and country settings should make intuitive sense. Why wouldn't an organization, whether it is an automobile manufacturer or a large hotel chain, want to be financially prosperous, responsive to customers, respectful of its employees, and a good corporate citizen? In fact, can you think of any for-profit company that would not want as one of its goals and objectives to be financially prosperous? The real surprise would be if a for-profit company did not mention in its mission statement a desire to be financially prosperous, financially secure, or some similar outcome.

The fact that there are often common threads to the goals and objectives pursued by organizations is simply recognition that the place organizations envision inhabiting is the same. In other words, the Promised Land looks the same for many organizations. Scholars who use resource dependency theory to explain how organizations structure themselves and undertake the design of their systems and processes would argue that the similarity in goals and objectives is to be expected. According to resource dependency theory, organizations strive for independence, while all the time knowing that such an ambition is not possible (Pfeffer, 1982). Organizations will inevitably find it necessary to build and maintain relationships with their various key stakeholders to ensure the continued access to these needed stakeholder resources. As such, organizations, in seeking to secure the financial resources they require, will want to ensure they meet their customers' expectations, and thereby retain their customers' business and the revenue and cash flow this provides. These organizations are also likely to find themselves dependent on the contributions of their employees. Such a dependency will encourage the organizations to ensure that their human resource policies are designed in such a way that will retain and motivate the employees who exhibit the best fit with the factors that underpin the organization's survival and success.

Having similar goals and objectives (i.e., financially prosperous, responsive to customers, etc.) does not mean organizations will operate in similar ways. In fact, Porter (1996) is adamant that that is the one thing that organizations must not do. Porter claims that any given organization must provide a different set of product/service attributes than any of its competitors. Unless an organization can attain this strategic differentiation, it will be unable to achieve its goals and objectives. The use of strategy to enable an organization to reach its goals and objectives and steer itself towards its Promised Land is the subject of Chapter 8.

Review Question 5.5: Why are the goals and objectives of many for-profit firms similar?
Answer: Please see the Answer section starting on page 283
Review Question 5.6: How is the mission statement of a not-for-profit related to its strategy?
Answer: Please see the Answer section starting on page 283

Review Question 5.7: Describe the relationships between an organization's mission statement, vision statement, strategy, and goals and objectives?

Answer: Please see the Answer section starting on page 283

Before concluding this chapter, it is worth noting that although most organizations, and
this is almost invariably true of for-profit firms, will feature overlapping sets of goals and objectives, this repetition is less likely to be the case for not-for-profit organizations. Often not-for-
profit organizations are created to provide a service that for-profit organizations are unable or
unwilling to provide. The fact that no other organization provides the service means that the
core of the single provider's goals and objectives, and the purpose these define, must of necessity
be different from all other organizations' goals, objectives, and purposes.

In some settings, laws may permit only one organization to deliver a particular service.
A prime example is the issuance of a country's passports. Countries will have a vested interest
in maintaining sole control over this activity. A defining characteristic of the sovereign state is
its ability to specify who can and cannot enter its borders. As a result, countries will be loath to
allow other individuals, groups, or organizations to issue passports and will specifically prohibit
others from doing so.

There are also occasions when for-profit organizations may be permitted to provide a
given service (i.e., there is no law prohibiting competition), but none choose to do so. As an
example, it would be highly unlikely that a for-profit company would be interested in providing budgeting services to low-income families experiencing financial problems. The fact that
these families are both low-income and struggling to pay their bills (for why else would they
require the budgeting services?) means the probability that a for-profit company would be paid
for its budgeting services is low. As a result, a for-profit company's desire to be involved in these
markets would be low as well.

In a situation where there is an inability or unwillingness on the part of other organizations
to offer particular services, and the provision of these services is held to be a necessary part of
maintaining the community or social fabric, the presiding government authority will create a
not-for-profit to offer the needed services. Since the purpose of the not-for-profit, and the goals
and objectives it is pursuing, are unlike any other organization's purposes, then the goals and
objectives of the not-for-profit will be unique. As a result, the need for formulating and implementing a competitive strategy to provide uniqueness relative to one's peers is not relevant. For
situations such as these, the mission statement also serves as the organization's strategy.

CONCLUSION

This chapter discussed the process whereby organizational goals and objectives are developed. The concept of stakeholders is central to understanding this process. In particular, key
stakeholder groups – which typically include employees, investors, customers, suppliers, and
government – influence an organization's establishment of its goals and objectives. More

dominant and powerful stakeholders will find they can impose more of their wishes on the focal organization than less dominant and powerful stakeholders can. It is the case, however, that even the wishes of the less dominant and powerful stakeholders must be accommodated in some way, for without their support the organization will be unable to function. Accordingly, a process of compromise, whether it is based on rational behaviour or political machinations, occurs.

The establishment of organizational goals and objectives are, as will be seen in Chapter 8, essential to organizations' development of competitive strategy. Organizational goals and objectives establish where an organization wants to be. Competitive strategy defines how an organization will pursue some form of sustainable uniqueness over its competitors (Porter, 1996) or commit to continuously improving the value proposition it offers its customers, such that this value proposition at any point in time is as good or superior to what is offered by any competing firm/organization (Cooper, 1995; Adler, 2011).

REFERENCES

Adler, R. W. (2011) Performance management and organizational strategy: how to design systems that meet the needs of confrontation strategy firms, *The British Accounting Review*, Vol. 43, No. 4, pp. 251–263.

Cooper, R. (1995) *When Lean Organizations Collide: Competing Through Confrontation*, Cambridge, MA: Harvard Business School Press.

Hickson, D.J. (1987) Decision-making at the top of organizations, *Annual Review of Sociology*, Vol. 13, pp. 165–192.

Pfeffer, J. (1982) *Organizations and Organization Theory*, Marshfield, MA: Pitman.

Porter, M.E. (1996) What is strategy?, *Harvard Business Review*, Vol. 74, No. 6, pp. 61–78.

Rasche, A. and Esser, D. (2006) From stakeholder management to stakeholder accountability. *Journal of Business Ethics*, Vol. 65, No. 3, pp. 251–267.

CHAPTER 6

Business ethics as an element of organizational strategy

INTRODUCTION

This chapter explores and discusses the relationship between ethics and performance management. As discussed in Chapter 2, the essence of performance management is ensuring employees do the right thing. The three main reasons employees fail to do the right thing are the lack of or a poorly articulated strategy, employees possessing inadequate skills, and the failure to ensure employees are properly motivated. The first issue is the topic of Chapters 7 and 8, while the second issue is covered as part of Chapter 11. The third issue is both central to the present chapter and a recurring theme throughout the book. More specifically, and in terms of the present chapter, employees who are unethically motivated will not be conforming to performance management's mandate of ensuring employees are doing the right thing.

This chapter argues that ensuring high levels of employee ethical behaviour are paramount to not simply the success but the very survival of all organizations, no matter their size or

DOI: 10.4324/9781003267195-8

industry. In spite of its criticality, time and again various organizations have shown significant lapses in ethical behaviour. Examples of organizations' depraved hubris, and in particular occasions when organizations believed they could either conceal their unethical behaviour or its detection would have an inconsequential impact, will be recounted to show the fallacy in believing unethical practices could ever constitute a strategy, even in the short term. Following this discussion, the chapter proceeds to discuss the factors that commonly lead to employee unethical behaviour. The chapter next examines various actions an organization can take to minimize the occurrence of unethical employee behaviour. These efforts include the healthy functioning of the Institute of Internal Auditors' (2013) three lines of defence system, the judicious use of employee incentives, and employee training on using Daniel Kahneman's system 2 thinking.

THE DEFINITION OF ETHICS

Ethics comprises how moral principles guide and proscribe individual behaviour. The word is derived from the Greek word *ethos*, which means custom, habit, character, or disposition. Ethics includes, but goes well beyond, knowing and obeying territorial laws. As such, ethics includes striving to live a good life, being a responsible citizen, and making good moral decisions.

Ethics is influenced by both secular (i.e., legal systems) and religious institutional concepts. Laws are meant to protect individuals' rights, as well as communicate individuals' responsibilities. Religions include principles by which individuals are meant to live. Many of the principles revolve around an individual's relationships with others. Honesty, respect, humility, and generosity are some of the more common themes which feature.

The practice of ethics includes addressing such major issues as abortion, human rights, systemic racism, climate activism, animal rights, and genetic engineering. In this chapter, however, only the ethics of professional/work conduct will be discussed. This focus is most relevant to the book's overall theme of performance management.

As noted above, abiding by the laws of one's jurisdiction forms a part of making ethical decisions and behaving ethically. In a subsequent section to this chapter, issues of bribes, kickbacks, and accountants' and senior managers' legal duties in financial accounting and reporting are discussed. Similar to the existence of laws that forbid insider trading, this discussion highlights laws that prohibit taking or receiving bribes or kickbacks and the requirement that organizations produce financial statements that fairly present their financial performances and positions.

Although laws incorporate many of the ethical standards to which most citizens subscribe, laws can either fail to fully express all of society's expectations or they may be based on a society's morally corrupt principles (e.g., US slavery in the 1600s–1800s, Nazi Germany's Aryanism, and South Africa's apartheid system). In terms of the former, a romantic relationship between two consenting adults is allowed under most, and certainly every western-based, countries' laws. Applying this legal threshold to a work environment would mean that a doctor could date a patient or a supervisor could date a subordinate. Although the doctor and supervisor could legally do this, in nearly all situations they would be disallowed from doing so because of the higher duty their respective professions' or organizations' ethical standards required of them. For doctors, their medical profession's code of conduct specifically prohibits romantic relationships between doctors and patients. For supervisors, their organizations typically have formalized rules, perhaps contained in an organizational code of ethics or in an employee handbook, that would forbid such relationships.

Readers who are familiar with the code of practice relating to accountants will know that accountants must display independence in both act and appearance. The former means that auditors, for example, must fully support their audit conclusions, including subjecting the claims of a client to independent verification and testing. The latter means that an accountant must avoid situations that could lead to or be reasonably perceived by another to lead to the receipt of special or preferential treatment from a client. Accordingly, accountants should not accept gifts from a client; nor, in most situations, would it be appropriate for an accountant to receive a home mortgage from the bank that they audit. The accounting profession deems both actions as putting at risk an accountant's professional judgement (i.e., the accountant's ability to act independently) and potentially sending a confusing signal to the public (i.e., the appearance of a lack of independence may undermine the public's faith in the accounting profession). A similar rationale for appearing independent explains why many senior politicians, at least those who are democratically elected, place their investment holdings in a blind trust while they are in office.

As these examples indicate, employees' work behaviour is often subject to a formalized set of ethical standards, and this is particularly the case for professional bodies (e.g., medicine, accounting, and law). In fact, the existence of a code of ethics is one of the distinguishing characteristics of a profession. Although some people commonly conflate professionalism with ethics, this is a mistake. For example, an accountant's expected behaviour exceeds what is demanded by the profession's code of ethics. Similar to other professions, such as medicine and law, accountants commit themselves to serving and protecting the public's interests. Wright (1951: 748), for example, argues that a professional's duty is to "… primarily [work] in the interests of others."

Koch (2019) traces this social ethic to the Latin root of the word "profession," which is "*profiteri*" and translates to declaring or professing publicly. Professions, in other words, are meant to be characterized by members who declare publicly their morally-shared commitment to work in the interests of society, a mandate that exceeds the set of rules comprising the profession's code of conduct. Flanagan and Clarke (2007) offer a very clear distinction between the constructs of ethics and professionalism when they describe a profession's ethics as typically represented by a code of ethics that serves to specify minimum levels of member conduct, whereas professionalism further embodies aspirational values (i.e., serving the public interest).

Review Question 6.1: Define ethics. How is it related to such concepts as morality and lawfulness?

Answer: Please see the Answer section starting on page 283

Review Question 6.2: In what way is ethics a fundamental part of a professional such as medicine, accounting, and law? Provide an example for each of these three types of professions.

Answer: Please see the Answer section starting on page 283

With the exception of global professions like accounting, whose ethical standards operate worldwide, the standard of ethical behaviour demanded of employees is often influenced by local/regional/national customs. In particular, history and cultural traditions help shape ethical practices and help explain why there are differences in the prevailing employee ethical standards in various geographical locations. As an example, the use of bribes and kickbacks are specifically forbidden by US law (i.e., the Foreign Corrupt Practices Act) and UK law (i.e., the UK Bribery Act). Yet, in some parts of the world, bribes and kickbacks are considered a customary part of doing business, with some people viewing them as no different from a diner who tips a *maître d* or a traveller who tips a porter. After all, the diner's and the traveller's largess likely includes the intention of influencing the *maître d'* (i.e., to get a preferred table and be assigned a good waiter) and the porter (i.e., to ensure the traveller's bags are safely transported to their destination). Some might even argue that the only difference between what distinguishes a bribe from acceptable practice is the amount being exchanged. Far from suggesting that bribes are in any way okay, the distinction being made here only seeks to illustrate how some of the very basic and everyday values one holds (and seldom questions) explain why employee ethical standards are not universal but setting specific.

For those organizations that operate in multiple locations, they will find that their prescribed ethical standards will be a product of the ethical values their stakeholders hold. Remember, as was discussed in Chapter 5, an organization's genesis and survival are based on the willingness of a variety of stakeholders to work together. Without their continued allegiance, the organization has no future. Fulfilling the collective stakeholders' expectations is an essential organizational mandate. In particular, all organizations must be conscious of the ethical standards of their stakeholders.

Legitimacy theory would also suggest that organizations must meet the ethical expectations of the communities in which they operate. Unless an organization does so, it risks losing the community support on which its existence relies, a situation which legitimacy theorists term losing one's social licence to operate. Maintaining one's social licence requires an organization to follow the rules, both legal and ethical, of the communities in which they reside.

Codes of ethics can be found in nearly all large and even most medium size organizations. Facebook's The Meta Code of Conduct (n.d.) makes seven references to its position on the ethical behaviour of its employees, ranging from the prohibition of bribes and kickbacks to avoiding conflicts of interest and insider trading. On page 7 of its Code of Conduct, employees are specifically instructed that they must "Act lawfully, honestly, ethically and in the best interests of Facebook and our Facebook users at all times." Facebook's VP of Product Design, Margaret Stewart, is quoted on page 30 of the Code of Conduct as saying:

> As technologists, we are all stewards of some of the most powerful communication tools ever created. These tools have generated a lot of good in the world, but their very power requires a deep sense of responsibility and a commitment to making the most ethically responsible decisions possible, every day.

Facebook's achievement of its espoused ambition of acting ethically has been the subject of many news stories, books, and US Congressional hearings. Critics charge that Facebook is aware of the detriment its social media causes to society. The company's proclaimed ideal of being ethically responsible to its users is inconsistent with accusations that it is a platform for bullying and misinformation. McNamee's (2019) book *Zucked* contends Facebook's business model is predicated on producing divisive Facebook communities and fostering anger and hatred between the groups, for research shows that these two emotions, more than any others, help create an "us versus them" mentality and lengthens user time spent on Facebook's website.

Walmart, Inc., which is an American multinational retail corporation that operates a chain of 10,500 hypermarkets, discount department stores, and grocery stores across 24 countries, has a 42-page Code of Conduct. Its Code of Conduct is couched in the concept of building and maintaining trust with all significant stakeholders. According to its president and CEO, Doug McMillon, Walmart's Code of Conduct serves as a behavioural compass. More specifically, he states:

> We remind ourselves each day that our work isn't just about what we achieve but how we achieve it. The way we conduct our business is as important as the products we sell and the services we provide. That means complying with the laws of the communities where we do business. But that is not enough. Associates who work at Walmart are expected to operate based on our values. Our expectation is you will put fairness, equity, justice, and integrity at the heart of everything you do. By working this way, each one of us will play an active part in shaping our culture, building trust, and making it possible for us to reach our purpose and potential as a company.
>
> (Walmart Code of Conduct 2021: 5)

Walmart's Code of Conduct refers to ensuring employee behaviour goes beyond merely following the laws of the communities in which it operates, which is consistent with this chapter's definition of ethics. As the company's president and CEO notes, the Code of Conduct calls for all employees to act with "fairness, equity, justice, and integrity."

Walmart's CEO's words are emblematic of what would be expected in a company's code of conduct. Walmart, however, has been consistently called out for its failure to pay its employees a living wage. The US's nonpartisan Government Accountability Office's October 2020 report "Federal Social Safety Net Programs: Millions of Full-Time Workers Rely on Federal Health Care and Food Assistance Programs" shows that workers at such food service and retail giants as Walmart, McDonald's, Amazon, Kroger, and Dollar General are among the top beneficiaries of Medicaid (a federal and state programme that helps low-income people with their healthcare costs) and the Supplemental Nutrition Assistance Program (a federal programme that helps low-income households buy the food they need for good health). These findings led US Senator Bernie Sanders to accuse Walmart (and several other large retailers and fast food restaurants) of "morally obscene" behaviour, whereby US taxpayers were being called upon to support "corporate welfare" because some of the largest and most profitable corporations in America are "paying their workers starvation wages" (Rosenberg, 2020).

As this brief discussion of Facebook and Walmart illustrates, what a company espouses and what it does can be two very different things. Having formal codes of ethics and employee codes of conduct can be useful. However, their mere existence will always pale to a company's culture, with the result being that formalised ethics programmes become window dressing and something to which only lip service is paid.

Review Question 6.3: What are the names of the common documents organizations and professional bodies use to convey ethical expectations and standards to their members?
Answer: Please see the Answer section starting on page 283

ETHICS' CONNECTION TO PERFORMANCE MANAGEMENT

As noted above, as well as was discussed in Chapter 5, organizations' stakeholders help to determine the goals any given organization will pursue. The successful pursuit of these organizational goals will be enabled by a competitive strategy, a topic that is discussed in Chapter 9. Although an unscrupulous organization could try to build a strategy around a covert programme of unethical behaviour (e.g., giving and accepting bribes, misrepresenting product/service features, and committing financial fraud), the reliance on such practices could never qualify as a strategy. The very essence of a strategy is about long-term, as opposed to short-lived, performance. Trying to scam stakeholders (i.e., customers, employees, investors, and suppliers) will not work in the long run. As the former President of the United States Abraham Lincoln once opined, "You can fool some of the people all of the time, and all of the people some of the time, but you cannot fool all of the people all of the time."

The relationship between ethics and performance management is much more than an implicit association between its needed presence and the pursuit of organizational strategy. An appreciation of its more explicit relationship can be gleaned from Boland (1982), who writes, "A well-controlled organisation would be one in which the ethical concerns of its members were identified, anaylzed and acted upon in a rational, coherent way." Notice the word "control." Chapter 2 discusses how previous conceptions of performance management were built on the idea of control, a concept that has evolved to now be referred to as "influence."

Boty-Lee and Moody (2010) further elaborate on the connection between ethics and performance management when they remark, "At their core, ethics programs are control systems designed to align employee behaviour with management's values." Again, notice these authors' use of the term "control system" and their reference to aligning employee behaviour with what management values/wants. This vision of ethics harmonizes with the definition of performance management presented in Chapter 2.

In summary, behaving ethically is an implicit assumption of strategy formulation and is fundamental to strategy implementation and evaluation. Since performance management is all about ensuring an organization's strategy is being implemented, then it follows that ethics and performance management are themselves interconnected. As will be discussed in the chapter's next section, organizational ethical failures are very costly. This fact reveals why performance management must be understood not only as ensuring an organization's strategy is being implemented, but also as detecting situations when the strategy is either not working or is experiencing drift due to employees making decisions that favour their self-interests over the needs of their organizations. Situations where this drift is likely to happen and how to avoid such situations are discussed in the subsequent sections of this chapter.

> *Review Question 6.4:* Explain how ethics is related to performance management.
> *Answer:* Please see the Answer section starting on page 283

THE COST OF ETHICAL FAILURES

There are a number of direct and indirect costs associated with ethical failures by organizations. The most studied forms of ethical failures involve corruption (i.e., the giving or receiving of bribes and kickbacks and the misstatement of companies' financial statements). In 2016 and 2017, more than USD 8 billion in cumulative corporate penalties and fines were collected by various countries' enforcement of anti-corruption laws (Gibson, Dunn, and Crutcher, 2018). While 8 billion is certainly no small sum, in 2020, Goldman Sachs alone was charged USD 5 billion in fines and penalties relating to its use of a third-party intermediary to bribe high-ranking government officials in Malaysia and the Emirate of Abu Dhabi (Gibson, Dunn, and Crutcher, 2021). Two and a half billion of the five billion total settlement was paid to the Malaysian government as part of Goldman Sachs' penalty for plundering the Malaysian sovereign wealth fund 1Malaysia Development Berhad by charging arranger and underwriter fees that were more than double what it charged for other Asia ex-Japan bond offerings during the similar time period.

In many instances of ethical failures, it is the senior leaders who have either directly or indirectly contributed to the outcome. For example, the Toshiba accounting scandal uncovered in 2015, was largely the product of its senior managers' top-down budgeting practices. Using what the company described as "Challenges," Toshiba's corporate leadership allocated a set of strict quarterly profit targets to its business units. These Challenges came with an implied understanding that failure would not be accepted. In some cases, the Challenges were handed down so close to the end of the quarter that there was no chance to genuinely/honestly impact performance. Believing that a failure to achieve the Challenges was not an option, the unit accountants began to engage in fraudulent accounting practices, including booking future profits early, pushing back losses, and pushing back charges.

The scandal caused the forced resignation of Toshiba's CEO Hisao Tanaka and tarnished the reputations of his two predecessors. More recently, in April 2021, Toshiba's then CEO Nobuaki Kurumatani was ousted for unethical behaviour relating to a USD 20 billion buyout bid from his former employer CVC Capital Partners. Although Toshiba may be the leader in an unenviable run of recent CEO malfeasance, its CEOs are far from the only ones being charged with unethical behaviour. In fact, a report by PricewaterhouseCoopers (PwC) found that in 2018 39% of all forced resignations of CEOs were due to unacceptable ethical behaviour, a percentage that PwC said was higher than the percentage of CEOs forced out for reasons of financial performance or struggles with their boards (PwC, 2019).

The leading piece of legislation responsible for anti-corruption legal actions is the Foreign Corrupt Practices Act (FCPA). The FCPA was introduced in 1977 by then US President Jimmy Carter. It was premised on the idea that corruption is bad business, and US persons, companies, and those operating within the US financial system should not profit from it. The FCPA is mostly known for its anti-bribery provisions. However, it also includes legislation relating to fraud in financial accounting and reporting. In particular, the Act requires entities to make and keep books, records, and accounts in reasonable detail and which accurately and fairly reflect an organization's transactions, as well as maintaining reasonable internal accounting controls aimed at preventing and detecting unauthorized payments. The US Department of Justice (DOJ) and the Securities and Exchange Commission (SEC), both of which oversee the FCPA's implementation, have increasingly sought to build a coordinated multinational network of law enforcers. The 2020 case against Goldman Sachs, which involved law enforcement authorities in the United States, United Kingdom, Singapore, Hong Kong, and Malaysia, is one example of these collaborative efforts.

FCPA violations can attract significant penalties. Violations of the anti-bribery provisions can result in organizations being fined up to $2 million for each criminal count or twice the pecuniary gain or loss resulting from the bribe. As was shown with Goldman Sachs, these penalties can add up to large sums. Violations of the accounting provisions can result in organizational fines of up to $25 million per violation, with individuals facing up to a $5 million fine and 20 years in prison. In spite of these high penalties, the annual number of FCPA enforcement actions has averaged around 36, with 2020's number being 32. Table 6.1 presents a list at 2021 of the top ten corporate settlements under the FCPA legislation. The settlement amounts are meant to represent all fines and penalties paid to all enforcement authorities. Although the US DOJ and the SEC both display on their websites the settlements reached on FCPA violations, the settlements reached with other national enforcement authorities are more opaque. For example, Goldman Sachs' total settlement is commonly estimated as exceeding USD 5 billion (Gibson, Dunn, and Crutcher, 2021). It is therefore best to view the table's settlements as close approximations rather than exact figures.

On top of the fines and penalties that an organization's ethical failings may bring, the organization will also likely find itself subject to a class action lawsuit initiated by aggrieved investors. Furthermore, and as part of its need to defend itself against FCPA investigations and class action lawsuits, the organization will find it must pay substantial legal, accounting, and consulting fees. As an illustration, Sampath *et al.* (2018) found that Siemens AG, throughout the legal defence of its 2008 bribery investigation, paid over USD 1 billion in consulting and legal fees. That sum equates to over 50% of the $1.78 billion it paid in penalties and fines for its wrongdoing.

TABLE 6.1 FCPA top ten violators 1977–2020

Rank	Company	Total settlement (USD '000s)	Date
1	Goldman Sachs	5,000,000	22 Oct 2020
2	Airbus	2,090,000	31 Jan 2020
3	*Petrobras*	1,780,000	27 Sep 2018
4	Siemens AG	1,780,000	15 Dec 2008
5	Ericsson	1,060,570	06 Dec 2019
6	Telia	965,000	21 Sep 2017
7	Mobile TeleSystems	850,000	06 Mar 2019
8	*VimpelCom*	795,000	18 Feb 2016
9	Alstom S.A.	772,290	22 Dec 2014
10	*Societe Generale*	585,000	04 Jun 2018

The financial costs from organizational ethical failings may be the most visible cost, but it is far from the only or even the most significant cost. Employee turnover and employee recruitment are also adversely affected by ethical failings. In particular, scholars have shown that companies with superior social performance – as represented by ethical work environments – not only tend to perform better financially (Bagnoli and Watts, 2003; Baron, 2001; Lev *et al.*, 2008; Orlitzky *et al.*, 2003), but they also have more satisfied and more committed employees, who are less likely to quit the organization for another employer (Nejati *et al.*, 2021; Wang *et al.*, 2013). Employee Benefit News (2017) calculates the cost of turnover at 33% of an employee's salary. These costs include both direct and indirect turnover costs, the latter of which are often neglected or overlooked. Table 6.2 lists the types of typical costs associated with these two categories of turnover costs.

A company's stock price invariably declines following the disclosure of an FCPA investigation. As an example, Willbros, a global engineering contractor, saw its stock price plummet by 31%. The stock was trading at $15.92 the day before the disclosure of the FCPA investigation on 17 May 2005 and fell to $11.00 at the close of trading on 18 May 2005. As another example, when Avon, the cosmetics company, made its initial disclosure on 20 October 2008 of being the target of an FCPA investigation, its stock price initially fell by 3% at the close of the following day's trading. However, the stock continued falling throughout the week and was down 26.8% by the week's end.

And finally, organizational ethical failings result in reputational harm. This damage includes not only the previously mentioned issues of finding it more difficult to retain and attract employees and a devalued stock price, but also the loss of other important stakeholders' loyalty and commitment. Suppliers, customers, and whole communities may shun or reduce their engagement with the organization. Suddaby *et al.* (2009) refer to this possibility as the consequential erosion of an organization's legitimacy and social licence to operate, which can produce a downward spiral of deteriorating company performance, fewer organizational resources, and increasingly discontented and less engaged employees.

Sampath *et al.* (2018) use abnormal stock market returns to calculate the total cost of an FCPA-initiated bribery investigation. The researchers then proceed to break this total cost into

TABLE 6.2 Cost of turnover

Direct costs	Indirect costs
• Recruitment of replacements • Administrative hiring costs • Costs of training	• Lost productivity associated with the time between the loss of an employee and hiring of a replacement • Lost productivity due to a new employee learning the job • Lost productivity associated with co-workers helping the new employee • Costs associated with the employee's lack of motivation prior to leaving • Sometimes, the costs of trade secrets and proprietary information divulged by the employee who leaves • Public relations costs

> *Review Question 6.5:* What are the main cost categories associated with organizational ethical failing? Give examples for each type of cost category?
>
> *Answer:* Please see the Answer section starting on page 283

three constituent parts of enforcement fines and penalties, class action lawsuits, and reputational harm. They find that for every $1 of share value loss, 18¢ can be attributed to enforcement fines and penalties, 0.2¢ to class action costs, and 81.8¢ to reputational loss. In other words, beyond the visible financial punishment a government and a court of law may impose, there is a much more severe, although less visible, 4.5 times greater penalty that customers, suppliers, investors, and other stakeholders collectively exact on the offending organization. A multiplier of 4.5, added to Goldman Sachs' USD 5 billion settlement, would suggest the real cost to its 2020 bribery case is about USD 27.5 billion.

BREAKING BAD: FACTORS ASSOCIATED WITH UNETHICAL EMPLOYEE BEHAVIOUR

Why is it that seemingly good people make bad judgements and, in the process, commit uncharacteristic, unethical behaviour? KPMG is one of the leading international professional services firms. With its strong links to the accounting profession, one would expect it to show a strong commitment to acting in the public interest, possess high ethical standards, and post a venerable record of good ethical behaviour. Instead, as the sidebar illustrates, KPMG has put up a very chequered performance over the past 20 years.

There exists among consulting practitioners a rule of thumb known as the 10-80-10 rule. It claims that 10% of employees are always honest, 80% are honest most of the time, and 10% will commit fraud or act unethically whenever an opportunity presents itself. These percentages are generic in the sense that they represent an average work setting. In reality, different organizations, different professional groupings, and even different country settings will display different percentages for the three categories. For example, a 2019 Gallop poll shows that the three most trusted professions are nurses, followed by engineers, and then medical doctors. The lowest trusted professions are insurance salesmen, politicians, and, at the very bottom, used car salesmen. Meanwhile, Transparency International provides an annual perceived corruption score for the world's 180 countries. In 2020's survey, the top three least corrupt countries are New Zealand and Denmark tied for first, with Finland occupying third place. The three most corrupt countries are Syria, Southern Sudan, and Somalia.

The percentages associated with the 10-80-10 rule are not nearly as important as recognizing the existence of the three employee categories. In an ideal world, an organization would only select and retain employees from the always honest category. It would, however, be fanciful to believe that an organization could have the luxury of only associating with this singular group of employees. Accordingly, an organization will want to try as best it can to avoid association with individuals from the always opportunistic group and put in place various controls,

Consider this …

From at least 2016 until early 2020, KPMG Australia engaged in a widespread exam cheating scandal, involving 1,131 of its employees or approximately 12% of the firm's workforce. Individuals implicated in the cheating included a large swathe of employees, ranging from junior accountants to senior partners. The cheating consisted of improper answer sharing when taking training tests, which included tests enabling its staff to satisfy requirements for maintaining their accounting licences. In particular, staff were found to have shared answers using email, text messages, and instant message services, as well as were found guilty of providing answers in hard copy documents, saving test answers to a shared server, and giving verbal answers to colleagues taking tests in the presence of others.

The cheating was a direct violation of the Public Company Accounting Oversight Board's (PCAOB) rules and quality control standards. The PCAOB (2021) found KPMG Australia guilty of failing to establish appropriate policies and procedures for administering and monitoring training tests. Ironically, some of the tests included topics on ethics. The PCAOB fined KPMG Australia USD 450,000 for its transgression. Furthermore, it ordered the firm to report back to the PCAOB within 120 days to show that it had complied with the regulatory body's order to establish and/or revise its testing policies and procedures for ensuring the integrity of its future training tests.

KPMG International Limited, which is the global umbrella of KPMG's network of firms operating in 145 countries, is no stranger to unethical practice. In 2019, KPMG US was fined USD 50 million for multiple misconduct scandals, including cheating on CPE exams. The cheating included KPMG staff manipulating computer servers and HTML code to lower the threshold for passing the tests.

In August 2005, the US DOJ and Internal Revenue Service (IRS) fined KPMG USD 456 million after the firm admitted criminal wrongdoing for enabling its clients to evade taxes. The DOJ described it as "the largest criminal tax case ever filed" (DOJ, 2005). KPMG admitted it conspired to defraud the IRS by designing, marketing, and implementing illegal tax shelters that generated at least $11 billion dollars in phony tax losses. It was further found that KPMG employees prepared false and fraudulent documents – including engagement letters, transactional documents, representation letters, and opinion letters – to deceive the IRS should it learn of the transactions.

Following the January 2018 collapse of Carillion, a British multinational construction and facilities management services company, inspectors from the Financial Reporting Council (FRC) examined KPMG's Carillion audit files for the years 2014 and 2016. It was subsequently found that KPMG supplied forged documents to the FRC audit quality inspectors. These documents included false spreadsheets and minutes of meetings, which were fabricated months after the audit occurred. KPMG partners blamed a junior member of the staff for this dishonesty. If it is true that this staff member committed the forgeries on their own, then, as Sika (2022) has charged, this would lead one to wonder about "… the supervision of staff, reviews by partners, prevalence of irregular practices and corrosive organisational culture."

As a further example of KPMG's chequered behaviour, in August 2021, the firm was fined £13 million for a serious conflict of interest. KPMG was also ordered to pay an additional £2.8 million in costs. The conflict of interest involved KPMG and one of its former partners, David Costley-Wood, acting for its client Silentnight, a large UK manufacturer of beds and mattresses, as well as for the firm H.I.G. Capital, which eventually acquired Silentnight. The FRC (2021) concluded that Costley-Wood, in an attempt to gain favour with H.I.G. Capital, helped H.I.G. "deliberately [bring] about the unnecessary insolvency of the original Silentnight Group in order to buy its business out of administration, while leaving its defined benefit pension scheme behind." The UK's Pensions Regulator argued that the crux of all the scheming was to help H.I.G. secure an unwarranted windfall of £47 million, which, in the process, put the savings of 1,200 Silentnight staff at risk (Pensions Regulator, 2021).

KPMG is far from the only large, international professional services firm to be singled out for poor practice and behaviour. According to the FRC, 29% of the audits delivered by the world's seven largest audit firms – BDO, Deloitte, Ernst & Young (EY), Grant Thornton, KPMG, Mazars, and PricewaterhouseCoopers (PwC) – fail to meet basic expected standards (FRC, 2021). However, even this latest report of the FRC gives extra attention to KPMG, stating, "Inspection results at KPMG did not improve and it is unacceptable that, for the third year running, the FRC found improvements were required to KPMG's audits of banks and similar entities."

Review Question 6.6: Beyond the committees and boards different professions may operate to investigate, judge, and discipline members' ethical violations, identify the main public bodies and organizations that police organizational ethical failings.

Answer: Please see the Answer section starting on page 283

---

systems, and programmes to dissuade individuals from the remaining group from giving in to temptation. These efforts will include ethics training, the adoption of codes of ethics, the use of internal controls, management oversight, internal audit activities, and channels for whistle blowing. Each of these mechanisms will be discussed more fully later in the chapter. First, it is useful to understand the set of known factors that commonly lead to employees committing fraud.

To help explain why employees commit unethical acts, researchers have proposed the fraud triangle. Although this model certainly applies to acts of fraud (e.g., embezzlement, insider trading, and improper financial reporting), it also applies more generally to employee decisions to behave unethically. The fraud triangle suggests that employee fraud/unethical behaviour is a function of

Review Question: 6.7 What is the 10–80–10 rule?

Answer: Please see the Answer section starting on page 283

Review Question 6.8: What are the main factors associated with employees making bad ethical decisions?

Answer: Please see the Answer section starting on page 283

three factors: opportunity, rationalization, and motivation. Unethical behaviour can occur when any of these three factors occur, but it will be most likely when all three factors are simultaneously present. Remember, according to the 10–80–10 rule, employees in the 80% group are honest most of the time. Generally, it is the simultaneous alignment of the three factors that lead these employees to go astray. In particular, an opportunity arises that coincides with a motivation to commit a fraud/unethical behaviour that the employee can rationalize as being okay.

The fraud triangle's opportunity factor includes a flaw in the organization's internal controls (i.e., none in place, not monitored, not enforced, or not effective), the granting of too much trust and employee autonomy, and insufficient senior management communication and leadership. The fraud triangle's employee motivation is partitioned into internal and external pressures. Internal pressures comprise employee greed, financial debt difficulties, and vices (e.g., drugs, gambling). External pressures consist of work pressure to perform (i.e., difficult/impossible budget targets) and having too much work. Finally, rationalization involves minimization of the behaviour by making such claims as "the company owes me," "everyone else is doing it," "no one will miss the money," "it's for a noble purpose," "there is no personal benefit," or "a decision by another employee has caused me take the action."

As already noted, it generally requires the presence of all three factors to trigger unethical employee behaviour. Since an organization has complete control over the opportunity factor, the likelihood that all three factors will coincide should be impossible without employee collusion. The organization also has significant influence over the other two fraud triangle factors. After all, it determines whether employees are being pushed too hard. It also is responsible for its organizational culture. A healthy organizational culture will prevent unethical musings and rationalizations from ever gaining traction. More will be discussed about this topic in Chapter 12. Suffice it to say, the organization has a significant ability to control, or at least influence, the incidence of unethical behaviour. The remainder of the chapter is devoted to a discussion of what organizations can do to minimize the occurrence of unethical behaviour.

HOW ORGANISATIONS CAN MINIMIZE UNETHICAL EMPLOYEE BEHAVIOUR

There are three ways an organization can reduce unethical employee behaviour. The organization should ensure whether its three lines of defence system are properly functioning, ensure whether it has judiciously designed and operated employee incentive systems, and also ensure whether it has promoted system 2 thinking over system 1 thinking. The remainder of the chapter is devoted to a fuller enumeration and discussion of these three approaches.

THE THREE LINES OF DEFENCE SYSTEM

The three lines of defence system offers a simple and effective way to help organizations manage operational risks and minimize the occurrence of unethical employee behaviour (Institute of Internal Auditors, 2013). The first line of defence comprises employee handbooks, ethics programmes, whistleblowing hotlines, the use of at-risk incentives for senior managers, and internal controls. Employee handbooks codify expected employee behaviour, identifying what employees are entitled to, what they must do, and what they must not do. Ethics programmes are aimed at helping employees understand the types of situations that may prompt the need to consider more carefully how a decision or participation in a decision might disadvantage the interests of the organization or confer an unwarranted preferential standing on the decision maker. Whistleblowing serves as one part of an organization's overall governance and risk management environment. A whistleblowing programme shows an organization's commitment to develop a "speak-up" culture, whereby employees are protected from retaliation for reporting organizational misconduct, including fraud, workplace bullying, and workplace health and safety violations.

At-risk incentives seek to curb unethical behaviour by postponing the full vesting of the financial incentives (cash bonuses, stock options, etc.) a manager may have been previously deemed to have earned. For a manager to receive the full incentive, they must ensure that prescribed standards are maintained throughout the vesting period. This provision helps to prevent a manager from making unethical decisions as a way to achieve their incentivized current performance. These decisions might involve accelerating sales into earlier time periods and deferring discretionary expenses (e.g., preventive maintenance) into later time periods. They could also involve cutting back on product/service quality programmes, employee training programmes, or leaving employee vacancies unfilled.

The final element in the first-line defence comprises an organization's internal controls. As mentioned above when discussing the fraud triangle, the fraud triangle specifies opportunity as one of the three main factors associated with unethical employee behaviour. This opportunity generally arises as the result of flaws in an organization's internal controls. Perhaps there are no internal controls, or the controls are not monitored, not enforced, or not effective. Organizations' accountants are responsible for the design and operation of internal controls. Internal audit departments will exist in large organizations, and it is the members of these departments who are responsible for ensuring their organizations' internal controls safeguard organizational assets, assist in the production of reliable financial reports, and enable compliance with all organizational policies, territorial laws, and government and industry regulations.

The typical organization's internal controls would include the separation of responsibilities. In particular, the individual who is responsible for working with an asset – whether it be cash, inventory, or company cars – should be different from the person responsible for the financial accounting of these assets. Other expected internal controls would feature the use of timecards/timesheets, having spending limits on the purchase orders employees can generate, the regular use of bank reconciliations, stringent rules and systems for the approval of new suppliers and entering them into the organization's supplier database, multiple records that show the requisitioning, ordering and receipt of assets before they are paid, and the requirement of multiple signatures for large payments or movements of cash. A well designed and operated internal control system should make it virtually impossible for an employee to commit fraud against the organization without the connivance of multiple employees involved in the deceit.

An organization's second line of defence against unethical employee behaviour involves the use of systems and processes designed to detect errors in a timely manner. Included in this second line of defence are violation and termination reporting, correlated trend analysis, staff engagement surveys, and customer surveys. Employee violations of organizational policies, and especially violations that have led to an employee's termination, should feature as part of an organization's regular reporting. Furthermore, these reports should form their own agenda item for every board of directors or board of trustees meeting. Correlated trend analysis involves looking for associations between problematic performance and likely causes. For example, a spike in the reporting of workplace bullying might be associated with a new hire or perhaps something as general as a shift in an organization's culture.

Unhappy customers may be the by-product of something that has gone amiss in the organization. Maybe it is the result of poorer product quality (perhaps due to a reduction in the funding of quality programmes), poorer trained employees (perhaps due to a cut in employee training), or long call centre wait times (perhaps due to not replacing departing employees). Regardless of whether these decisions are due to a decisionmaker trying to gain a personal advantage (e.g., a bonus), which would be an example of unethical behaviour, or due to some other factor, the organization will want to address the customers' concerns.

Unhappy employees may be the result of poor working conditions, poor work relationships, or poor leadership. Again, these factors may be the result of a decisionmaker trying to gain a personal advantage and would therefore be unethical. Knowing why employees are unhappy is key to not only detecting possible unethical behaviour, but it is critical to minimizing situations where employees rationalize their unethical behaviour by blaming the organization for some perceived wrong. One example might be an employee believing that their organization's failure to replace a departed employee has resulted in having to work longer hours and experiencing greater stress. This employee might rationalize their unethical behaviour by asserting their behaviour compensates for the extra work they are doing. Another example might be an employee feeling underinvested in due to a cutback in employee training. Again, the employee might rationalize their unethical behaviour by claiming the organization has been unfair and they are merely evening things up.

The third line of defence involves assuring or improving the first two lines of defence. An organization's internal audit department is responsible for this third line of defence. As part of its duties, the internal auditor will conduct analytical reviews of significant activities and accounts (e.g., reported employee violations and new customer and supplier account openings), evaluate the robustness and readiness of the organization's risk management processes and coverage, and conduct studies of the integrity of management and governance reporting.

JUDICIOUS DESIGN AND USE OF EMPLOYEE INCENTIVES

In addition to ensuring healthy functioning of the three lines of defence system, an organization can also reduce the risk of unethical employee behaviour by ensuring it judiciously uses employee incentives. As will be discussed in Chapter 11, the literature offers at best mixed results for the motivational benefits associated with employee incentives. If employee motivation is merely thought of as energizing employees, then incentive programmes are useful (Kohn, 1993). However, if employee motivation is framed as energizing employees to accomplish organizationally-beneficial outcomes in both short and longer terms, then employee incentives have questionable efficacy (Herzberg, 2003).

Organizations that chose to use employee incentives should only do so when the incentives are tied to reasonable performance targets. Many organizational ethical failings can be traced to organizations' use of unrealistic targets. Imposing too high of a target can lead employees to engage in dysfunctional behaviour (e.g., an engineer who avoids collaborating with colleagues to avoid sharing a bonus the organization offers for production process improvement ideas) and even unethical behaviour (e.g., creating slack in a budget).

Wells Fargo, a large California-headquartered financial services company, presents a poignant example of a company's injudicious use of incentives that led to unethical employee behaviour. In the early to mid-2010s, Wells Fargo introduced an incentive compensation programme for its branch employees. The incentives formed part of the bank's "Go for Gr-Eight" marketing initiative, which required getting eight financial products (e.g., a credit card, savings account, mortgage) into the hands of each customer. To reach this ambition, cross-selling goals for employees were set, with some reported to be as high as 20 per day. Employees who reached their goals were rewarded with incentives. Personal bankers were offered bonuses of 15–20% of their salary, and tellers could earn up to 3% of their salary.

To place into context Wells Fargo's Go for Gr-Eight programme, the incentivized goal was a more than 33% increase on its 2010 performance. Some critics charge that even this base period included years of aggressive cross-selling (Public Citizen, 2016). According to the consulting firm A.T. Kearney, the average bank customer in the mid-2010s had 2.71 financial products at their primary bank. In other words, the Go for Gr-Eight goals represented a nearly 200% increase on what the average bank was achieving.

Daily and monthly "Motivator" reports were used to track and rank individual, branch, and regional cross-selling performance. These reports assigned quotas for the number and types of products to be sold. Any shortfall in an individual's, branch's, or region's daily target was added to the next day's goals.

Employees describe how the reports not only encouraged a high-pressure work environment but also produced a culture of shaming those who were deemed to be poor performers. For example, Wells Fargo branch manager, Rita Murillo, recalls the dread that came with the hourly conference calls initiated by regional bosses who wanted to check up on her Florida branch's cross-selling (Reckard, 2013). She also recounts how employees who lagged behind on their quotas were threatened with termination and were required to stay late and work weekends to meet their goals. Murillo states, "We were constantly told we would end up working for McDonald's. If we did not make the sales quotas … we had to stay for what felt like after-school detention, or report to a call session on Saturdays" (Reckard, 2013).

Following media reports into the high-pressure, aggressive cross-selling tactics at Wells Fargo and the negative publicity this engendered, the bank's board commissioned the law firm Shearman and Sterling to conduct an independent investigation into the scandal. The Shearman and Sterling report is particularly damning of Wells Fargo's Go for Gr-Eight and associated incentive plan. It found that the company's practice of publishing performance scorecards put

> *Review Question 6.9:* Name three approaches an organization can take to minimize the
> likelihood that employees will behave unethically?
>
> *Answer:* Please see the Answer section starting on page 283

"… pressure on employees to sell unwanted or unneeded products to customers and, in some cases, to open unauthorized accounts" (Shearman and Sterling, 2017: i). It labelled the bank's cross-selling plans and targets as "unattainable" and criticized the bank's top managers for failing to acknowledge the relationship between these unattainable goals and the ensuing fraudulent employee behaviour. The report notes that the bank's own records showed that "[a]s sales goals became more difficult to achieve, the rate of misconduct rose" (Shearman and Sterling, 2017: 43), and this information was common knowledge among senior managers. In a 2012 email that Wells Fargo's head of strategic planning for the Community Bank Division Matthew Raphaelson sent to Chief Risk Officer Michael Loughlin, the connection between the two was laid bare. Raphaelson stated that the goal-setting process was a "balancing act," one in which "[l]ow goals cause lower performance and high goals increase the percentage of cheating" (Shearman and Sterling, 2017: 65).

To conclude this section on employee incentives, organizations should only adopt employee incentives if they can ensure the performance targets are reasonable. Approaches to help achieve reasonable performance targets starts with avoiding top-down budgets. Organizations should instead incorporate employee participation into the budget-setting process. Targets that employees contribute to will have their buy-in and will not be viewed with the scepticism top-down budgeting generally engenders. It is important that organizations also ensure a good employee line of sight. This objective involves helping employees to understand their particular organization's goals and what they must do to contribute toward the realization of these goals. Finally, organizations should adopt multiple performance measures. Focusing on one or even a small group of performance measures will likely lead employees to maximize their achievement on the selected measures while ignoring or allowing performance to slip on other operationally and strategically important activities. Together, budget participation, strong line of sight, and multiple performance measures will help attenuate the risk of dysfunctional and unethical employee behaviour when an organization uses employee incentives.

PROMOTING SYSTEM 2 THINKING

Daniel Kahneman, in his book *Thinking, Fast and Slow*, described the human brain as having two broad systems for thinking. He termed these types system 1 and system 2. Whereas system 1 is impulsive, instinctive, and effortless, system 2 is characterized by control and reflectivity. Table 6.3 presents the main features of each system.

System 1 thinking accounts for the vast majority of a person's beliefs and attitudes, and ultimately their decision making. It is predicated upon quick assessments of a situation and uses past experiences as benchmarks. These benchmarks act as heuristics that allow swift decisions to

TABLE 6.3 The characteristics of Daniel Kahneman's system 1 and system 2 thinking

System 1	System 2
• Fast	• Slow
• Unconscious	• Conscious and controlled
• Automatic	• Deliberate
• Effortless	• Effortful
• Responsible for 98% of thinking and decision making	• Responsible for 2% of thinking and decision making

be reached and enable the person to move on to the next decision. In contrast, system 2 thinking accounts for a very small percentage of a person's beliefs, attitudes, and ultimate decision making. It is highly rational, logical, sceptical, and mentally demanding. Unlike system 1's use of heuristics, system 2 eschews using interpolation and extrapolation. Instead, it seeks multiple forms of corroborating information or, if these do not exist, then it requires the search for missing information or the collection of new information.

System 2 thinking's rigour and thoroughness lend themselves to superior decisions being made. The problem with system 2 thinking is its time-consuming and mentally-taxing nature. If a person used system 2 thinking to make all decisions, they would only get through a small subset of the typical number of decisions they make during the day. Imagine using system 2 thinking while at the grocery store. Even if a person arrived at its opening, they likely would not get through the first aisle before the store closed. Or imagine employing system 2 thinking every time you wanted to choose music to listen to. Before choosing a song, it would not be enough to know your top choice of the songs you know. Instead, you would need to know the world's full catalogue of songs, from which you could then choose the right one to listen to.

System 1 thinking prevents such decision paralysis and allows a person to take timely action. With system 1 thinking, a person uses heuristics or rules of thumb to reach a quick decision. For example, a person might say,

> I am feeling a bit down and I want to hear a happy song to cheer me up. I know a handful of songs on my playlist just for this occasion. I will play Pharrell Williams' 'Happy' and follow that with Walk the Moon's 'Shut Up and Dance'.

Or maybe Christmas is a few days off, so the person says, "I want to get into the Christmas spirit, and I see on my Christmas playlist both Mariah Carey's 'All I Want For Christmas Is You' and Ariana Grande's 'Santa Tell Me'. I am going to listen to the first." Notice how the person did not try to identify all the existing songs for either situation. Rather, the person merely looked at what they had on their playlist and chose from there.

Behavioural economists call heuristic-based behaviour satisficing, a concept that is linked to 1978 Economics Nobel Prize winner Herbert Simon's (1957) bounded rationality. Under bounded rationality, it is asserted that people have neither the access to nor the ability to assimilate and digest all the information needed to make optimal decisions. Accordingly, people will make choices that are not optimal, but instead are satisfactory and sufficient for a given set of circumstances. For example, a common company practice when negotiating a major purchase (e.g., a truck, a new security system, or insurance for its property) is to seek out three quotes and choose the best one from these three. Such an approach may not produce the lowest cost for best value, but it will produce a "good enough decision" that the organization is willing to live with.

The purpose of system 1 thinking is to protect a person's system 2 thinking from cognitive overload. In other words, system 1's use of instinct and habit allows a person to rapidly sift through information and ideas, prioritizing the most relevant data and filtering out the rest. Without these cognitive and behavioural shortcuts, an individual would at the end of the day still be struggling with what to wear and what to have for breakfast.

Despite the dominant role system 1 thinking plays in a person's decision making, people invariably underestimate this reality and overestimate what they deem to be their rationally-motivated behaviour. People overlook the fact that their instinctive, gut feeling, heuristically-driven decision making is predicated on incomplete (i.e., due to satisficing) and sometimes just plain erroneous (e.g., when a person tries to make connections between a current problem and one they experienced previously) data sets. In contrast, system 2 thinking's slow, conscious, and deliberate approach enables a person to reflect on rules, view them from different perspectives, develop different courses of action, and ultimately select an option that is grounded in evidence and reason. System 2 thinking, therefore, is especially relevant to recognizing and resolving ethical dilemmas by enabling a person to make thoughtful judgements about the potential impacts, the magnitude of those impacts, and parties likely to be affected by the decisions a person makes. Consequently, it is important that a person not only recognizes the irrationality and bias that their primary system 1 thinking generates, but that they also take regular pauses throughout the day to take stock of the decisions they have made by purposefully employing system 2 thinking.

Current and retrospective examinations of the type of thinking employees are using will help ensure serious matters are receiving the more mentally-taxing system 2 thinking. Using system 1 thinking to decide where to have the company Christmas party, who should captain the company's soccer team, and how the company's social committee should use the money earned on the company's cafeteria vending machines is fine. However, when it comes to deciding such issues as whether to hire a relative or friend, how and when to use employee participation in the budgeting process, and how best to deal with an employee conflict of interest, it is important that system 2 thinking prevails. Training employees to differentiate between different decision situations and when to use the significantly more time-consuming system 2 thinking feature as important aids to reducing unethical employee behaviour.

CONCLUSION

This chapter discussed the relationship of ethics to performance management. Noting how the essence of performance management is getting employees to implement organizational strategy, the promotion of ethical employee behaviour will be key to any organization's performance management efforts. Strategy has an implicit long-term orientation. Unethical behaviour is antithetical to such a focus.

The chapter proceeded to show the high cost of organizations' ethical failings. Some of these costs are direct (i.e., regulatory fines and penalties), while others are indirect (e.g., employee turnover and harm to an organization's reputation). Research findings suggest that the latter set of costs dwarf the financial costs by a ratio of more than 4:1. Together, the inability to achieve an organization's strategy and the substantial cost of ethical failings make it imperative for organizations to understand what factors lead employees to behave unethically and what actions the organization can implement to minimize the occurrence of such behaviour. Armed with these understandings, an organization's senior managers and its governing board will be in a better position to ensure its performance management system is operating effectively.

REFERENCES

Bagnoli, M. and Watts, S.G. (2003) Selling to socially responsible consumers: competition and the private provision of public goods, *Journal of Economics and Management Strategy*, Vol. 12, pp. 419–445.

Baron, D. (2001) Private politics corporate social responsibility, and integrated strategy, *Journal of Economics and Management Strategy*, Vol. 10, pp. 7–45.

Boland, R.J. (1982) Organizational control, organizational power and professional responsibility, *Business and Professional Ethics Journal*, Vol. 2, No. 1, pp. 15–25.

Bolt-Lee, C.E. and Moody, J. (2100) Highlights of finance and accounting ethics research, *Journal of Accountancy*, Vol. 210, No. 4, pp. 38–41.

DOJ. (2005) Retrieved from https://www.justice.gov/archive/opa/pr/2005/August/05_ag_433.html on 25 January 2022.

Employee Benefit News. (2017) Retrieved from https://www.benefitnews.com/news/ avoidable-turnover-costing-employers-big on 14 January 2022.

Financial Reporting Council. (2021) Retrieved from https://www.frc.org.uk/news/july-2021/frc-annual-audit-quality-inspection-results-2020-2 on 25 January 2022.

Flanagan, J. and Clarke, K. (2007) Beyond a code of professional ethics: a holistic model of ethical decision making for accountants, *Abacus*, Vol. 43, No. 4, pp. 488–518.

Gibson, Dunn and Crutcher. (2018) 2017 Year-End FCPA Update, Retrieved from https://www.gibsondunn.com/2017-year-end-fcpa-update/ on 13 January 2022.

Gibson, Dunn and Crutcher. (2021) 2020 Year-End FCPA Update, Retrieved from https://www.gibsondunn.com/2020-year-end-fcpa-update/ on 13 January 2022.

Herzberg, F. (2003) One more time: how do you motivate employees?, *Harvard Business Review*, Vol. 81, No. 1, pp. 87–96. Reprinted from 1968.

Institute of Internal Auditors. (2013) Retrieved from https://na.theiia.org/standards-guidance/Public%20 Documents/PP%20The%20Three%20Lines%20of%20Defense%20in%20Effective%20Risk%20 Management%20and%20Control.pdf on 13 January 2022.

Koch, T. (2019) Professionalism: an archaeology, *HEC Forum*, Vol. 31, pp. 219–232.

Kohn, A. (1993) Why incentive plans cannot work, *Harvard Business Review*, Vol. 71, No. 6, pp. 54–63.

Lev, B.I., Petrovits, C. and Radhakrishnan, S. (2008) Is doing good, good for you? How corporate charitable contributions enhance revenue growth, *Strategic Management Journal*, Vol. 31, pp. 182–200.

McNamee, R. (2019) *Zucked: Waking Up to the Facebook Catastrophe*, London: HarperCollins Publishers.

Meta Platforms, Inc. (n.d.) The Meta code of conduct, retrieved from https://scontent.fhlz2-1.fna. fbcdn.net/v/t39.8562-6/306923411_3179863872263267_4034325136788139641_n.pdf?_nc_cat=110&ccb=1-7&_nc_sid=ad8a9d&_nc_ohc=XIbD6MougFcAX_tfFBX&_nc_ht=scontent.fhlz2-1. fna&oh=00_AT_T8cDZ3BsF2h5wcatnYWE-PNylG19GmLe26-myzQ1Tfw&oe=6326014E on 13 September 2022.

Nejati, M., Brown, M.E., Shafaei, A. and Seet, P.S. (2021) Employees' perceptions of corporate social responsibility and ethical leadership: are they uniquely related to turnover intention?, *Social Responsibility Journal*, Vol. 17, No. 2, pp. 181–197.

Orlitzky, M., Schmidt, F.L. and Rynes, S.L. (2003) Corporate social and financial performance: a meta-analysis, *Organization Studies*, Vol. 24, No. 3, pp. 403–441.

PCAOB. (2021) Retrieved from https://pcaob-assets.azureedge.net/pcaob-dev/docs/default-source/enforcement/decisions/documents/105-2021-008-kpmg-australia.pdf?sfvrsn=81a97edf_6 on 25 January 2022.

Pensions Regulator. (2021) Retrieved from https://www.thepensionsregulator.gov.uk/en/document-library/enforcement-activity/regulatory-intervention-reports/silentnight-group-db-scheme-regulatory-intervention-report on 25 January 2022.

Public Citizen. (2016) Retrieved from https://www.citizen.org/wp-content/uploads/wells-fargo-king-of-cross-sell.pdf on 19 January 2022.

PwC. (2019) Succeeding the long-serving legend in the corner office. Retrieved from https://www.strategy-business.com/article/Succeeding-the-long-serving-legend-in-the-corner-office on 23 February 2022.

Reckard, E.S. (2013) Retrieved from https://www.latimes.com/business/la-fi-wells-fargo-sale-pressure-20131222-story.html on 19 January 2022.

Rosenberg, E. (2020) Walmart and McDonald's have the most workers on food stamps and Medicaid, new study shows, *The Washington Post*, 18 November.

Sampath, V.S., Gardberg, N.A. and Rahman, N. (2018) Corporate reputation's invisible hand: bribery, rational choice, and market penalties, *Journal of Business Ethics*, Vol. 151, No, 3, pp. 743–760.

Shearman and Sterling Report. (2017) Retrieved from https://www08.wellsfargomedia.com/assets/pdf/about/investor-relations/presentations/2017/board-report.pdf on 19 January 2022.

Sika, P. (2022) Retrieved from https://leftfootforward.org/2022/01/accounting-firms-are-at-the-heart-of-corruption-in-the-uk/ on 25 January 2022.

Simon, H.A. (1957) *Models of Man*, New York: John Wiley.

Suddaby, R., Gendron, Y. and Lam, H. (2009) The organizational context of professionalism in accounting. *Accounting, Organizations and Society*, Vol. 34, pp. 409–427.

Walmart Code of Conduct. (2021) Retrieved from https://www.walmartethics.com/content/dam/walmartethics/documents/code_of_conduct/Code_of_Conduct_English_US.pdf on 13 January 2022.

Wang, Y.J., Tsai, Y.H. and Lin, C.P. (2013) Modeling the relationship between perceived corporate citizenship and organizational commitment considering organizational trust as a moderator, *Business Ethics: A European Review*, Vol. 22, pp. 218–233.

Wright P. (1951) What is a profession? *Canadian Bar Review*, Vol. 29, pp. 748–57.

CHAPTER 7

Introduction to organizational strategy

CHAPTER OBJECTIVES

- Define organizational strategy and discuss its importance to an organization's success.
- Identify the two types of organizational strategy: corporate-level and business-unit-level.
- Discuss the three types of corporate-level strategy: single-industry, related-diversified, and unrelated-diversified.
- Discuss the basic associations between corporate-level strategy and performance management system design.

INTRODUCTION

This chapter introduces the concept of organizational strategy. It discusses how organizational strategy is often narrowly misconstrued as financial strategy (i.e., providing good returns to shareholders) or marketing strategy (i.e., developing good distribution channels). This chapter proceeds to describe types of strategy: corporate-level and business–unit-level. The former is the focus of the present chapter, while the latter is comprehensively discussed in Chapter 8. In addition to describing corporate–level strategy, the present chapter reveals basic associations between corporate–level strategy and performance management design.

THE IMPORTANCE OF STRATEGY

Earlier, in Chapter 1, the Japanese proverb about an organization's imperative to not just formulate strategy, but to also ensure its implementation was discussed. The quoted proverb, "Strategy without action is a daydream," is actually only the first half of the entire proverb. The second half is "Action without strategy is a nightmare." In other words, doing things without a clear plan of the specific set of activities the organization should be undertaking is a recipe for disaster.

DOI: 10.4324/9781003267195-9

In the Bible's book of Genesis, it is stated, "In the beginning there was nothing." For organizations that have yet to formulate and implement a strategy, there is at best a state of nothingness. At worse, as the Japanese proverb suggests, a state of nightmarish chaos may reign. In a similar way, though operating on a highly separate and very distant ontological plane, just as God reportedly imposed form and meaningfulness on what was previously emptiness and nothingness, so too is strategy capable of giving life, discipline, and direction to what was previously an organization's state of disorder.

As this chapter and Chapter 8 will show, strategy is both an organization's driving force and its very life source. Strategy communicates to employees the what, how, why, when, and where of the actions they are meant to perform. In other words, it provides focus and direction to employee behaviour. An organization's strategy will also provide, assuming the strategy has the hallmarks of a winning strategy, a topic discussed in Chapter 8, the basis for the organization's continued success. Scholars refer to this state as a sustained competitive advantage (Porter, 1996).

THE CATALYST FOR STRATEGY

As mentioned in Chapter 5's discussion, an organization's purpose is defined by its goals and objectives. There is a high degree of commonality in the goals and objectives pursued by different organizations. For example, every for-profit company seeks to be profitable, making the goal and objective of profitability common to all for-profit companies.

Further shared goals, beyond the single goal of profitability, are likely to be held by various organizations. As noted in Chapter 5, key stakeholders, who each operate with their own set of self-interests, must come together for the purpose of sustaining any given organization. Unless there is sufficient regard given to these stakeholders' interests, the organization cannot exist. As a consequence, the typical organization will find it must make room for and accommodate the desires of employees who want adequate pay and safe working conditions, suppliers who want to receive timely payment for the goods and services they provide, customers who want to be treated fairly and with respect, the wider community (as well as the governments that represent these communities) who want the organization to act responsibly and lawfully, and (at least for for-profit companies) investors who want good returns on their invested capital. The ultimate result of these various stakeholder wants and desires is that the typical organization will have a list of goals and objectives similar to the following:

- Good employee remuneration
- Safe working environment
- Good corporate citizenship
- Satisfactory returns on invested capital (returns can be market yields for investors of for-profit companies or psychological returns for donors of not-for-profits)
- Profitability (if a for-profit company).

We can see that for many organizations, especially for-profit organizations, the set of goals and objectives they hold are not unique to other organizations – whether these others reside in the same or different industries. Accordingly, any given for-profit organization and its peers are likely to possess similar views about where they need to be. This place was referred to in Chapter 5 as the Promised Land.

Knowing where the organization wants to be, while clearly important, forms only part of senior management's task of ensuring organizational health and survival. The other part of this task, and what is arguably the much more significant part, is working out how the organization will succeed in reaching its desired destination. In other words, strategy answers the question of *how* an organization will navigate the waters between where it is now and where it wants to be. As we will soon see, strategy provides the plan, and, in particular, the unique way that an organization will go about marshalling its capabilities and resources to reach its Promised Land.

WHAT IS STRATEGY?

Strategy is often mistakenly viewed in narrow, parochial terms. Sometimes, for example, it is equated with financial strategy, which involves an organization's planning of its financial needs and the sources from which the required capital will be raised. In particular, an organization can raise capital by issuing debt, selling shares, or tapping into its internal capital reserves (i.e., its retained earnings).

Strategy is also sometimes misconstrued as marketing strategy. For example, someone may incorrectly say a company's strategy is mass marketing (i.e., appealing to potential customers through mass media and mass distribution) or relationship marketing (i.e., focusing on customer loyalty and long-term customer engagement). Marketing strategies such as mass marketing and relationship marketing are best viewed as functional strategies, which are subordinate to and meant to be supportive of an organization's overall strategy. As an illustration, mass marketing would be supportive of an organization that was employing an organizational strategy that relied on high-volume sales. Meanwhile, relationship marketing would be conducive to an organizational strategy that depended on creating and maintaining high-quality customer interactions.

Unlike functional strategy's subordinate and supportive role, organizational strategy is meant to be the answer and provide the broad roadmap to show how an organization will achieve its goals and objectives. During its early descriptions, organizational strategy was largely viewed as long-term planning. It is instructive to note that the first academic journal devoted to the study of strategy was titled *Long Range Planning*. The centrality of time to the concept of strategy is captured by Miyamoto (1974: 21), who argues for the need "to see distant things as if they were close and to take a distanced view of close things" when formulating organizational strategy.

A more contemporary view of organizational strategy (i.e., post-1980) regards it as comprising how an organization will marshal its resources into a coordinated set of activities that provide a value proposition for customers that will enable their continued patronage of the organization's products or services. Robert Shirley (1982: 262) provides a definition of organizational strategy that certainly captures the concept at its broadest level when he states: "[T]he strategy of an organization consists of those decisions that (a) define the relationship of the total organization to its environment and (b) give guidance to administrative and operational activities on an ongoing basis."

> *Review Question 7.1:* What is strategy?
> *Answer:* Please see the Answer section starting on page 283
> *Review Question 7.2:* Why is strategy important to organizations?
> *Answer:* Please see the Answer section starting on page 283
> *Review Question 7.3:* What is the difference between organizational strategy and functional strategy?
> *Answer:* Please see the Answer section starting on page 283

Organizational strategy can be broken apart into two elements: corporate-level strategy and business-unit-level strategy. Corporate-level strategy relates to what market(s) an organization chooses to compete in. Business-unit-level strategy, which is also commonly referred to as competitive strategy, comprises the astute choices managers make when deciding upon, constructing, and linking together the set of activities that define an organization's value proposition. The current chapter focuses on corporate-level strategy. Business-unit-level strategy is discussed in Chapter 8.

TYPES OF CORPORATE-LEVEL STRATEGY

Organizations can choose between three types of corporate-level strategy. The first features the adoption of a highly focused approach of concentrating on an individual industry. This strategy is called a single-industry strategy. High-profile companies that pursue this strategy include Google, SAS, American Express, Toyota, Marriott, Telefónica, and KPMG. These companies, and many more could be listed, have made a conscious choice to stick to their knitting and focus on what they do best (Peters and Waterman, 1982).

In contrast to confining themselves to a single industry, some firms may choose to span several industries. Firms may choose this path of industry diversification to take advantage of synergies that can be gained from a firm's choice to operate in either related or unrelated industries. Firms that pursue a related-diversified strategy create synergy by sharing operating/manufacturing facilities, logistics, and/or marketing systems between their family of sister companies.

An unrelated-diversified strategy, the third type of corporate-level strategy, derives from the application and transfer of superior management expertise and/or financial resources to firms in unrelated industries. The senior managers of these organizations frequently display a level of confidence in their management abilities that borders on arrogance. Harold Geneen, the then CEO of ITT, was purported to have told a fellow airline passenger who mispronounced Geneen's name that the beginning "g" in his name was pronounced like the soft "g" in Jesus and not the hard "g" in God.

A common misconception prevails that if a firm buys a competitor, what some scholars call concentric diversification, it becomes a related-diversified firm. This belief, however, is not correct. Concentric diversification may help a firm take advantage of economies of scale and may even have the added bonus of reducing competition, but this act of buying a competitor does not move the firm outside of the single industry. If, for example, KPMG buys out a regional accounting firm, its market share will increase and the opportunity for higher profits, due to the potential for greater economies of scale, may exist. Such a purchase, however, has not changed the fact that KPMG still operates in the same industry: the provision of accounting and consulting services.

To classify as a related-diversified strategy, KPMG would have to expand outside its current industry, while ensuring the attainment of some operating/delivery system synergy. Branching out into accounting software development could be one example of how a firm like KPMG could achieve this multiple industry synergy. In fact, the 2015 strategic alliance between Xero and KPMG Australia, the purpose of which was to deliver cloud accounting to small businesses, is a step on the path to such a related-diversified strategy. Other examples of companies enacting a related-diversified strategy are Avon Products' backward vertical integration, whereby it brought in-house the production of some of its cosmetics, and Levi Strauss & Co.'s forward vertical integration from a manufacturer of clothing to the additional operation of retail stores to sell and market its clothing.

As previously noted, firms that pursue unrelated-diversified strategies possess supreme confidence in the superiority and transferability of their management expertise and/or financial resources. Kyocera, for example, believes that its amoeba management system is the primary engine for its unparalleled financial success. Throughout its 50-plus years of existence, it has moved well beyond its original mission of manufacturing ceramic insulators for television sets and now produces semiconductor components for automobiles, office equipment, and mobile phones, as well as manufacturing dental implants and solar panels. The company also owns and operates hotels, and even has a consulting division that has advised on and facilitated the implementation of a plethora of companies' adoption of amoeba management.

Samsung is another example of a company pursuing an unrelated-diversified strategy. In addition to its manufacture of smartphones, tablets, and televisions, the company also produces military hardware and ships, constructs apartments, and even operates a Korean amusement park. Further examples of companies with unrelated-diversified strategies are Siemens, 3M Company, General Electric, Pentair Ltd, Tyco International, Asea Brown Boveri, United Technologies, and The Trump Organization.

When firms pursue unrelated diversification, the purpose should be to achieve synergy by applying and transferring superior management expertise (an expertise that is generic across industries rather than being specific to any one industry) and/or financial resources to firms in unrelated industries. The purpose should not be to minimize market risk. This responsibility belongs to the investors, who possess ample equity and bond market-related options for altering the risk-return mix of their investments.

General Electric (GE) used a diversified portfolio rationale to justify its operation as an unrelated-diversified firm, an approach that was aggressively pursued by former GE CEO Jack Welch. Although GE's stock price consistently outperformed its peers under Welch's tenure (1981–2001), producing a return on investment of 1,120.6% during the 1990s alone, the stock began to falter during the final year of Welch's leadership. Welch grew GE's market capitalization from USD 14 billion when he started in 1981 to USD 400 billion when he retired in September 2001. However, starting in 2000, GE's stock began a prolonged and deep descent to sit at around USD 100 billion at the start of 2022. Stock analysts have blamed its fall on the incompatibility of GE's conglomerate model with today's need for organizational quickness and agility. For its part, GE decided in November 2021 to divide the company into three public companies: aviation, health care, and energy. Various Wall Street commentators predict other unrelated-diversified companies will follow suit and have singled out the likes of Emerson, Roper Technologies, and 3M. According to Nick Heymann of William Blair, an American multinational independent investment bank and financial services company, "It's over now. In a digital economy, there's no real room for it" (AP, 2021).

One of the possible sources of success for a firm that pursues an unrelated-diversified strategy can be its ability to transfer financial resources across its network of firms. The Boston Consulting Group (BCG) Growth-Share Matrix and the GE/McKinsey Matrix offer senior managers of unrelated-diversified firms insight into how they might manage this transfer of financial resources. While the two matrices are quite similar to each other, many organizational scholars and practitioners (see, for example, Collis *et al.*, 1999) consider the GE/McKinsey Matrix, which was developed by McKinsey and Company in the early 1970s, to be an improvement on the BCG Matrix, which was developed in the mid-1960s by Bruce Henderson. Consequently, the current discussion focuses on the GE/McKinsey Matrix. Those readers who are interested in learning about the BCG Matrix should consult Henderson (1970) or simply search the internet, where a myriad of information about this matrix can be found.

The GE/McKinsey Matrix argues that the unrelated-diversified company's success rests on its ability to maintain a portfolio of products/services in different stages of its lifecycle. Products/services with plateauing or declining market growth opportunities are meant to provide the financial resources to nourish products/services exhibiting low market share but offering high growth potential. In other words, some companies within the unrelated-diversified company's portfolio of companies will be assigned the mandate of growing and building, with cash flowing to these companies. Meanwhile, other companies under the unrelated-diversified company's umbrella will be instructed to hold or possibly even divest their market positions, with cash transferring from these companies to the growing/building companies. Table 7.1 provides a visual representation of this set of circumstances.

Porter's (2008) Five Forces Model can be used to assess industry attractiveness. Alternatively, a set of relevant factors such as the following list can be used:

1   Market growth rate
2   Market size
3   Demand variability

TABLE 7.1 GE/McKinsey Matrix

		Business unit strength		
		High	Medium	Low
Industry attractiveness	High	Grow	Grow	Hold
	Medium	Grow	Hold	Harvest
	Low	Hold	Harvest	Divest

4   Industry profitability
5   Industry rivalry
6   Global opportunities
7   Macroenvironmental factors (including political, economic, sociocultural, and technological).

When using a list like the one above, a user may wish to weight each factor by its perceived importance rather than treat each factor equally. For example, if industry profitability is deemed to be twice as important as global opportunities, then the latter will carry a weighting that is half of the former. To help determine the factor weightings, managers may wish to use an analytical technique such as conjoint analysis.

Following the assignment of weightings to each factor, the user next scores each factor using a nine-point scale. The bottom end, denoted by "1," indicates "extremely unattractive." The top end, shown as "9," signifies "extremely attractive." The scale's midpoint of "5" represents an "average" rating.

Table 7.2 provides an example of an industry attractiveness analysis using a set of factors similar to the ones illustrated in the above list. As this table reports, Industry B, with its total score of 7.6, exhibits the highest industry attractiveness score of the three industries examined.

Business unit strength represents a business unit's relative competitiveness within its industry of operation. A business unit's market share is an important determinant of a business unit's strength, but it is not the only determinant. One possible listing of the factors that could be included in the determination of business unit strength is:

1   Market share
2   Growth in market share
3   Production capacity
4   Brand equity
5   Distribution channel access
6   Profit margins relative to competitors.

Similar to what was done when assessing an industry's attractiveness, weightings are assigned to each factor. These weightings are then multiplied by the scores assigned to each factor to yield a weighted score. The summation of these scores represents the business unit's strength. Table 7.3 provides an illustration of a business unit strength analysis involving three different business units. As this table reveals, Business Unit 3 shows the highest score, followed by Business Units 2 and 1, respectively.

Following the calculations of industry attractiveness and business unit strength, each business unit is plotted on the matrix. Assuming Business Unit 1 is associated with Industry A, Business Unit 2 is associated with Industry B, and Business Unit 3 is associated with Industry C results in the completed matrix shown in Figure 7.1.

Superimposing Table 7.1 on Figure 7.1 suggests the following action:

1   Business Units 1 and 3 should adopt hold strategies.
2   Business Unit 2 should adopt a growth strategy.

Some readers may notice that the circles in Figure 7.1 are different sizes. This representation is purposeful. When plotting a business unit's position on the matrix, the typical advice is to represent market size by the size of the circle. As indicated in Table 7.2, the market size for Industry B, in which Business Unit 2 operates, is the largest, followed by Industry A (Business Unit 1) and finally Industry C (Business Unit 3). The GE/McKinsey Matrix literature also suggests that users may wish to represent a business unit's market share by displaying this as a pie chart in the circle. Furthermore, it is also suggested that an arrow can be added to each circle to represent the expected future position of the business unit. For example, if the expectation for Business Unit 1 were a less attractive industry and eroded business unit strength, then an arrow pointing to the lower right-hand corner of the GE/McKinsey Matrix would be attached to the circle in Figure 7.1 representing Business Unit 1. This added information would suggest to a manager that the hold strategy presently suggested might need to be supported by a contingency plan that provides for the divestment of the business unit.

TABLE 7.2 An illustration of industry attractiveness assessment

	Weighting (%)	Industry A		Industry B		Industry C	
		Raw score	Weighted score	Raw score	Weighted score	Raw score	Weighted score
Market growth rate	15	4	0.6	8	1.2	2	0.3
Market size	10	6	0.6	9	0.9	2	0.2
Demand variability	10	6	0.6	7	0.7	2	0.2
Industry profitability	20	5	1.0	7	1.4	4	0.8
Industry rivalry	20	2	0.4	7	1.4	2	0.4
Global opportunities	10	4	0.4	8	0.8	3	0.3
Macroenvironmental factors	15	4	0.6	8	1.2	4	0.6
Totals	100	31	4.2	54	7.6	19	2.8

TABLE 7.3 An illustration of business unit strength assessment

	Weighting (%)	Business Unit 1		Business Unit 2		Business Unit 3	
		Raw score	Weighted score	Raw score	Weighted score	Raw score	Weighted score
Market share	15	4	0.6	6	0.9	8	1.2
Growth in market share	20	5	1.0	6	1.2	9	1.8
Production capacity	10	7	0.7	5	0.5	7	0.7
Brand equity	20	4	0.8	6	1.2	8	1.6
Distribution channel access	20	5	1.0	7	1.4	7	1.4
Profit relative to competitors	15	6	0.9	6	0.9	6	0.9
Totals	100	31	5.0	36	6.1	45	7.6

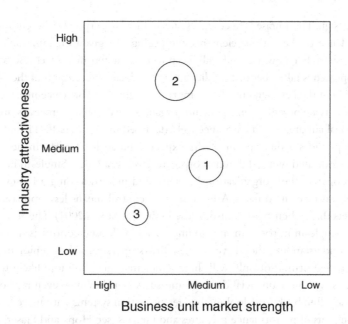

FIGURE 7.1 An illustrated mapping of strategic business units on the GE/McKinsey Matrix.

Review Question 7.4: What are the three types of corporate-level strategy? Describe and give examples of each.

Answer: Please see the Answer section starting on page 283

Review Question 7.5: How does the GE / McKinsey Matrix link with an organization's pursuit of an unrelated-diversified strategy?

Answer: Please see the Answer section starting on page 283

The GE/McKinsey Matrix offers senior managers of unrelated-diversified firms advice on how they might plan and manage their strategic business unit portfolios. In particular, the information conveyed in the matrix should help these managers plan where financial resources will be sourced and where they will be applied. These insights, though useful in the management of cash flows between subunits, do not address the issue of how a strategic business unit's core competencies are arranged to lead to value creation and competitive success. This latter issue is the focus of discussion in Chapter 8.

CORPORATE-LEVEL STRATEGY AND PERFORMANCE MANAGEMENT SYSTEM DESIGN

At this point, it is worthwhile to pause, take stock, and reflect on how corporate-level strategy is related to performance management design. In fact, you are encouraged throughout this book to continually contemplate how each chapter's featured topic affects and is affected by performance management design. The phrase "affect and is affected by" is purposely chosen to reinforce the mutual dependence of the various elements comprising any given organization's performance management system. For now, we will only keep to general and high-level discussions of these affects. This approach is taken because a fuller and more detailed discussion of the affects requires an understanding of the key elements that comprise any given performance management system. These key elements are organizational structure; organizational systems, processes, and procedures; and organizational culture, which are, respectively, discussed in Chapters 10, 11, and 12.

Table 7.4 provides a description of the expected broad-level performance management characteristics associated with different corporate-level strategies. Single-industry firms are more likely to operate their organizational systems and processes using a looser style of control than unrelated-diversified firms. A loose style of control means less emphasis is placed on meeting budgets than when tight control is used (Van der Stede, 2001). The reason that senior managers of a single-industry firm are willing to adopt looser control is a direct function of the greater understanding they have of their firm's operations than senior managers of an unrelated-diversified firm. Not only will these senior managers be more likely to supplement financial budgets with non-financial data and measures, but they may even replace their firm's largely historical, often backward-looking budget evaluation systems with more lead-indicating, forward-looking sets of performance measures and metrics (see Hope and Fraser, 2003).

In contrast to single-industry firms, unrelated-diversified firms will adopt tight control. The senior managers of these latter firms will not possess the same level of familiarity with the diverse markets in which they operate relative to the senior managers of single-industry firms who specialize in one industry. Lacking the industry knowledge and experience to know how or when to make adjustments to their firms' budgets, senior managers of unrelated-diversified firms will cling to the systems and processes they know, including the budgeting systems they operate.

A further reason behind unrelated-diversified firms' senior managers' strict adherence to their organizations' set of organizational systems and processes is the synergy that is meant to underlie the pursuit of an unrelated-diversified strategy. In particular, this pursuit is often based on a belief in the firm's superior meta-industry management expertise. In other words, these firms believe they have developed best-practice organizational systems, processes, and procedures that transcend industry categories. For example, Kyocera uses the same hourly efficiency measure to evaluate the business unit performance of each of its subunits because its senior management team is confident that its hourly efficiency measure is as relevant for evaluating a business unit that makes solar panels as it is for a business unit that operates hotels.

The organizational structure of single-industry firms will be simple. In contrast, unrelated-diversified firms will likely display complex structures. According to organizational scholars

TABLE 7.4 Relationship between performance management characteristics and corporate-level strategy

	Single-industry	Related-diversified	Unrelated-diversified
Systems and processes	Loose	↔	Tight
Organizational structure	Simple	↔	Complex
Organizational culture	Singular	↔	Plural

(see, for example, Hall and Tolbert, 2009), organizational structures are directly associated with the complexity of a firm's internal and external environments. As will be examined in Chapter 10, single-industry firms, especially ones that operate in environments exhibiting high stability and predictability, are likely to benefit from adopting simpler, more centralized organizational structures. This form of organizational structure will almost certainly be the case if a cost-focused strategy (see Chapter 8) is being pursued.

Unrelated-diversified firms will benefit from adopting decentralized organizational structures. Once again, a fuller understanding of the reasons for this association must await the reading of Chapter 10. For now, it is sufficient to realize that due to the wide range of companies operating under an unrelated-diversified firm's umbrella, it is unlikely that any one manager or a small group of managers will possess sufficient, timely information or have the multi-industry skills and understandings to make high-quality decisions.

The organizational cultures of single-industry and unrelated-diversified firms are likely to be quite different. While any given single-industry firm is likely to have a single, unitary organizational culture, an unrelated-diversified firm will display plural cultures. Through its operation in a single industry, the single-industry firm will likely find that its marshalling of resources will coalesce around and be evidenced by a single expression of its core values and beliefs. In contrast, the unrelated-diversified firm will find that its subunits have assembled heterogeneous mixes of resources from one another, which will produce different expressions of core values and beliefs and result in these firms having pluralistic cultures.

Firms that pursue related-diversified strategies will typically exhibit characteristics that fall somewhere in the middle between the two ends of the continua shown in Table 7.4. In other words, related-diversified firms are likely to operate organizational systems and processes that require a medium level of adherence. While senior managers of these firms may not possess the same high degree of industry experience as their single-industry counterparts, their moderate levels of familiarity will allow them to supplement a strict reliance on budgets, for example, with a wider set of measures and metrics. The related-diversified firms will also feature organizational structures that are neither as simple as single-industry firms nor as complex as unrelated-diversified firms. And finally, related-diversified firms will have organizational cultures that lack the singular focus of single-industry firms but are not as plural as the unrelated-diversified firms.

It must be remembered that the associations described here are only what might be generally expected. They are not meant to be rigid axioms. As this book has already stated, and the following chapters continue to amplify, the exact performance management design of any given organization must await a full and comprehensive enunciation of the organization's particular, idiosyncratic facts and circumstances. While general statements like the ones above apply to the "average" firm pursuing each of the three corporate-level strategies, departures from these typical profiles do occur. For example, Kyocera, the large Japanese multinational conglomerate previously mentioned, operates a performance management system that features a singular organizational culture. This fact runs counter to the expectation that a firm like Kyocera, which is pursuing an unrelated-diversified strategy, should display multiple organizational cultures across its diverse set of subunits. Instead, Kyocera exhibits a singular organizational culture that is characterized by high performance, high trust, significant employee empowerment, and high altruism. As Adler and Hiromoto (2012) show, Kyocera's organizational culture acts as a key organizational integrating mechanism. Without a strong integrating mechanism like its singular

> *Review Question 7.6:* What are the general associations between corporate-level strategies and performance management design?
>
> *Answer:* Please see the Answer section starting on page 283

organizational culture, Kyocera's use of extreme decentralization would likely produce substantial subunit competition and ultimately undermine the collaborative culture needed to support the confrontation strategies its subunits pursue.

CONCLUSION

This chapter defined organizational strategy and discussed its importance to an organization's survival and success. Organizational strategy consists of two types: corporate-level strategy and business-unit-level strategy. The former comprised the focus of the present chapter, while the latter becomes the focus of Chapter 8. There are three types of corporate-level strategy: single-industry, related-diversified, and unrelated-diversified. The chapter discussed these three types of strategy and offered multiple examples of each. The GE/McKinsey Matrix was introduced as a tool that managers of unrelated-diversified firms can use to plan and manage the allocation of resources within their respective firms' strategic business units. In the chapter's penultimate section, the basic associations between corporate-level strategy and performance management design were discussed.

REFERENCES

Adler, R. and Hiromoto, T. (2012) Amoeba management: lessons from Japan, *Sloan Management Review*, Vol. 54, No. 1, pp. 1–7.

Associated Press (AP). (2021) GE to end its run as a conglomerate, split into 3 companies, Retrieved from https://apnews.com/article/business-0efa0e45cba17ec5e51011b83bdd52f1on 23 February 2022.

Collis, D.J., Montgomery, C.A., Campbell, A., Goold, M., Prahalad, C.K. and Lieberthal, K. (1999) *Harvard Business Review on Corporate Strategy*, Boston, MA: Harvard Business School Press.

Hall, R.H. and Tolbert, P.S. (2009) *Organizations: Structures, Processes, and Outcomes* (10th Edition), Upper Saddle River, NJ: Pearson Prentice Hall.

Henderson, B.D. (1970) *The Product Portfolio*, Boston, MA: The Boston Consulting Group, Inc.

Hope, J. and Fraser, R. (2003) Who needs budgets?, *Harvard Business Review*, Vol. 81, No. 2, pp. 108–115.

Miyamoto, M. (1974) *A Book of Five Rings* (translated by Victor Harris), London: Allison & Busby; Woodstock, NY: The Overlook Press.

Peters, T.J. and Waterman, R.H. (1982) *In Search of Excellence*, New York: Harper & Row.

Porter, M.E. (1996) What is strategy? *Harvard Business Review*, Vol. 74, No. 6, pp. 61–78.

Porter, M.E. (2008) The five competitive forces that shape strategy, *Harvard Business Review*, Vol. 86, No. 1, pp. 79–93.

Shirley, R. (1982) Limiting the scope of strategy: a decision based approach, *Academy of Management*, Vol. 7, No. 2, pp. 262–268.

Van der Stede, W.A. (2001) Measuring tight budgetary control, *Management Accounting Research*, Vol. 12, No. 1, pp. 119–137.

CHAPTER 8

Competitive strategy

CHAPTER OBJECTIVES

- Introduce the concept of business-unit-level strategy, or what is commonly referred to as competitive strategy.
- Discuss and critique the competitive strategy taxonomies of Miles and Snow, Porter, Cooper, and Kim and Mauborgne.
- Using the concept of order-winning criteria (OWC), compare and contrast the four showcased competitive strategy taxonomies.
- Discuss the basic associations between competitive strategy and performance management system design.

INTRODUCTION

This chapter discusses strategy as it relates to business units, a topic that is commonly termed competitive strategy. Various popular competitive strategy taxonomies are reviewed and critiqued. The concept of order-winning criteria (OWC) is used as a prism through which to view each taxonomy. The chapter ultimately leverages these understandings of strategy, and in particular competitive strategy, to illustrate the implications of competitive strategy on performance management design and operation. Advice is offered about the typical influence the pursuit of different competitive strategies has on organizational systems, processes, and procedures, organizational structures, and organizational cultures.

BUSINESS-UNIT-LEVEL STRATEGY

Business–unit-level strategy, what is also commonly referred to as competitive strategy, comprises the astute choices managers make when deciding upon, constructing, and linking together the set of activities that define an organization's value proposition. The development of a unique value proposition featuring high customer utility endows a firm with a competitive advantage. Uniqueness is defined in relation to one's competitors, and it can only be claimed if a firm's product/service offerings provide at least one characteristic that is perceived by customers as

DOI: 10.4324/9781003267195-10

being superior to competitors' offerings. According to Clulow *et al.* (2003: 221), "A firm is said to have a competitive advantage when it is implementing a value creating strategy not simultaneously being implemented by any current or potential player."

It is senior management's task to devise a unique competitive strategy for each of its key business units. Often these key business units are referred to as strategic business units or SBUs. Hoque (2003: 48–49) offers a cogent definition of SBU when he writes:

> A Strategic Business Unit (SBU) is an organisational operating or sub unit that has a distinct set of products or services sold to a customer/group of customers, facing a well-defined set of competitors, and a mission distinct from those of the other operating units in the firm.

SBUs can be distinguished by the following four attributes:

1   Usually found in large diversified companies
2   Possess distinct missions relative to other SBUs in the same organization
3   Compete for customers against a set of competitors that are distinct from and external to other SBUs in the same organization
4   Possess high decision-making autonomy.

Several scholars have contributed significantly to the field of competitive strategy. In this chapter, we discuss the theoretical and practical contributions made by four groups of scholars: Miles and Snow (1978), Porter (1985), Cooper (1995), and Kim and Mauborgne (2005, 2015). As this discussion will show, competitive strategy has its tangible representation in what can be called OWC. Put very simply, OWC are the reason customers buy from one organization and not another. Customers may, for example, buy from Firm A because it offers the most innovative products/services. In contrast, customers may buy from Firm B because it provides the lowest-priced products/services. When choosing which firm to buy from, customers will generally, and almost invariably, need to make trade-offs between innovation and low prices. A competitive strategy that is characterized by a single order-winning criterion can be seen in Porter's (1985) conceptions and descriptions of strategy, which are comprehensively discussed in this chapter.

In addition to firms using a singular product/service attribute to attract customers, firms can also use multiple product/service attributes to win customers. Firms that pursue this latter strategy must meet minimum thresholds across the entire set of product/service attributes, as opposed to simply being better than their competitors on one of these attributes. As an example, a landscape company may focus on providing a combination of low prices, high customization, and on-time delivery. This situation illustrates a multiple OWC strategy. Although the use of multiple OWC may be inconsistent with Porter's ideas, such an approach is recognized and even encouraged by others (for example, Cooper, 1995; Kim and Mauborgne, 2005).

The idea of a single criterion and multiple OWC is returned to at the end of this chapter, when Miles and Snow, Porter, Cooper, and Kim and Mauborgne's conceptions of competitive strategy are summarized. In particular, a diagram offering comparisons of the key underlying assumptions comprising each of the four strategy taxonomies is provided.

Review Question 8.1: What is competitive strategy?

Answer: Please see the Answer section starting on page 283

Review Question 8.2: What are strategic business units (SBUs), and how do they relate to competitive strategy?

Answer: Please see the Answer section starting on page 283

MILES AND SNOW'S FOUR STRATEGIC ARCHETYPES

Miles and Snow contend that the strategy a company adopts is a function of its beliefs about and experiences with three fundamental management problems:

1   Deciding how to select and adjust its product/service offerings (the entrepreneurial problem)
2   Deciding how to produce and deliver its products/services (the engineering problem)
3   Creating organizational structures capable of establishing roles, relationships, and organizational processes that are consistent with and support the decisions made on (1) and (2). This final problem is termed the administrative problem.

How an organization approaches and makes decisions about these three fundamental problems determines the competitive strategy the organization pursues. Although different solutions to these three problems will be chosen by different organizations, Miles and Snow suggest that the solutions can be grouped around similar themes, which will in turn produce competitive strategies that fall into one of four groups: enthusiastic prospector, domain defender, anxious analyzer, and reluctant reactor.

Prospectors crave change. They view change as analogous to opportunity, which explains the reason Miles and Snow preceded the word "prospector" with the word "enthusiastic." Accordingly, they try to create or, at a minimum, influence change. They are well versed in active experimentation and are constantly on the lookout for new products and market opportunities. In other words, the prospector's answer to the entrepreneurial problem is to seek renewal and innovation.

Prospectors adopt a proactive approach to meeting, anticipating, and shaping customer needs and demands. Not wanting to be too dependent on any one product/service or technology, they choose to deliver a broad range of products/services. The prospector's answer to the engineering problem is to horizontally integrate.

The dramatic innovation they seek and the diverse set of business activities they operate characterize the administrative problem they must address. In particular, the unpredictability of their environment (which is characterized by significant change) and their high level of product/service renewal and innovation (which is characterized by frequent product/service introductions and revampings) influence prospectors to decentralize and adopt divisionalized organizational structures. The classic example of a prospector is 3M Company.

Defenders strive to protect their market shares, hence the reason Miles and Snow prefaced this strategic orientation with the word "domain." Defenders prefer internal and external environments characterized by stability and predictability. This preference is the polar opposite of what prospectors want. Due to the relative stability that characterizes their environments, defenders can and do make greater use of long-term planning.

Defenders commonly use two methods for protecting their market shares. The first method involves lobbying government for the adoption of legislation that supports their (the incumbents') dominant competitive positions (called protective legislation) or lobbying government to refrain from adopting legislation that could inhibit or blunt the defenders' dominant competitive positions (called liberalized legislation). One example of an industry's use of protective legislation is described in Box 8.1. Another example is accountants, and in particular those from large accounting firms, who have benefited greatly over the years from government regulation requiring the auditing of the financial statements of listed companies to be restricted to accountants who have specific professional accreditation. This legislation serves as an important barrier to entry and helps ensure the Big Four international accounting firms' dominant market share in the auditing of listed companies' financial reports.

In addition to lobbying for protective legislation, defenders have also been known to lobby against liberalization in legislation. A classic example of this resistance to legislative reform was the strategy adopted by the large national phone companies during the latter part of the 20th century (e.g., AT&T in the US, British Telecommunications plc in the UK, and SFR in France). In an attempt to maintain their essentially monopolistic positions, these companies fought strongly against legislation that would separate the business of phone line transmission (involving the construction and maintenance of the physical infrastructure) from the business of phone retailing (the selling of phone calling plans). A further example of a company that lobbied its government to prevent legislation that would blunt its competitive position is Microsoft. In particular, Microsoft resisted legislative attempts to curtail its alliances with computer hardware manufacturers, who preloaded Microsoft software on the machines they sold to customers. Although the large telecoms and Microsoft eventually lost their bids to prevent legislation in their respective industries, it is likely that their attempts were successful in delaying this legislation, which helped to extend, albeit temporarily, these defenders' dominant competitive positions.

The second way defenders seek to maintain their market dominance is through cost leadership. They achieve this cost leadership by assiduously pursuing cost-minimization programmes. The adoption of standardized operating practices, product/service specialization, benchmarking, and vertical integration are commonly used tactics to underpin the defenders' provision of their respective industries' lowest-cost products and services. Defenders are further known to adopt centralized decision-making and functionally-based organizational structures. These solutions to what Miles and Snow term the "administrative problem" help defenders achieve cost efficiencies, which they can pass on to their customers in the form of lower prices.

Analyzers forge their competitive advantage through the adoption of calculated change. Unlike the prospector, who seeks change and continuously evolves themself to benefit from the change, analyzers are more circumspect about change and their response(s) to it. Furthermore, unlike the defender, which is eager to avoid change and maintain the *status quo*, analyzers are neither averse nor unwilling to change. They will not, however, rush into change, and will leave

BOX 8.1

The defender strategy and ethics

Defenders commonly implement aggressive tactics aimed at preventing other companies from entering their territory. The use of this strategy in the pharmaceutical industry brings into sharp relief the juxtaposition of strategy and ethics. A small number of US and European-based companies dominate the pharmaceutical industry. The three largest companies are Johnson & Johnson, Roche, and Pfizer. These companies have adopted the accounting profession's strategy of cultivating protective legislation, especially through the workings of the US FDA (Food and Drug Administration), as well as relying on the telecom's and Microsoft's previous strategy of trying to thwart legislative liberalization.

Firms in the pharmaceutical industry are notorious for devoting a substantial portion of their annual budgets to lobbying. During the ten-year period of 2006–2015, pharmaceutical companies in the US spent over US$ 880 million on lobbying politicians and contributing to their political campaigns. To put this dollar amount into perspective, this figure is more than eight times the amount US gun lobbyists spent. Represented by a prodigious army of 1,350 lobbyists, these US pharmaceutical companies contributed to the election or re-election campaigns of approximately 7,100 politicians in an attempt to influence the political agenda and legislative process.

Commenting on the brazen methods used by the US pharmaceutical companies to prevent competition to their opioid products, a 2016 *New York Times* story, which referred to a report by Mulvihill *et al.*, described how drug makers and their allies have stymied the use of potentially safer non-opioids like cannabis, for fear that the latter's uptake would erode the pharmaceutical companies' profits. Public health officials have pointed out that opioids are highly addictive and their replacement by medical marijuana could offer an equally effective but far safer alternative.

The pharmaceutical industry's use of lobbying to prevent legislative liberalization in the treatment of patients with pain, combined with this industry's desire to see its markets protected by US FDA regulations, clearly raises the question, "Is the pharmaceutical industry endangering patient welfare in its pursuit of profits?" As such, a significant ethical issue pervades the defender approach adopted by the large pharmaceutical companies.

the pushing of the technological envelope to the prospectors. Analyzers take a highly studied approach to needed change, and this is why Miles and Snow included the adjective "anxious."

Analyzers seek to steer a path that lies between the prospector's focus on innovation and the defender's focus on efficiency. Their dual focus, which comprises the exploitation of existing markets and exploration of new markets, has similarities to organizational ambidexterity, especially in how this concept has been defined and illustrated by O'Reilly and Tushman (2011). In other words, the analyzer's answer to the engineering problem posed by Miles and Snow is to maintain product/service efficiency, while displaying sufficient agility and readiness to pursue new business opportunities as and when they arise.

To help it achieve its dual efficiency and innovation focus, analyzers seek to cultivate intergroup (including between divisions, departments, and work units) collaboration. Analyzers strive to create network opportunities among their respective organizational members and the groups they comprise. As such, they are likely to adopt matrix structures. Good examples of analyzers are IBM, Anheuser-Busch, and Kyocera.

Miles and Snow's fourth strategy category is called the reactor. This strategy is essentially a default category. Firms that do not fit one of the first three categories will by default fall into this category. Reactors display a lack of systematic response to any of Miles and Snow's three fundamental questions. These firms follow no programme of strategic planning or thinking. Instead, they only choose to make decisions about what their organizations do (i.e., the sets of product and service attributes that define their offerings), where they do it (i.e., the structural characteristics that determine the scope and geographical dispersion of their operations), and how they do it (i.e., the set of operating processes and work practices they use) because they are pressured into making these decisions. It is for this reason that Miles and Snow preface this strategy with the adjective "reluctant."

Miles and Snow contend that any of the first three strategies can be viable. Furthermore, none of these three is necessarily superior to any of the other two. The success from pursuing one of the three strategies will depend on whether the firm can ensure synergy in the net-worked set of activities that underpin its strategic approach. In contrast, the reactor strategy is not viable. It lacks the essential ingredients of proactivity and deliberateness that characterize the first three. Being reactive and the product of incremental *ad hoc* decisions, the reactor strat-egy displays no consistent or coherent sequencing to its strategic decision-making. The strategy dooms a firm to an unsustainable and ultimately failed existence. Table 8.1 summarizes Miles and Snow's four strategic archetypes and their unique responses to each of the three fundamen-tal problems.

Various scholars have attempted to verify the reliability and validity of the Miles and Snow taxonomy. In an examination of nearly 450 organizations in the hospital industry, Shortell and

TABLE 8.1 Miles and Snow's four strategic archetypes' responses to the three fundamental management problems

Fundamental problem	Prospector	Defender	Analyzer	Reactor
Entrepreneurial	Renewal and innovation	Refinement and efficiency	Innovation and efficiency	No systematic response
Engineering	Broad range of products/services	Government lobbying and/or specialized product/service offerings	Technical efficiency	No systematic response
Administrative	Decentralized, divisionalized	Centralized, functional	Networked, matrix	No systematic response

Zajac (1990) observed significant associations between the Miles and Snow taxonomy and how these health-related organizations designed their respective business activities. Organizations with prospector strategic orientations were more likely to be first-movers in the adoption of new products and services, which Shortell and Zajac (1990) operationalized as:

1 Emphasis given to new services and new market development activities
2 Number of diversified services offered (adjusted for the size of the hospital)
3 Number of diversified services started in the two years preceding data collection
4 Ratio of outpatient to inpatient services offered
5 Number of high-technology services offered (adjusted for the size of the hospital)
6 Number of new diversified services planned for the future.

Shortell and Zajac further observed that analyzers were generally more likely to be first-movers in the adoption of new managerial procedures and systems. Moore (2005) applied Miles and Snow's taxonomy to the retail environment and similarly found the taxonomy to be largely applicable to retail contexts. And finally, and again in support of the predicted associations between Miles and Snow's strategic orientations and organizational activities, Subramanian *et al.* (1993) observed that prospectors were the most proactive of the four archetypes in their environmental scanning. Analyzers were the second most proactive, while defenders were found to be more *ad hoc* than proactive in their approach to environmental scanning.

PORTER'S COST LEADER, DIFFERENTIATOR, AND FOCUS STRATEGY

Porter has had a major, and arguably perhaps the most major, impact on strategy theory and practice. Ever since the publication of his book *Competitive Advantage: Creating and Sustaining Superior Performance* (1985), his influence has been profound and enduring. According to Porter, the effectiveness of a firm's strategy is a function of the attractiveness of the industry it operates in and the ability to establish and maintain a favourable competitive position in the adopted industry.

Porter argues there are two basic types of competitive position: cost leadership and differentiation. As he states:

> Competitive advantage grows out of value a firm is able to create for its buyers that exceeds the firm's cost of creating it. Value is what buyers are willing to pay, and superior value stems from offering lower prices than competitors for equivalent benefits or providing unique benefits that more than offset a higher price. There are two basic types of competitive advantage: cost leadership and differentiation.
>
> (Porter, 1985: 3)

Both cost leadership and differentiation can be pursued using a broadly-based competitive scope (i.e., the generalist) or a narrowly-based competitive scope (i.e., the specialist). A generalist strives for presence in most, if not all, customer and geographical segments of its given industry.

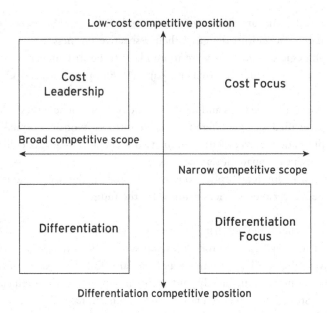

FIGURE 8.1 Generic strategy as a function of competitive scope and competitive position.
Source: Adapted from Porter (1985: 12).

Large, well-known banks such as Chase Bank, Bank of America, HSBC, and National Australia Bank are prime examples of generalists. In contrast, specialists focus on serving the needs of a subset of its industry's customer and/or geographical segments, and sometimes just a single segment. Keeping with the banking industry, specialists would include banks that provide small business loans like SmartBiz and Celtic Bank. Figure 8.1 provides an illustration of the competitive scope and competitive position factors that define a firm's generic strategy.

A competitive position predicated on cost leadership can only be attained by one firm in any given industry, for this strategy involves laying claim to the lowest prices. Having the second-lowest prices may be highly praiseworthy, but it provides no rallying cry for attracting customers. Accordingly, the first defining characteristic of cost leadership is that it applies to only one firm operating in each industry.

Firms that pursue a cost leadership strategy cannot neglect other factors that define their product/service, including such factors as product/service innovation, quality, or after-sales service. Successful cost leaders must achieve proximity to what their competitors deliver on these other product/service dimensions. If the cost leader cannot accomplish this objective, then the product/service becomes unrecognizable from its competitors' offerings and can no longer be seen as a low-cost version of these offerings.

The main way cost leaders achieve their competitive advantage is through economies of scale, lean manufacturing, tight direct-cost and overhead-cost control, avoidance of marginal customer accounts, cost savings through modifications of the supply chain, and cost minimization in areas like research and development, service, sales force, and advertising. Cost leaders are notable for their ability to exert industry stability through the strong influence, if not their outright dominion, to set a price floor in their industry. Other competitors, the differentiators, that is, who typically incur higher costs due to the differentiated products/services they provide, will set prices above the cost leader's established price relative to the additional customer value the differentiators' products/services offer.

The industry stability a cost leader provides can, however, be undermined when more than one firm within the same industry strives for cost leadership. The outcome can be significant and mortal for not just one of the two firms vying for cost leadership, but for any differentiator which finds the price premium it charges is no longer supported by the new – and perhaps continuing to fall – price floor that the battle to claim cost leadership precipitates.

A differentiation strategy is achieved by virtue of a firm offering uniqueness on some non-price-based dimension/attribute of the product/service. The ability to deliver uniqueness derives from doing some activity or set of activities better than one's competitors and, as a result of this better execution, being able to lay claim to providing products/services that are superior on one or more attributes. A firm can emphasize superiority, and therefore differentiate, on any one of the following five main factors/sub-factors:

- Product/service features (innovation, quality, scope, delivery, etc.)
- Service (before, during, and/or after the sale)
- Distribution (warehousing, dealer networks, etc.)
- Marketing (placement, relationships, etc.)
- Company image/reputation.

As an illustration, Nike differentiates its athletic shoes on image, while Mercedes-Benz chooses product design for its point of differentiation. Irrespective of the particular manner a firm seeks to differentiate its products/services, to achieve this superiority, or what Porter likes to call "uniqueness," the firm must have relatively better – in comparison with its competitors, that is – capabilities in one or more of the following areas: pioneering scientific research, highly-skilled and creative product-development personnel, a strong sales force, and/or a strong reputation for quality and innovation.

Just as firms that pursue a cost leadership strategy must achieve proximity to what their differentiation-based competitors offer on various product/service attributes, differentiators need to be conscious of the cost leader's price and always ensure the price premium they charge is commensurate with the additional/superior product/service features they offer. To stray too far above the price floor set by the cost leader, without adequate justification for this price premium, will imperil the differentiator's survival.

Porter's final generic competitive strategy is called focus. As previously noted, firms that pursue a focus strategy are deliberately choosing to concentrate on a piece of, and not across the whole of, their industry. Firms with a focus strategy may, for example, concentrate on a particular customer (e.g., demographic, behavioural) or geographic segment of their chosen industry. It is for this reason that some scholars and practitioners refer to this strategy as a segmentation strategy.

The focus strategy is often chosen by smaller businesses, for they typically lack the resources required to pursue a cost leadership or differentiation strategy. The limited operations of these smaller companies prevent them from realizing economies of scale. Accordingly, the main driver of a cost leadership strategy is not available. Furthermore, their smallness means that they do not possess the specialized resources that are required for a differentiation strategy.

To be successful, a focus strategy requires:

- The target niche to be large, profitable, and growing
- Industry generalists to view the niche as uneconomical for them to pursue and unimportant to their own success
- Few rivals trying to compete in the same niche.

Microbreweries are good examples of companies that pursue focus strategies, especially differentiation focus strategies. These brewers typically provide a product that appeals to a particular market niche. The niche could be one that appreciates some premium, even exotic, blend of ingredients. For example, some microbrewers use various herbs and spices (such as curry, cumin, and cayenne), while others use recipes involving coffee, vanilla bean, and peppers. There are also microbrewers who appeal to customers' environmentalism by selling organic beers, and still other brewers who build their customer base around parochialism (i.e., pride in/loyalty to one's local region).

COOPER'S CONFRONTATION STRATEGY

Cooper's (1995) conceptions of strategy have largely slipped under the radar. This circumstance is most unfortunate, for Cooper's ideas are well evidenced by actual competitive practice, being based on 20 in-depth case studies involving a broad cross section of Japanese manufacturers. The case companies included Sony Corporation, Kirin Brewing Company, Mitsubishi Kasei Corporation (now named Mitsubishi Chemical Corporation), and Olympus Optical Company (now named Olympus Corporation). In spite of the significant time and care Cooper invested investigating the strategic approaches adopted by Japanese manufacturers, his work has been largely overlooked. Why this anonymity should prevail is worthy of further consideration, and it forms a topic of discussion at the end of this section.

Cooper sees the world very differently from his previous Harvard colleague Michael Porter. Whereas Porter preaches the virtues of uniqueness, Cooper speaks about the effects of globalization on the commoditization of products and services, and the implications these effects have on competitive strategy. Cooper argues that as products/services reach mature lifecycle stages, they become more susceptible to survival zone collapses; and when these collapses occur, the industry's competitors are faced with a more limited competitive space and the need to compete in closer quarters in a more head-to-head fashion.

Cooper contends that price, quality, and functionality – what he terms the survival triplet – determine the number of competitors within an industry and the nature of the competition. In an industry setting where the competitive space is large, firms can strive for competitive advantage using the strategy literature's traditional strategic orientations (e.g., Porter's cost leader and differentiator).

Price, says Cooper, is a direct function of cost. It includes all costs required to produce the product/service, including not only all production costs (e.g., materials, labour, and overhead) and marketing and selling costs, but also all investment costs (e.g., research and development). Quality is defined in terms of customer perceptions about how well the product/service conforms to its specifications, or what some like to call "doing what it says on the tin." Finally, functionality encompasses three dimensions: vertical product differentiation, horizontal product differentiation, and the provision of full customer solutions. The reader who wants to learn more about these three dimensions should refer to Page 15 of Cooper's *When Lean Entreprises Collide: Competing Through Confrontation* (1995).

Cooper uses three-dimensional space to illustrate the size of an industry's competitive space and the associated positions a firm can occupy. In an attempt to provide a simplified visual illustration, quality is redefined here as the ability to meet customer expectations. Customer expectations, as described in the total quality management literature, take a more liberal view of the range of purposes and higher standards that products/services must achieve than is the case when a conformity to company specifications approach is used. As such, a customer expectations approach captures both Cooper's quality and functionality dimensions. This simplification allows the use of two-dimensional space to depict the relationships Cooper is trying to portray.

Figure 8.2 is a customer resource grid that illustrates an industry setting where price/cost and quality plus functionality allow ample competitive space for competing firms to occupy their own unique positions, which in the language of Porter constitutes their competitive strategy. Price/cost is shown as the y-axis and customer expectations as the x-axis. The points which populate the figure represent customers with specific utilities for price, quality, and functionality. Some customers will be interested in low cost and have little appetite or no need for quality and functionality. These customers are represented in the lower left-hand corner of Figure 8.2. Other customers will demand extremely high quality and functionality, and be willing to pay a substantial price premium for this need. Meanwhile, a further set of customers will desire medium levels of quality and functionality and will pay a medium price premium for the product/service. These varied customer preferences allow sufficient competitive space for a cost leader and differentiators to emerge as is shown in Figure 8.2.

The relatively minor amount of overlap among the competitive spaces of the five firms suggests that in a stable market the strategic competitive positions of the five firms could endure. Markets, however, are fluid and dynamic. Changes in market supply are bound to happen. Existing competitors will exit, new competitors will arrive (and may subsequently exit), and substitute products/services will appear. These changes will invariably cause movement in the competitive positions firms assume. Also affecting an industry's supply are the significant technological advances (e.g., computer-aided design, computer-aided manufacturing, factory automation) that have dramatically reduced production costs and improved product quality. Supporting these technological advances and helping to fuel further efficiency gains and boosts in quality are such organization-wide and systemically-oriented improvements systems as total quality management and just-in-time (see Adler, 1999). The end result of these various producer-initiated changes is a near-constant downward pressure on price and a near-constant upward pressure on quality. These forces pave the way for the producers' inexorable migration towards the lower right-hand corner of Figure 8.2. This reality is well captured by Toshiro Shimoyama, the former chairman and CEO of Olympus Optical Co., Ltd, who stated, "Competition has become a treadmill of exhaustion from which there appears to be no escape" (as cited in Cooper, 1995: 2).

In addition to producer-related, supply-side influences, demand-side, customer-driven influences further serve to shape an industry's competitive space. Just think how often we hear companies describe themselves as "customer-centric" or utter the refrain, "The customer is

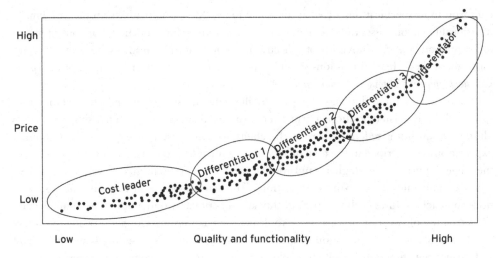

FIGURE 8.2 Visual portrayal of cost leader and differentiators operating in unique competitive spaces.

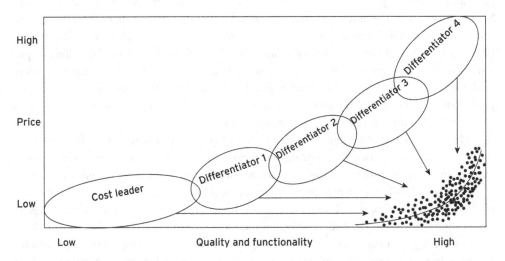

FIGURE 8.3 Collapse of survival zones and implications for cost leaders and differentiators.

always right." According to Cooperstein (2013), today's market environment has moved well beyond these superficial adages. He believes the business world has moved from the age of manufacturing (1900–1960) to the age of distribution (1960–1990) to the age of information (1990–2010) to now the "age of the customer."

Customers have grown quite fond of their new power. The purchasing benefits globalization has brought to customers are readily evidenced by their ability to flit between producers with minimal to no switching costs. Increasingly, a change between providers can be made at the stroke of a few keys on a keypad. As a result, customers increasingly, if they do not already, expect producers to be both low price and high quality.

The combination of supplier actions and customer expectations culminates in the customer utilities being concentrated in the lower right-hand corner of an industry's customer resource grid. This situation is visually illustrated in Figure 8.3. The arrows pointing from each firm to the figure's lower right-hand corner indicate the migration path each firm must undertake to relocate itself where the customers now reside.

According to Cooper (1995), industries whose main products/services have reached the mature stage of their product lifecycles and which feature high levels of competition are likely to experience the shrinking survival zone illustrated in Figure 8.3. While Cooper has recounted the experiences of the automobile, computer, and telecommunications industries to demonstrate his point, Adler (2011) has identified further industries (e.g., whiteware and banking) that have followed a similar trajectory towards a limited industry competitive space.

Firms that operate in mature industries with high levels of competition will be both unable to distance themselves from their competitors and unable to adopt a unique competitive strategy. Instead, these firms must learn how to compete head-to-head and toe-to-toe. They will be required to pursue what Cooper calls a confrontation strategy. Cooper (1995: 11) offers the following description of this strategy:

> A generic strategy that does not rely on avoiding competition is confrontation. Firms that adopt a confrontation strategy do not attempt to collude nor do they attempt to become cost leaders or differentiators. Instead, they compete head-on for their share of the market by developing and exploiting *temporary* competitive advantages. While they still try to differentiate their products by introducing new features or try to develop a price leadership position by dropping prices, they do not expect such actions to lead to a sustainable competitive advantage. Instead, they assume that their competitors will rapidly bring out products that are equivalent and match any price changes.
>
> (Emphasis in original)

Cooper's confrontation strategy is not unlike Mintzberg and Waters' (1985) idea of an imposed strategy. Mintzberg and Waters view organizational strategies as spanning a continuum, with deliberately-planned strategies at one end of the continuum and emergent, environmentally-determined strategies at the other end. Imposed strategies, one of the eight strategies identified in Mintzberg and Waters' model, occupy a space close to the environmentally-determined end of the continuum. According to these scholars, the environment strongly influences the organization's action to the point that the environmental pressures become "inescapable" (p. 268). This idea of inescapability is similar to Cooper's ideas, although the latter largely views the environment in terms of competition. Lee (2004) and Melnyk et al. (2010) represent two additional sets of scholars who have more recently discussed the need for blended strategies when strategic positions such as cost leadership or differentiation no longer offer long-term defendable positions on their own.

Why Cooper's confrontation strategy has failed to resonate with practitioners and scholars is a mystery. While Cooper's book *When Lean Enterprises Collide: Competing Through Confrontation* had 525 Google Scholar citations at the time of 12 August 2022, Porter's book *Competitive Advantage: Creating and Sustaining Superior Performance* has accumulated thousands of citations, has had over 30 printings, and has been translated into 13 languages. As previously noted, Porter's impact on the field of strategy has been immense and enduring, and the fact that his seminal book has received such rave attention is far from surprising and richly deserved. But it remains a strange curiosity why Cooper's work has attracted signficantly less interest.

Three likely reasons help to explain the comparative anonymity of Cooper's work. One reason is the largely esoteric nature of the scholarly peer review process and what ultimately receives the nomenclature of "quality" research. Cooper's use of largely qualitative research methods, which predominantly consisted of interview data, is an example of swimming against the tide. In particular, accounting research during the 1990s, and this was especially true in the US, was associated with the rise of quantitative research methods and the associated demise of qualitative research methods. Bennis and O'Toole (2005) discussed the then newfound fascina-tion of US business schools with quantitative research methods and the detrimental effects they were having on scholarship and student learning. In spite of Bennis and O'Toole's (2005) and Ghoshal's (2005) passionate admonitions against this trend and their calls for the re-evaluation of business schools' research and teaching agendas, the hegemony of the quantitative research method, which has now established itself far beyond the shores of the US, certainly did not help Cooper's ideas become mainstream.

A second likely reason that scuppered Cooper's ideas from garnering greater attention is related to his sample's setting. During the 1980s and early 1990s, Japan was a darling of the eco-nomic world, and research on Japanese companies and their management practices frequently featured in the scholarly and practitioner literatures. But when Japan's economic bubble burst in the mid-1990s, so too did scholarly and practitioner interest in Japan and its companies. Unfortunately for Cooper, it was a classic case of bad timing.

A third reason for the failure of Cooper's work to resonate more widely may be traced to Porter, who was a colleague of Cooper's at Harvard up until the mid-1990s. Cooper's ideas were in significant opposition to Porter's ideas. Although others were beginning to question Porter's strident opposition to the possibility of hybrid strategies (see, for example, Johnson and Scholes, 1993), Cooper, as a colleague who shared office space with Porter in the Harvard Business School, must have been a particularly irritating thorn in Porter's side. In fact, when reading Porter's 1996 *Harvard Business Review* article "What is strategy?", the reader gains the impression that Porter is feeling cornered by scholars like Cooper. From the opening sen-tence, and even the very heading that precedes this sentence (i.e., "Operational Effectiveness Is Not Strategy"), it appears as though Cooper's 1995 book *When Lean Enterprises Collide: Competing Through Confrontation* has released a ghost that is haunting Porter and causing him significant angst and turmoil. On Page 3 of Porter's article, he includes a sidebar on "Japanese Companies Rarely Have Strategies." While Porter does an excellent job in his 1996 article defending and further enunciating his cost leader and differentiator taxonomy, his article misses the point that Cooper is trying to make about the effects a maturing industry and high competition will have on the competitive strategies firms can pursue. Cooper, who failed to receive tenure at Harvard, lost his foothold there. Being cast adrift from Harvard meant he lost the preferential privileges Harvard faculty have in publishing their work in the *Harvard Business Review*. Without these platforms for name recognition (i.e., Harvard Business School) and publication outlets (i.e., *Harvard Business Review*), Cooper's ideas concerning confronta-tion strategy largely withered.

KIM AND MAUBORGNE'S BLUE OCEAN STRATEGY

Blue ocean strategy is meant to conjure up the idea of a firm being so unique in the value proposition it offers customers that there is no competitor in sight. The successful pursuit of blue ocean strategies enables the firm to trawl customer-rich seas without interference from any competitors and the need to share this market space with any competitor(s). The path to these blue waters involves creating new markets. In contrast to seeking finer segmentation of existing markets, blue ocean strategies involve converting non-customers into customers. More specifically, it comprises converting customers using alternative or substitute products/services to the blue ocean firm's set of product/service offerings. Southwest Airlines qualifies as a successful implementer of a blue ocean strategy. Through its introduction of low-cost and friendly service, it converted ground transport users (train and bus riders) into fliers. Uber Technologies, Inc., is another example of a blue ocean strategy. This firm is transforming the short-distance transportation habits of people throughout the world. Some of its customers were previous bus riders, while others simply would not have made the trip previously.

Blue oceans move beyond Porter's ideas of building sustainable competitive advantage through either differentiation or low cost. Blue ocean strategies demand the simultaneous pursuit of differentiation and low cost. As Kim and Mauborgne state: "In reality, a market-creating move breaks the value-cost trade-off. It is about pursuing differentiation and low cost simultaneously … A market-creating move is 'both-and,' not an 'either-or,' strategy" (2015: 72). The need for a dual differentiation and low-cost focus explains why blue ocean strategy firms' products/services are characterized by their ability to offer "a leap in productivity, simplicity, ease of use, convenience, fun, or environmental friendliness" (Kim and Mauborgne, 2015: 72). Kim and Mauborgne's dual focus can be contrasted with Porter's admonition to eschew such conflation. It is also worth noting how Southwest Airlines is used by Porter to showcase the quintessential cost leader, while Kim and Mauborgne use Southwest Airlines to illustrate the successful pursuit of a blue ocean strategy. While Southwest Airlines' emergence and disruption of the airline industry occurred largely due to its low airfares, a fact which supports Porter's choice to classify Southwest as a cost leader, Kim and Mauborgne are equally correct in contending that Southwest's customer value proposition went beyond low fares, adding further weight to the growing numbers of scholars who view the successful pursuit of hybrid strategies as possible and even necessary.

COMPARING MILES AND SNOW'S, PORTER'S, COOPER'S, AND KIM AND MAUBORGNE'S TAXONOMIES

Earlier in this chapter, the topic of OWC was discussed. We now use this concept of OWC to gain further understanding of the four strategic orientations just presented. A single order-winning criterion is fully consistent with Porter's ideas and also captures Miles and Snow's defender and prospector strategic orientations. Porter is quite adamant that each firm must, if it wants to be successful, excel on a particular product/service attribute. Focusing on more than one product/service attribute is likely to result in the firm being what Porter calls "stuck in the middle" and with no demonstrable sustainable competitive advantage, which will ultimately imperil the firm's survival. Miles and Snow, although not nearly as prescriptive as Porter, also advocate a single order-winning criterion, or at least this is true with its defender and prospector strategies. Defenders will typically excel at low cost as a way to minimize competition and maintain their market dominance. Prospectors will seek to push boldly into the lead by emphasizing a particular non-cost product/service attribute.

In contrast to adopting a single order-winning criterion approach, Cooper's and Kim and Mauborgne's views on strategy, as well as Miles and Snow's analyzer, promote a multiple OWC approach. What distinguishes the strategic orientations of these respective models is the extent of manager choice. Kim and Mauborgne argue that blue ocean strategy is the "both-and" (i.e., dual differentiation and low-cost) focus that managers will undertake in their quest to create new markets. In other words, managers will choose to adopt multiple OWCs. Analyzers' multiple OWC approach derives from their pursuit of a strategy that lies between the prospector's focus on innovation and the defender's focus on efficiency. Again, managers choose this path. In contrast, Cooper's confrontation strategy is environmentally mandated (it results from the collapse of an industry's survival zone) and lacks manager choice. As previously noted, a confrontation strategy is equivalent to an imposed strategy. Figure 8.4 summarizes the relationship between these ideas on OWC and the strategic orientation taxonomies of Miles and Snow, Porter, Cooper, and Kim and Mauborgne.

As shown in Figure 8.4, there are situations where external environmental forces determine either the price an organization charges or the non-cost-related OWC an organization must deliver. The latter situation commonly occurs when a product, but more often a service, is government or industry regulated. For example, a notary public (who is a government appointee with the primary responsibility of witnessing signatures on legal documents), a US enrolled tax agent (who is a federally-authorized tax practitioner), and a health practitioner or centre that is a registered government service provider all must ensure their services conform to a set of regulated standards. Although there is no flexibility on the nature of the provided service, there is flexibility in pricing, or at least the pricing used for a non-government party. The notary public can charge different prices, and even offer services *pro bono*, for different clients. So too can the enrolled tax agent. Meanwhile, health care practitioners can levy surcharges on top of what the government pays. These surcharges can be different for different groups of patients. In New Zealand, patients under the age of 14 or who hold a Community Services Card are charged reduced doctors' fees or no fees at all.

Situations where a product's OWC is cost-based and the price being charged is determined by external environmental forces invariably involve a commodity product. For example, a seller of crude oil would find itself subject to an imposed, price-taker strategy. Crude oil is priced based on its established chemical characteristics: the oil's American Petroleum Institute (API) gravity and its sulphur content. Oil with lower API gravity and lower sulphur content is more highly prized and therefore commands a higher price. North Sea Brent Crude, which is extracted from the part of the Atlantic Ocean located between the UK, Scandinavia, Germany, the Netherlands, Belgium, and France, has relatively low API gravity and low sulphur content. It commands a higher price than other types of crude oil such as North America's West Texas Intermediate Crude (WTI) and the UAE Dubai Crude.

Since the characteristics of crude oil are straightforward functions of where the oil is sourced, there is nothing an oil producer can do to customize or change the properties of its product. Once an oil producer transports its product to the appropriate collection point (e.g.,

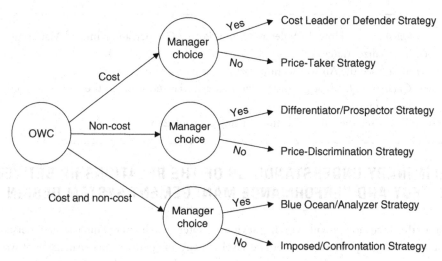

FIGURE 8.4 The relationship between OWC and the strategy taxonomies of Miles and Snow, Porter, Cooper, and Kim and Mauborgne.

Sullom Voe, an island north of Scotland, for Brent Crude), the producer receives the prevailing spot price (the current market price at which an asset is bought or sold for immediate payment and delivery). Whether it is Royal Dutch/Shell or British Petroleum that delivers the oil has no influence on the spot price, for any given barrel of Brent Crude is deemed indistinguishable and is wholly substitutable by another barrel. Neither Royal Dutch/Shell nor British Petroleum can do anything to alter the product they deliver. Both companies will find they must accept the fact they are price-takers and do whatever they can to keep their cost structures as low as possible.

Other companies that produce commodity products will also likely find themselves beholden to a price-taker position. Agricultural producers of such commodities as corn, wheat, and soybeans will typically be price-takers. So too will miners of copper, silver, and gold, as well as producers of energy. Commodities by definition are fungible, which means that due to their equivalence any unit of a particular commodity can be replaced by another unit of this same commodity in satisfaction of a contractual obligation. For example, every bushel of Number 2 corn (which is defined as possessing 15.5% moisture content) can be substituted by any other bushel of Number 2 corn. This idea of indistinguishability explains why commodity producers' products can be mixed together and why these producers are price-takers.

Although it is generally true that producers of commodities are price-takers, it must also be recognized that even with commodities like maize, wheat, and energy, opportunities for differentiation are increasingly occurring. In particular, farmers who employ organic farming practices can differentiate their products. Likewise, energy producers who use renewable sources (wind, hydro, and solar power) can also differentiate their products from energy producers who rely on non-renewables (coal, gas, and nuclear power). Accordingly, the number of organizations with commodity-like products that demand a price-taker position is far smaller than the number of organizations that fall into the other strategic classifications of cost leaders, differentiators, defenders, prospectors, analyzers, blue ocean, and confrontation.

> *Review Question 8.3:* How do Miles and Snow, Porter, Cooper, and Kim and Mauborgne conceptualize strategy?
>
> *Answer:* Please see the Answer section starting on page 283
>
> *Review Question 8.4:* What are order-winning criteria, and how do they relate to competitive strategy?
>
> *Answer:* Please see the Answer section starting on page 283

PRELIMINARY UNDERSTANDINGS OF THE RELATIONSHIP BETWEEN STRATEGY AND PERFORMANCE MANAGEMENT SYSTEM DESIGN

Similar to the discussion provided in the previous chapter, which offered high-level understandings of the relationships between corporate-level strategy and performance management system design, we now examine some of the basic patterns in the relationships between competitive strategy and performance management system design. As noted in Chapter 7, a fuller and more detailed discussion of these relationships require your understanding of the key performance management elements that are the featured topics of Chapters 10–12.

Table 8.2 provides a description of the expected generalized performance management characteristics associated with different competitive strategies. Cost leaders and defenders will be likely to operate performance management systems exhibiting high formality and high standardization. In particular, these organizations, which crave stability, will want their members to follow tried-and-tested work procedures. Formalized rules that are standardized and repeatable will be prized by these organizations. Since these organizations are committed to keeping their costs low, they will eschew organizational structures that feature duplication. As a result, these organizations are likely to adopt functional structures. And finally, these organizations will possess cultures characterized by conservatism. Such cultures reinforce these organizations' desires to maintain stability and retain the *status quo*.

In contrast to cost leaders and defenders, differentiators and prospectors will adopt systems and processes that accentuate informality and are customized to the setting. These organizations embrace change and will therefore want to allow and encourage their employees to seek out new ways of undertaking work tasks and procedures. Differentiators and prospectors recognize that the recipe that may work for today is unlikely to be the one that will succeed tomorrow. Consequently, the formalization/codification of systems and processes will be unhelpful, wasteful, and merely interfere with their employees' abilities to seize new opportunities and devise better ways of conducting their work. The organizational structures will be divisional, for these structures are associated with quicker organizational action and decision-making. The organizational cultures will be distinguished by high entrepreneurialism.

The performance management systems of the organizations pursuing analyzer, blue ocean, and confrontation strategies will feature characteristics that borrow from both ends of the continua shown in Table 8.2. It is premature and unnecessary at this point in the book to discuss the general performance management design features of this final set of competitive strategies until more developed understandings about organizational systems, processes, and procedures, organizational structures, and organizational cultures have been achieved. Accordingly, this discussion is postponed until later in the book.

TABLE 8.2 Relationship between performance management characteristics and competitive strategy

	Cost leaders Defenders	Analyzers blue ocean confrontation	Differentiators prospectors
Systems and processes	Formal, standardized	↔	Informal, customized
Structure	Functional	↔	Divisional
Culture	Conservative	↔	Collaborative

Review Question 8.5: Provide an example of at least one firm for each of the following competitive strategies: cost leader, differentiator, defender, prospector, analyzer, and blue ocean.

Answer: Please see the Answer section starting on page 283

Review Question 8.6: What are the general associations between the competitive strategies of Miles and Snow, Porter, Cooper, and Kim and Mauborgne and performance management design?

Answer: Please see the Answer section starting on page 283

CONCLUSION

This chapter discussed business-unit-level strategy, or what is often referred to as competitive strategy. Many scholars have significantly contributed to the competitive strategy literature. This chapter highlighted four of the most significant contributions: Miles and Snow (1978), Porter (1985), Cooper (1995), and Kim and Mauborgne (2005). Each of these competitive strategy taxonomies was extensively discussed and critiqued. The concept of OWC was used as a prism through which to understand more fully each of the taxonomies. These understandings of competitive strategy were used to provide preliminary advice on the associations between competitive strategy and performance management design.

REFERENCES

Adler, R.W. (1999) *Management Accounting: Making It World Class*, Oxford: Butterworth-Heinemann.

Adler, R.W. (2011) Performance management and organization strategy: how to design systems that meet the needs of confrontation strategy firms, *British Accounting Review*, Vol. 43, No. 4, pp. 251–263.

Bennis, W.G. and O'Toole, J. (2005) How business schools lost their way, *Harvard Business Review*, Vol. 58, No. 3, pp. 96–104.

Clulow, V., Gerstman, J. and Barry, C. (2003) The resource-based view and sustainable competitive advantage: the case of a financial services firm, *Journal of European Industrial Training*, Vol. 27, No. 5, pp. 220–232.

Cooper, R. (1995) *When Lean Enterprises Collide: Competing Through Confrontation*, Cambridge, MA: Harvard Business School Press.

Cooperstein, D.M. (2013) *Competitive Strategy in the Age of the Customer*, Cambridge, MA: Forrester Research.

Ghoshal, S. (2005) Bad management theories are destroying good management practices, *Academy of Management Learning and Education*, Vol. 4, No. 1, pp. 75–91.

Hoque, Z. (2003) *Strategic Management Accounting Concepts, Processes, and Issues*, Oxford: Chandos Publishing (Oxford) Limited.

Johnson, G. and Scholes, K. (1993) *Exploring Corporate Strategy*, London: Prentice Hall International.

Kim, W.C. and Mauborgne, R. (2005) *Blue Ocean Strategy: How to Create Uncontested Market Space and Make the Competition Irrelevant*, Cambridge, MA: Harvard Business School Press.

Kim, W.C. and Mauborgne, R. (2015) Red ocean traps: the mental models that undermine market-creating strategies, *Harvard Business Review*, Vol. 93, No. 3, pp. 67–73.

Lee, H.L. (2004) The triple – a supply chain, *Harvard Business Review*, Vol. 82, No. 10, pp. 102–111.

Melnyk, S.A., Davis, E.W., Spekman, R.E. and Sandor, J. (2010) Outcome-driven supply chain, *MIT Sloan Management Review*, Vol. 51, No. 2, pp. 33–38.

Miles, R.E. and Snow, C.C. (1978) *Organizational Strategy, Structure, and Process*, New York: McGraw-Hill.

Mintzberg, H. and Waters, J. (1985) Of strategies, deliberate and emergent, *Strategic Management Journal*, Vol. 6, No. 3, pp. 257–272.

Moore, M. (2005) Towards a confirmatory model of retail strategy types: an empirical test of Miles and Snow, *Journal of Business Research*, Vol. 58, No. 5, pp. 696–704.

Mulvihill, G., Perrone, M., Whyte, L.E. and Wiederassan, B. (2016) Media partnership examines influence of opioid industry, *New York Times*, 18 September.

O'Reilly, C. and Tushman, M.L. (2011) Organizational ambidexterity in action: how managers explore and exploit, *California Management Review*, Vol. 53, No. 4, pp. 5–22.

Porter, M.E. (1985) *Competitive Advantage: Creating and Sustaining Superior Performance*, New York: Free Press.

Porter, M. E. (1996) What is strategy?, *Harvard Business Review*, Vol. 74, No. 6, pp. 61–78.

Shortell, S.M. and Zajac, E.J. (1990) Perceptual and archival measures of Miles and Snow's strategic types: a comprehensive assessment of reliability and validity, *Academy of Management Journal*, Vol. 33, No. 4, pp. 817–832.

Subramanian, R., Fernandes, N. and Harper, E. (1993) An empirical examination of the relationship between strategy and scanning, *Mid-Atlantic Journal of Business*, Vol. 29, No. 3, pp. 315–330.

CHAPTER **9**

Digital business transformation
Connections to competitive strategy

CHAPTER OBJECTIVES

- Define digital business transformation.
- Describe and provide examples of some of the early manifestations of digital business transformation.
- Discuss why digital business transformation is often described as a journey that requires the holistic integration of business practices.
- Discuss how digital business transformation is related to performance management.
- Describe how the three levers of performance management are influenced by and influence the adoption of digital business transformation.

INTRODUCTION

This chapter examines organizations' evolving use of digital business transformation (DBT) and the effect on performance management design and practice. As the chapter will show, an organization's use of DBT has impacts on its strategy, organizational structure, employee work practices, leadership, and organizational culture. Accordingly, this concept comprises themes that address multiple aspects of the book's performance management model. In recognition of the wide-ranging influence DBT has on performance management design and practice – especially in terms of how an organization conceives, implements, and tracks the progress of its strategy – this chapter has been purposefully positioned to appear just after to the book's twin chapters on strategy.

The chapter begins by discussing the distinguishing characteristics of DBT, including the organizational outcomes it is intended to promote. Being more customer-centric, promoting deeper engagement with stakeholders, and developing additional revenue streams are some of

DOI: 10.4324/9781003267195-11

the more commonly expressed outcomes. In fact, the significantly consequential nature of the strategic and operational opportunities DBT makes possible means that a manager's task of designing and implementing performance management systems in a DBT environment is both especially challenging and potentially highly advantageous. Accordingly, the issue of performance management design comprises much of the chapter's focus.

WHAT IS DBT?

DBT describes an organization's journey to harness a digitized environment by leveraging the opportunities and evolving practices of digital technologies and their impact on society in an operationally optimal and strategic manner. This definition is worthy of some closer unpacking. First, the term digitized refers to an environment that consists wholly of binary coding (i.e., a world where 0s and 1s are used to represent characters, instructions, and literally everything). A digital environment can be contrasted with its analogue counterpart, the latter which uses electrical impulses to emulate the audio waves of sound. Today's world is dominated by digital/binary coding due its cost advantage, convenience in saving and retrieving data, and its ability to survive long distances without signal decay.

In addition to harnessing a world of 0s and 1s, DBT is defined by its adoption of digital technologies and solutions that are intended to help an organization enhance customer value, increase efficiency, promote innovation, and improve decision making. In other words, far from being an end in themselves, digital technologies are intended to enable a more customer-centric environment that will ultimately provide an organization with higher revenues, added revenue streams, and greater profitability. As one example, Starbucks' integrated use of digital technologies led to reducing customers' time-in-line by 900,000 hours per year (Marchand *et al.*, 2014). This reduction not only saved customers time, but it also saved its partners (the term Starbucks uses when referring to its frontline staff) time in receiving and processing customers' orders. Meanwhile, the New Zealand IRD's digitalization initiative has shortened the time it takes a taxpayer to request and receive an IRD number from weeks to hours.

The digital technologies DBT relies upon are commonly captured under the umbrella term "AMPS" (Analytical tools and applications, Mobile tools and applications, Platforms to build shareable digital capabilities, and Social media). As such, digital technologies include video technologies for working from home, GPS-locating services, 5G and virtual reality, smart homes, cloud computing, Artificial Intelligence (AI), deep fake and AI, and bitcoin and blockchain.

The promised advantages of DBT occur from being able to combine and integrate large quantities of data (i.e., the concept of big data) in a way that offers genuine business insight. Large sets of multifaceted data are essential for DBT. However, it must be remembered that data are nothing more than simple records of raw facts. To achieve DBT, an organization must be able to transform the data first into usable information and thereafter into relevant and useful knowledge that can guide managers' decision making. This transformation is aided by the use of sophisticated enterprise application software (e.g., Enterprise Resource Planning [ERP], Customer Relationships Management [CRM], Business Intelligence [BI], and Supply Chain Management [SCM]), data analytics software (e.g., Python, Microsoft Power BI, and Tableau), and Artificial Intelligence decision support systems.

The early roots of DBT can be traced back to organizations' efforts in the early 1990s to offshore the processing of accounting data, populating of call centres, and undertaking of research and development. Since these attempts were invariably pursued for the purpose of reducing costs, they fail to meet today's threshold requiring the holistic use of digitized environments, digital technologies, and redesigned organizational structures, organizational cultures, and organizational systems, processes, and procedures to achieve improved organizational agility, more satisfied customers, and better financial performance. Other slightly more recent, but still embryonic, examples of DBT can be observed in Dell's late 1990s strategy of using the World Wide Web to sell personal computer systems directly to customers and Netflix's 1997 founding as the world's first online DVD-rental store. Again, these examples are emblematic of DBT's budding beginning, rather than representative of its contemporary defining characteristics. In particular, these early manifestations lacked today's expected standard of AMPS integrated use and had yet to implement the management, organizational culture, and system and process changes needed to realize the full set of benefits DBT offers.

In contrast to its initial foray into DBT and as an example of a firm's sophisticated use of big data and AMPS, Netflix now not only digitally delivers films to the internet-enabled devices of its subscribers, but it routinely collects and analyzes data on each subscriber's film watching habits, including what they watch (i.e., what kind of movie genres) and when they watch. This information helps the company to improve its marketing of existing films to customers, as well as determine the type of future films it should commission.

It is important to realize that far from being only relevant to high-tech companies, DBT is equally relevant to more ordinary, less sexy organizations. As an example, Howden, a UK-based application engineering company that provides solutions in air and gas handling, is known for its use of DBT to improve its service offerings and provide better customer support (PTC, n.d.). Furthermore, i-SCOOP (n.d.) claims DBT is relevant to all organizations wishing to become "..agile, people-oriented, innovative, customer-centric, streamlined, efficient and able to induce/leverage opportunities to change the status quo and tap into big data and new, increasingly unstructured data sources."

DBT's customer-centric focus and its use of AMPS, which serves to produce fuller and deeper engagement with its stakeholders, has a variety of implications for the practice of performance management. These include impacts on strategy formulation, organizational structure, organizational culture, and organizational system, process, and procedure design. In other words, DBT affects four major elements of the book's performance management model. The reader should note that the succeeding sections' discussion of DBT's impact on performance management is preliminary. More will be said about its impact in later chapters dedicated to each of the four topics.

Before discussing the impact of DBT on performance management design, it is important to caution against interpreting DBT's creation of greater engagement with outside stakeholders, especially in regard to customers becoming co-creators in the company's value proposition, as an invitation to expand the definition of performance management to include influencing external stakeholders' implementation of an organization's strategy. Although it can undoubtedly be highly beneficial for an organization to leverage DBT to gain these co-creation opportunities, performance management should, and only where applicable, go as far as influencing employees to encourage customer engagement/participation in value co-creation. In other words, performance management's reach should be indirect, as opposed to direct, on customers and other key stakeholders.

Review Question 9.1: Define each of the following terms: data, information, knowledge, digitized, digital technology, and digital business transformation.

Answer: Please see the Answer section starting on page 283

Review Question 9.2: Describe and provide examples of some of the early manifestations of digital business transformation.

Answer: Please see the Answer section starting on page 283

ORGANIZATIONAL STRATEGY

To the uninformed, DBT may sound like a functional strategy that can be pursued by an organization's marketing department. For example, DBT may be mistakenly seen as a marketing-level strategy that attempts to create extra sales channels or enable more customized advertising. Such a view is gravely misguided and neglects DBT's potential for enabling and supporting competitive advantage. As noted above, DBT requires organization wide, coordinated action aimed at leveraging a range of digital technologies to improve customers' value propositions (i.e., the benefit/utility customers receive relative to the cost they pay).

Just as it is incorrect to view DPT as a functional strategy, it is also wrong to view it as equivalent to a competitive strategy. For our present purposes it is useful to view DPT as an important element of, and perhaps even a linchpin to, an organization's existing competitive strategy. DBT should further be understood as an enabler of a new competitive strategy. In other words, DBT affects both strategy formulation (due to its role in enabling a new competitive strategy) and strategy implementation (due to its role in supporting existing competitive strategy).

DPT's ability to support an organization's existing competitive strategy is largely a function of the deeper, real-time insights it offers into customer preferences. These insights allow an organization to calibrate better the value proposition it offers its customers. As an example, DBT can help an organization understand how customers value (i.e., what utility they attach to) the various pieces of its product/service. An organization can use these insights to make and prioritize decisions about what product/service attributes to change, as well as the prices to charge. For example, airlines for the past two decades have employed DBT to segment their customers and optimize ticket pricing by collecting and analysing data that is useful to identifying individual product features (e.g., seat location) and their perceived customer utility (i.e., customer willingness to pay).

In addition to supporting an organization's existing competitive strategy, DBT also offers organizations the opportunity to alter their existing business models, build new ones, and migrate to entirely new strategies. Customer product/service reviews help an organization identify areas for improvement (e.g., problematic product features, call centre performance). DBT further offers organizations the opportunity to enhance their product lines and create additional revenue streams. Some organizations, for example, provide a basic version of a product or service for free but impose a charge for users who want to use advanced versions of the product/service. These advanced versions offer additional features and capabilities. Adobe uses this strategy, which is popularly known as a freemium strategy, for its Adobe Acrobat products. Adobe Acrobat Reader DC is offered free, while the company's premium Adobe Acrobat Pro DC product is offered to those who are willing to pay for such added features as advanced search and editing options, convenience with working with interactive objects, and the ability to be used on nonstandard documents. USA Today, the American daily newspaper and news broadcasting company, also uses this freemium strategy, whereby it offers many of its news stories for free while reserving others for its fee-paying subscribers.

DBT additionally offers organizations the chance to migrate their competitive strategies to whole new ones. For example, DBT can unshackle an organization from a geographically-constrained market. DBT can also permit an organization to move from a generalist market position (i.e., catering to the average customer) to a more focused market position (i.e., focused on a particular group or groups of customers). A fuller and more comprehensive discussion of these generalists and focused competitive strategies is provided in Chapter 8.

ORGANIZATIONAL STRUCTURE

DBT seeks to streamline customer processes as part of its quest to enhance the customer experience. To accomplish this objective, it is essential that an organization's customer-serving employees are given both the means (i.e., real-time access to complete sets of customer data) and the authority to make customer-related decisions. Ideally, an organization's structure should be flat, allowing networked employee groups to transcend functional silos.

Customers commonly have queries or needs that cut across multiple, traditionally-constituted organizational departments. For example, a new customer might want to place a purchase order, provide special delivery instructions, and negotiate customer credit. A conventionally structured organization would require the customer to contact several internal departments, starting with its customer credit department. After the credit terms were negotiated, the customer would then be directed to the sales order department. Finally, the customer would be connected with the shipping department. Far from being streamlined, this process is time-consuming and customer unfriendly.

The New Zealand IRD offers a good example of how DBT has improved the customer/taxpayer experience. Whereas in the past a taxpayer wishing to apply for child support and having questions about their student loan and their business' GST would have been required to make multiple phone calls to speak with multiple specialists (a child support specialist, a student loan specialist, and a GST specialist), now the taxpayer can speak with one IRD agent who can resolve all three matters. This change has been facilitated primarily by DBT's decentralizing of information that was once shuttered in separate IRD departments and other government agencies. Aided by this integrated database, an IRD agent can view a taxpayer's full set of tax information and provide a seamless, one-stop customer solution service.

The enablement of streamlined, customer-centric services requires an organization's continuous facilitation of frontline workers engagement with IT specialists and business intelligence analysts. Frontline workers will have detailed understandings of customers' expectations and requirements. Supported by business intelligence analysts, these understandings can be complemented by other sets of customer-specific information (e.g., socially-informed knowledge that

> *Review Question 9.3:* Is digital business transformation more or less relevant for certain types of organizations? Explain your belief.
>
> *Answer:* Please see the Answer section starting on page 283
>
> *Review Question 9.4:* Digital business transformation is often described as a journey that requires the holistic integration of business practices. Discuss and provide examples of why digital business transformation is likened to a journey and provide examples of what business practices require holistic integration.
>
> *Answer:* Please see the Answer section starting on page 283

is perhaps gained through such big data sets as FB and Google) to enable the creation of fuller customer profiles. These in turn can be used to hone advertising campaigns and predict/nudge customer behaviour. IT specialists will, of course, be an essential piece of the overall process, for they will be the designers of the hardware and software systems needed to collect the various data and instruct the frontline workers on how to use this hardware and software. Remember, a main purpose of DBT is to enable frontline staff to leverage relevant digital technology for the purpose of providing customers an improved experience. Organizations may find that their DBT journeys lead to a point where organizational structures, especially physical locations, become redundant. As Joe Whittinghill, Microsoft's Corporate Vice President of Talent, Learning, and Insights, has remarked, "In the digital age, the modern workplace is no longer a place, it is a mindset in which both people and organizations support and celebrate purpose, creativity, and growth" (CECP, Imperative, and PWC, 2018).

ORGANIZATIONAL SYSTEMS, PROCESSES, AND PROCEDURES

DBT requires that organizational systems, processes, and procedures contribute to an organization's efforts to become more agile and customer-focused. Computer-driven processes and AI-supported decision making offer part of the answer, for they provide broader and faster communication among relevant organizational stakeholders. These stakeholders may be internal to the organization (e.g., frontline workers and IT specialists) or internal and external to the organization (e.g., customers and employees producing co-designed customer solutions). An example of the latter can be found in towns and cities' increasing use of citizens to identify and report on problems needing fixing. In particular, municipalities throughout the world have adopted electronic "fix it" forms. These forms allow citizens to use their internet-enabled devices to report a problem they are seeing in a public space (e.g., a leaking pipe, an abandoned vehicle, overgrown vegetation, a pothole in a road, an issue with a public toilet). The citizens benefit by seeing the problem fixed quickly, while the town/city benefits from helping ensure a satisfied citizenry and addressing a problem in its early and less costly stages.

In addition to enabling faster and broader communication channels to promote data-driven decision making, DBT requires the presence of organizational systems, processes, and procedures that can successfully bridge the in-store and virtual experiences. Virtual shopping seeks to embed human interaction into the traditional online shopping experience, which relies on shoppers self-navigating product catalogues. The objective of virtual shopping is to produce an omnichannel experience that offers customers the same shopping experience regardless of whether they are shopping in-store or online. This seamless shopping experience is accomplished by providing in-store sales associates with simple and reliable virtual interfaces to instantly connect via text, chat, or video with a customer shopping from home. It is important that the virtual shopping experience includes the ability for the customer to ask questions, view all parts of the product line, and receive recommendations from a knowledgeable sales associate. A good example of such a shopping experience is Gucci Live, something which Gucci advertises as the virtual replication of its personalized in-store service experience.

As part of supporting sales associates' ability to provide the high level of personal service an omnichannel approach requires, organizations will find they need to create an environment that encourages community knowledge sharing. Again, this means dismantling the typical silo mentality that pervades traditional organizational structures, thinking, and action. To help enable the realization of highly-networked communities of knowledge sharing, organizations must be willing to delayer their organizational structures (i.e., create flatter organizational structures), upskill and provide the technical/digital support to allow employees to make effective data-driven decisions, and provide the tools and discretion to allow employees to work from anywhere and at any time.

ORGANIZATIONAL CULTURE

For many people, change can be worrying and even alarming. The phrase that humans are creatures of habit is not merely the product of anecdotal musings. Neuroscience provides support for the assertion. To begin with, it is important to recognize that everything a person does, feels, or thinks is a function of their brain's neuron activity. In particular, every thought and action of an individual is the result of a circuit of neurons firing/communicating with neighbouring neurons in a specific pattern. As Donald Hebb, a Canadian neuroscientist, has shown, once a pattern/circuit of neurons has been establihsed, when one neuron fires, the others fire too. Over time, the circuit becomes strengthened to the point that the interconnected set of neurons are the internal body's formula for what others see as a person's set of habits. The important point to understand here is that there is a physiological reason for why habits form and why people are generally averse to change.

DBT is all about change (Moll and Yigitbasioglu, 2019; Warren *et al.*, 2015). Some would even term it highly disruptive change. The challenge for managers who are responsible for overseeing their organizations' introductions of DBT is ensuring that workers will not merely accept it, but will actively welcome and support its introduction and future development. As history points out, this task can be difficult, which is illustrated in the following story.

In the early 19th century, textile workers in England formed a radical faction called the Luddites. The group opposed textile factories' use of machines, believing that their introduction would lead to workers losing their jobs. Calling the use of machines a fraudulent and deceitful practice intended to circumvent standard labour practices, the Luddites regularly destroyed textile machinery (Conniff, 2011). Although initially confined to Nottingham, the

Luddite movement grew into a region-wide and bloody rebellion that lasted from 1811 to 1816. Rebelling workers were shot by textile mills and factory owners, and it was only when the might of legal and military force was applied that the movement was finally suppressed.

Although this story of the Luddite movement is a classic example of workers' fear of change and loss of jobs, more contemporary examples can be found. For example, US coal workers blame their loss of jobs on the political lobbying efforts of environmentalists. While this is partially true, the main reason for today's lower demand for coal is the presence of cheaper alternative forms of energy. Whether there is a rational or irrational basis to a person's fear of losing their job is not what matters. All that matters is that the person is likely to resist change. Should an organization find that there is a widely held belief among its employees that a proposed organizational change will lead to job losses, then this is not a conducive environment for implementing change. The consulting firm i-SCOOP (n.d.) describes the danger of adopting a change like DBT when workers are not ready when it writes:

> However, change management first and foremost obviously is about the human dimension: internal customers, stakeholders, the broader ecosystem within which organizations reside. No organization, business, government or NGO, can realize a profound digital transformation without putting people first and having people on board. If things change too fast for people or we are not taking into account the individuals that are touched, as well as their concerns, this can be a recipe for failure and at broader scale even resistance.

It is imperative, therefore, that the introduction of DBT is accompanied by a human resource plan that helps workers visualize their place in the future of work. This plan should include programmes to upskill employees who are willing to be part of the DBT. The upskilling programmes should prepare employees for job roles that will revolve around transforming increasingly large and varied amounts of data into knowledge that can benefit how organizations interact with their customers and create value for all their stakeholders.

For those workers who are not interested in being part of an organization's DBT, they need to be encouraged to relocate to alternative jobs (both within and outside the organization) where the pace of change is less pronounced. It is important for these employees to understand that this solution is likely to be a temporary fix. Remember, DBT is an organization-wide initiative. Hoping to hide in a pocket of the organization in an unchanging role is implausible. A report by the World Economic Forum (2020) predicts that the top 15 work skills needed in 2025 will be led by skills of problem solving (e.g., analytical thinking, complex problem solving, and critical thinking) and self-management (active learning, resilience, and flexibility). In other words, being a confident, self-motivated learner with strong cognitive skills and a willingness to find and take advantage of changing opportunities are the hallmarks of a future successful worker. The full list of World Economic Forum (2020) skills is shown in Table 9.1.

The successful implementation of DBT requires information to be shared among employees. This idea of ensuring employees have full access to all information relevant to maintaining and growing customer relationships was discussed in the previous section. Organizations will find that attaining a knowledge sharing community requires the democratization of information and the empowerment of people to use this information. In other words, there must be an organizational culture of trust. This trust will include believing that employees will use the information in organizationally beneficial and ethical ways, as well as trust in believing that

TABLE 9.1 World Economic Forum's list of top 15 skills workers will need in 2025

Rank	Skill
1	Analytical thinking and innovation
2	Active learning and learning strategies
3	Complex problem solving
4	Critical thinking and analysis
5	Creativity, originality, and initiative
6	Leadership and social influence
7	Technology use, monitoring, and control
8	Technology design and programming
9	Resilience, stress tolerance, and flexibility
10	Reasoning, problem solving, and ideation
11	Emotional intelligence
12	Troubleshooting and user experience
13	Service orientation
14	Systems analysis and evaluation
15	Persuasion and negotiation

Review Question 9.5: Identify and explain which elements of the book's performance management model are affected by an organization's adoption of digital business transformation.

Answer: Please see the Answer section starting on page 283

Review Question 9.6: Explain how and provide specific examples showing the influence of digital business transformation on performance management practice and design.

Answer: Please see the Answer section starting on page 283

---

employees will make correct decisions without the need for continuous supervision. It is worth noting that the need to operate with trust is not the same as granting employees a free pass to do anything. As will be discussed in later parts of this book, placing trust in employees does not mean an organization loses its ability to manage or influence employees. High-trust organizational cultures and strong processes for employee accountability can be mutual. In fact, in a DBT environment, an organization will find that its newly created systems and processes offer improved real-time information on business activities and performance. Employee accountability therefore will be easier to demonstrate by the employee and determine by the organization.

CONCLUSION

DBT is best viewed as a journey involving an organization's strategic and prioritized use of digital technologies to enable and support its competitive strategy. The fresh technologies DBT allows organizations to leverage leads to new strategic opportunities and challenges, evolving market environments, and changing competitive landscapes. However, in addition to influencing the formulation and implementation of an organization's strategy, DBT also influences the operation of an organization's three main levers of performance management: organizational structure; organizational systems, processes and procedures; and organizational culture.

DBT's presence is only likely to increase in the years ahead. Its uptake has been boosted by the COVID-19 pandemic, mainly in the form of people being required to work and shop from home. Climate change is likely to further increase its adoption. Assuming international agreement can be reached on limiting the burning of fossil fuels and until clean fuels can become a regular part of daily travel, people will likely perform more work and shopping from home. Additionally, the further evolution of AMPS will continue to drive and enhance the benefits organizations can receive from DBT.

REFERENCES

CECP, Imperative, and PWC. (2018) Making work more meaningful, Retrieved from https://d0cb2f2608c10c70e72a-fc7154704217aa017aa46150bf00c30c.ssl.cf5.rackcdn.com/pwc-building-a-fulfilling-employee-experience.pdf on 5 March 2022.

Conniff, R. (2011) What the Luddites really fought against, Smithsonian, Retrieved from https://www.smithsonianmag.com/history/what-the-luddites-really-fought-against-264412/ 13 February 2022.

i-SCOOP. (n.d.) What is digital business transformation? The essential guide to DX, Retrieved from https://www.i-scoop.eu/digital-transformation/ on 05 February 2022.

Marchand, D.A., Wade, M.R. and Liu, F. (2014) Digital business transformation, Retrieved from https://www.imd.org/research-knowledge/articles/digital-business-transformation/ on 10 February 2022.

Moll, J. and Yigitbasioglu, O. (2019) The role of internet-related technologies in shaping the work of accountants: new directions for accounting research, *British Accounting Review*, Vol. 51, No. 6, pp. 1–20.

PTC. (n.d.) Howden adapted and accelerated digital transformation in the face of disruption, Retrieved from https://www.ptc.com/en/case-studies/howden-adapted-and-accelerated-digital-transformation-in-the-face-of-disruption on 10 February 2022.

Warren, Jr., J.D., Moffitt, K.C. and Byrnes, P. (2015) How big data will change accounting. *Accounting Horizons*, Vol. 29, pp. 397–407.

World Economic Forum. (2020) The future of jobs report. Employment, skills and workforce, Retrieved from https://www3.weforum.org/docs/WEF_Future_of_Jobs_2020.pdf on 13 February 2022.

PART **3**

Levers of control

Organizational structure

CHAPTER OBJECTIVES

- Define organizational structure.
- Describe the dimensions of organizational structure and how these influence employee behaviour and ultimately strategy implementation.
- Discuss the interrelationships between various dimensions of organizational structure.
- Define the term responsibility centre and discuss each of the four main types.
- Discuss senior managers' imperative to ensure their chosen responsibility centre is fit for purpose.

INTRODUCTION

Chapter 3 traced the history of performance management, identified key milestones in performance management thinking, compared and critiqued various leading scholars' attempts to develop performance management frameworks, and presented an original, unified model of performance management. As that chapter showed, one of the three main levers of performance management is organizational structure.

Different organizational structures will have different influences on employee behaviour. These different influences result from an organizational structure's simultaneous ability to permit as well as constrain specific types of employee behaviour. For example, the purpose of some organizational structures is to permit/constrain employee behaviour in a manner that will promote business innovation and/or market growth. These types of organizational structures, however, would be inappropriate for organizations that are pursuing other outcomes. For example, when an organization is pursuing goals that involve the minimization of costs and/or the minimizing of business risk, other organizational structures are likely to be favoured.

At present, or at least in terms of the current chapter, the discussion will focus on how different forms of organizational structure can be successfully matched with expected or desired organizational outcomes. Later in the book, in Chapters 13 and 14, the discussion will recognize the fuller richness of an organization's setting (e.g., the organization's size, life-cycle stage, and ownership, as well as its industry, national culture, and labour markets) as it offers prescriptions on how

DOI: 10.4324/9781003267195-13

organizational structure, in combination with the other two main performance management levers (i.e., organizational systems, processes, and procedures and organizational culture), should be designed to promote employees' implementation of the organization's strategy.

DEFINITION OF ORGANIZATIONAL STRUCTURE

Some scholars liken organizational structure to the structure of a building. Just as buildings can have many different types of design, so too can organizational structures. Buildings can be compact or sprawling, single-storied or multiple-storied, and feature fixed or flexible floor plans. In a similar manner, organizations can be located in single or multiple sites, comprise many or few layers of middle-level management, and feature formality (i.e., many rules and procedures) or flexibility (i.e., few rules and procedures). According to organizational theorists, the structure an organization adopts is connected not merely to the costs an organization incurs, but, even more importantly, serves as a critical driver of an organization's performance.

An obvious question to ask is why senior managers at different organizations choose different organizational structures. In answering this question, it must be understood that structure, whether it is the structure of a building or that of an organization, influences the behaviour of those who use or are governed by it. It should not be surprising therefore that churches exhibit different physical designs than factories, and factories that produce cheeses have different designs from factories that produce automobiles.

The idea of superiors leveraging their power to influence/control their subordinates' behaviour is a key defining element of organizational structure (Ranson *et al.*, 1980). As Blau (1974: 12) pointed out long ago, organizational structure involves "the distributions, along various lines, of people among social positions that influence the role relations among these people." In other words, the ultimate purpose of organizational structure is to establish order in an organization's social relationships. In particular, it is about controlling who performs what tasks and with whom.

Hall and Tolbert (2005) contend that organizational structure serves three main purposes:

- Aids the production of organizational outputs and the achievement of organizational goals.
- Minimizes/attenuates the effects of employee mistakes/variations on an organization's production of outputs.
- Determines the flow of information in an organization and how and by whom organizational activities are performed.

It should be readily recognized that all three purposes of organizational structure outlined by Hall and Tolbert are relevant to performance management. In particular, all three purposes are associated with influencing employee behaviour to help ensure the execution of particular

---

Review Question 10.1: What is organizational structure?

Answer: Please see the Answer section starting on page 283

sets of actions/activities that will aid in the organization's implementation of its strategy and achievement of its goals and objectives. And it is for this reason that organizational structure serves as a key lever of performance management.

THE COMPONENTS OF ORGANIZATIONAL STRUCTURE

The designing of organizational structure involves deciding how an organization will group its human resources, as well as control and coordinate these groups' interactions. Employees are typically grouped among specific organizational departments. At the typical bank, for example, each employee will report to the manager of (or be the manager of) one of the following departments:

- Retail banking
- Loan servicing
- Wealth management
- Investment banking
- Deposit operations
- Wire transfer operations
- Cash management
- Electronic banking
- Commercial banking
- Mortgage banking.

While the use of departments is certainly the most visible manifestation of organizational structure, the less evident, but arguably more powerful mechanisms that define organizational structure are complexity, formalization, and centralization. Each of these mechanisms is discussed below.

Complexity

Complexity is measured by the amount of horizontal differentiation, vertical differentiation, and spatial dispersion an organization displays. Horizontal differentiation is defined as the range of tasks or activities a worker has the authority to undertake. It equates to specialization. For example, a factory employee working on one of Bosch's dishwasher production lines would probably have a very limited number of job tasks and responsibilities (i.e., high specialization) and would therefore be viewed as having low horizontal differentiation. In contrast, teachers of primary school students, who are responsible for teaching an inevitably non-homogenous group of students (due to IQ, family backgrounds, etc.) on a variety of subjects (mathematics,

---

Review Question 10.2: What are the three dimensions of organizational structure?

Answer: Please see the Answer section starting on page 283

history, science, etc.), will be required to carry out a wide range of constantly fluctuating roles and duties. These teachers will accordingly display low specialization and therefore high horizontal differentiation.

It is worth noting that horizontal differentiation can differ not only across organizations operating in different industries but also within the same organization. For example, a hospital's kitchen workers will probably be highly specialized and feature low horizontal differentiation, while the same hospital's emergency department's nurses and doctors, who are responsible for treating patients with a variety of ailments ranging from bee stings to severe traumas, will display low specialization and therefore high horizontal differentiation.

Vertical differentiation is defined as the number of supervisory levels in an organization. It is often measured as the number of supervisory layers between an organization's CEO and the employees who deliver the organization's outputs (e.g., the factory workers who produce iPhones at Samsung or the nurses who care for patients on a hospital ward). Organizational charts are a common method used to express an organization's vertical differentiation. Figure 10.1 depicts the organizational chart of a hypothetical landscaping firm. As this organizational chart shows, there are three layers between the landscape firm's owner/CEO and the workers providing the landscaping services (i.e., the crew members for each of the three main work units of earthworks, lawn care, and garden care).

As can be well imagined, some organizations display tall structures featuring many organizational levels, while other organizations display squat structures that feature few layers. The classic case of the former would be a large governmental agency like the US Internal Revenue Service (IRS), or what is often termed an Inland Revenue Department by other governments. A commissioner sits at the top of these organizations, with many layers existing between this commissioner and the employees who answer taxpayer queries, input tax returns, and undertake field investigations. In contrast to various governments' tax agency's tall organizational charts, a firm like Scribd, the San Francisco-based digital library and document-sharing platform company, maintains a very flat structure. The close interface between its nearly 100 employees and its CEO makes this company not only flat, but also a good example of a network structure. Instead of the rigid reporting lines that dominate the typical organizational structure, a network structure prioritizes soft structure connections between individuals, groups, and communities. A visual representation of the linkages produces a map that resembles a spider web design.

Spatial dispersion, which is the final element of complexity, is defined as the extent of geographic range associated with an organization's units, activities, and personnel. A small family-operated commercial cleaning service might operate from and provide cleaning services in one localized area. Meanwhile, a firm like Cleaning Services Group, a UK commercial cleaning company, provides cleaning services to customers and employs personnel from throughout the UK. Accordingly, the Cleaning Services Group would be viewed as possessing high complexity on spatial dispersion.

Since organizational complexity is the combination of horizontal differentiation, vertical differentiation, and spatial dispersion, any attempt to characterize a particular organization's complexity will require an assessment and summation of these three dimensions of complexity. Figure 10.2 provides a three-dimensional portrayal of three firms' organizational complexity. As this figure shows, Firm A exhibits low horizontal differentiation, vertical differentiation,

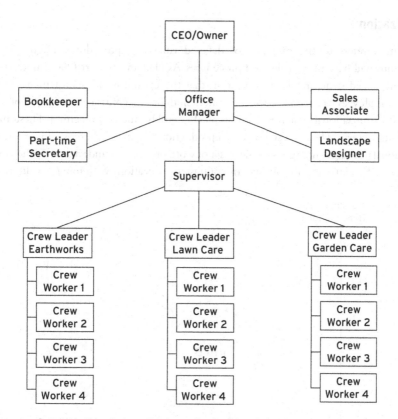

FIGURE 10.1 Organizational chart for hypothetical landscaping business.

and spatial dispersion, and therefore it would be classified as possessing low organizational complexity. Meanwhile, Firm B, which displays medium amounts of the three forms of organizational complexity, would be classified as having medium organizational complexity. Finally, Firm C, which is characterized by high amounts of each form of organizational complexity, would be classified as featuring high organizational complexity.

Although Figure 10.2 displays each dimension of organizational complexity as being similarly low, medium, or high for Firms A, B, and C, respectively, it is possible for heterogeneous classifications to prevail across the three complexity dimensions for any given organization. For example, an organization could be high on two of the dimensions of organizational complexity and medium on the third dimension. This organization would most likely still be viewed as displaying high organizational complexity. An even more common occurrence might be an organization exhibiting offsetting combinations of low and high complexities, which might result in it being classified as possessing medium organizational complexity.

As will be discussed in more detail later in this chapter, the adoption of complex organizational structures is often associated with the presence of challenging, turbulent, and unpredictable environments. These environmental conditions are often caused by shifts in technology or the changing circumstances of competitors and the methods of competition. Not surprisingly, and as will subsequently be discussed more fully, certain corporate and competitive strategies are associated with different patterns of organizational complexity.

Formalization

Formalization refers to the presence of detailed rules and procedures. Highly-formalized organizations will have many rules and procedures. As Hall and Tolbert (2005) note, the adoption of formalized structures is an indication that the organization's senior managers do not trust their employees to exercise good judgement and/or self-control. An example of a highly-formalized organizational structure is the typical assembly-line manufacturer. These manufacturers are characterized by their standardized production practices, whereby all work moves in a unidirectional flow and undergoes the same set of work procedures undertaken by the same set of employees in the same amount of time. In contrast, organizations with low formalization allow

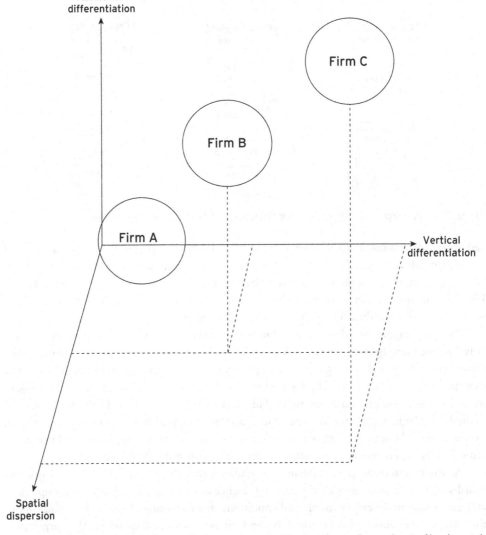

FIGURE 10.2 Organizational complexity represented by the three dimensions of horizontal differentiation, vertical differentiation, and spatial dispersion.

their employees to exercise individual judgement and discretion in the performance of tasks. A classic example of a low-formalized work environment is a computer games software developer.

In general, less formality is likely to feature at organizations that rely on employee creativity and innovation. Innovation is by its very nature the opposite of abiding by proven recipes. It requires a willingness to experiment, be novel, and accept the possibility of failure. Creativity, which is the driver of innovation, is customarily viewed as synonymous with risk-taking. In other words, risk-taking involves removing the safety nets (i.e., formalized rules and procedures) and taking (calculated) bets or leaps of faith about a new way of doing something.

In addition to high-tech companies, universities are further examples of organizations that rely on creativity and innovation to power their success. Although university structures have historically featured low-formalization environments, ever since the New Public Management (NPM) approach was introduced throughout parts of the Anglo-American world in the 1980s universities have and continue to become more formalized. NPM was developed by various governments to make the public services more "business-like" (Hood, 1991). The motivating idea was to make these public service organizations, whether they were universities or social services departments, more efficient by using private sector management models.

Many managers of public sector organizations show their commitment to NPM practices by adopting highly-formalized structures. These managers have adopted a one-size-fits-all approach. They have essentially regressed 70 years back in time in their desire to embrace Weber's (1947) bureaucratic model, including its high reliance on hierarchal authority, limited employee discretion, high division of labour, incentive-based rewards, and extensive rules and procedures. These public sector managers have apparently either never learned or forgotten that private sector firms that rely on creativity and innovation, such as Apple and Google, use less formalized structures. These same managers have also either never learned or forgotten that the NPM approach, in its encouragement of "customer service," often promotes decentralized service delivery models, whereby the employee who interfaces with the customer is given greater decision-making authority.

It is interesting to note that a growing number of Fortune 500 companies are becoming less formalized and more decentralized. In the process, many companies are abandoning their once-a-year employee performance evaluation programmes. These companies, which include Microsoft, Yahoo, and Accenture, want to change the focus from after-the-fact control and evaluation to creating opportunities to support and position workers to perform better in the future. As Accenture CEO Pierre Nanterme says:

> The art of leadership is not to spend your time measuring, evaluating. It's all about selecting the person. And if you believe you selected the right person, then you give that person the freedom, the authority, the delegation to innovate and to lead with some very simple measure.
>
> (Cunningham, 2013)

In spite of the changed approach being adopted by today's for-profit companies, especially those that pursue strategies based on innovation, universities are increasingly adopting formal, centralized structures that feature backward-looking, quantitatively-focused performance measurement. As Kallio *et al.* (2016) have noted, this choice is having negative effects on university employees. These authors describe the views of one lecturer in business and economics who stated:

> [It is] yet another thing that consumes our time [with] administrative nonsense and for which we need to hire more administrative staff (so that we can hire more administrative staff in order to run their business, so that we can hire more administrative staff in order to …). It's an endless bloody cycle, and the administrators not only make up work for themselves and each other, but also for us here at the operational level. It annoys me a lot.
>
> (Kallio *et al.*, 2016: 696)

Meanwhile, a lecturer in humanities who responded to Kallio *et al.*'s (2016) survey said:

> I do not understand how anyone could be tempted by the never-ending reporting and accountability. People get used to it, however, little by little. Maybe the younger people do not know anything else and think that control is a part of the job.
>
> (Kallio *et al.*, 2016: 699)

Kallio *et al.*'s (2016) study serves as a strong reminder of the need to ensure a good fit when designing a performance management system. Academics, or at least those who have earned a PhD, are meant to have been trained and inculcated with the ability and desire to be intellectually curious, self-motivated, and hard-working. In other words, their social programming should assure harmony between the academics' goals and those of their academic institutions. Although some level of formalization may be useful in universities, adopting the same high levels of formalization as banks, meat processing plants, or nuclear power stations is unlikely to prove helpful for universities. Since university academics are, at least in theory, meant to arrive at their respective universities highly motivated and with goals about teaching and research that should be similar to their universities' goals, creating a high-formalization environment is more likely to be counterproductive. Remembering that Hall and Tolbert (2005) refer to the adoption of formalized structures as an indication that the organization's senior managers do not trust their employees to exercise good judgement and/or self-control, it is no wonder that Kallio *et al.*'s business and economics lecturer complained that his university's high reliance on formalization annoyed him a lot.

Centralization

Centralization refers to the distribution of organizational power. When power is held mainly by employees occupying the top echelons of an organization, the organization is said to be centralized. Conversely, when power has been devolved throughout the organization, the organization is seen to be decentralized.

Although some scholars, and in particular accounting scholars who uncritically borrow concepts from other disciplines, view centralization (and formalization as well) as related to organizational decision-making processes but not organizational structure, this view is not supported by the organizational theory literature. Since it is the latter literature that has a significantly longer history studying the concept of organizational structure, and since the vast majority of the research on organizational structure is housed in this body of literature, this book adopts the organizational theorists' treatment of centralization as part of organizational structure.

It is important to understand that the assessment of an organization's centralization/ decentralization is based on the types and not simply the quantity/number of decisions being made. In particular, it is necessary to know who makes the critical and meaningful organizational decisions that matter most as opposed to the ordinary and mundane ones that have small and/or highly localized impacts. In general, decisions relating to an organization's strategy are the ones that truly matter. These decisions typically involve determining or influencing an organization's product/service offerings, the scope and geographical dispersion of its operations, and/or the key sets of operating processes and work practices it uses. Decisions about where to hold the company Christmas party, who should captain the company's social softball team, or who should decide whether a kosher option should be included among the company's cafeteria offerings represent non-strategic, non-critical, ordinary decisions. Whether senior managers or low-level subordinates make these decisions has no bearing on the assessment of an organization's degree of centralization/decentralization.

In centralized organizations, relevant information is captured by lower-level employees, who then pass this information up the organizational hierarchy. During its transmission up the organizational hierarchy, the information becomes increasingly consolidated and analyzed. As an example, each of Cadbury's manufacturing departments (e.g., Cadbury Roses, Cadbury Favourites) will assemble information about its production defect rates. This information will be combined to produce section-wide defect rates and manufacturing plant defect rates. Further consolidations of these defect rates will occur at regional levels (i.e., country and continent) until a worldwide defect rate has been produced and presented to a senior manager or the senior management group. Sometimes analyses and even recommendations are appended to the information flowing up the organization's hierarchy, but it is only when the information reaches the senior management ranks that the decisions are made or finalized. Senior managers' decisions in the form of commands and expectations for how employees should best act are then returned down the hierarchy, where they become actioned by the appropriate lower-level employee(s).

Centralized structures, due to their reliance on a few key decision-makers at the upper organizational levels, reduce the need for conflict resolution among lower-level departments and work units. Without the authority to make key decisions, middle- and lower-level employees will be unlikely to come into conflict over such issues as who should take leadership on a given initiative, the price to charge for the transfer of products/services between departments, and the circumstances that permit the internal movement of employees from one department to another.

Centralized organizational structures are usually a lower-cost option compared with decentralized organizational structures. The latter normally feature duplication of responsibilities/duties. As will be discussed more fully in Chapter 14, centralized structures work best in environments that are more certain and predictable. In contrast, decentralized structures are better suited to less certain and more unpredictable environments.

Decentralized structures are usually preferred when an organization's environment features substantial change – perhaps because of rapid changes in product or process technology, or perhaps due to changes in customers' preferences – which makes it impossible for any single individual or small group of individuals to keep up to date. It is also the case that in some industries more democratic cultures are expected and therefore decentralized structures are required.

Review Question 10.3: How does organizational structure influence employee behaviour? Provide some examples.
Answer: Please see the Answer section starting on page 283

Review Question 10.4: How are the three dimensions of organizational structure related to one another?
Answer: Please see the Answer section starting on page 283

Hospitals, universities, and software manufacturers are examples. Finally, some countries, especially European countries, have legislation that mandates employee participation in their companies' decision making, including representation on company boards. More will be said about these issues in Chapters 13 and 14.

ORGANIZATIONAL STRUCTURE INTERRELATIONSHIPS

While it is generally the responsibility of an organization's senior managers to influence the amount of complexity, formalization, and centralization present in their organizations, there are some natural limits to this influence. For instance, formalization and centralization are linked. When all other relevant factors (e.g., company size) remain constant, when formalization (centralization) is increased (decreased), centralization (formalization) will also increase (decrease). For example, it should be obvious that a decision by senior managers to exert greater formalization will in turn produce greater centralization. The imposition of more rules, systems, and procedures means less discretion is available to the average worker and more power is held by the rule makers: the senior managers.

As another example of the linked nature of complexity, formalization, and centralization, when an organization becomes more complex – usually as the result of an increase in its size – the organization finds it needs to decentralize. It is often the case that the senior managers simply do not possess the time or detailed level of information necessary to make the kind of real-time decisions required. Of course, when an organization experiences greater complexity and adopts greater decentralization, there is a risk of losing organizational control and coordination. Senior managers, as a consequence, will commonly increase their organization's amount of formalization – often adopting or adding further standard operating procedures (SOPs) – as a way of counteracting this problem.

RESPONSIBILITY CENTRES

One way organizations attempt to ensure the success of their operations is through the appointment of particular individuals to lead specific elements of their respective organization's activities.

This lead employee, who is generally termed a manager, and the employees he/she supervises create what is called a responsibility centre. Each responsibility centre will be responsible for a given type and breadth of work activities. Some units, which are headed by employees at lower levels of the organization's hierarchy, will frequently be responsible for a small set of operationally-focused activities (e.g., number of units of product produced, number of employee hours worked). Other units, especially ones headed by employees working at senior organizational levels, will be assessed using financial and non-financial metrics across a wide range (or the entire range if it is the CEO) of organizational activities.

The creation of responsibility centres is closely related to an organization's use of centralization and decentralization, an idea that is discussed more fully below. There are four main types of responsibility centres: revenue centres, expense centres, profit centres, and investment centres. Each type of responsibility centre is now discussed.

Revenue centre

Revenue centres are responsible for their sales. Senior managers provide each of their revenue centres with a sales target, which is usually decided as part of the organization's budgeting process. Since sales are solely an output measure, there is no opportunity to measure efficiency; for such a measurement would require comparing outputs to inputs.

Revenue centres are mainly used by marketing/sales departments. These organizational units frequently have control over the amount and mix of products/services they sell, but generally do not have control over the cost of the goods they are selling. Other organizational units, such as manufacturing or purchasing, control these costs. Under such conditions, and especially when the purpose of the performance measurement is to evaluate managers, the use of a revenue centre is the correct choice of responsibility centre. Generally, the performance evaluation will consist of comparing actual sales or orders booked against budgets or predetermined sales quotas. It is sometimes the case that the revenue centre will also be held accountable for expenses incurred directly within the revenue centre (i.e., salespersons' salaries, salespersons' travel expenses, etc.). However, such accountability will be secondary to the revenue centre's primary focus on revenues.

Expense centre

Expense centres are responsible for managing the costs associated with their respective centres' activities. For example, the fire chief of any given fire department would normally be responsible for managing his/her fire department's costs relative to a budget. Unlike a revenue centre manager, the fire chief would not be responsible for sales. Not only are most fire departments government funded, but it is also the case that there would be something perverse about making a fire department responsible for revenues. The objective of fire departments is to extinguish fires. Although it might be reasonable to encourage fire departments to advertise and be responsible for an ancillary service like their fire prevention services, the same cannot be said about its core activity of extinguishing fires. Surely it is not in a community's interest to have its fire department promoting/encouraging fires so that it can then extinguish them and charge for this service.

There are two types of expense centres: discretionary expense centres and engineered expense centres. Discretionary expense centres are used to focus manager attention on input and process costs alone. The managers of these units are given a set amount of resources to operate their respective units. In other words, they are given the authority to spend up to a certain amount. No attempt is made to assess the outputs associated with the discretionary expense unit's efforts (i.e., its input and conversion costs). As such, and as was the case with revenue centres, no opportunity exists for measuring the unit's efficiency.

In spite of this inability to measure efficiency, discretionary expense centres still serve the useful purpose of drawing their managers' attention to managing their units input and process costs within the means (i.e., the budget) they have been allocated. Furthermore, for some types of discretionary expense centres it is possible to use surrogate measures of output. For example, although an organization is unlikely to measure each of the outputs of its human resource (HR) department, it may benchmark the size of its department's discretionary expense budget and the number of employees served against the size of another organization's HR department's discretionary expense budget and the number of employees it serves. Should the size of the discretionary expense budget of the benchmarked organization not be available, this fact alone may not prevent calculating a relative performance comparison. A head count of the two organizations' HR departments can be used in lieu of the budget size. For support departments like an organization's HR department, the primary expense it incurs is the payroll costs of its staff. Nonwage costs – including computer costs, office occupancy costs, and consumables – usually represent a minor amount of these departments' costs. It is important to note, however, that relative comparisons between an organization's support department and an outside organization's support department assume that the activities performed and the workforce it supports are reasonably equivalent. Deviations from these assumptions would call into question the utility of benchmarking.

Typical discretionary expense centres are administrative and support units. The latter include the accounting, finance, research and development, human resources, customer relations, legal, and public relations departments that comprise most organizations, or certainly most large organizations. Each discretionary expense centre is given a budget at the start of the year to cover the coming year's expected quantum of work. A senior manager, usually the CEO or his/her designated vice president, will set these expense centres' budgets, hence the reason for the adjective "discretionary" that precedes this type of expense centre. The employee who sets a unit's budget will not only need to anticipate likely events (e.g., how much customer service will be demanded in the coming year), but will also probably need to make trade-offs between the size of an administrative or support service's budget and the expected quality (including the timeliness) of the work. For example, the senior manager responsible for setting the customer service department's budget will have to trade off the amount of resources devoted to his/her company's call centre with the waiting times customers will experience.

Engineered expense centres are used when there are predictable relationships between the amount of inputs required and the number of saleable outputs produced. In particular, engineered expense centres conform to the following characteristics:

1 Their inputs can be measured in monetary terms.
2 Their outputs can be measured in physical terms.
3 The optimum amount of inputs required to produce one good unit of output can be accurately specified.

Although factories are classic examples of situations where optimum relationships between inputs and outputs can be specified in advance, there are many service companies where this relationship can also hold. For example, an auto insurance company's claims department would normally be able to predict the number of hours needed to process and pay an approved claim. Similarly, a bank would generally know how many hours are required to process a loan application for an average customer's purchase of a new home. Accordingly, with engineered expense centres it is possible to measure efficiency, and therefore the managers of these units will be responsible for their respective centres' costs relative to their achieved levels of production. Although a budget will probably be prepared for engineered expense centres, differences in the volume of planned versus actual production will be recognized. If the production volume is 50% greater than what was budgeted, then the allowable variable costs will be increased to reflect this increase in volume. If the production volume is 10% lower than what was budgeted, then the allowable variable costs will be decreased to reflect this decrease in volume. In other words, the budget for engineered expense centres is flexed.

Profit centre

Profit centres are responsible for managing both their revenues and expenses. As such, they are responsible for their unit's bottom lines (e.g., revenues minus expenses). Although some organizations like Kyocera create profit centres at their lowest hierarchical levels – such as a plating department in one of its factories – for many organizations the creation of profit centres occurs at higher organizational levels when revenue and expense centres come under the combined control of a higher unit/manager. For example, a hotel manager at one of Hilton Hotel's properties would be responsible for his/her hotel's revenue centres (e.g., its sales department) and expense centres (e.g., housekeeping department).

Since profit is an integral objective of most organizations, profit centres are viewed as an ideal way to align employees' goals with the company's profit motives. Horngren *et al.* (2009) report how Office Products Depot (OPD), an office products distributor, changed its sales department from a revenue centre to a profit centre. Prior to the change, OPD's salespeople received a 3% commission on all sales, regardless of such cost considerations as ordering and delivery costs. Based on a customer profitability study, many of OPD's customers with high numbers of orders but low quantities per order were found to be unprofitable. After changing the sales department to a profit centre and amending its sales incentive system from a straight 3% commission on sales to a 15% bonus on a salesperson's customers' monthly profits, the salespeople began encouraging their customers to consolidate their many separate orders into fewer orders. The change in customer ordering behaviour produced a 40% reduction in ordering and processing costs for OPD, leading to greater profits per order and increased overall customer profitability.

In addition to helping to align employee and organizational goals, profit centres are associated with the following further advantages:

- Quicker decision making because the decisions are being made at the profit-centre level and do not require head office approval.
- Senior managers, by virtue of being relieved of the day-to-day decision making that the profit-centre employees have assumed, can now focus on strategic issues.

- Higher-quality decision making because the employees most familiar with the issues are making the decisions.
- The decision making required of profit-centre managers helps them acquire all-important general management skills, which assists with their career development and helps senior-level managers identify and target employees for promotion to higher-level jobs.

Although profit centres certainly possess several key advantages, they are not panaceas for organizational success. Some of the challenges associated with their use are as follows:

- The increased decentralization inherent in profit centres often produces duplication of services and additional total organizational costs.
- A lack of coordination can develop because more localized decision making is occurring, which often does not pay sufficient regard to the organization's set of wider activities.
- The goal of maximizing profit may be a necessary goal for many organizations but by itself is an insufficient goal. Broader measures, especially lead-indicator measures that offer insights into future profitability, are needed.
- Inter-unit rivalry can foster employee behaviour that transcends healthy rivalry and leads to dysfunctional organizational behaviour, which may include the hoarding of resources (information, employees, customers, etc.) and attempts to sabotage sister profit centres (especially when profit centres are ranked relative to one another).

Investment centre

An investment centre has responsibility for the profits it generates and the asset base it operates. Profits on their own convey only part of an organization's health. For example, a convenience store that achieves a $300,000 profit and has an investment base of $1 million offers a better current financial return than a large utility company that achieves a $100 million profit and has an investment base of $1 billion. Using a measure like return on investment (ROI), it can be shown that the convenience store has an ROI of 30% ($300,000/1,000,000), and the utility company has an ROI of 10% ($100 million/$1 billion). Although a profit centre may help promote goal congruence between employees and their organization, an investment-centre approach possesses heightened potential for supporting employee and organizational goal harmony. More specifically, an investment-centre approach encourages employees to invest only in additional resources when the expected return is equal to or greater than the organization's cost of capital and disinvest in resources when the ROI falls below its cost of capital.

As with profit centres, it is often the case that investment centres will operate at higher hierarchical levels of an organization. In particular, as profit centres are consolidated under a high-level organizational unit/manager, these units/managers will be responsible for the profits the consolidated profit centres generate as well as the investment bases they use. Returning to the Hilton Hotel example referred to previously, a regional manager will be responsible for supervising the individual hotel managers. This regional manager, who has authority for new hotel projects, will be responsible for the profits generated by his/her region's hotel managers and the investment base associated with all the hotel properties.

Various financial metrics support an organization's use of an investment-centre structure. ROI, residual income, and economic value added (EVA) are the three most popular metrics. It is worth noting that many organizations which claim to be using ROI are in fact using return on assets (ROA). ROA, as the name implies, simply involves creating a ratio that places an organization's net income in the numerator and its total assets in the denominator. ROI, in contrast, requires more thought on the part of its users. In particular, it requires nuanced determinations of the value to ascribe to the investment base that is used to generate the organization's profits. Although working capital will certainly be part of the computed investment base, adjustments to cash, receivables, and inventories are often needed. For example, sometimes an investment unit's cash is controlled by the company's headquarters. Usually, this centralization is done to minimize the organization's overall cash holdings. For organizations that use centralized cash holdings, an obvious challenge involves how much cash to report for any given investment centre. Making adjustments to an organization's centrally-controlled cash account is especially important if senior managers are interested in comparing a unit's performance with other industry competitors. Failure to do so would mean that the centrally-controlled unit's cash balance would be artificially lower than its competitor's cash balance and the ROI comparison would potentially be less meaningful.

Further challenges exist for the treatment of accounts receivable and inventories. In particular, users of ROI must decide whether to value these accounts at their cost or selling price. The cost to produce a product or provide a service will almost invariably be lower than the sales price. Some practitioners and scholars argue that accounts receivable and inventories should be valued at their cost as opposed to their realizable value unless the latter is lower than the former. Implementing such an approach would result in accounts receivable being recorded at their cost of goods sold value and inventories being recorded at their cost to manufacture or purchase. Proponents of this approach believe that a company's costs should dictate the value of the investment. Meanwhile, there are other practitioners and scholars who argue that it is the opportunity cost that is relevant to these accounts' valuations. In other words, accounts receivable and inventories should be valued at their balance sheet amounts.

Users of ROI must also decide the date on which to measure the capital investment base. Since the numerator of ROI is net income, which is a period-long figure, it is conceptually more consistent to report accounts receivable, inventory, and other assets at their average-period amounts. Expediency, however, often prevails, and these accounts are reported at their end-of-period balances.

When calculating an organization's investment base, consideration must also be paid to the organization's liabilities. In particular, current liabilities should be closely examined for "free" capital. Assume, for example, that an organization always pays its accounts 30 days after an invoice's receipt. In such a situation, the organization has free capital for this 30-day period. Some organizations will subtract this free capital from the asset-derived investment base. In fact, some organizations subtract all of their current liabilities from their asset-derived investment base as a way of reflecting the free capital of these current liabilities.

It is important to note that ROI is not the only performance measure an investment centre can use. In fact, relative to residual income (RI) and EVA, ROI is an inferior performance measure. ROI's two main shortcomings are its failure to provide reliable investment signals and its failure to encourage consistent inter-unit project investment. In terms of the first shortcoming, subunits and their managers should always be encouraged to invest whenever the projected returns equal or exceed the strategic business unit's cost of capital. If the benchmark cost of capital is 15%, then all projects with expected returns equal to or greater than 15% should be accepted. Instead of basing their investment decisions on cost of capital benchmarks, managers who are evaluated using ROI will accept/reject projects based solely on whether a contemplated project will increase their respective units' currently-achieved ROIs. Such decision making relies on irrelevant benchmarks that may discourage investment when it should be occurring and encourage investment when it should not be occurring.

As a second shortcoming, ROI fails to encourage consistent inter-unit project investment. Unless the inconsistency solely derives from senior management's beliefs about the risks of the different organizational units, the outcome will be suboptimal for the organization as a whole. For example, if one business unit is currently achieving a 20% pre-tax ROI, it will be uninterested in any projects that offer returns below 20%. Meanwhile, a different business unit that is achieving a 5% pre-tax ROI will be uninterested in projects with expected returns below 5%, but interested in projects with returns above 5%. As such, this second business unit will accept a range of projects that the first business unit will reject (i.e., projects earning returns between 5% and 19%).

In contrast to ROI, RI and EVA offer reliable and consistent inter-unit project investment signals. In particular, any project earning returns equal to or above an organization's cost of capital will be accepted by all business units of this organization. Scholars have demonstrated that ROI is an unreliable management tool when used to aid proforma investment decision making. As such, ROI should never be used for budgeting purposes. Instead, its use should be limited to measuring past business unit performance and evaluating this performance relative to some benchmark or expectation. As an example, a vineyard might measure its ROI performance over the past ten years and compare this ROI with either its cost of capital or with the expected return that could have been generated if the land were used for some other purpose than growing grapes and making wine (e.g., to grow another plant or to subdivide the land into a housing development). Meanwhile, for all budgeting purposes, RI or EVA should be used.

Whether an organization chooses RI or EVA is irrelevant; for as Adler and McClelland (1995) have shown, the two are one and the same. The only difference is that EVA has been backed up by a very slick marketing campaign to make it appear as if it is new wine when it is really only old wine in new bottles.

Review Question 10.5: What is a responsibility centre?

Answer: Please see the Answer section starting on page 283

Review Question 10.6: What are the four main types of responsibility centres an organization can choose from? Describe each type and give examples of the organizational units that are likely to adopt each type.

Answer: Please see the Answer section starting on page 283

TABLE 10.1 Types of responsibility centres and their appropriateness

		Responsibilities			
		Expenses	Revenues	Revenues and expenses	Revenues, expenses, and assets
Authority	Sufficient	Expense centre	Revenue centre	Profit centre	Investment centre
	Insufficient	Pseudo expense centre	Pseudo revenue centre	Pseudo profit centre	Pseudo investment centre

> *Review Question 10.7:* What is meant by the terms controllability and separability? How
>   are they relevant to responsibility centre design?
> *Answer:* Please see the Answer section starting on page 283
> *Review Question 10.8:* From a contingency theory perspective, what organizational struc-
>   tures are commonly encouraged for each of the competitive strategies discussed in
>   Chapter 9? Explain why.
> *Answer:* Please see the Answer section starting on page 283

Which responsibility centre is best to use?

At this point in the discussion, it might be asked why an organization would not simply choose
to use investment centres for all its business units. As noted above, investment centres encourage profit awareness and disciplined investing/divesting of organizational assets. The reason that
investment centres are not the default option is due to the need to ensure fitness for purpose. In
particular, investment centres may not be the appropriate type of responsibility centre because
insufficient cause-and-effect relationships exist between the efforts of a business unit and its
managers and the type of performance being measured. For example, when evaluating a business unit manager, it is crucial that the performance measure be composed solely of factors that
are under the control (or at least the influence) of the manager. Meanwhile, when evaluating a
business unit's performance, it is essential that the performance measure only includes factors
that are directly traceable to the business unit.

   Spiller (1988) refers to these twin organizational mandates as the principles of controllability and separability. Violation of the principle of controllability means that if employees view
the basis of their performance as being outside their control, they will view the performance
evaluation as unfair. Such a determination will likely erode employee motivation and may cause
dysfunctional behaviour, including gaming and fraud. Meanwhile, the violation of the principle
of separability will undermine organizational decision making. Table 10.1 communicates the
importance of equating managerial authority (i.e., the power to control/influence) with managerial responsibility. Although it is possible for an organization to create any type of responsibility centre it desires, only in situations where managerial authority equates to managerial
responsibility is the responsibility centre fit for purpose. In situations where managers lack the
authority implied by the chosen responsibility centre, the name of the assigned responsibility
centre should be preceded by the term "pseudo" to highlight its fictional status.

CONCLUSION

Organizational structure represents one of the three main levers of performance management. Organizational systems, processes, and procedures and organizational culture represent the other two main levers and will be discussed in Chapters 11 and 12, respectively. Senior managers can utilize different organizational structures to influence employee behaviour. These organizational structures will include different amounts of complexity, formalization, and centralization. Although managers can systematically vary these three dimensions of organizational structure, these dimensions are not mutually exclusive. Changes in one may cause changes in another. Senior managers must be cognizant of this fact when choosing the type of structural configurations they desire.

Certain organizational structures are more likely to support particular corporate and competitive strategies. Single-industry firms, especially ones that exhibit stability and predictability, are likely to benefit from adopting centralized structures. This form of structure will almost certainly be the case if a cost-focused strategy is pursued. It is also likely that these firms (i.e., single-industry and cost-focus) will adopt high formalization. In particular, because these organizations crave stability, they will want their employees to adhere to well-established rules and procedures based on documented best-practice assessments. And finally, it is likely that these firms will adopt high specialization. This practice is well suited to high-volume approaches, which are commonly associated with cost-focused strategies.

Unrelated-diversified firms will benefit from decentralized structures. Due to the range of companies operating under an unrelated-diversified firm's umbrella, it is unlikely that any one manager or small group of managers will possess sufficient, timely information or have the multi-industry skills and understandings to make high-quality decisions. Since organizational size is positively correlated with formalization, unrelated-diversified firms will typically exhibit high formalization. It is also the case that their supposed superior management expertise and/ or control of abundant financial resources, which form the guiding rationale for an unrelated-diversified firm's existence (see Chapter 7), will lead to greater formalization. Kyocera is an example of a conglomerate with supreme confidence in its superior management expertise, which is embodied in its amoeba management system. All divisions, departments, and units must use amoeba management. The requirement produces high formalization in Kyocera's internal financial and management reporting.

For unrelated-diversified firms that base their success on the adroit ability to transfer financial resources among their respective network of firms, a formalized programme for contributing and receiving financial resources will prevail. In particular, a set of formalized rules and procedures will determine by whom, how much, and when financial resource transfers will occur.

Responsibility centres are a key manifestation of organizational structure. An organization's choice of revenue centre, expense centre, profit centre, or investment centre should be based on the criterion of fitness for purpose. Part of the process of ensuring fitness for a purpose is ensuring that managerial responsibility is commensurate with managerial authority.

REFERENCES

Adler, R.W. and McClelland, L.A. (1995) EVA: reinventing the wheel, *Chartered Accountants' Journal*,Vol. 74, No. 4, pp. 35–36.

Blau, P.M. (1974) *On the Nature of Organizations*, New York: John Wiley and Sons, Inc.

Cunningham, L. (2013) Accenture CEO explains why he's overhauling performance reviews, *Washington Post*, 23 July. Retrieved from www.washingtonpost.com/news/on-leadership/wp/2015/07/23/accenture-ceo-explains-the-reasons-why-hes-overhauling-performance-reviews/?utm_term=.b82492d120e4.

Hall, R.H. and Tolbert, P.S. (2005) *Organizations: Structures, Processes, and Outcomes* (9th Edition), Upper Saddle River, NJ: Pearson Prentice Hall.

Hood, C. (1991) A public management for all seasons? *Public Administration*, Vol. 68, No. 1, pp. 3–19.

Horngren, C.T., Data, S.M., Foster, G., Rajan, M.V. and Ittner, C. (2009) *Cost Management: A Managerial Emphasis*, Upper Saddle River, NJ: Pearson.

Kallio, K., Kallio, T.J., Tienari, J. and Hyvönen, T. (2016) Ethos at stake: performance management and academic work in universities, *Human Relations*,Vol. 69, No. 3, pp. 685–709.

Ranson, S., Hinings, R. and Greenwood, R. (1980) The structuring of organizational structures, *Administrative Science Quarterly*,Vol. 245, No. 2, pp. 1–17.

Spiller, E.A. (1988) Return on investment: a need for special purpose information, *Accounting Horizons*, Vol. 2, No. 2, pp. 1–9.

Weber, M. (1947) *The Theory of Social and Economic Organization*, New York: Oxford University Press.

Organizational systems, processes, and procedures

CHAPTER OBJECTIVES

- Identify the three primary types of organizational systems, processes, and procedures used by organizations for effective performance management.
- Identify and discuss the types of performance measurement systems organizations use to motivate and direct employee behaviour.
- Identify and discuss the types of employee incentive systems organizations use to motivate and direct employee behaviour.
- Identify and discuss the human resource systems organizations use to motivate and direct employee behaviour.

INTRODUCTION

The previous chapter discussed one of the three main levers of performance management, namely organizational structure. The present chapter discusses the second main lever of control: an organization's systems, processes, and procedures. This lever of control has consumed the bulk of the performance management literature's descriptions of how organizations seek to influence their employees' implementations of their organizations' strategies (see, for example, Malmi and Brown, 2008). Organizational systems, processes, and procedures represent formalized approaches to directing and encouraging specific types of employee behaviour (i.e., those behaviours that will support the implementation of an organization's strategy). As such, this lever of performance management is similar to what Hopwood (1974) terms "administrative control" and what Anthony (1956) calls "formal control."

The primary organizational systems, processes, and procedures relied upon by organizations are performance measurement systems, employee incentive systems, and human resource systems. Each of these is separately discussed in the three main chapter sections that follow.

DOI: 10.4324/9781003267195-14

PERFORMANCE MEASUREMENT SYSTEMS

Performance measurement systems comprise the collection and reporting of relevant organizational data. Organizations operate performance measurement systems for five main reasons/purposes, which are to:

- Establish position
- Communicate direction
- Influence behaviour
- Stimulate action
- Facilitate learning.

The characteristics of a good performance measurement system include the use of financial and non-financial performance measures (Cheng *et al.*, 2007; Franco-Santos *et al.*, 2007; Ittner *et al.*, 2003); the ability to translate business strategies into deliverable results (Hall, 2008), alignment of management processes (including target setting, decision-making, and performance evaluation) with the achievement of chosen strategic objectives (Ittner *et al.*, 2003), and the adoption and linking of diverse key performance indicators (KPIs) to the organization's business strategy (Franco-Santos *et al.*, 2012). The succeeding chapter sections discuss each of these topics, beginning with the collection and reporting of organizational data that is financial, non-financial, or a combination of these two.

Financial performance measurement systems

Performance management draws liberally on financial performance measurement systems, with the most common being the use of budgets. The next two subsections discuss two financial measurement systems: budgets and economic value added.

Budgets

Budgets can range from operating budgets to fixed asset budgets; the former is the main type of budgetary system relied upon. An operating budget has several key characteristics, including:

- It covers a future period of time, predominantly one year.
- It is stated in monetary terms.
- It conveys organizational members' tacit or stated commitment to achieving the revenue and expense goals it shows.
- Irrespective of whether a budget is created from the ground up (participatory budgets) or top down (authoritarian budgets), the budgeting process requires an authority higher than the one to which the budget pertains to review and approve the budget.

Review Question 11.1: What are the main purposes of a performance measurement system?
Answer: Please see the Answer section starting on page 283

- Once approved, the budget is fixed and should only be modified under exceptional conditions (e.g., a major and unexpected currency devaluation).
- At specified intervals, often monthly, any differences between the budgeted and actual figures are analyzed and explained.

The process of creating budgets, and in particular what types of budgeting approaches to use, has received significant scholarly and practitioner attention. As a general rule of thumb, incremental budgeting is found to be best suited for stable environments. For example, the relatively stable demand a utility company experiences would enable its use of incremental budgeting. Meanwhile, zero-based budgeting is recommended for unpredictable environments. These latter environments are characterized by instability, complexity, and resource scarcity, requiring organizations to be nimble and highly responsive/highly opportunistic to the rapidly occurring changes. A company operating in the nanotechnology field would likely benefit from a zero-based budgeting approach.

Many organizations combine the performance measurement aspects of budgets with the use of employee incentive systems. Although the use of incentive and reward systems will be discussed more fully later in this chapter, for now, it is worthwhile to understand that budgets on their own have significant motivating potential. Goal-setting theorists would argue that the use of budget targets acts to motivate behaviour. As Latham and Baldes (1975) showed, when the drivers of logging trucks were set the ambitious goal of filling their trucks to at least 94% of their capacities, log loads per truck increased significantly from their pre-goal level. Moreover, this increase in load capacity occurred despite there being no effect on employee remuneration (i.e., there were no rewards or punishments offered).

Budgets can be used in a tight or loose manner. Tight budget control means employees are expected to achieve the budget. Excuses for its non-achievement are not tolerated. It is the responsibility of employees to ensure they meet their budgets. Often a reward for achieving the budget or a penalty for failing to do so is used to incentivize employees. Although the use of tight budgets is associated with a unit's/manager's more consistent reporting of budget attainment, such reporting may or may not be genuine. It may be the product of manipulation or fraud. Employee manipulation occurs when managers, in an attempt to meet the budget, accelerate sales (e.g., encourage a customer to place an order earlier than it would otherwise do by offering a higher sales discount for doing so) and/or defer expenses (e.g., delay repairing or overhauling a piece of machinery). In contrast to employee manipulation, fraudulent behaviour could involve the fictitious reporting of events (e.g., a sale that never occurred) and/or the purposeful misrepresentation of financial statements (e.g., omitting liabilities from the balance sheet as Enron did). Senior managers must be very careful when budgets are used in a tight-control manner, for they must guard against the possibility that these budgets will spawn dysfunctional employee behaviour.

Loose budget control means the budget serves primarily for planning and coordination purposes. The evaluation of sub-units or employees is not undertaken, and no thought is given to attaching incentives and rewards to a budget's achievement. The use of loose budget control can avoid the dysfunctional employee behaviours that can occur under tight budget control.

One large French multinational reportedly used its annual strategic retreat to develop ambitious stretch budgets. The company's CEO would encourage his senior managers at the retreat to put forward best-case scenarios. He would ask them to develop a budget based on the organization experiencing favourable conditions and the organization doing everything right to match this favourable environment. The organization's senior managers would then create an organization-wide budget based on these best-case scenarios. The CEO would end the retreat by remarking on the exceptional performance this budget heralded and would encourage his senior managers to do all they could to realize the budget's goals. Interestingly, and something that all the senior managers knew, the CEO would file the budget in his bottom desk drawer and never refer to it again. Accordingly, it can be understood that the CEO was using the budget purely as a signalling tool. He wanted to signal to his managers that they should be prepared to achieve high goals; for unless they did, they would be undermining the efforts of their peers (e.g., the production department needed to achieve high production volumes to support the high sales orders the sales department was forecasting and vice versa). Essentially this CEO was following the advice of Henry David Thoreau, who wrote: "If you have built castles in the air, your work need not be lost; that is where they should be. Now put the foundations under them" (1854: 241).

Tight budget control is more suited to stable and predictable environmental conditions. In particular, the internal and external environments should feature foreseeable customer demand, stable production technologies, and predictable competitive conditions. A refiner of petroleum would typically fit this set of conditions and therefore tight budget control would be suitable. In contrast, when an organization's internal and external environments are not stable and predictable, then loose budget control would be preferred. A start-up organization or an organization in a high-growth phase like Scribd, the world's largest online digital library, would be prime candidates for loose budget control.

Cost drivers play an important role in the development of budgets. Although many academics and practitioners would argue that cost drivers should be primarily selected on their ability to provide high cause-and-effect relationships between cost objects (e.g., products/services, departments, customers) and cost pools, others would argue that cost drivers need to focus more on an organization's strategic intent rather than on being faithful to a cause-and-effect maxim.

Toshi Hiromoto (1991) offers a good example of a Japanese manufacturer that used cost drivers in a highly strategic manner. He recounts a story of a factory with high levels of factory automation using direct labour hours to allocate its manufacturing overhead. The western academics and practitioners who were touring this plant scoffed at the idea of using direct labour hours when machine hours seemed like the much more logical choice. Labour costs represented only a small fraction of the product's cost, while the costs associated with its automation (i.e., machines and robots) were significant. The Japanese accountants, however, were unfazed by the criticism and replied that since the goal of the factory was its full automation, using direct labour provided a very clear and strong message to the factory's department managers to ensure full automation. Using direct labour hours as the cost driver meant that departmental managers who were slow to automate would be allocated relatively large amounts of manufacturing overhead. If a manager wanted to reduce the amount of manufacturing overhead allocated to his/her department, then all he/she needed to do was to increase his/her department's level of automation faster than others were doing. In fact, a department manager could eliminate all allocations of manufacturing overhead to his/her department by fully automating.

Budget slack, whereby employees underestimate revenues and overestimate expenses, is a perennial problem for organizations that rely on budgets to evaluate employee performance. Employees, being eager to increase their likelihood of receiving organizational rewards and avoiding penalties, may try to introduce slack into their budget targets. Although too much budget slack is certainly detrimental to organizations, it is not necessarily the case that organizations should insist on no budget slack. According to some scholars, slack in an organization is crucial to discovery and innovation. Having the time and freedom to be curious has led to major scientific advancements (Soyer and Hogarth, 2015). Companies like Google and 3M give their employees free time during work hours to follow their passions. This free time usually equates to one day a week. And it is not just large companies that claim to benefit from using innovation time off (ITO) programmes. Atlassian, a Sydney-based developer of collaboration software, credits its innovation success to the ITO it operates.

As Merchant and Manzoni (1989) point out, some budget slack can actually be useful. It may, for example, reduce hoarding, free management from the otherwise more frequent need to follow up on unfavourable variances, and promote innovation. Readers interested in delving deeper into the topic of setting budget targets are advised to read Stringer and Shantapriyan (2012).

As the above discussion indicates, although some budget slack may actually benefit an organization, excessive budget slack is detrimental and should be avoided. There are two main ways to minimize the occurrence of excessive budget slack. One way is to separate budget evaluation from employees' performance evaluation. Lacking the same incentives to game the budgeting process, employees will be more likely to provide accurate budget estimates. The second way to avoid excessive slack is to encourage/incentivize employee honesty in the budget-setting process. The generic term used to describe this technique is truth-seeking budgets.

In contrast with the typical budget, which rewards employees when a certain level of performance has been achieved, truth-seeking budgets contain both explicit rewards and penalties. In particular, employees are:

- Rewarded when goals are achieved
- Penalized for underestimating goals
- Penalized for overestimating goals.

The following bonus-based formula is used to support this set of rewards and penalties:

Bonus = Actual performance $\star$ incentive multiplier – Performance in excess of budget $\star$ penalty multiplier 1 – Performance below budget $\star$ penalty multiplier 2

Since actual and budgeted performance variances can only be favourable (actual performance is better than planned) or unfavourable (actual performance is worse than planned), only one of the penalty multipliers can apply in the above formula. Furthermore, although different senior managers are likely to choose multipliers of different sizes – mostly due to these individual managers' preferences for encouraging/discouraging risk – it is always the case that the multipliers will be ordered in the following way:

penalty multiplier 1 < incentive multiplier < penalty multiplier 2

This ordering is purposeful. Since the penalty associated with underestimating performance is smaller than the penalty associated with overestimation, employees are encouraged to be ambitious without overpromising what they can deliver. There are significant costs and reputational risks associated with overpromising. If, for example, a manufacturing unit's budgeted production prompts its sales division to source orders for all its budgeted production, then customers who fail to have their purchase orders delivered will be unhappy. This circumstance may lead to a customer's cancelation of their current or future order(s). If, on the other hand, the sales department has overpromised on what it can achieve in sales orders, then the manufacturing department will have overproduced. This overproduction will result in excess inventory and lead to higher costs of working capital. As Table 11.1 illustrates, employees will maximize their compensation when budgets are set high and attained.

Economic value added (EVA)

EVA is a measure of corporate performance that was developed by Joel Stern. It was created to reinforce management's supposed prime imperative: to enhance shareholder value. In particular, EVA alerts managers to the necessity of earning rates of return on total investor capital that are, at a minimum, equal to the prevailing market rate of return that applies to the particular business. When a firm exceeds the required rate of return, shareholder value is added. When it fails to meet the required rate of return, shareholder value is lost.

Since its introduction in the late 1980s, EVA has developed a long list of corporate converts. Included in this list are such US behemoths as AT&T, Briggs & Stratton, Coca-Cola, GE, NCR, Quaker Oats, Scott Paper, TransAmerica, and Whirlpool. Of course, there are scores of large and small companies from all over the world that have also adopted EVA. For instance, in New Zealand, Airways Corporation, Fay, Richwhite & Co., Fletcher Challenge, New Zealand Dairy Industry, Sanford Limited, Skellerup Group, PGG Wrightson, Telecom, and Trans Power New Zealand Ltd use EVA. At Volkswagen Group, EVA is viewed as a cornerstone of their performance measurement system and an engine to their success. The following excerpt comes from the company's 2013 annual report:

> The Volkswagen Group's financial target system centers on continuously and sustainably increasing the value of the Company. We have been using value contribution … which

---

Review Question 11.2: What are the distinguishing characteristics of a budget?
Answer: Please see the Answer section starting on page 283
Review Question 11.3: What are tight control and loose control? Provide examples of each.
Answer: Please see the Answer section starting on page 283
Review Question 11.4: What are strategic cost drivers?
Answer: Please see the Answer section starting on page 283
Review Question 11.5: What are the limitations of using profit as a measure of performance?
Answer: Please see the Answer section starting on page 283
Review Question 11.6: What is budgetary slack? Is it good or bad? How can senior managers influence its occurrence?
Answer: Please see the Answer section starting on page 283
Review Question 11.7: Why might a manager submit a budget that is biased, and how should senior management respond?
Answer: Please see the Answer section starting on page 283

TABLE 11.1 An illustration of truth-seeking budget bonuses calculated for conditions of underachieving, overachieving, and exactly meeting budget

Budget amount	Actual amount	Condition	Bonus 1 Incentive multiplier = 0.10 Penalty multiplier 1 = 0.05 Penalty multiplier 2 = 0.15	Bonus 2 Incentive multiplier = 0.10 Penalty multiplier 1 = 0.01 Penalty multiplier 2 = 0.30
$105,000	$100,000	Overestimate	$9,250[1]	$8,500[4]
$95,000	$100,000	Underestimate	$9,750[2]	$9,950
$100,000	$100,000	Actual = budget	$10,000[3]	$10,000[6]

1 $100,000*0.10 – ($105,000 – $100,000)*0.15.

2 $100,000*0.10 – ($100,000 – $95,000)*0.05.

3 $100,000*0.10.

4 $100,000*0.10 – ($105,000 – $100,000)*0.30.

5 $100,000*0.10 – ($105,000 – $100,000)*0.01.

6 $100,000*0.10.

corresponds to the Economic Value Added (EVA) … for a number of years, in order to use resources in the Automotive Division efficiently and to measure the success of this.

The concept of value-based management allows the success of our innovative, environmentally oriented product portfolio.

EVA is calculated as the difference between the net operating profit after tax and the cost of all capital employed to generate such profit. The following formula is used to calculate EVA:

$$EVA = (r - c) \star K$$
where:
r = return on capital employed
c = cost of capital
K = economic value of capital invested in the business

The return on capital employed is essentially ROI, with some adjustments made to both the profit figure and investment base as a means of better approximating the economist's definition of wealth creation. Some of the more common adjustments involve modifications to deferred income taxes; operating leases; last-in-first-out (LIFO) inventory reserves; unrecorded goodwill and its amortization; asset revaluations; successful efforts expensing; unusual gains and losses; provisions for bad debt, inventory obsolescence, warranties, and deferred income; and such intangibles as research and development (R&D), patents, trademarks, new product development, and up-front marketing costs. Table 11.2 sets out the effect each of the adjustments has on the computation of a firm's net operating profit after tax (NOPAT) and capital employed.

An adjustment should also be made to the depreciation charge whenever the book amount (i.e., the amount appearing on the financial statements) does not closely approximate the economic depreciation. Should this occur, the asset should be revalued at its current economic cost,

TABLE 11.2 EVA adjustments needed to capital and NOPAT

Adjustments to capital:	Items to include in NOPAT:
Deferred tax reserve	Increase in deferred tax reserve
Present value of the next five years' worth of	Operating lease expenses
minimum lease payments	Increase in LIFO reserve
LIFO reserve	Goodwill amortization (Note: no adjustment is
Cumulative goodwill amortization	needed for unrecorded goodwill)
Unrecorded goodwill	Asset revaluations
Asset revaluations	Increase in full cost reserve
Full cost reserve	Unusual loss (gain) after tax
Cumulative unusual loss (gain)	Increase in reserve for bad debt
Bad debt reserve	Increase in reserve for inventory obsolescence
Inventory obsolescence reserve	Increase in reserve for warranty costs
Warranty reserve	Increase in reserve for deferred income
Deferred income reserve	R&D expense
Capitalized R&D	Patents expense
Capitalized patents	Trademarks expense
Capitalized trademarks	New product development expense
Capitalized new product development costs	Up-front marketing expense
Capitalized up-front marketing costs	

minus any estimated residual value, and depreciated on a straight-line basis over the estimated life of the asset. Estimated asset lives should be based on such considerations as likely obsolescence through technological change, deterioration through use, and the effects of the competitive environment.

In addition to the various adjustments noted above, NOPAT must always be adjusted for interest expense. In particular, interest expense must be added back to net income when calculating NOPAT. This adjustment is made for the purpose of maintaining the division between a company's operating performance and how it chooses to finance its activities (i.e., the proportion of debt versus shareholder funds used).

The following example provides a comprehensive illustration of the various equity and NOPAT adjustments that are necessary for calculating EVA. When reviewing the example, keep the following two points in mind: the company's first year of operations was 2015, and its cost of capital is assumed to be 12%.

Before calculating Solar Panel, Inc.'s EVA, let's first perform some traditional financial accounting analyses. First, an examination of the income statement reveals that net income has increased from $157,000 to $197,000. This is an increase of 25.6% to 25.5%. Next looking at the balance sheet we see that total assets have increased from $1,536,000 to $1,772,000, an increase of 15.&5 to 15.4%. Combining these measures of net income and total assets we can calculate Solar Panel, Inc.'s return on assets (ROA). In 2015 its ROA was 10.2%. In 2016 the ratio rose to 11.1%. In sum, traditional accounting performance measures are providing signals that the company is performing well. Now let's look at the answers that an EVA analysis provides. This EVA analysis is presented in Tables 11.3–11.6.

There are two important lessons to be learned from the above EVA example. First, accounts payable are generally not included in the calculation of a firm's capital employed. Instead, due to what is a generally constant or expanding dollar amount of vendor financed working capital, it is commonly viewed as a free source of capital.

Solar Panel, Inc. Income Statement For the Years Ended 31 December 2015 and 2016

	2015 (in US$'000s)	2016 (in US$'000s)
Revenue	1,000	1,200
Cost of goods sold	500	600
Gross margin	500	600
Operating expenses:		
Selling & administration	53	75
Depreciation	75	100
R&D	50	60
Amortization of goodwill	10	10
Miscellaneous expense	10	11
Total operating expenses	198	256
Net income before interest and taxes	302	344
Interest expense	93	82
Net income before taxes	209	262
Tax expense (at 25% tax rate)	52	65
Net income	157	197

Solar Panel, Inc. Balance Sheet As of 31 December 2015 and 2016

	2015 (in US$'000s)	2016 (in US$'000s)
Assets		
Cash	10	30
Inventories	30	52
Prepaids	6	10
Land	450	450
Factory and equipment	1,000	1,200
Intangibles – goodwill	40	30
Total Assets	1,536	1,772
Liabilities		
Accounts payable	35	50
Provision for deferred taxes	10	20
Provision for warranties	20	30
Short-term bank loan	200	154
Bonds payable	700	750
Total Liabilities	965	1,004
Shareholders' Equity		
Common stock	414	414
Retained earnings	157	354
Total Shareholders' Equity	571	768
Total Liabilities and Shareholders' Equity	1,536	1,772

TABLE 11.3 Calculating NOPAT for 2015 and 2016

	2015 (in US$'000s)	2016 (in US$'000s)
Net income	157	197
Add:		
Interest	93	82
R&D expense	50	60
Amortization of goodwill	10	10
Increase in deferred tax	10	10
Increase in provision for warranties	20	10
Deduct:		
Amortized R&D	—	20
Total NOPAT adjustments	183	152
NOPAT	340	349

TABLE 11.4 Calculation of economic capital for 2015 and 2016

	2015 (in US$'000s)	2016 (in US$'000s)
Capital employed per balance sheet:		
Common stock	414	414
Retained earnings	157	354
Bank loan	200	154
Bonds payable	700	750
Add:		
R&D capitalized	50	90
Cumulative goodwill amortization	10	20
Capitalized deferred taxes	10	20
Capitalized provision for warranties	20	30
Adjusted capital employed	1,561	1,832

TABLE 11.5 EVA for 2015 (assuming a 12% cost of capital) (in US$)

EVA = NOPAT – (Capital employed * 12%)

= 340,000 – (1,561,000 * 12%)
= 340,000 – 187,320
= 152,680

TABLE 11.6 EVA for 2016 (assuming a 12% cost of capital) (in US$)

EVA	= NOPAT – (Capital employed * 12%)
	= 349,000 – (1,832,000 * 12%)
	= 349,000 – 219,840
	= 129,160

The second lesson to be learned from the EVA example is the sometimes contrary signals that EVA and other accounting performance measures may provide. In contrast with the improvement in performance that ROA indicates, EVA suggests a very different view. In particular, although Solar Panel, Inc. has managed to add shareholder value in both 2015 and 2016, its performance *worsened* between the two years. EVA fell by 15.4% from $152,680 in 2015 to $129,160 in 2016. Due to EVA's focus on company performance in relation to what a company's investors expect, it is the preferred technique for measuring corporate financial performance and should therefore be relied upon.

Non-financial performance measurement systems

The exclusive use of financial performance measurement systems is becoming increasingly rare. The size and scale of today's organizational operations and the types of CEOs who run these organizations are markedly different from what they once were. Organizations are becoming increasingly diversified and multinational, and their CEOs are becoming more akin to the roving sheriffs during the days of the American Wild West. They enter as outsiders (i.e., CEOs are headhunted from what has developed into a pool of professional CEOs), are expected to bring law and order (commonly translated as a new drive and strategic direction), and are summarily dismissed the moment financial performance falters (current average CEO tenure is at a historic low of five years, see Marcec, 2018).

The combination of today's complex organizations and CEOs' peripatetic habits means modern CEOs rarely possess the same level of knowledge about company operations and the workers who drive these operations as their predecessors did. Unlike such CEOs as Carnegie, DuPont, and Sloan, who had a visceral feel for the companies they ran and were able to see beyond the reported financial performance measures, today's CEOs are often less knowledgeable about the business operations they oversee and less able to make the same *ad-hoc* adjustments.

To ensure successful organizational management, senior executives must either include other sources of information in their decision-making – such as measures about shipment rates, machine utilization, and lead times required to introduce new products – or risk the consequences of taking action on a set of incomplete data. Unfortunately, the number of

---

Review Question 11.8: What are the benefits of using EVA rather than ROI?

Answer: Please see the Answer section starting on page 283

senior managers who continue to put at peril their organizations' fortunes remains high. These managers neglect to rein in excessive inventories, overlook cost-reduction opportunities, and fail to harness their respective organizations' intellectual capital.

The singular use of financial performance measurement systems fails to capture the competitive bases of today's organizations. In the past, cost efficiency largely determined an organization's success. As a result, the need for financial information, particularly cost information, was essential and, by itself, largely sufficient. Today's organizations compete on a range of factors, including cost, quality, flexibility, and innovation.

The need for non-financial performance measures results from twin causes. On the one hand, it is partly in response to the changed characteristics of businesses and CEOs, and on the other hand, it is partly due to the changed basis of firm competition. In the ensuing subsections, two of the more notable non-financial performance measurement systems are discussed.

Drucker's views on non-financial performance measures

Drucker (1995) has written extensively about the need for organizations to collect information about their core competencies. Although he believes that the set of core competencies of one organization may, and typically does, differ from the set of core competencies of another organization, he is quick to add that "Every organization – not just businesses – needs one core competence: innovation" (1995: 60). As a consequence, Drucker devotes most of his attention to fleshing out the various performance measures that help an organization appraise and record its innovation.

According to Drucker, the starting point for assessing an organization's innovation begins not with a review of one's own performance, but with a careful assessment of the innovations in one's industry over a given period. As such, Drucker calls for organizations to ask questions like:

- Which of the innovations were truly successful?
- How many of them were ours?
- Is our performance commensurate with our objectives? With the direction of the market? With our market standing? With our research standing?
- Are our successful innovations in the areas of greatest growth and opportunity?
- How many of the truly important innovation opportunities did we miss? Why? Because we did not see them? Or because we botched them?
- How well did we convert an innovation into a commercial product?

Unlike Hall *et al.*'s (1991) non-financial performance measurement system and the hybrid performance measurement systems to be discussed later in this chapter, Drucker's system, if one can label it as such, stays well clear of providing formulas or setting forth categories on which to judge performance. Instead, he seeks to highlight the management mindset that must prevail during the development of measures of performance. The qualitative measures he proposes, which are actually more akin to open-ended questions, are more concerned with assessment than they are with measurement. However, as Drucker properly points out, the ability to answer questions is not nearly as important as the ability to pose the right questions. Senior management's value-added contribution is less about answering questions, for this is typically the job of the various operating and support groups. Instead, the value senior managers add comes from posing the right questions, which equates to focusing employee attention on truly important matters, and providing a framework within which the employees can address these matters.

Hall, Johnson, and Turley's four dimensions of performance measurement

Hall *et al.* (1991) propose a performance measurement system consisting of four broad measures: quality, lead time, resource use, and people development. These measures are primarily geared for manufacturers. Nevertheless, with a little bit of imagination, they can be adapted to service enterprises.

Quality

Quality measures are divided into three main groups: external quality, internal quality, and quality improvement processes. External quality defines the product or service goodness that customers or other people outside the organization ascribe to its products or services. Examples of external quality measures include customer surveys, service call effectiveness, and warranty and reliability rates. Internal quality represents the calibre of the organization's operations and processes. Examples of internal quality measures include overall yields, process capabilities, inspection ratios, and defect and rework rates.

The quality improvement process defines the programme or set of formalized steps an organization adopts to ensure high levels of external and internal quality. As such, today's quality improvement process determines tomorrow's internal and external quality. Although generally difficult to measure, Hall *et al.* point to the measurement and scoring criteria used to determine the winner of the Malcolm Baldrige National Quality Award as an excellent point of reference when trying to assess an organization's quality improvement process.

Lead Time

Lead time defines the length of time required to transform raw materials into finished products. Examples include tooling turnaround time, equipment repair time, time to change layout, engineering change time, tooling design time, and tooling build time.

The measurement of lead times is important for two reasons. First, such measures help the firm to focus on potentially rich areas of value-added or, more to the point, non-value-added activities. Any lead-time measure greater than zero implies waiting time. Although it may be said that wines improve with age, this relationship seldom holds with other business activities. How, for instance, does waiting in a queue at the supermarket or waiting for the product to be shipped improve value? Surely it does not.

A second important reason for measuring lead times is the valuable information such measures provide about an organization's flexibility. In today's business markets, where the "customer is king," the ability to tailor products and services to customers' unique needs is critical. To accomplish this, organizations must evolve their businesses in the direction of make-to-order. Lead-time measures show just how far an organization has progressed.

Resource Use

Measurements of resource use quantify the amount of particular resources consumed and the cost associated with their consumption. Examples of some typical measures of resource use are direct labour dollars, materials consumption, space utilization, and machine utilization. While the first two measures quantify the direct costs associated with using labour and materials to make products or provide services, the latter two measures contain both a direct cost element and an indirect, opportunity cost element.

One of the factors that limits the precision, if not usefulness, of resource use measures is the reliance placed on the accountant's conception and formulation of costs. As Hall *et al.* point out, the various assumptions and aggregations that generally go into the computation of a cost figure make its use suspect. In particular, how can one distinguish between small, but still unfavourable, changes? Might they be indications of something wrong or mere "measurement chatter?"

People Development

People measures comprise Hall *et al.*'s fourth category. Other than noting the need for organizations to maintain human resource inventories and implement systems that fairly and appropriately recognize and reward employees, Hall *et al.* offer little additional advice on this category. This is an unfortunate occurrence, especially in light of the fact that scholars and practitioners alike are underscoring the increasingly important role played by an organization's human resources. Later in this chapter, we discuss how human resource systems contribute to performance management.

It appears that Hall *et al.*'s underdeveloped set of people measures could be substantially improved by incorporating into it Thomas Stewart's work on intellectual capital. In particular, Thomas Stewart (1994) has studied various companies' attempts to record and report their intellectual capital. One company, Skandia Assurance and Financial Services (AFS), a Swedish company selling annuities, variable life insurance policies, and other savings and insurance instruments, appears to be leading in this area. Rather than relying on such conventional practices as the skill levels attained by its employees or the amount of money spent upgrading employees' skills, AFS is more interested in developing ratios that reveal how effectively it leverages its intellectual assets. As Stewart (1994: 9) notes in his summary of AFS's approach to intellectual capital,

> It is less important to find the grand total value of intellectual capital than to develop gauges that show whether AFS is moving in the right direction – creating more of the stuff this year than last, and using it better.

Examples of the trends that AFS charts are the growth in its broker network and the size of the accounts they manage.

Hall *et al.* stress the need for the average organization to make substantial improvements across all four performance fronts or risk elimination by its competitors. Although Hall *et al.* realize the difficulty (if not impossibility) of making a simultaneous across-the-board improvement, they are confident that organizations can make incremental improvements over time to each of the four performance criteria without jeopardizing the organization's past achievements. For instance, improvements in lead times should be sought without regression on some other measure, such as quality. Similarly, improvements in quality should occur without sacrificing resource use.

Review Question 11.9: What are non-financial performance measurement systems, and why are they used?

Answer: Please see the Answer section starting on page 283

Hybrid performance measurement systems

Performance measurement systems that rely upon a combination of financial and non-financial performance measures are termed hybrid systems. Two of the more popular hybrid performance measurement systems are discussed below.

Kaplan and Norton's balanced scorecard

Kaplan and Norton's (1993) balanced scorecard is a hybrid performance measurement system consisting of financial and non-financial measures. The balanced scorecard assesses enterprise performance from four broad perspectives: financial, internal business, customer, and organizational capacity. Together, these perspectives are meant to help an organization identify, design, and deliver the set of factors that will enable the provision of the right processes at the right time to create stakeholder satisfaction, which will allow the organization to attain its outcomes and achieve its vision (Kaplan and McMillan, 2020).

Over time, there has been a minor evolution in the conception and naming of aspects of the balanced scorecard.

The financial perspective seeks to answer the question: How should we appear to our shareholders? This perspective offers insight into how well the organization is meeting its shareholders' needs. Some of the typical measures used to assess financial performance are return on capital, cash flow, project profitability, and profit forecast reliability.

The customer perspective seeks to answer the question: How should we appear to our customers? This perspective provides insight into how well the organization is meeting its customer needs. Some of the measures that characterize the customer perspective are customer surveys, customer-satisfaction indices, customer-retention rates, market-share trends, on-time delivery statistics, product reliability, and product safety. Again, similarities should be apparent between these measures and Hall *et al.*'s quality measures.

The internal business perspective seeks to answer the question: At what business practices must we excel? This perspective sheds light on how well the organization is executing its core activities. Some of the measures that commonly appear under this category are cycle times, unit costs, yield rates, scrap rates, machine utilization, set-up times, and manufacturing lead times. The reader should be able to see similarities between these measures and Hall *et al.*'s lead-time and resource measures.

The organizational capacity perspective, which was originally named "innovation and learning" and subsequently "learning and growth," seeks to answer the question: How can we continue to improve and create value? This perspective sheds light on an organization's ability to improve and create value. Some of the measures that are commonly associated with this perspective are employee satisfaction, employee retention, and employee productivity; percentage of processes with real-time feedback; number of employee suggestions; and measures of team building and team performance.

Information from each of these perspectives is vital to the organization's continued success. As Kaplan and Norton (1993) like to point out, the successful management of an organization requires the ability to view performance in several areas simultaneously. Similar to an aeroplane pilot – who needs constantly updated information on fuel, air speed, altitude, bearing, and destination – an organization and its managers need information comprising a broad set of performance criteria.

All organizations need information from each of the four performance perspectives; however, the specific set of items comprising each perspective will most likely be different for each organization. The differences will arise from variations in organizational strategies, as well as factors that are unique to an organization's internal and/or external environments. As Kaplan and Norton (1993: 135) note: "The balanced scorecard is not a template that can be applied to businesses in general or even industry-wide. Different market situations, product strategies, and competitive environments require different scorecards." Accordingly, effective balanced scorecards are ones that have been tailored to fit the organization's mission, strategy, and internal and external environments. The decisive test of a well-designed balanced scorecard is an observer's ability to see beyond the specific scorecard measures and correctly divine the organization's strategy.

As a way to illustrate likely differences in the balanced scorecards between organizations pursuing dissimilar strategies, imagine an organization with OWC (order-wining criteria) that include sustainability and good corporate citizenship. This organization will find that its financial perspective will benefit from such measures as the percentage of sales earned from socially and environmentally targeted products/services, dollars saved from accident reductions, dollars saved from product life cycle reviews, dollars spent on employee health and safety projects, dollars spent on remediation programmes (e.g., habitat restoration), dollars spent on worker accident prevention programmes, and dollars spent on community improvement projects. Customer perspective measures might include the tonnes of post-consumer waste recycled, number of consumer-focused environmental education campaigns conducted, number of safety/environmental safety brochures downloaded, number of products with safety failures, dollar amount of products/services donated, and number of good citizenship awards won. Internal business process measures could feature CO_2 and methane emissions produced, percentage of solvents recycled, tonnes of solid waste produced, tonnes of hazardous waste produced, number of environmental fines received, and energy used. And finally, the organizational capacity perspective might have measures for the number of ergonomic reviews conducted, workforce diversity achieved relative to the organization's region of operation and/or customer base, number of ISO 14001 (which relate to international standards specifying requirements for effective environmental management systems) certifications, and number of product life cycle reviews performed.

A number of organizations have adopted the balanced scorecard. A partial list of such adopting organizations includes Apple, Rockwater, CIGNA Corporation, Bank of Montreal, Airways Corporation, Telecom New Zealand, ICI Australia, New Zealand Post, and Ericsson Australia Limited. According to Kaplan and Norton, the typical company testimonial centres on the balanced scorecard's ability to help drive organizational change and enhance management planning and control.

If there is one major shortcoming with the balanced scorecard it is the often inconsistent set of performance measures that appear under the organizational capacity perspective. For example, in their seminal 1993 *Harvard Business Review* article showcasing Rockwater's experience with using the balanced scorecard, Kaplan and Norton placed under this perspective (which had the original name of "innovation and learning perspective") such measures as percentage of revenue from new services, rate of improvement index, staff attitude survey, number of employee suggestions, and revenue per employee. It seems, however, that many of these performance measures can be, and perhaps are better, categorized under different performance perspectives from the one Kaplan and Norton used. Percentage of revenue from new services, which is essentially a specific type of market-share statistic, appears better categorized with customer performance measures. Likewise, the rate of improvement index, which is defined for Rockwater as the improvement made in relation to product rework and safety issues, appears better categorized with internal business performance measures. Furthermore, staff attitude surveys might be better placed with measures of internal business performance, and revenue per employee might be better placed with financial performance measures. In sum, Kaplan and Norton have never offered a compelling list of measures that might feature as part of their organizational capacity perspective.

In fairness to Kaplan and Norton, they appear to be aware of the deficiency inherent in their organizational capacity perspective. In their book, *Translating Strategy into Action: The Balanced Scorecard* (1996: 146), they admit that the measures in the organizational capacity perspective are "less developed than those of the other three balanced scorecard perspectives." In their most current rendition of this perspective, as shown on the Balanced Scorecard Institute's webpage, the historical confusions associated with this perspective are slowly being addressed.

To help reduce the confusion relating to this fourth balanced scorecard perspective, it is suggested that the name of this perspective be changed to the "learning perspective." In fact, such a name change is more a rediscovery than a reorientation. In the balanced scorecard's original version, the perspective was labelled "innovation and learning." Additionally, the name change would mirror the importance that today's writers are ascribing to an organization's ability to learn.

Focusing on learning and avoiding words like "growth" will improve the conceptual clarity of this perspective and harmonize better with the management literature on continuous improvement. In particular, the idea of growth or improvement should not be seen as unique to any one perspective. Improvement is required across all four perspectives. To operate otherwise jeopardizes an organization's survival. When organizations become complacent and merely seek to maintain performance, they are in danger of slipping backwards and losing competitiveness.

The measures to assess this renamed learning perspective can be researched in the management literature focusing on learning organizations. Measures comprising an organization's learning capacity will draw attention to the organization's ability to generate new ideas and subsequently generalize and disseminate them on an organization-wide basis. In more specific terms, items likely to feature under this learning perspective are measures of an organization's ability to harness its human assets and should include measures of employee empowerment, the adoption of best practices, the creation of flatter organizations, and unlocking synergies between employees and structural capital.

Most recently, Kaplan and McMillan (2020) have provided an amended version of their balanced scorecard as a way to accommodate those organizations wishing to align their balanced scorecards with a triple bottom line approach. The main changes feature changing the organizational capacity perspective to enablers, changing the customer perspective to stakeholders, and changing the financial perspective to outcomes. These changes in terminology allow recognition of the fact that, when compared with earlier balanced scorecard versions, a triple bottom line approach requires a wider purview of the groups one must account for and the consequences (i.e., financial, social, and environmental) one must report on.

Before leaving this topic of the balanced scorecard, it is worth noting some similarities between Kaplan and Norton's work and the work of Brignall and his colleagues. Based on a multi-year field project seeking to uncover key performance measures in for-profit service businesses, Brignall *et al.* (1991) propose a set of six generic performance dimensions: competitiveness, financial, quality, flexibility, resource utilization, and innovation. Although in some respects the framework is very much like Hall's, sharing many of the same performance category names, it has even more in common with the balanced scorecard. The similarity becomes increasingly evident when the performance measures underlying Brignall *et al.*'s six dimensions are compared with the performance measures comprising the balanced scorecard's four perspectives. In particular, the competitiveness and financial performance measures tap the same theme as the balanced scorecard's financial perspective. Additionally, the quality performance measures map onto the balanced scorecard's customer perspective, while the flexibility and resource utilization performance measures equate to the balanced scorecard's internal perspective. And finally, the innovation performance measures are similar to the balanced scorecard's organizational capacity perspective. It is interesting to note that the Brignall *et al.* and Kaplan and Norton performance measurement systems were developed at about the same time, although on different sides of the Atlantic Ocean, and largely ended up with the same results.

Cross and Lynch's performance measurement hierarchy

Cross and Lynch (1990) propose a performance measurement system that links operational and strategic goals and integrates financial and non-financial information. To help underscore their message about the importance of linking strategy with measures of performance, they illustrate, using what they have termed a performance pyramid, the intertwining nature of strategic objectives and operational performance measures. An adapted version of the pyramid is presented in Figure 11.1.

At the top of the pyramid is the organization's strategy. Strategic objectives are developed from this strategy and translated down the organization, ultimately to the very work centres themselves. With a sound knowledge of the organization's strategic objectives, the work centres can now begin developing appropriate operational performance measures to indicate how well they are meeting the strategic objectives. Data in the form of these operational performance measures are then sent back up the organization's line of command. Based on the feedback contained in these measures, senior managers can, as needed, fine-tune either the presentation or substance of future strategic objectives.

The process of communicating strategic objectives is cascading in nature. Strategic objectives are first communicated down to the business-unit levels where market satisfaction and financial performance targets are developed. In terms of Kaplan and Norton's balanced scorecard, these terms resemble the customer and financial perspectives, respectively.

The strategic objectives are next translated down to departments in the form of customer satisfaction, flexibility, and productivity targets. The actual performance achieved on customer satisfaction and flexibility combine to comprise an organization's market satisfaction measure, and the actual performance achieved on productivity comprises an organization's financial performance measure.

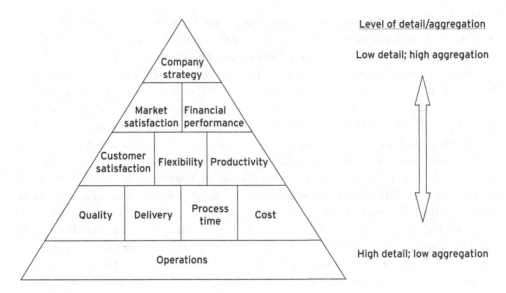

FIGURE 11.1 The performance pyramid.
Source: Adapted from Cross and Lynch (1990).

Finally, the strategic objectives are translated to the work centres. Here they are represented by quality, delivery, process time, and cost targets. The actual performance achieved for quality and delivery combines to comprise an organization's customer-satisfaction measure, while delivery and process time combine to comprise an organization's flexibility measure, and process time and cost combine to comprise an organization's productivity measure.

Performance measurement information is meant to percolate up through the organization as actual performance is achieved. As these measures of performance move up the organization, they undergo increasing aggregation and summarizing. Senior managers, the ultimate target of the performance information, will use the information to focus their organization's future strategic objectives and the communication of these objectives.

In addition to highlighting the critical role played by organizational strategy in determining performance measures, Cross and Lynch's performance pyramid makes two further important contributions. First, it shows the intertwined nature of performance targets and performance measures. Second, it reveals the cascading and iterative process by which strategic targets move down and operational measures move up through various levels of an organization's hierarchy.

The main weakness of the Cross and Lynch performance pyramid is its failure to recognize or mention the importance of organizational learning. As noted above, scholars and practitioners are increasingly emphasizing this critical organizational factor. Perhaps, therefore, it is this lack of comprehensiveness that explains the model's low rate of adoption by organizations.

Performance measurement systems summary

There is increasing awareness that performance measurement systems comprised solely of financial measures or solely of non-financial measures are inadequate for today's environment. The demands of today's business environment, especially the bases of competitive success coupled with the modern CEO's common lack of tenure and experience with the company he/she runs, have given impetus to the need for hybrid performance measurement systems. These hybrid systems must incorporate a sufficiently broad-based set of performance measures. Otherwise, employees' strategies for maximizing their own goals, typically at the expense of the organization's goals, may develop.

As examples of the dysfunctional behaviour that can occur when the performance measurement focus is too narrow, consider the following two real-life stories. The first story is about a major UK airport that tried to improve the speed of delivery of passengers' luggage to the baggage collection area by measuring how long it took for the initial bag to arrive at the baggage carousel. The performance measure became commonly known as "the first bag to the belt." Although the airport's measurement approach would appear quite logical, it did not take long for the baggage handlers to figure out a successful strategy, at least when viewed from their perspective. Upon a plane's arrival, one of the baggage handlers would quickly unlock the cargo door, disappear for a few moments inside the cargo hold, reappear with as small a bag as he/she could find without spending too much time searching, throw this bag to another waiting baggage handler, who would then sprint directly to the baggage claim carousel. Based on the airport's performance measurement system, the baggage handlers' performance was judged excellent. In reality, however, their performance was anything but exemplary. They stepped on other passengers' bags in the process of selecting the small and easily portable bag, sometimes dropped this bag when making the throwing exchange, and generally undertook a lot of wasteful activities trying to beat the system.

A second story about a performance measurement system that had too narrow a focus involves Penfold Wineries. Penfold implemented a performance measurement system that measured productivity as the number of litres of wine produced per worker hour. The employees quickly recognized that they could improve this productivity measure by decreasing their performance on a range of other non-recorded activities, including product waste and overtime. Consequently, although the measured productivity was quite high, the performance measurement system was actually undermining the firm's competitiveness.

As the above two case examples highlight, performance measurement systems must tap a broad range of organizational activity or risk unleashing dysfunctional employee behaviour. Of course, it must also be understood that just as there is a danger in having too few foci and too narrow a focus, there is also a danger in having too many foci and too broad a focus. The existence of too many performance measures may produce information overload or may trivialize the importance of any single performance measure. Either way, the performance measurement system breaks down and loses its motivational purpose.

But even when the "right" number of performance measures is used, which according to Kaplan and Norton is about 15–20, there is still the problem of knowing what to do when the performance measures provide mixed messages. In other words, what action should a manager take when one performance measure signals good news while another performance measure, either within or across performance categories, signals unfavourable news?

There appear to be two approaches a manager can take when confronted with conflicting performance signals. The first approach is based on Hall *et al.*'s idea that performance on a given measure should be maintained or improved without any sacrifice of performance on any other measure. In other words, slippage or backtracking on any given dimension of performance is unacceptable.

Review Question 11.10: What are hybrid performance measurement systems, and why are they used?

Answer: Please see the Answer section starting on page 283

The second approach involves the weighting of the various performance criteria and thereby constructing a composite score. The weighting scheme is based upon senior management's preferences for successfully achieving the various performance measures. Multiple methods can be used to develop a weighting system, ranging from Delphi techniques to paired-comparison rankings. A discussion of these techniques, however, is beyond the scope of this book. Readers who are interested in gaining more information about these weighting techniques can read the ample, primarily management-based literature that exists on this topic. In addition, Chan and Lynn's (1991) *Journal of Management Research* article, which is referenced at the end of this chapter, can be consulted.

As one final comment before leaving this discussion about performance measures, it can sometimes be the case, despite its counterintuitive feel, that good performance could comprise doing less. For example, success for an organization providing budgeting services for low-income people might be viewed as the number of people being offered budgeting services, with more meaning more success. However, if the budgeting service is actually changing how people behave, and these individuals find they are now capable of balancing their financial inflows and outflows and are no longer coming into financial strife, then seeing fewer people could be a good thing. The same could be said for a foodbank. Serving fewer people could be a very good sign, for it is hopefully showing that the foodbank has succeeded in serving as a temporary backstop until people regain their feet and can now be independent again. In other words, for both the budgeting service provider and the foodbank, achieving lower on a measure could be the very best outcome.

EMPLOYEE INCENTIVE SYSTEMS

Employee incentive systems feature prominently at many organizations. There is a belief among these organizations, and especially among the business consulting fraternity that advises organizations on pay practices, that financial incentives in particular motivate employees to achieve better performance. In contrast with popular organizational practice, the scholarly literature on pay for performance shows this relationship to be much more complex and less straightforward than the consultants apparently perceive it to be. The next two subsections discuss first the types of existing incentives and second the theory and literature that support their use.

Types of incentives

Incentives can be categorized in several ways. First incentives can be non-financial or financial. The former consists of:

- Recognition
- Promotion opportunities

- Increased job responsibilities
- Increased autonomy.

Non-financial incentives are more closely associated with the use of intrinsic factors to motivate workers. Although past worker surveys suggest that non-financial incentives are more influential than financial incentives in attracting and retaining employees, some recently conducted surveys suggest the opposite. For example, *The 2016 Deloitte Millennial Survey: Winning over the Next Generation of Leaders* states, "Pay and financial benefits drive Millennials' choice of organization more than anything else" (p. 19). Many organizations point to these results as evidencing the primacy of financial incentives over non-financial incentives. However, a more recent, 2018 study conducted by CECP (a CEO-led coalition of more than 200 of the world's biggest companies), Imperative (an enterprise peer coaching platform), and PricewaterhouseCoopers suggests that foremost on employees' minds is the desire for meaningful work, which is defined as work that aligns with employees' values and leads to a sense of purpose and fulfilment. The study finds that 70% of its surveyed employees would consider leaving their current role for a more fulfilling job opportunity. Furthermore, one in three employees were willing to accept lower pay for more meaningful work. Susan Podlogar, the Executive VP and Chief Human Resource Officer at MetLife, hints at the benefits organizations can obtain by the introduction of more meaningful work when she says, "Fulfilment goes beyond engagement and productivity to maximize human energy, spirit, and potential" (CECP, Imperative, and PWC, 2018: 8). As will be shown when discussing the theory and literature examining what motivates employees, the usefulness of financial incentives has long been questioned by scholars and practitioners alike.

Financial incentives consist of:

- Salary increases
- Bonuses
- Benefits
- Perquisites.

Salary increases usually result from an employee's promotion. For example, a bank teller may be promoted to head bank teller. With this promotion comes further job responsibilities, and this in turn is accompanied by greater remuneration.

Bonuses are typically one-off payments to employees who perform particularly well. A bank teller, as an example, may receive a bonus because he/she exceeds a performance target. As an illustration, Wells Fargo recently offered its employees bonuses for cross-selling the bank's products.

While many bonuses, especially at the senior management level, are individual-based, group-based bonuses are quite common for lower-level employees. The only real difference between individual- and group-based bonuses is that the former is based on a single individual's accomplishments, while the latter is based on a group's accomplishments (e.g., a particular department or branch of a company). Generally, a predetermined quantitative formula is used to determine the size of the overall bonus, which is then divided among the group of employees. Some scholars are critical of such programmes, citing the potential for free riders, for individuals to see themselves as detached from the group, and for a lack of perceived equity in the distribution of rewards. Other scholars argue that group-based programmes engender peer/social pressure that creates a culture of ownership and responsibility. Merchant and Van der Stede (2007) and Rosen *et al.* (2005) conclude group-based plans are effective and argue for their greater use.

Bonuses can be further distinguished based on whether the bonus is available immediately to employees or whether they must wait until some future point in time. The reason for deferring the bonus payment is to ensure the performance is genuine and not the result of either employee manipulation (accelerating revenues or deferring/delaying expenses) or an accounting artefact.

Handelsbanken Group provides an illustration of a group-based bonus system with a deferred payment structure. Each year, if certain conditions have been met, a portion of the bank's profits are paid to a profit sharing pool for employees. The main criterion used to determine whether and how much of the bank's profits will be contributed to the profit sharing plan is a comparison of Handelsbanken's return on shareholders' equity to its peer group. The bank places an upper limit on its contribution to the profit sharing plan at 25% of the total dividends paid to shareholders. Furthermore, employees are only eligible to a share of the monies when they reach the age of 60, at which point they receive a payout based on the number of years they worked for the bank.

Some companies operate company-wide bonus plans that allow employees to earn company stock. Proctor & Gamble's long-running stock ownership programme has resulted in an estimated 10–20% of its shares being owned by a wide cross section of its employees. About 13% of Southwest Airlines stock is owned by its employees, while H-E-B, the Texas-based supermarket chain, pledged in 2015 to give its employees 15% of the company's shares. H-E-B employees who were at least 21 years old, had worked for the company at least a year, and had logged a minimum of 1,000 hours of work during 2015 were rewarded with stock equal to 3% of their salary plus $100 for each full year of work at the company. Although it is true that higher-paid employees typically benefit the most from these profit sharing and stock ownership plans, the bonuses can still meaningfully benefit lower-paid workers, who can earn bonuses that often range between 10 and 15% of their base compensation.

The third category of financial incentives is benefits, which are non-wage incentives given to employees. Examples include employer-provided or paid housing, insurance (health, dental, life, disability, etc.), sick leave, holiday/vacation (paid and unpaid), retirement benefits, childcare, profit sharing, university tuition reimbursement, and matching of employee charitable giving. At Netflix, employees are granted unlimited family leave, providing employees the autonomy to decide what works best for them.

In spite of the literature's compelling evidence for how employee benefit programmes motivate employees and more than pay for themselves (sometimes multiple times over), many organizations eschew this advice and limit their employee benefits to full-time employees. Major retailers – including Walmart, Home Depot, and Target – are only hiring temporary workers (i.e., employment contracts specifying less than 35 hours of work per week) and are converting full-time employees to part-time as a way to avoid paying health and holiday/vacation benefits.

Perquisites, or simply perks as they are more commonly called, are the fourth and final type of financial incentive. Perks are specific kinds of benefits that are discretionary in nature and generally only offered to employees with high-rank or long seniority. Perks include take-home

> *Review Question 11.11:* What types of employee incentives can an organization use?
> *Answer:* Please see the Answer section starting on page 283

vehicles, hotel stays, free refreshments, leisure activities during work time (company gyms, squash courts, etc.), and allowances for lunch. The senior employee team, and only the senior employee team at Comcast, for example, enjoys executive dining on the company's 52nd floor of the Rockefeller Center that features linen tablecloths and a daily lunch menu with sushi, a selection of salads, seasonal soups, fresh-baked breads, and much more.

Theory behind the use of incentives

The use of employee incentives is commonly linked to goal-setting theory and agency theory. In terms of goal-setting theory, popular wisdom asserts that employees will be more motivated and more likely to achieve their assigned goals if rewards are attached to the goals' achievement. Compensation consultants have modified the earlier goal-setting acronym of SMART, which was discussed in Chapter 4. The letters in this acronym stand for "specific," "measureable," "ambitious," "reasonable," and "time-targeted." The more recent addition of the letters "E" (the need to evaluate) and "R" (the need to reward) to the SMART acronym have created the new acronym "SMARTER."

The SMARTER acronym may suggest some superior and improved organizational mandate, but in reality, it is just another mostly empty marketing jingo. As mentioned earlier in this chapter, goal-setting theorists steadfastly argue that motivation is chiefly driven by the act of setting goals. Although the goal-setting literature includes reference to the use of rewards, this inclusion of rewards is similar to goal-setting theory's advice on employee participation. In particular, the use of rewards and employee participation can further support the benefits associated with goal setting. Many organizations and their compensation consultants, however, have misrepresented these research findings to suggest that goal-setting theory requires rewards to be attached to goals. Not only is this characterization false, but, as will shortly be shown, the majority of the literature on the use of employee rewards also suggests that their use is ephemeral.

Agency theorists also subscribe to the belief that the use of employee rewards helps align employee goals with those of the organization. According to agency theory's dour view of humankind – including its preception of workers as lazy, greedy, and untrustworthy – rewards are seen as necessary to curb the likelihood of workers behaving in a dysfunctional manner. Agency theory's assumptions about workers have limited empirical backing, and Ghoshal (2005), among other scholars, has roundly criticized the legitimacy of the theory's assumptions.

Agency theory has also been criticized for encouraging shady and unethical behaviour. Wells Fargo offers a good case in point. The bank wanted to improve the number of bank products its average customer held. In an ambitious bid to align employees' goals with the bank's goal of raising its customers' average number of products from 6.1 to 8, the bank implemented its "Gr-eight initiative." Since agency theory believes employees need an incentive, or what others call a bribe, to overcome their inherent laziness, Wells Fargo attached a bonus scheme to its "Gr-eight initiative." As readers who are familiar with Wells Fargo will know, in attempting to meet this lofty goal, the bank's employees engaged in a variety of dishonest behaviour. In particular, the employees resorted to using fraudulent and unethical cross-selling tactics, including fabricating customers and assigning PIN numbers to ATM cards without the customer's authorization. The US Congress held hearings into the fraud and, following the filing of a case against the bank by regulators and the city and county of Los Angeles, Wells Fargo agreed to pay a fine of $185 million.

Frederick Herzberg (2003), who first wrote on this subject of employee rewards 50 years ago, argues that monetary rewards can never motivate employee behaviour. Instead, they can only serve to demotivate employees. In particular, when employees believe their remuneration is too low, they will become demotivated. Increasing these employees' pay will alleviate their feelings of demotivation. Once the pay reaches a level that the employees perceive as being fair, the employees will no longer feel demotivated. Not feeling demotivated, however, is not the same as feeling motivated. Rather than residing at opposite ends of a single continuum, motivation and demotivation occupy two separate continua. Other factors beyond pay are what ultimately motivate workers; and these factors include responsibility, achievement, and learning and growth opportunities.

Pay constitutes what Herzberg terms a hygiene factor. Similar to poor work conditions or poor relationships with one's supervisor, these hygiene factors can either be unmet and therefore lead to employees' dissatisfaction, or the hygiene factors can be met and lead to no employee dissatisfaction. Although hygiene factors on their own cannot produce satisfied and motivated workers, it is always the case that organizations must ensure the hygiene factors have been met before they can successfully use motivating factors to stimulate employee behaviour.

Alfie Kohn is equally dismissive of the use of monetary rewards to motivate employees. Kohn (1993: 55) writes: "Research suggests that, by and large, rewards succeed at securing one thing only: temporary compliance. When it comes to producing lasting change in attitudes and behavior, however, rewards, like punishment, are strikingly ineffective." Meanwhile, Dan Ariely (2016), the James B. Duke Professor of Psychology and Behavioral Economics at Duke University, similarly debunks the idea that incentives increase performance. In his book *Payoff*, Ariely not only calls into question the positive effect of incentives on human motivation, but he explicitly notes their potential to be *demotivating*.

Patty McCord, the Chief Talent Officer at Netflix from 1998 to 2012, recounts a set of experiences that echoes the sentiments of Herzberg, Kohn, and Ariely (McCord, 2014). She describes how Netflix didn't pay performance bonuses, because they believed they were unnecessary. According to McCord (2014), if you hire the right people, and in particular, "[i]f your employees are fully formed adults who put the company first, an annual bonus won't make them work harder or smarter." Netflix's employee compensation philosophy was based on paying market-based rates, being honest, and treating employees fairly. McCord (2014) further states that she always encouraged her employees to talk with head hunters and tell her the salary they were being offered. This information allowed her to ensure Netflix was in fact paying market-based salary rates.

The sceptic at this point might argue that Herzberg, Kohn, and Ariely, however eminent their scholarly reputations may be, as well as the compensation practices reported at Netflix are examples of employee compensation outliers. Surely others have contributed work on this subject, and what do these other findings show? The reality is hundreds of laboratory and field experiments examining the association between financial incentives and employee performance appear in the management, accounting, and economics literatures. The overall picture this research paints is one of no consistent relationship. For example, in a meta-analysis drawing on the findings of 98 studies examining the impact of worker incentives on employee performance, Guzzo et al. (1985) observe no significant overall effect. They further find that the number of workers who were absent or quit their jobs was virtually unrelated to financial incentives. Bonner et al. (2000), who conduct a review of 85 financial incentive studies, reach a similar conclusion. They observe that only about half of the studies show a positive relationship between financial incentives and employee performance. Furthermore, for the studies that do report a positive relationship, it is invariably for the quantity of work (i.e., doing more of something or doing it faster) and not the quality of work (Jenkins et al., 1998).

Compounding the lack of a consistent relationship between financial incentives and employee performance, more recent research shows both a failure to lift employee performance and an increase in dysfunctional risk-taking behaviour. A 2017 publication by Financial Institute Services of Australasia (FINSIA), co-authored by Elizabeth Sheedy and Le Zhang, shows that study participants whose compensation was profit-based exhibited no significant increase in productivity relative to their fixed-pay counterparts. The former group of employees did, however, exhibit significantly less risk-management compliance than the fixed-compensation group. Labelling these findings as "surprising," since the whole purpose of incentives is to encourage staff to work harder, Sheedy and Zhang conclude their research by writing: "Given the significant adverse impact on compliance noted above, the study supports the elimination of profit-based incentives currently being debated within the financial services industry" (2017: 3).

The unconvinced reader may wonder if the failure to find supporting evidence for pay-for-performance plans is due to the failure to focus on the right groups of people. For example, CEOs of major corporations, whose mandate is to maximize shareholder wealth, would surely be positively influenced by financial incentives. Again, disappointment awaits. A tongue-in-cheek story by the New York Times published in 1998 describes a study that searched for CEO-related factors associated with a company's stock performance (Bryant, 1998). The lone statistically significant factor was a CEO's golf handicap. Lower handicaps were correlated with higher performance, which led Graef Crystal, a consultant on executive compensation, to quip, "… corporate directors may want to give out stock options that vest only if the chief executive lowers his handicap by a certain amount."

Recent data that focuses on CEO pay and company performance provides even more sobering news, showing a negative association between the two. As an example, MSCI, a US-based, global finance company, found that "[t]he best-paid CEOs tend to run some of the worst-performing companies and vice versa – even when pay and performance are measured over the course of many years" (Francis, 2016). In particular, the 2016 study shows that $100 invested in the 20% of companies with the highest-paid CEOs would have grown to $265 over ten years, whereas the same amount invested in the companies with the lowest-paid CEOs would have grown to $367.

In contrast to the absence of reliable findings linking incentive pay schemes with improved performance, a more consistent set of findings emerges when employee motivation is separated into intrinsic and extrinsic motivation (Kuvaas et al., 2017; Pink, 2011). Intrinsic motivation is defined as the desire to perform an activity for its own sake because of the inherent pleasure and satisfaction it offers, while extrinsic motivation is defined as the desire to perform an activity because of the tangible rewards (e.g., incentive pay) it brings (Deci *et al.*, 1989; Deci and Ryan, 2000). Research undertaken in the field of behavioural economics shows that the use of extrinsic motivators reduces individuals' willingness to perform a task for its own sake **and** is associated with a decline in performance (e.g., Bowles and Polanía-Reyes, 2012; Frey, 1993; Frey and Jegen, 2001). Frey and Jegen (1999) refer to this effect as "crowding out." In other words, far from being additive or synergistically positive, extrinsic and intrinsic motivation are negatively correlated.

Support for this crowding out effect is observed in Deci *et al.*'s (1999) meta-analysis of 128 laboratory experiments. Similar and more recent findings are observed by Kuvaas *et al.* (2017) and Cerasoli *et al.* (2014). Kuvaas *et al.*'s (2017) work is particularly instructive. In their field study of 106 gas station managers and employees, they find not only a negative correlation between intrinsic and extrinsic motivation but also an insignificant correlation between extrinsic motivation and employee performance, as well as a significant positive correlation between extrinsic motivation and turnover intentions. In contrast, a significant positive correlation was observed between intrinsic motivation and employee performance and a significant negative correlation between intrinsic motivation and turnover intentions. When summarising their work, Kuvaas *et al.* (2017: 253) state:

> Our data are consistent with the widely held belief that intrinsic motivation has a greater influence on performance than does extrinsic motivation, and they refute the hypothesis that "if there is an undermining effect on intrinsic motivation, it is usually dominated by the positive effect of PFIP (pay-for-individual-performance) on extrinsic motivation" … Nevertheless, we do not suggest that extrinsic motivation cannot positively influence work performance … extrinsic motivation can be a potent motivator where there is little potential for intrinsic motivation and when it is relatively easy to monitor and measure results and outcomes. Kuvaas *et al.* (2016), for instance, found a small positive association between extrinsic motivation and increased sales effort, but they also found a positive relationship between extrinsic motivation and increased turnover intention (which is in line with the findings of the present study). This small increase in work effort may be outweighed by the increase in turnover intention.

Carl Davidson, the founder of Research First Ltd, an NZ-based business market research and consulting firm, in drawing upon his experiences with helping organizations improve, succinctly captures the essence of the above discussion. He states, "Most professionals care about their craft, they care about performing well for the people around them, and if you set them up to compete with one another, you will undermine the team dynamic as well as their performance" (as cited in Leggatt, 2021). Davidson's counsel is clear and simple: if you want to motivate workers, then build an environment with "lots of laughter" and institute an intrinsic reward culture that supports and acknowledges performance (as cited in Leggatt, 2021).

In spite of what the literature's findings reveal, pay-for-performance plans continue to be a mainstay of many organizations' attempts to influence employee behaviour. They have proven especially popular among higher-skilled individuals working with low (easy) versus

> *Review Question 11.12:* How do scholars and practitioners generally perceive the value of
> employee incentive systems?
> *Answer:* Please see the Answer section starting on page 283

high (hard) thresholds (Banker *et al.*, 2001; Dohmen and Falk, 2011; Román, 2009; Shields and Waller, 1988). While it is one matter for a production worker to be paid a piece rate for each good unit of product produced, it is a very separate matter to institute a pay-for-performance scheme for a senior executive. In the former case, it is quite evident what has been produced. For senior managers, however, their quantity and quality of performance are not nearly as clear. As an example, basing a senior manager's incentive compensation on a formula that compares his/her company's actual and budgeted earnings per share neglects such important factors as accounting-related timing issues, the quality of the earnings, and the opportunistic influence senior employees can exert on the setting of incentivized targets. Enron serves as a classic case in point. Organizations that insist on using pay-for-performance plans should proceed with a high level of caution.

HUMAN RESOURCE SYSTEMS

Human resource management (HRM) is primarily concerned with the relationship between the management of an organization's human resources and the organization's performance. Typically, this performance is viewed in terms of achieving organizational objectives and competitive advantage. As Delery (1998: 303) notes, HRM practices influence a "firm's resources, such as the human capital of the firm, or employee behaviours, and it is these resources and behaviours that ultimately lead to performance."

As noted earlier in this chapter's discussion of hybrid performance measurement systems, the effective management of an organization's employees is a critical lead factor to customer satisfaction and an organization's financial performance. Becker and Gerhart (1996) show that good people management practices produce positive and significant economic results. HRM practitioners and scholars have a long tradition of trying to understand and design good people management practices aimed at encouraging high employee commitment, motivation, and performance. Some of the efforts have focused on building resilient organizational cultures, which are defined as work settings that help employees to concentrate on what matters by encouraging them to learn from the past and providing them time and training to develop innovative thinking. Other efforts have focused on building high-performing work cultures. This term refers to a shared workforce expectation whereby all employees want to set and achieve challenging, organizationally relevant goals in a manner that supports, or at least does not harm, the efforts and ambitions of other stakeholders (e.g., co-workers, customers, owners).

According to the HRM literature, worker performance is a function of individual worker characteristics (Cardy *et al.*, 1995). The critical importance ascribed to the individual worker means that the prime imperative of an organization is to recruit and select the right people. In particular, organizations must initially develop recruitment and selection systems, processes, and procedures that ensure they attract employees with the right knowledge, right skills, and right attitudes. Upon successfully hiring these employees, the organization will next want to ensure they continually perform at a high level. To enable this ongoing high level of employee performance, organizations must put in place systems and processes that ensure the proper training and effective management of their workforce.

Every organization, regardless of the strategy it pursues, desires a high-performing work culture. Whether it is a cost leader, which wants its workers to remain vigilant to cost-saving approaches, or an innovator, which wants its workers to develop its next generation of unique products/services, all organizations will be interested in ensuring their HRM systems are capable of attracting, training, and retaining the right types of employees. Unlike the choice an organization can make about whether to operate an employee incentive system, no similar choice exists when it comes to the use of HRM practices. There are benefits to be gained (or lost) from operating (or not) best practice HRM systems, processes, and procedures.

When it comes to recruiting, many organizations employ sophisticated psychometric testing. These tests measure a job applicant's job-relevant cognitive abilities (which are sometimes referred to as a candidate's aptitude) and personality, and are used to help identify applicants who are best suited to a given job.

Cognitive abilities tests typically comprise test items that measure an applicant's verbal reasoning, numerical reasoning, abstract reasoning, spatial ability, technical ability, and clerical ability. These tests are usually delivered as paper and pencil exercises (although they can be computer-administered) and are generally time-limited. An applicant's results are measured against those of others who have previously taken the test in order to make relative assessment comparisons. Examples of cognitive reasoning tests are the Rust Advanced Numerical Reasoning Appraisal (RANRA), the Watson Glaser Critical Thinking Appraisal (WGCTA), and the GTI Online Solutions (GTIOS) psychometric tests. The GTIOS is especially popular among the main accounting firms.

Personality tests are used to explore the way applicants do things (e.g., do they enjoy taking risks), how they behave in certain situations, and their preferences and attitudes. Unlike cognitive ability tests, personality tests do not have right and wrong answers. Instead, applicants' results are compared with the characteristics considered essential for the job to gauge if these individuals are suited for the given work environment and job. These tests are usually paper-based questionnaires, but some are taken on computers. Classic examples of these tests are the Minnesota Multiphasic Personality Inventory (MMPI), Myers-Briggs Type Indicator (MBTI), and Millon Clinical Multiaxial Inventory (MCMI).

Good recruiting practices will be of little help unless an organization can retain its employees. The low, single-digit employee resignation rates of the mid-2010s, which averaged around 2% in the US, spiked to over 8% in the US in early 2020 (Economic Policy Institute, 2021). Anthony Klotz, a professor of management at Mays Business School at Texas A&M University, termed the mass exodus the Great Resignation. Causes for the unprecedented quantity of resignations have included changed worker perceptions triggered by the COVID-19 pandemic. Workers not only reassessed their employment because of the risk their jobs exposed them to in catching COVID-19 but also because they discovered that the lockdowns that forced them to work from home offered freedom from the drudgery and expense of long commutes to work. Furthermore, workers found work from home offered greater work flexibility and greater scope to gain better work-life balance.

Other countries are preparing for high levels of employee resignations to reach their shores. In Australia and New Zealand, for example, various worker surveys show a significant amount of pent-up worker dissatisfaction. PwC's 2021 report *What Workers Want: Winning the War for Talent* shows that 38% of surveyed workers plan to leave their employer within the next year. Meanwhile, Auckland University of Technology's Wellbeing@Work study found a substantial increase in workers with the intention to change jobs, rising from 35% in May 2020 to 46% in April 2021. The desire to be part of organizations that offered flexible working arrangements, hybrid working guidelines, and greater scope for paid and unpaid leave opportunities were commonly aired themes. In addition, workers expressed a call for more autonomy in the work they do and greater support from their bosses/leaders. The latter were expected to show empathy, and to prize and promote worker wellbeing.

Ongoing employee training is a further essential ingredient for retaining good employees, as well as promoting optimal employee performance. Unlike the previous section's discussion of the absence of reliable evidence linking incentive pay with employee performance, Guzzo *et al.* (1985) report that training and goal-setting programmes have far more influence on worker productivity than pay-for-performance plans. When devising employee training and development programmes, it is important that these programmes:

- Are strategy-driven
- Are adequately resourced, both in terms of financial resources and time resources (i.e., employees are provided time off from work to complete the training)
- Employ the most appropriate delivery method, whether this is a classroom lecture, e-learning, simulation, case study, role plays, etc.
- Are rigorously evaluated to assess the short- and long-term benefits achieved.

Discovery Health, a South African health insurer, operates a training programme called "The Discovery Person," which is intended to support the organization's strategy by growing employees who are optimistic, entrepreneurial, results-driven, intelligent, honest, and humble. Kyocera's ongoing training includes daily group-based meetings, which often include reading excerpts from the company founder's book on being successful in business, to showcase and reinforce the toughness and hunger it expects its employees to display. Meanwhile, at Adobe, employees are supported with access to learning funds that offer up to $10,000 per year for an employee's study of certain degrees and certificates (Adobe, n.d.).

In addition to ensuring an organization attracts employees with the right knowledge, right skills, and right attitudes, and then invests in these employees' ongoing training and development, organizations must also ensure the right organizational culture prevails. Although human resource systems certainly have a role to play in making this happen, organizational culture is impacted by a myriad of internal and external organizational elements. For example, such factors as the leadership styles of an organization's senior managers, the professional orientations of the employees, and the societal norms that comprise an organization's environment all serve to shape an organization's culture. The next chapter discusses what defines an organization's culture and how senior managers can shape their organizations' cultures to encourage employee motivation and commitment to implementing their respective organizations' strategies.

Review Question 11.13: Describe how organizations use human resource management systems to attract, train, and retain employees.

Answer: Please see the Answer section starting on page 283

CONCLUSION

This chapter discussed how an organization uses operating systems, processes, and procedures to influence employees' implementation of the organization's strategy. This particular lever of control relies on formalized approaches to directing and encouraging specific types of employee behaviour. Three main organizational systems (and the processes and procedures embedded in these systems) were discussed. Performance measurement systems are the most popular type of organizational system, with budgets representing the classic and ever-enduring method to motivate and focus employee attention. In addition to discussing other types of financial, non-financial, and hybrid performance measurement systems, this chapter discussed the role employee incentive systems and human resource systems play as part of an organization's overall performance management system.

It is important to note that just because an organization can measure some elements of input, process, or output does not mean that it necessarily should be doing so. Two examples of the dysfunctional employee behaviour that can occur if an organization's performance measures are not fit-for-purpose were provided. Unfortunately, there is a growing trend in such industries as healthcare and education to track and continuously monitor performance. Governments, which are often the main benefactors of these two industries, are rightfully concerned about ensuring they are receiving good value for the investments they are making. Using simplistic measurements of performance, however, and this often occurs because no other measures exist, will not prove helpful. In education, for example, the desired outcome is not simply to graduate students but to graduate engaged citizens who can effectively contribute to their country's economy and wider set of societal institutions. Accordingly, concentrating on graduation rates alone is a foolhardy measure. Government employees, who have oversight for their respective countries' education sectors, must either show the needed patience to await multi-year longitudinal performance data or be willing to rely upon other, more informal and subjective forms of control. Ensuring that the right organizational culture exists in these harder-to-measure industries is one highly useful measure of control, which is the topic of the next chapter.

REFERENCES

Adobe. (n.d.) Education reimbursement, Retrieved from https://benefits.adobe.com/us/employee-discounts-and-perks/learning-fund/education-reimbursement on 3 March 2022.

Anthony, R. (1956) *Management Accounting: Text and Cases*, Homewood, IL: Irwin.

Ariely, D. (2016) *Payoff: The Hidden Logic That Shapes Our Motivations*, New York: TED/Simon & Schuster.

Auckland University of Technology. (2021) Wellbeing@Work, Retrieved from https://www.stuff.co.nz/business/126696547/great-resignation-coming-to-nz-more-people-ponder-quitting-their-job on 3 March 2022.

Banker, R.D., Lee, S.Y., Potter, G. and Srinivasan, D. (2001) An empirical analysis of continuing improvements following the implementation of a performance-based compensation plan, *Journal of Accounting and Economics*, Vol. 30, No. 3, pp. 315–350.

Becker, B.E. and Gerhart, B. (1996) The impact of human resource management on organizational performance: progress and prospects, *Academy of Management Journal*, Vol. 39, No. 4, pp. 779–801.

Bonner, S.E., Hastie, R., Sprinkle, G.B. and Young, S.M. (2000) A review of the effects of financial incentives on performance in laboratory tasks: implications for management accounting, *Journal of Management Accounting Research*, Vol. 12, No. 1, pp. 19–57.

Bowles, S. and Polanía-Reyes, S. (2012) Economic incentives and social preferences: substitutes or complements? *Journal of Economic Literature*, Vol. 50, No 2, pp. 368–425.

Brignall, T., Fitzgerald, L. Johnston, R. and Silvestro, R. (1991) Performance measurement in service businesses, *Management Accounting*, Vol. 69, No. 10, pp. 34–36.

Bryant, A. (1998) Duffers need not apply, *New York Times*, 31 May 1998.

Cardy, R., Dobbins, G. and Carson, K. (1995) TQM and improving performance appraisal research: theory and practice, *Revue Canadienne des Sciences de l'Administration*, Vol. 12, No. 2, pp. 106–115.

CECP, Imperative, and PWC. (2018) Making work more meaningful, Retrieved from https://d0cb2f2608c10c70e72a-fc7154704217aa017aa46150bf00c30c.ssl.cf5.rackcdn.com/pwc-building-a-fulfilling-employee-experience.pdf on 5 March 2022.

Cerasoli, C.P., Nicklin, J.M. and Ford, M.T. (2014) Intrinsic motivation and extrinsic incentives jointly predict performance: a 40-year meta-analysis, *Psychological Bulletin*, Vol. 140, No. 4, pp. 980–1008.

Chan, Y.C. and Lynn, B.E. (1991) Performance evaluation and the analytic hierarchy process, *Journal of Management Research*, Vol. 3, pp. 57–87.

Cheng, M.M., Luckett, P.F. and Mahama, H. (2007) Effect of perceived conflict among multiple performance goals and goal difficulty on task performance, *Accounting and Finance*, Vol. 47, No. 2, pp. 221–242.

Cross, K. and Lynch, R. (1990) Tailoring performance measures to suit your business, *Journal of Accounting and EDP*, Vol. 6, No. 1, pp. 17–25.

Deci, E.L., Connell, J.P. and Ryan, R.M. (1989) Self-determination in a work organization, *Journal of Applied Psychology*, Vol. 74, No. 4, pp. 580–590.

Deci, E.L. and Ryan, R.M. (2000) The "what" and "why" of goal pursuits: human needs and the self-determination of behaviour, *Psychological Inquiry*, Vol. 11, pp. 227–268.

Deci, E.L., Ryan, R.M. and Koestner, R. (1999) A meta-analytic review of experiments examining the effects of extrinsic rewards on intrinsic motivation, *Psychological Bulletin*, Vol. 125, No. 6, pp. 627–668.

Delery, J.E. (1998) Issues of fit in strategic human resource management: implications for research, *Human Resource Management Review*, Vol. 8, No. 3, pp. 289–309.

Dohmen, T. and Falk, A. (2011) Performance pay and multidimensional sorting: productivity, preferences, and gender, *American Economic Review*, Vol. 101, No. 2, pp. 556–590.

Drucker, P.F. (1995) The information executives truly need, *Harvard Business Review*, Vol. 73, No. 1, pp. 54–62.

Economic Policy Institute. (2021) Retrieved form https://web.archive.org/web/20211112142251/https://www.epi.org/indicators/jolts/# on 3 March 2022.

Francis, T. (2016) Best-paid CEOs run some of worst-performing companies, *The Wall Street Journal*, Retrieved from https://www.wsj.com/articles/best-paid-ceos-run-some-of-worst-performing-companies-1469419262 on 5 December 2021.

Franco-Santos, M., Kennerley, M., Micheli, P., Martinez, V., Mason, S., Marr, B., Gray, D. and Neely, A. (2007) Towards a definition of a business performance measurement system, *International Journal of Operations & Production Management*, Vol. 27, pp. 784–801.

Franco-Santos, M., Lucianetti, L. and Bourne, M. (2012). Contemporary performance measurement systems: a review of their consequences and a framework for research, *Management Accounting Research*, Vol. 23, pp. 79–119.

Frey, B.S. (1993) Motivation as a limit to pricing, *Journal of Economic Psychology*, Vol. 14, No, 4, pp. 635–664.

Frey, B.S. and Jegen, R. (1999) Motivation crowding theory: a survey of empirical evidence, *Institute for Empirical Research in Economics, University of Zurich Working Paper Series*, ISSN 1424–0459.

Frey, B.S. and Jegen, R. (2001) Motivation crowding theory, *Journal of Economic Surveys*, Vol. 15, No, 5, pp. 589–611.

Ghoshal, S. (2005) Bad management theories are destroying good management practices, *Academy of Management Learning & Education*, Vol. 4, No. 1, pp. 75–91.

Guzzo, R.A., Jette, R.D. and Katzell, R.A. (1985) The effects of psychological based intervention programs on worker productivity: a meta-analysis, *Personnel Psychology*, Vol. 38, No. 2, pp. 275–291.

Hall, M. (2008) The effect of comprehensive performance measurement systems on role clarity, psychological empowerment and managerial performance, *Accounting Organizations and Society*, Vol. 33, No. 2–3, pp. 141–163.

Hall, R.W., Johnson, H.T. and Turley, P.B. (1991) *Measuring Up: Changing Pathways to Manufacturing Excellence*, Homewood, IL: Business One Irwin.

Herzberg, F. (2003) One more time: how do you motivate employees?, *Harvard Business Review*, Vol. 81, No. 1, pp. 87–96. Reprinted from 1968.

Hiromoto, T. (1991) Another hidden edge – Japanese management accounting, *Harvard Business Review*, Vol. 66, No. 4, pp. 22–26.

Hopwood, A.G. (1974) *Accounting and Human Behaviour*, London: Prentice Hall.

Ittner, C.D., Larcker, D.F. and Randall, T. (2003) Performance implications of strategic performance measurement in financial service firms, *Accounting, Organizations and Society*, Vol. 28, No. 7–8, pp. 715–741.

Jenkins, G.D.J., Mitra, A., Gupta, N. and Shaw, J. (1998) Are financial incentives related to performance? A meta-analytic review of empirical research, *Journal of Applied Psychology*, Vol. 83, No. 5, pp. 777–787.

Kaplan, R.S. and McMillan, D. (2020) Updating the balanced scorecard for triple bottom line strategies, Harvard Business School Accounting & Management Unit Working Paper No. 21-028.

Kaplan, R. and Norton, D. (1993) Putting the balanced scorecard to work, *Harvard Business Review*, Vol. 70, No. 5, pp. 134–142.

Kaplan, R. and Norton, D. (1996) *Translating Strategy into Action: The Balanced Scorecard*, Boston, MA: Harvard Business School Press.

Kohn, A. (1993) Why incentive plans cannot work, *Harvard Business Review*, Vol. 71, No. 6, pp. 54–63.

Kuvaas, B., Buch, R., Gagné, M., Dysvik, A. and Forest, J. (2016) Do you get what you pay for? Sales incentives and implications for motivation and changes in turnover intention and work effort, *Motivation and Emotion*, Vol. 40, No. 5, pp. 667–680.

Kuvaas, B., Buch, R., Weibel, A., Dysvik, A. and Nerstad, C. (2017) Do intrinsic and extrinsic motivation relate differently to employee outcomes?, *Journal of Economic Psychology*, Vol. 61, pp. 244–258.

Latham, G.P. and Baldes, J.L. (1975) The practical significance of Locke's theory of goal setting, *Journal of Applied Psychology*, Vol. 60, No. 1, pp. 122–124.

Leggatt, J. (2021) Retrieved from https://www.acuitymag.com/business/how-to-build-a-high-performance-team on 16 February 2022.

Malmi, T. and Brown, D.A. (2008) Management control systems as a package – opportunities, challenges and research directions, *Management Accounting Research*, Vol. 19, No. 4, pp. 287–300.

Marcec, D. (2018) CEO tenure rates, *Harvard Law School Forum on Corporate Governance*, Retrieved from https://corpgov.law.harvard.edu/2018/02/12/ceo-tenure-rates/ on 20 February 2022.

McCord, P. (2014) How Netflix reinvented HR, Retrieved from https://hbr.org/2014/01/how-netflix-reinvented-hr on 3 March 2022.

Merchant, K.A. and Manzoni, J. (1989) The achievability of budget targets in profit centres: a field study, *The Accounting Review*, Vol. 64, No. 3, pp. 539–558.

Merchant, K. and Van der Stede, W. (2007) *Management Control Systems: Performance Measurement, Evaluation and Incentives* (2nd Edition), Harlow: Prentice Hall.

Pink, D.H. (2011) *Drive: The Surprising Truth about What Motivates Us*, New York: Penguin.

PwC. (2021) What workers want: winning the war for talent, Retrieved from https://www.pwc.com.au/important-problems/future-of-work/what-workers-want-report.pdf on 3 March 2022.

Román, F.J. (2009) Analysis of changes to a team-based incentive plan and its effects on productivity, product quality and absenteeism, *Accounting, Organizations and Society*, Vol. 34, No. 5, pp. 589–618.

Rosen, C., Case, J. and Staubus, M. (2005) *Equity: Why Employee Ownership Is Good for Business*, Boston, MA: Harvard Business School Press.

Sheedy, E. and Zhang, L. (2017) *Are Profit-Based Incentives Compatible with a Risk Culture?* Sydney: FINSIA.

Shields, M.D. and Waller, W.S. (1988) A behavioral study of accounting variables in performance-incentive contracts, *Accounting, Organizations and Society*, Vol. 13, No. 6, pp. 581–594.

Soyer, E. and Hogarth, R.M. (2015) Fooled by experience, *Harvard Business Review*, Vol. 93, No. 5, pp. 73–77.

Stewart, T.A. (1994) Your company's most valuable assets: intellectual capital, *Fortune*, Vol. 130, 10 October, pp. 2–10.

Stringer, C. and Shantapriyan, P. (2012) *Setting Performance Targets*, New York: Business Expert Press.

The 2016 Deloitte Millennial Survey: Winning over the Next Generation of Leaders. Retrieved from https://www2.deloitte.com/content/dam/Deloitte/global/Documents/About-Deloitte/gx-millenial-survey-2016-exec-summary.pdf on 10 December 2021.

Thoreau, H.D. (1854) *Walden; or, Life in the Woods*, Boston, MA: Ticknor and Fields.

CHAPTER 12

Organizational culture

CHAPTER OBJECTIVES

- Define organizational culture.
- Identify and describe the six dimensions of organizational culture.
- Discuss the process an organization's senior managers undertake to identify poor alignment between the organization's culture and the organizational strategy being pursued.
- Discuss the two main ways senior managers can create change in organizational culture.

INTRODUCTION

This chapter discusses organizational culture and its role as one of the three main levers of performance management. As noted in Chapter 11, the study and practice of performance management have typically focused on the operation of performance measurement systems. The use of organizational culture as a lever of performance management has been much less studied and practised (Malmi and Brown, 2008). Such an underuse of organizational culture is unfortunate, for it misses an important opportunity for influencing employee behaviour and supporting organizational success. As an example, Deloitte's 2016 Global Human Capital Trends (n.d.), which surveyed 7,000 business and human resource leaders in more than 130 countries, shows that 86% of respondents believe corporate culture is important or very important to business success, and 82% of respondents believe that culture is a potential competitive advantage.

The present chapter begins by defining organizational culture. It next identifies and discusses the six dimensions of organizational culture. The discussion draws on various organizational examples to illustrate the six dimensions. Based on these developed understandings, this chapter proceeds to discuss how senior managers can create organizational cultures that encourage employees to implement their respective organizations' strategies.

DOI: 10.4324/9781003267195-15

WHAT IS ORGANIZATIONAL CULTURE?

Despite the fact that organizational culture is intangible, to the attentive person its existence is unquestionable. If you have worked at an organization, you will have felt its presence. Think back to one of these work experiences and try to attach descriptors to how your fellow work-mates behaved or what McKinsey and Company refer to as "how people do things around here." Would you, for example, describe your work colleagues as hardworking or lazy? Did you find them friendly or exclusive? Were they entrepreneurial or creatures of habit? Did they come across as unassuming or elitist? While far from exhaustive, these descriptors help to define an organization's culture; which in turn influences, for better or worse, how people behave. This behaviour determines the overall mood of the organization and is responsible for establishing whether a worker is accepted or shunned, whether teams will feature harmony or disharmony, and ultimately whether the individual and collective behaviour of an organization's members will support or detract from the implementation of the organization's strategy.

Organizational cultures are invariably idiosyncratic. Furthermore, they take time to develop and are slow, and even resistant, to change. These characteristics help to explain why the merger of two companies can be so fraught with uncertainty both before the combination (i.e., when project-ing the anticipated synergies) and after the amalgamation (i.e., when trying to realize the planned synergies). A merger will be especially problematic when one of the combining organizations fea-tures a culture marked by secrecy and elitism. Without the level of sharing and transparency that is generally needed to support a merger's success, the likelihood of a successful outcome is reduced.

Schein (2004, 2017) refers to culture as the pattern of shared, basic assumptions of how people are to behave in the organization. Organizational culture, at least implicitly, specifies the roles, norms, and values inherent in an organization. According to Camerer and Vepsalainen (1988: 115), organizational cultures form when organizational members agree to be governed by a specific "set of broad, tacitly understood rules." These rules become the organization's guiding principles. They determine which behaviours are deemed acceptable. Should members exhibit unacceptable behaviour, they will be pressured to conform or, assuming they refuse to conform, will be ostracized or exiled.

Norms and expectations of behaviour are often influenced by organizational policies, pro-cedures, and even prevailing reward systems. When employees observe who gets rewarded/punished, powerful signals about the organization are revealed. An organization's leaders, by virtue of being the overseers of employee reward systems, will play a pivotal role in shaping organizational strategy. In addition, organizational leaders' behaviour will significantly shape an organization's culture. Employees observe the actions of their leaders and come to associate the organization's values with what these leaders do (Willmott, 1993). Leaders who "walk the talk" will find their employees have reinforced conceptions of what is expected. However, when leaders act inconsistently with what they preach, employees will interpret the leaders' actions as the more important cue for what is expected and accepted (Willmott, 2003).

According to Camerer and Vepsalainen (1988), effective cultures require both appropriate-ness and consistency. Appropriateness means the culture is well aligned to the strategic needs of the organization. Consistency involves an organization's managers and employees being in agreement about the unwritten rules that define the organization's culture. The benefits a healthy and conducive organizational culture can provide an organization are manifold. They include more committed employees, longer-serving employees, and more productive employees. Jon Katzenbach, the founder of The Katzenbach Center at Strategy&, PwC's strategy consulting business, refers to organizational culture as:

> … a source of positive emotional energy that you can't get anywhere else. When an organization is at its best, the culture will energize people, and they will feel good about what they are doing to advance the strategic and operating goals of the company.
>
> (CECP, Imperative, and PWC, 2018: 11)

Organizational culture can exist at the macro/organizational level as well as at the micro/subgroup level. The latter might be a division, department, or work team. At the macro level, certain institution-wide tacit beliefs and rules will operate. These beliefs and rules influence behaviour. It is also the case that the unique cultures that operate in subparts of the organization will exert a further influence on employee behaviour. For some employees, especially those who are part of tightly-knit work groups that feature member stability and a sense of separateness (perhaps due to functional specialization and/or geographical location), the employees' work groups and their cultures strongly govern employee behaviour.

A good example of the operation of micro-level cultures comes from the Broadway play *A Few Good Men*. In this play, the accused US Marine recites his order of personal identification and accountability as "unit, corps, country, God." In other words, the implicit set of rules that the Marine felt most governed his behaviour, and thus the reason for his unwillingness to divulge information about the investigated murder, was his Marine unit. And this Marine unit's culture, which demanded in the circumstances that he remains silent, took precedence over the Marine Corps' obligation to investigate the murder, the victim's family's desire to discover the truth, and his Christian upbringing. It is essential that senior managers understand that these micro-level organizational cultures can exist; for, without this understanding, they will not be able to shape or leverage their organization's culture for the purpose of encouraging the type of employee behaviour they desire.

The influence and management of organizational culture are thought to occur in a variety of ways. Critical or novel incidents can set precedents that serve to define an organization's culture (Adler and Hiromoto, 2012). These incidents may include the embedding of the personality of an organization's founder into the organizational culture (Akroyd and Kober, 2020; Collier, 2005; Giovannoni *et al.*, 2011; Koiranen, 2003). Strong or charismatic leadership may also guide culture (Camerer and Vepsalainen, 1988). Finally, employment policies and practices that feature strong socialization practices and/or selection strategies that emphasize person-culture fit can further shape organizational culture (Guest, 1994; O'Reilly *et al.*, 1991). In the remainder of this chapter, we look at the six dimensions of organizational culture and how senior managers can shape and subsequently leverage these dimensions as part of the total performance management package these managers are responsible for overseeing. The six dimensions of organizational culture are:

- Shared beliefs
- Shared values
- Shared experiences

- Symbols
- Exemplars
- Power structures.

Table 12.1 is used to connect these dimensions of organizational culture with actual organizational practice and helps guide the ensuing discussion. *The Wolf on Wall Street*, which is one of the three organizations referred to in Table 12.1, is a major film based on Jordan Belfort's founding and operation of the brokerage house Stratton Oakmon, Inc. Enron, the second organization featured in Table 12.1, was the American energy, commodities, and services company that spectacularly failed and went into bankruptcy in 2001. The final organization is Kyocera, the Japanese conglomerate that has been referred to in previous chapters.

Shared beliefs

For any given organization, employees will possess shared beliefs about the purpose of the organization and the collective role they are meant to play in realizing this purpose. Employees at one organization might view their organization's purpose and their employee role as serving others. These "others" might be shareholders, customers, or benefactors. In contrast, another

TABLE 12.1 Portrayals of three different organizational cultures

Culture characteristic	The Wolf on Wall Street	Enron	Kyocera
Shared beliefs	Money is the scorecard of life	Screw or be screwed	Act as the customer's servant Contribute to the advancement of society and mankind
Shared values	Unbridled greed Vanity Misogyny	Macho Risk-taking Competitive	Long hours Respect Humility
Shared experiences	Drug-fuelled parties	Daredevil expeditions	Reading Dr Inamori's books on management
Symbols	Expensive cars Big yachts Lavish parties	Corporate jets Ferraris Strip clubs	Open-plan work areas
Exemplars	Leonardo DiCaprio	Jeff Skilling, the company's CEO	Dr Inamori, founding CEO
Power structures	You eat what you kill	Rank and yank	Employee ability and perceived competence

Review Question 12.1: What is organizational culture?
Answer: Please see the Answer section starting on page 283
Review Question 12.2: What six dimensions comprise organizational culture?
Answer: Please see the Answer section starting on page 283

organization's employees might view their organization's purpose and their employee role as a vehicle for maximizing their individual self-interests. Such an organization would be described as displaying highly egocentric behaviour. Although this behaviour is highly dysfunctional and undermines an organization's long-term success, it is endemic in some undeveloped countries' governmental offices and agencies (e.g., police departments, customs departments) and has been observed among what were once considered some of the most venerable firms (e.g., Waste Management, Enron, Parmalat, and Worldcom).

As shown in Table 12.1, Kyocera's set of shared beliefs comprise employees viewing their role as being their customers' servants. Customers, incidentally, are defined as anyone, whether internal or external to the organization, who is provided with a good or service by a Kyocera employee. Moreover, far from being seen as a means to an end (e.g., treating customers well to create loyal and more profitable customers), Kyocera employees forge these excellent employee-customer relationships as an end in itself. Kyocera's mission statement is, after all, to "contribute to the advancement of society and mankind."

Unlike Kyocera, the shared beliefs displayed in *The Wolf on Wall Street* and Enron were highly self-centred. The former's shared beliefs could be summed up as "Money is the scorecard of life," while the latter's would be "Screw or be screwed." At both Enron and the Wall Street firm, employees subscribed to the idea that the end justifies the means. They also felt that monetary incentives and rewards serve as the best motivators of workers. In many ways, the underlying gestalt at these two companies was the belief that money is everything.

Shared values

Organizational culture is also defined by the values its employees share. When defining these values, it is often the case that adjectives can be used. For example, Ahmad (2010) describes AirAsia's shared values as innovation, openness, youthfulness, an audacious sense of fun, and a never-say-die attitude. Founded as an innovator and disruptor of the Southeast-Asia market by Tony Fernandes, it seems quite logical and helpful for the airline's employees to share the founder's values of innovation and disruption. For other organizations, especially ones that are pursuing a cost leadership strategy, sharing such values as conservativeness, cost consciousness, and frugality would seem appropriate.

At Kyocera, which pursues a confrontation strategy, its shared values include long hours, respect, and humility. The first value of long employee working hours would certainly appear to support its strategy. Although it would also seem that its strategy would require emphasis on innovation, this value is implicit in its values of respect and humility. In particular, being a respectful and humble servant of the company's customers includes being attentive to and anticipating their needs.

The most defining shared value at both the Wall Street firm and Enron was ultra-materialism. A poignant anecdote from each firm serves to capture their respective greed. At the Wall Street firm, it was the employee who brought a house plant to personalize his work cubicle on the same day the firm was managing its first initial public offering (IPO) on behalf of a client. The employee was ridiculed and immediately fired for his whimsical sentimentalism. There was money to be made, and his supervisors were offended that anything should interfere with their quest for wealth. The plant creates the perfect foil for the firm's quintessential employee. The former is an oxygen-producer, life-enabler and the latter is an oxygen-sapping, business parasite.

Likewise, at Enron, one of its former employees stated in an interview, "If I'm going to my boss's office to talk about compensation, and if I step on some guy's throat and that doubles it, then I'll stomp on that guy's throat."

In addition to its ultra-materialism, the Wall Street firm was further characterized by its unbridled selfishness, vanity, and misogyny. Its employees would stop at nothing in their pursuit of money. Far from believing they had any ethical responsibility relating to how they made their money, the employees felt they were inherently deserving of the money. This culture of greed and entitlement, which operated in a predominantly male work environment, helped fuel a misogynistic orientation.

Complementing Enron's ultra-materialism were the shared values of risk-taking, machoism, and hyper inter-employee competition. Each year employees were ranked against one another, and the bottom 20% were automatically fired. This performance evaluation system promoted a high-risk, dog-eat-dog environment. The top performers were respected and unquestioningly obeyed, while the poorer performers were mocked and bullied.

Shared experiences

The shared experiences of employees further help to determine an organization's culture. These shared experiences can come in several forms. Being part of an organization's start-up and the struggles that are usually associated with these experiences can serve as a particularly formative shared experience. So too can being part of an organization's successful emergence from a bankruptcy. Shared experiences can also occur through social, after-work-hours events like company sports teams and parties.

At Kyocera, a significant shared experience is employees' reading of Dr Inamori's books on management. Dr Inamori was the founder of the company. Prior to his role as the company's CEO, he was a recent university graduate and an engineer at Shofu Inc., a ceramics manufacturer that now specializes in dental products. Being inexperienced and with no one to mentor him, he had to figure out his Kyocera CEO role on his own. He quickly decided that his success depended on empowering and turning those around him into valued business partners. Dr Inamori felt that by working together he and his "business partners" could share their business experiences and help one another to become more effective leaders. Towards this end, Dr Inamori wrote a series of books on management for his colleagues to read. At today's Kyocera, employees at all levels read Dr Inamori's books. Often, a work team's daily morning meeting includes reading a page from one of these books. With titles like *Respect the Divine and Love People* (1999) and *A Passion for Success* (2007), these shared reading experiences serve to support the company's values of hard work, respect, and humility.

The shared experiences of the Wall Street firm primarily revolved around drug-fuelled parties. Nothing was out of bounds at these parties. Everything was seen as having its price, and money was seen as no obstacle to ensuring whatever was wanted could be purchased.

At Enron, there were legendary tales of daredevil expeditions to the Australian outback, the glaciers of Patagonia, and a 1,200-mile dirt-bike race through Baja, Mexico. These senior management bonding experiences were so extreme that the managers often returned not simply a little bruised and tired, but with lacerations and broken bones. Ken Rice, the chief executive of Enron's High-Speed Internet Unit, believed Enron's CEO Jeff Skilling's goal was to find an adventure "where someone could actually get killed." Photo albums of these out-of-control adventures were disseminated throughout the company, allowing all of Enron's employees to at a minimum vicariously share the experiences that served to support the company's values of risk-taking, machoism, and hyper inter-employee competition.

Symbols

Symbols are physical manifestations that communicate meaning. Students, for example, will be very familiar with the grading symbols used to evaluate their work. An "A+" and an "F," as two examples, have significant meanings, even though both are really nothing more than a series of lines arranged in a particular manner. Nevertheless, an A+ has come to represent much more than five lines. Instead, it stands for academic performance and achievement at the highest level. Furthermore, its appearance on a piece of academic work – whether it is that of a school-aged child or university student – is highly likely to produce a smile and elicit great pride.

The most prominent organizational symbols usually comprise company logos, the look of a company's headquarters (e.g., a tall skyscraper or a modest building adjoining a factory), and the dress code it has. Each of these symbols is intertwined with and helps constitute an organization's culture. The informal dress codes of Silicon Valley firms and the formal dress codes of London banks reinforce the values held by these two very different sets of business organizations. The former holds the values of innovation and uniqueness, whereas the latter represents values of trustworthiness and discretion. Of course, these symbols may be more fancied than real. Some banks may wish to project an image of being trustworthy, even though they are charlatans. These occurrences of inauthenticity retain their claim as potent organizational symbols, but they do so because they are sham symbols.

Arthur Andersen, the former "Big Five" international accounting firm, had a set of oak doors at each of its offices. The oak was a symbol of its unbending service to the needs and interests of the public. This commitment to the public included exhibiting high integrity and moral judgement. This author still remembers, when being recruited to join Arthur Andersen's Minneapolis, Minnesota office, having lunch with two junior Arthur Andersen accountants who waxed lyrical about the firm's oak doors and the meaning they conveyed.

The author can also remember audit assignments at General Mills and Cargill, Inc. The former is a Fortune 500 company. Its employees were impeccably tailored and groomed. The latter company is a private company. Its annual revenue of US$ 120 billion and 153,000 employees is significantly larger than General Mills' annual revenue of US$ 16 billion and 39,000 employees. In contrast with General Mills' employees, the average Cargill, Inc. employee wore un-ironed shirts and didn't sport nearly the same amount of hair gel and make-up. This simple matter of dress and grooming spoke volumes about the company's unassuming ways and concentrated focus on getting jobs done.

As Table 12.1 shows, the defining symbols at the Wall Street firm were expensive cars, big yachts, and lavish parties. Enron's symbols were corporate jets, Ferraris, and strip clubs. In contrast to the Wall Street firm and Enron's bacchanalia, a telling symbol at Kyocera is its open-plan work designs. All employees work in a common, shared area. No one, and this includes the company's president, has their own private office. These open-plan designs help to support and reinforce the company's values of hard work (for it can easily be seen if someone is working) and humility (no one is more privileged than another).

Exemplars

Exemplars comprise who and what the company chooses to immortalize. An organization's exemplars identify its values and help convey what is perceived as superior behaviour. Founding members often comprise an organization's exemplars. This is certainly the case at Kyocera. In particular, the rags-to-riches story of the company's founder, Dr Inamori, is known by all employees. Kyocera's employees exhibit the same respect, awe, and admiration for their company's founder as music fans do for their favourite pop musician. Employees at Kyocera can tell endless stories about Dr Inamori's business acumen, work ethic, and generosity.

The exemplar at the Wall Street firm was Jordan Belfort, the antihero played by Leonardo DiCaprio. Belfort epitomized his firm's unquenchable thirst for wealth. He was dismissive of anything that did not contribute to his accumulation of greater wealth.

Jeff Skilling was Enron's exemplar. He exemplified Enron's arrogance. It is reported that during his interview at Harvard Business School he was asked if he was smart. His reply was, "I'm fucking smart." His answer shows how superior he considered himself to others; and it was this belief that helps explain how he and others at Enron were so certain that they deserved whatever they could take.

Power structures

As described in Chapter 10, all organizations exhibit different concentrations of power. In some organizations, one or two key senior executives are all powerful. In other organizations, a whole group of executives or even a whole department (e.g., the marketing departments at Nike and Budweiser) wields the main power. Remember, power is based on who in the organization has the greatest amount of influence on the organization's strategic decisions and direction.

At Kyocera, power is shared broadly and deeply in the organization. Dr Inamori's goal to create business partners meant that he was willing to share power. This sharing of power extended well beyond his immediate group of senior executives and included the team leaders who oversaw their respective groups' production activities, housekeeping activities, etc. Dr Inamori always thought of the amoebas, the base work units, and the leaders who manage these units as akin to mobile food carts and their owners. He wanted his amoeba leaders and their teams of employees to exhibit the same agility that a food stall seller experiences when making decisions about location, menu/product offerings, and pricing.

At the Wall Street firm, power was held by whoever brought in the largest amount of money in the current period. Past performance was irrelevant. Either you earned your keep and had sufficient influence to be retained or you were thrown out. Accordingly, an employee who was powerful one day could be on the scrap heap the next day.

Enron's power was also a function of who was making the company money. Perhaps due to its large size, Enron formalized its power structure by rating all its employees every six months. Employees were rated from 1 (best) to 5 (worst). The ratings were almost exclusively based on how much money a worker made for the company. To reinforce its competitive, cutthroat environment, the company specified a particular distribution of ratings. The top 5% were designated "superior" and the bottom 15% were labelled "needs improvement." In between these two ends of the distribution were the categories "excellent" (30% of employees), "strong"

(30% of employees), and "satisfactory" (20% of employees). Anyone who remained rated as needing improvement in the succeeding half-yearly evaluation was summarily fired. This system of ranking and yanking, something *Time* magazine likened to "cull[ing] employees as if they were head of cattle," placed power with those employees rated as "1"s. These employees received the designation of "superior" and exercised their "superiority" for self-aggrandizement at every opportunity (Greenwald *et al.*, 2001: 38).

DETECTING MISALIGNED ORGANIZATIONAL CULTURES

When viewing Table 12.1, it is clear that Kyocera's organizational culture is markedly different from the other two firms. From a performance management perspective, the interesting point about the variation seen in the three organizational cultures has less to do with the actual differences than how their respective organizational cultures link together with the other two main levers of performance management (i.e., an organization's structure and its organizational systems, processes, and procedures) to support and promote employees' implementation of the organization's strategy. At Kyocera, the three performance management levers fit well with each other to support the company's confrontation strategy. In particular, the company's organizational culture (as shown in Table 12.1) complements its use of:

- An organizational structure that is highly decentralized.
- A simple performance measurement system – what the company refers to as "hourly efficiency" – that is easily understood and therefore capable of supporting its high employee empowerment, management-by-all philosophy.
- An employee incentive system that is based on the company's overall performance, which thereby promotes the coordinated integration of its more than 3,000 amoebas (work groups).
- Human resource practices that enable a high-performing work culture, both in terms of the close attention paid to attracting and recruiting the right type of employee and the ongoing training and development offered to employees.

In contrast to Kyocera, the organizational cultures of the Wall Street firm and Enron, while seemingly well suited to their respective organizational structures, performance measurement systems, and employee incentive systems, could never have supported anything other than an organizational strategy premised on short-term profit maximization and short organizational life. These latter two firms' organizational cultures were simply too toxic to support long-term sustainability. As the sidebar describes, Uber, the transportation network company, hit the news in early 2017 for all the wrong reasons when a story appeared in the *Financial Times* reporting a growing problem with its own toxic organizational culture.

Although organizational cultures can be difficult to objectively assess and define, they are certainly amenable to subjective measurement and understanding. In addition to being able to measure and understand organizational culture, it is also true that an organization's employees – and especially its senior managers – can influence the culture.

The detection of misaligned organizational cultures involves measuring what currently exists and comparing this with an ideal state. When an organization's senior managers detect

Consider this ...

Susan Fowler, a former site reliability engineer at Uber, published an entry on her personal blog in February 2017 called "Reflecting on one very, very strange year at Uber." In her blog, she describes alleged incidents of sexual harassment by her superiors. She further describes how Uber's human resource department refused to discipline a manager who propositioned her on her first day of work. The human resource department claimed this was the manager's first complaint against him and no formal disciplinary action would be taken. Fowler was told she had two choices: she could accept a transfer to another part of the company or she could remain in her current role with the understanding that this decision could lead to unfavourable performance reviews from her superior. Fowler elected to leave Uber and has since learned that other female Uber employees experienced similar forms of sexual harassment that preceded Fowler's complaint and were reported to Uber's human resource department. Since some of the complaints involved the same manager who sexually harassed Fowler on her first day of work, the representations made by the human resource department to Fowler appear untrue. In response to Fowler's blog, early Uber investors Mitch and Freada Kapor reported that that they had tried in vain for years to change Uber's "destructive culture."

gaps between their organization's current and ideal states, they will want to effect organizational culture change. This change can be achieved in two main ways. The first is a function of an organization's leadership, and the second involves how an organization operates its human resource systems. More will be said about each of these forms of influence later in the chapter.

The measurement of an organization's organizational culture involves what is called an organizational culture audit. When undertaking such an audit, the assessor will pose a series of questions related to each of the six dimensions of organizational culture discussed above. Each of these six dimensions and the questions associated with each are now separately discussed.

Shared beliefs

Different organizations strive to fulfil different purposes. The purpose of a car manufacturer, for example, is quite different from the purpose of a real estate developer. As a result, the shared belief among Google employees that you can be serious without the need to wear a suit and that being formal does not equate to being productive may not be as applicable to a major bank like JPMorgan Chase & Co. Furthermore, even for organizations operating in the same industry, their different strategies will invariably demand different purposes. H&R Block, the US tax-preparation company with operations in North America, Australia, Brazil, and India, states its purpose as being "the leading global consumer tax company bringing tax and related solutions to clients year-round." This purpose would differ from a small, regionally-focused tax firm's purpose. Unlike H&R Block's cost leader approach, small tax practitioners would typically seek to provide personalized tax return preparation and advice to a particular set of geographically-targeted customers. Based on these different strategies and purposes, we can expect to find different shared beliefs operating at different organizations. Answers to the list of questions below will help identify what an organization's shared beliefs are:

- Does the organization have a mission statement?
- Do the employees believe in its purpose?
- How does the organization define success?
- What issues do employees pay most attention to in the long run? For example, is it sales, market share, company growth, cutting costs, innovation, employee turnover, etc.?
- What issues do employees pay most attention to in the short run? For example, is it sales, market share, company growth, cutting costs, innovation, employee turnover, etc.?
- When faced with a new problem, what rules, processes, and procedures do employees use to solve it?
- What core beliefs do these rules, processes, and procedures reveal?

Shared values

An organization's shared values are connected to its shared beliefs. Beliefs, for example, about what an organization sees as important in the short and long run and how its employees should approach new problems will inevitably help shape and be shaped by the organization's shared values. At Google, shared values revolve around being actively involved, working with great people, and earning customer trust every day (Li, 2020). The following list of questions can be used to gain insight into an organization's shared values:

- Does the organization have a mission statement?
- Are values included in the mission statement?
- Do the employees believe in its values? For example, do they walk the talk of the espoused values?
- How important is planning?
- How important are budgets?
- How important is stability?
- How important is creativity?
- How important is punctuality?
- How important is collegiality?
- What are the employees' attitudes towards its customers? What about towards each other?
- What is the company's attitude towards mistakes?
- What events are causes for celebration? For example, does the organization celebrate employees' promotions, retirements, or other achievements? Does the organization celebrate the introduction of new products or the acquisition of new customers or suppliers?
- Does the organization celebrate public holidays with company parties? Which public holidays? Who can attend? Just the employees or the employees and their partners and/or children?
- What would customers, suppliers, and other key stakeholders identify as the organization's values?

Shared experiences

An organization's shared employee experiences, whether these experiences have been directly or vicariously lived, will significantly influence an organization's culture. Often it is the handed-down folklores that exert the strongest influence on an organization's culture, for these stories are frequently tweaked, embellished, and retranslated to match the organization's evolved culture. An organization's founders are usually immortalized as trendsetters if the organization's strategy is based on innovation or as financial geniuses if the organization's strategy is based on cost leadership. Apple Computers' official website, for example, describes the company's start-up as a "fairytale of one garage, three friends and very humble beginnings." Although it is true that three young inventors began work in a garage, the garage was located in Los Altos Hills, California. This neighbourhood was at the time and continues to be one of the wealthiest suburbs in the US according to *Forbes Magazine*, which provides an annual ranking of the wealthiest zip codes in the US. Thus, to say that the beginnings of Apple were very humble appears to be an intentional disregard of the company's location advantages for the apparent purpose of promoting the narrative of a company that rose to prominence against the odds and disrupted an established industry with its innovative ideas and products.

The following set of questions helps assess and understand an organization's shared experiences:

- What are the main stories/myths/folklores that employees most often hear and tell?
- What do employees talk about when they think of the history of the organization?
- What stories do they tell new people who join the organization?
- What do these stories say about what the organization believes in?
- How does it feel to be a worker at the organization?
- What employee behaviours (and the organizational routines that support these behaviours) are most common?
- How are work practices and procedures created? How are they enforced?
- Do employees work in groups or individually?
- How are key decisions made?
- How do employees learn about important organizational news? Is it through such formal, written forms as memos, emails, and newsletters? Or is it through formal but oral channels like group meetings and company assemblies? Or does it happen through informal grapevines?
- What is the tone of communication between employees?
- Is profanity commonplace?
- Are first names or are titles and last names used to greet people?
- Do employees socialize together during breaks or after work?
- Are these social groups exclusive to some employees or open to all employees? Are new hires included?
- What programmes are in place to develop employees?
- Does the organization operate an employee mentoring programme?
- Do mentors and mentees believe the programme is effective?

Symbols

All organizations possess symbols that give clues about their organizational cultures. As noted above, these symbols can range from company logos to the look of a company's headquarters to the dress code it enforces. Each of these symbols reveals something about an organization's culture. For example, if the manager of a supermarket wears a suit and tie that says something very different about an organization's culture than if he/she wears a shopkeeper's apron. Likewise, the use of colour can be very revealing. As an illustration, the use of single, bright, garish colours often symbolizes an organization's no-frills, no-nonsense approach to business. Similarly, the use of stickmen in advertising, as opposed to notable celebrities, can also convey a cost leader's frugal intentions to provide the lowest prices.

Answers to the following list of questions can help reveal what an organization's symbols suggest about the organization's culture:

- Where is the organization located? Is it located in the central business district or in the outskirts of a town/city?
- Do the organization's external premises comprise a large amount of undeveloped, unused land? Does this land have a water feature such as a lake, river, or fountain?
- If the organization is located in a building in a town/city's central business district, does the organization occupy one of the building's top floors?
- Does the organization lease or own all or part of an iconic building?
- What do the work areas look like? Are they clean? Are they tidy? Are they small or large? Are they minimalist or extravagant?
- What is on the walls or displayed in the organization's common areas (e.g., foyers, vestibules, meeting rooms, corridors)? Are these displays expensive artworks, company history lines, or company products?
- How do people dress? Does the organization have different dress codes for different occasions?
- What kind of gift, if any, is presented to a retiring employee?

Exemplars

Exemplars are usually highly successful organizational members, either current or retired, who have been elevated to exaggerated levels of conspicuous prominence. These individuals occupy a canonized status that is not unlike the sainthoods the Roman Catholic Church bestows on those it deems to be miracle workers. The main difference between the two is that the latter is a highly formalized process with plenty of pomp and pageant attached to the distinction, whereas the former is the informal manifestation of an organizational group's collective belief that someone epitomizes the essence of the organization and deserves to be idolized. Generally, the idolized person is a current or former employee. It is, however, possible that the exemplar could come from outside the organization. W. Edwards Deming, the prominent total quality management innovator and practitioner, could (and the author has seen this to be the case for several manufacturing companies he consulted for) serve as an exemplar. So too might a team like the All Blacks (New Zealand's national rugby team) serve as an exemplar for other sporting codes. In fact, National Football League (NFL) teams from the US have increasingly attempted to study and understand the basis of the All Blacks' winning formula, in the hope that they can apply these learnings to their own success.

Exemplars do not always have to be people. Not only can the exemplar transcend one person, as was just discussed in the above paragraph about how a team can serve as an exemplar, but it can also be an event or an idea. For example, Apollo 11, which produced the first man to walk on the moon, can be an exemplar. This space mission might, for example, be used as an exemplar by an organization that sees itself as trying something very new and challenging. Remember, exemplars are simply an organization's elevation of somebody or something to an idolized state. Accordingly, when assessing an organization's exemplars, the following set of questions will prove useful:

- In the stories employees recount about their organization, who are the stories' heroes, villains, and mavericks?
- What employee behaviours get rewarded?
- What employee behaviours get punished?
- What is the typical reward offered? For example, is it a raise or bonus? Or is it a plaque, gift, or time off?

Power structures

Understanding an organization's power structure is essential to understanding the organization's culture. Organizations that operate highly-centralized structures, especially when these occur in environments characterized by significant change and unpredictability, convey a lack of faith and trust in their employees. For some senior managers, this lack of faith and trust in their employees is based on the belief that employees are inherently untrustworthy (see Chapter 4's discussion of agency theory). For other managers, their lack of faith and trust in their employees is rooted less in their wariness of their employees and more in their micro-managing leadership style (see Chapter 13's discussion of leadership styles based on initiating structure).

Just as highly-centralized power structures reveal insights into an organization's culture, so too do highly-decentralized structures. Although decentralization can indicate an organization has faith in and trusts its employees to make good decisions, it is also possible that it denotes senior management laziness and incompetence. US journalists have questioned whether President Donald Trump's management style is simply a cover for his laziness and incompetence, for instance.

When judging an organization's power structure, and what it reveals about the organization's culture, answers to the following set of questions will be helpful:

- Who has the real power in the organization to make or influence decisions?
- What do these people believe and champion within the organization?
- How does the organization define leadership?
- Is there a predominant leadership style and, if so, what is it?
- How is power used or abused by the leaders?

The sidebar summarizes a news story about the changed power structures employees at the University of Otago staff claimed to have experienced in the mid- to late 2010s under the leadership of its vice-chancellor. Notice the news story's use of such terms as centralized control, low trust, and fractured communication. These terms describe a power structure that is opposite to what a knowledge-based organization should possess. A supportive power structure should instead be one that is characterized by decentralization, high trust, and collaborative, highly networked employees.

The University of Otago employees' description of their organization's power structure as "toxic" would have likely set off alarm bells among the university's board of trustees. Time and again, these types of organizational settings have been shown to be not only counterproductive to an organization's achievement of its goals, but they are prime breeding grounds for unethical employee behaviour. As discussed in Chapter 6, such environments permit one of the three triggering factors for employees acting unethically: the ability to rationalize the unethical behaviour. It is for this very reason that astute organizations conduct annual employee surveys. In fact, an organization's failure to organize regular employee surveys should be viewed as a problem in itself, for it invariably signals a senior management team that is fearful of constructive criticism.

The disregard for and discouragement of employee input prominently featured at Wells Fargo in the mid-2010s. In particular, the independent report into the bank's cross-selling scandal noted that the head of the Community Banking Division Carrie Tolstedt and her inner circle "… were insular and defensive and did not like to be challenged or hear negative information. Even senior leaders within the Community Bank were frequently afraid of or discouraged from airing contrary views" (Shearman and Sterling, 2017: 8). As will be discussed later in this chapter, particularly perceptive organizations conduct not simply annual employee surveys but also perform periodic cultural audits.

Consider this …

On 9 March 2020, the newspaper the *Otago Daily Times* reported on a story about University of Otago staff members feeling betrayed and disheartened by the actions of top management. The staff members called the University "very sick" and in need of "radical action." Those interviewed described and decried an organization that had "… gone from a place of devolved responsibility, high trust, collegiality and strong goodwill to centralised control, fractured communication, curtailed freedoms, low morale and high stress."

The news story cited a 2019 survey undertaken by the union representing the University's staff members, which found that 68% of the University's employees said their job satisfaction was either worse or much worse than before, 21% reported being bullied in the previous six months, 40% felt their health and wellbeing had suffered because of work, and only 44% would recommend the University as a good place to work. One of the interviewees said several years ago close to 100% of the University's staff would have recommended the

University to prospective employees. The interviewed employee went on to say, "Every time I think about that result, I want to cry." Underlying causes for the poor survey results included the University's top-down management style, its increasing culture of micromanagement, and its failure to support and respect personal autonomy.

One of the news story's more stunning revelations was the reservation of academics to be interviewed from their offices (either on their office phones or writing from their official email accounts). They reported feeling unsafe "... express[ing] critical views on work emails, university-hosted websites or university phones." Several of the interviewed staff members feared risking their careers by speaking up. Although no names were used in the news story, these individuals still worried they might be identified.

The staff members claimed the University's changed power structure had precipitated a "climate of suppression" and "loss of academic freedom." One individual stated, "There used to be a social contract between academics and the university. The job requires long hours and quite a bit of stress because you have a lot of responsibility. But we would be trusted to get on with it. In return, there was a certain amount of job security and a culture of mutual respect. But that social contract has been well and truly destroyed. I'm prioritizing my students... but I'll be damned if I'm going to spend my evenings and my weekends doing other parts of my job."

The news story sought to include a response from the University. The response largely ignored the issues of staff disillusionment, faltering morale, and employee turnover. Instead, the response was highly defensive and even combative. It challenged the reporter's newspaper "... to take a brave look at their own culture and seek to improve." The University's response mainly consisted of reeling off a list of University accomplishments, including topping all the highly competitive research funding pools, earning the highest level of research income in the University's history, receiving student ratings showing more satisfaction with its teachers, and continuing to attract outstanding academic and professional staff from within New Zealand and internationally. Either with naivety or calculation, no mention was made of the fact that these measures are largely indicative of historical efforts. Winning research grants and being recognized for good teaching are the results of previous years' work. For research, it might involve the conduct of earlier pilot studies and the investment of time in building up networks of research colleagues. For teaching, it might involve making wider connections between the topics one teaches and what occurs in practice and other relevant fields of study. Good teaching is a journey of improvement that is built on reflection of one's teaching practice and refinements to it. To contend that research or teaching are products of the moment is disingenuous. The University's response concludes by claiming, "On the whole, our culture here is good." This shallow assertion sounds reminiscent of the classic admonishment by police at an accident scene, where they say, "There is nothing to see here. Move along."

The dire and dysfunctional nature of the University's power structure had been enabled or at least allowed to continue by the university's senior management group, which consisted of the vice-chancellor, chief financial and operating officers, a director of human resources, two other directors, three deputy vice-chancellors and four pro-vice chancellors. The collective culpability of this group led one of the interviewees to wonder, "Is this a situation where the entire [university] government needs to be swept away, so we get a new set of leadership we have confidence in?" (Otago Daily Times, 2020).

PROMOTING EFFECTIVE ORGANIZATIONAL CULTURES

Answers to the six sets of questions listed above provide a composite of an organization's culture. This profile can then be compared with the organization's ideal profile. This ideal profile is the one which best fits with the other performance management elements shown in Figure 3.1 (i.e., organizational structure; organizational systems, processes, and procedures; and internal and external contingent factors) for the purpose of supporting employees' implementation of the organization's strategy.

Should an organization find differences or gaps between the actual and ideal organizational culture, it will want to implement changes to close these gaps. Implementing cultural change is far from easy. It involves re-moulding employee values, beliefs, and behaviour. Although the challenges involved in effecting organizational culture change must not be underestimated, its difficulty should not be a reason for lack of action.

Before leaping into organizational culture change, the organization's senior managers should be quite clear about what they are trying to change. For example, if an organization's senior managers discover that their organization's work environment is highly competitive and not the collaborative setting it was hoping for, then these managers must carefully consider how this supposed gap interferes with their employees' implementation of the organization's strategy.

As a way of more fully teasing out this last point, imagine a research and development department that prior to the audit of its organization's culture prided itself on having a collegial work environment. Imagine further that the results of the audit identify its employee culture as competitive. Such a finding should not be assumed to mean that a problem exists and needs correction. Employee competition is neither bad in itself nor indicative that collegiality cannot exist. Healthy employee competition is both possible and can in fact be quite useful. Inter-employee rivalry that might focus on the number of published articles between employees of a research and development department need not undermine collegiality, and its presence may enhance the chances of positive organizational outcomes.

There are of course limits to the amount of employee competition that can occur before it becomes dysfunctional. For example, the employee competition discussed above involving the Wall Street firm and Enron was far from healthy. Competitions that result in employees demeaning one another or allowing someone to brag about stomping on a colleague's throat if doing so will better one's bonus, as the Enron employee stated, are harmful to any organization that maintains ambitions of long-term survival. Accordingly, any organization with similar levels of employee competition will want to find ways to create greater employee cooperation and empathy.

An organization's employees, and especially its senior managers, can influence their organization's culture in two main ways. The first is through leadership. Senior managers can act as leading lights and model the behaviour they expect. This behaviour is commonly referred to as "leading by example." Mayer *et al.* (2009) have studied what they term to be the trickle-down effects of ethical leadership. Their findings report a direct negative relationship between ethical leadership and group-level deviance, and a positive relationship between ethical leadership and group-level organizational citizenship behaviour (OCB). This topic of leadership is discussed more fully in Chapter 13. For now, it is sufficient to realize that managers, in their role as organizational leaders, influentially shape their respective organization's cultures, either for the better or for the worse. Cecily Joseph, the VP of Corporate Responsibility at Symantec, well captures this idea when he says,

> Leadership style matters…it's critical to the kind of culture we want. If we want a culture that's inclusive—that wants you to bring your whole self to work—we want leaders who aren't afraid to be themselves, and even to acknowledge their weaknesses.
>
> (CECP, Imperative, and PWC, 2018: 13)

The second main way senior managers shape their organizations' strategies is through the human resource systems they operate. Chapter 11 discussed how human resource systems can be used to encourage high employee commitment, motivation, and performance. It is no wonder that organizations with superior human resource practices are commonly perceived as the better place to work. In fact, Glassdoor, a Californian company, regularly collects salary and other feedback from employees working at over 600,000 predominantly large companies located throughout the world about what it is like to work at these organizations. Each year, Glassdoor publishes its list of "The Best Places to Work" in the US. In 2017, the top ten companies were:

1 Bain & Company
2 Facebook
3 Boston Consulting Group
4 Google
5 World Wide Technology
6 Fast Enterprises
7 In-N-Out Burger
8 LinkedIn
9 Adobe
10 Power Home Remodelling.

A common thread among these companies is their ability to build organizational cultures that recognize and value the contributions of their employees. For example, Jane Gonnerman,

Review Question 12.3: What is a cultural audit?

Answer: Please see the Answer section starting on page 283

Review Question 12.4: How can a cultural audit be used to create a better performance management system?

Answer: Please see the Answer section starting on page 283

a partner of Bain & Company, stated, "We create an environment where people want to come to work and can individually create a career that works for them." An examination of exactly how today's organizations promote the development of high-performing organizational cultures is the topic of the ensuing discussion.

HUMAN RESOURCE MANAGEMENT PRACTICES AND ORGANIZATIONAL CULTURES

Flextime, compressed workweeks, extended holidays (six weeks and sometimes more), gyms at work, and opportunities to work from home are just some of the ways that today's organizations are trying to improve their employees' perceptions of their work environments and ultimately the organizational cultures that operate. A study conducted by the Society for Human Resource Management reveals that 57% of employers in 2016 offered workers the option of telecommuting. This and other novel approaches to reshaping work practices are not intended as quirky fads. As Michael Mahoney, the vice-president of consumer marketing at GoHealth Insurance, a health insurance comparison website, says, his company's decision to move to a more casual dress code was not predicated on making the employees more comfortable but making the employees more productive. He further states, "if we were able to measure an increase in productivity for everyone who wears suits and a tie, then great." In other words, if coming to work dressed as one's favourite superhero resulted in higher employee productivity, then for companies like GoHealth that would be their adopted dress code.

Grant McCracken (2013), an anthropologist and research affiliate at Massachusetts Institute of Technology, notes that employees are working longer hours and technology is continuing to blur the line between work and personal life. Employees can now, no matter the time of day or whether they are in or out of the office, access emails and other work documents. In response, and in an attempt to make these extra working hours tolerable, companies are permitting telecommuting.

Some managers may be uneasy with the practice of allowing employees to work from home. However, such reservations are not supported by the literature. Studies have consistently shown that telecommuting workers are equally as productive or more productive than their office-dwelling colleagues (Bloom *et al.*, 2015). More recently, the COVID-19 pandemic has provided the conditions for a natural experiment, offering the opportunity to compare employee performance between the two modes of working. A study by Awada *et al.* (2021) reports that pre-COVID-19 and working from home productivity levels were unchanged.

Meanwhile, some positive correlations were observed between female, older, and high-income workers and increases in reported productivity. In addition, studies that have examined the correlation between telecommuting and employee creativity show a positive correlation between the two (Covarrubias *et al.*, 2021).

Today's conflating of work and personal life is certainly recognized at Burton Snowboarding, a snowboard manufacturer in Burlington, Vermont. Burton recognizes the strain that company travel places on employees, especially employees with families. Accordingly, in addition to operating a subsidized childcare centre, when employees are away travelling for work, the company will pay babysitters either to watch the employees' children at home or to accompany the employees and their children if they travel together. The company also allows its employees to bring their dogs to work.

Keen to see its employees practice their snowboarding skills, Burton encourages them to grab a workmate and get in a few runs of snowboarding before or after work. The company even gives its employees a free season pass to a local mountain and free snowboarding lessons. Moreover, on days when it snows more than 60 cms in 24 hours, the company closes its business for the day, and everyone heads to the mountains.

GoHealth has implemented unlimited vacation days, shorter hours on Fridays, and a gym membership subsidy. Each of these programmes was developed as part of the company's initiative to help its employees juggle their many work and non-work tasks and find some balance between the two. The unlimited vacation days, for example, alleviate employees' fears about having to come to work sick (because they are out of days they can take off) or having to use vacation days at the end of the year because of a "use-it-or-lose-it" policy. Far from abusing these generous human resource policies, companies find that these human resource policies often help to support an organization's work-hard, play-hard culture. Senior managers at Morningstar, the Chicago-based investment research firm, find that they must encourage their employees to take vacation/holiday time and the paid sabbaticals for which they are eligible.

Of course, just because employees are not at work – whether it is because they are working from home, on vacation, or on a sabbatical – does not mean that they are not engaging with their work. Often these employees will be checking their work emails and checking in with their colleagues while away from the office. As Morningstar's CEO Joe Mansueto says, his workers are "overachievers." The purpose of adopting more flexible human resource policies, especially ones that allow greater employee discretion about where and when they do their work, is to create organizational cultures that allow workers the freedom to think in new and

---

Review Question 12.5: Explain the need for organizational cultures to support organizational strategy and align with an organization's structure and the systems, processes, and procedures it operates.

Answer: Please see the Answer section starting on page 283

Review Question 12.6: If a cultural audit identifies a mismatch between the organization's culture and the desired culture, what are the two main ways senior managers can create organizational culture change?

Answer: Please see the Answer section starting on page 283

creative ways. Since the success of many of today's organizations depends on their employees' ability to be creative innovators, it is far from surprising that these organizations are willing to invest significant resources into promoting organizational cultures that value employee creativity and innovation.

CONCLUSION

Organizational culture exerts a strong influence on employee behaviour. This influence, depending on how well it links with the other elements of an organization's performance management package, can be for the better or the worse. Organizational cultures that reinforce and support employees' implementation of their organizations' strategies should be leveraged to their full potential. Unsupportive organizational cultures will require increased reliance on organizational structure and organizational systems, processes, and procedures in the short term to counteract and compensate for the organizational culture's shortcomings. In the medium and long term, an organization's senior managers will want to promote changes that serve to enhance the alignment between the organization's culture and the other elements of the performance management system.

The present chapter's discussion of the six factors that comprise organizational culture, its exposition of how to identify gaps between an organization's actual and ideal organizational cultures, and its discussion of how to effect change in organizational culture completes this book's discussion of the three main levers of performance management. In the next two chapters, we examine internal and external contingent factors that influence a manager's choice of and the manner in which the three levers of performance management are operated.

REFERENCES

Adler, R.W. and Hiromoto, T. (2012) Amoeba management: lessons from Japan, *Sloan Management Review*, Vol. 54, No. 1, pp. 83–89.

Ahmad, R. (2010) AirAsia: indeed the sky's the limit!, *Asian Journal of Management Cases*, Vol. 7, No. 7, pp. 7–31.

Akroyd, C. and Kober, R. (2020) Imprinting founders' blueprints on management control systems, *Management Accounting Research*, Vol. 46, pp. 1–18.

Awada, M., Lucas, G., Becerik-Gerber, B. and Roll, S. (2021) Working from home during the COVID-19 pandemic: impact on office worker productivity and work experience, *Work*, Vol. 69, No. 4, pp. 1171–1189.

Bloom, N., Liang, J., Roberts, J. and Ying, Z.J. (2015) Does working from home work? Evidence from a Chinese experiment, *Quarterly Journal of Economics*, Vol. 130, No. 1, pp. 165–218.

Camerer, C. and Vepsalainen, A. (1988) The economic efficiency of corporate culture, *Strategic Management Journal*, Vol. 9, No. S1, pp. 115–126.

CECP, Imperative, and PWC (2018) Making work more meaningful: building a fulfilling employee experience, Retrieved from https://d0cb2f2608c10c70e72a-fc7154704217aa017aa46150bf00c30c.ssl.cf5.rackcdn.com/pwc-building-a-fulfilling-employee-experience.pdf on 11 August 2022.

Collier, P.M. (2005) Entrepreneurial control and the construction of a relevant accounting, *Management Accounting Research*, Vol. 16, No. 3, pp. 321–339.

Covarrubias, L.P.C., Pérez, P.A., Cruz, P.D.A. and Silva, A.A. (2021) Factors related to the willingness of employees to accept telecommuting: preceding the pandemic crisis, *Journal of Organizational Psychology*, Vol. 21, No. 6, pp. 14–24.

Deloitte. (n.d.) Deloitte's 2016 global human capital trends, Retrieved from https://www2.deloitte.com/us/en/insights/focus/human-capital-trends/2016/human-capital-trends-introduction.html on 10 March 2022.

Giovannoni, E., Maraghini, M.P. and Riccaboni, A. (2011) Transmitting knowledge across generations: the role of management accounting practices, *Family Business Review*, Vol. 24, No. 2, pp. 126–150.

Greenwald, J., McCalope, M., Marchant, V. and Terdiman, D. (2001) Rank and fire, *Time*, Vol. 157, No. 24, pp. 38–40.

Guest, D. (1994) Organizational psychology and human resource management: towards a European approach, *European Work and Organizational Psychologist*, Vol. 4, No. 3, pp. 251–270.

Inamori, K. (1999) *Respect the Divine and Love People*, Singapore: McGraw-Hill.

Inamori, K. (2007) *A Passion for Success*, San Diego, CA: University of San Diego Press.

Koiranen, M. (2003) Understanding the contesting ideologies of family business: challenge for leadership and professional services, *Family Business Review*, Vol. 16, No. 4, pp. 241–250.

Li, L. (2020) 10 reasons why Google's company culture works, Retrieved from TINYpulse: https://www.tinypulse.com/blog/10-great-examples-of-googles-company-culture#:~:text=Google%20is%20a%20firm%20believer, in%20the%20way%20they%20work on 25 February 2022.

Malmi, T. and Brown, D.A. (2008) Management control systems as a package – opportunities, challenges and research directions, *Management Accounting Research*, Vol. 19, No. 4, pp. 287–300.

Mayer, D.M., Kuenzi, M., Greenbaum, R., Bardes, M. and Salvador, R.B. (2009) How low does ethical leadership flow? Test of a trickle-down model, *Organizational Behavior and Human Decision Processes*, Vol. 108, No. 1, pp. 1–13.

McCracken, G. (2013) Apple's trojan horse, *Harvard Business Review*, 13 May. Retrieved from https://hbr.org/2013/05/apples-trojan-horse.

O'Reilly, C.A., Chatman, J. and Caldwell, D.D. (1991) People and organizational culture: a profile comparison approach to assessing person-organization fit, *Academy of Management Journal*, Vol. 34, No. 3, pp. 487–516.

Otago Daily Times. (2020) Retrieved from https://www.odt.co.nz/lifestyle/magazine/culture-control on 14 January 2022.

Schein, E.H. (2004) *Organizational Culture and Leadership*, 3rd ed. San Francisco, CA: Jossey-Bass.

Shearman and Sterling (2017) Independent Directors of the Board of Wells Fargo & Company Sales Practices Investigation Report, Retrieved from https://www08.wellsfargomedia.com/assets/pdf/about/investor-relations/presentations/2017/board-report.pdf on 11 April 2022.

Willmott, H. (1993) Strength is ignorance; slavery is freedom: managing culture in modern organizations, *Journal of Management Studies*, Vol. 30, No. 4, pp. 515–552.

Willmott, H. (2003) Renewing strength: corporate culture revisited, *M@n@gement*, Vol. 6, pp. 73–87.

PART 4

Contingent factors

Internal environment

INTRODUCTION

This and the following chapter identify and discuss internal and external contingent factors that help determine an organization's use of the three levers of performance management. Internal contingent factors, which are the focus of the present chapter, consist of factors that reside inside the organization. These internal factors comprise leadership styles, organizational lifecycle, organizational size, and organizational ownership. External factors, which are examined in Chapter 14, are factors that reside outside the organization. These external factors consist of industry, national culture, government regulation, and labour markets.

As this chapter and the succeeding one will demonstrate, successful performance management design requires not only ensuring good fit between an organization's strategy and the three primary levers of performance management, but it also requires ensuring alignment – or at least understanding when alignment is not present and compensating for it – between an organization's contingent factors and the types of performance management levers it uses. As a point of illustration, some organizations have CEOs whose leadership style is democratic. These CEOs like to empower their employees by encouraging their participation in decision-making. In contrast, other organizations' CEOs exhibit an autocratic leadership approach. These leaders are loath to delegate responsibility and instead make all the organizationally important

DOI: 10.4324/9781003267195-17

> *Review Question 13.1:* What are internal contingent factors? Why are they important to performance management design?
>
> *Answer:* Please see the Answer section starting on page 283

decisions themselves. These two contrasting leadership styles can significantly impact the choice of performance management design an organization uses. For example, an organization that is pursuing Miles and Snow's prospector strategy is generally best advised to adopt a decentralized organizational structure. For CEOs with democratic leadership styles, this is not a problem. However, for prospectors with autocratic CEOs, the ability to implement decentralized organizational structures may prove difficult.

Some people may rightly argue that it is possible to replace a CEO. It must be understood, however, that this decision is the prerogative of the organization's board and not the performance management designer. Accordingly, the latter will need to adjust the performance management design to take account of this contingent factor. A performance management designer might, for example, recommend the adoption of a balanced scorecard that features an organizational capacity measure related to the number of employee suggestions made over a specific period of time. Formalizing an organizational expectation requiring employees to participate in suggesting new and/or improved products, services, and processes will help counteract the autocratic leader's propensity to be the sole decision maker. Although this type of leader will likely wish to determine alone the value of the employee suggestions being made, the institutionalized support for an employee suggestion system will ensure that a more diverse set of viewpoints and opinions are being offered than would otherwise be the case. Such an outcome is sure to benefit a prospector.

Just as leadership style will impinge on what performance management design an organization can adopt, so too might the other internal and external contingent factors. This and the following chapter identify and describe these contingent factors, as well as discuss how each factor influences performance management design.

LEADERSHIP

Understandings of leadership have evolved substantially over the years. In its early discussions, leadership was dominated by case studies of larger-than-life, "known" leaders. Typically these case studies focused on high-profile statesmen or military generals. The intention was to glean core, common characteristics that defined these archetypal leaders.

Beginning in the 1940s, researchers embarked on a purportedly more scientific approach to the study of leadership. Similar to the research approach taken by the Yale University-based psychologist William Sheldon, whose somatotypes research sought to connect people's personalities with their body types (e.g., a belief that overweight people, whom he termed endomorphs, are extroverted and jolly, while thin people, whom he termed ectomorphs, are introverted and anxious), the study of leadership began a phase of studying connections between physical traits and skills and the likelihood of being a leader. For example, this research examined such physical traits as height and attractiveness and the propensity to be a leader. The research also studied relationships between aptitudes (e.g., being an extrovert) and communication (e.g., being a good orator) and leadership likeliness. This stream of research failed to find any scientifically-demonstrable evidence to connect physical traits and skills with leadership capability, and eventually it withered as a field of enquiry.

By the 1950s, the seat of leadership study became consolidated at the universities of Ohio State and Michigan. Researchers at these two universities embarked on a set of pioneering leadership studies that became referred to as the Ohio State Leadership Studies. Unlike the previous trait approach used to study leadership, the Ohio State and Michigan University researchers sought to identify observable behaviours of leaders. Drawing upon a variety of research methods, including surveying leaders and observing them in laboratory settings, these studies culminated in the production of two broad factors of leadership: initiating structure and consideration. Initiating structure involved a leader being task oriented. Such a leader exhibits a keen interest in determining the set of tasks that should be accomplished and by whom. Furthermore, this leader seeks to define and ensure conformity with specific task standards. In his/her attempt to minimize worker deviation from task standards, this type of leader will promulgate rules and procedures aimed at regulating worker behaviour.

Unlike the task focus of the initiating structure leader, the consideration leadership style is characterized by a leader who is people-focused. This leader consults with his/her staff, keeps them apprised of changes that could affect their working conditions, and is willing to be flexible to help the worker balance the demands of work and life more generally. In other words, this leader is attentive to the psychological needs of the staff and is committed to protecting their personal welfare. The application of this leadership style can be seen in the leader who spends time learning about the jobs of his/her subordinates. For example, a former CEO at Christchurch International Airport reported that when he was hired, he inherited an airport with disgruntled and disengaged employees. As a way of demonstrating his sincerity in valuing the contributions they make, he spent a half day each month working alongside employees in each of the major airport functions (fire brigade, parking services, airport security, etc.). Far from trying to gain insight into how the work processes could be improved, he used these half day work experiences to meet with his employees, learn their names, and understand how they were hoping to contribute to the airport. The employees displayed an immediate positive response. After getting over their initial shock of meeting with the CEO, for some employees reported having worked at the airport for over 30 years and never once meeting with the CEO, the employees reported feeling like they were being listened to and felt more willing to increase their engagement with the company.

According to the Ohio State researchers who led the research project on leadership during the 1950s, depending on the organizational situation, the preferred leadership style might be initiating structure or consideration. Additionally, since the researchers defined the two leadership styles as being mutually exclusive (i.e., a leader who is high on initiating structure must be low on consideration and vice versa), this conception of leadership dictates that there is a right type of leader for each organizational setting. As a result, this theory of leadership became known as the theory of situational leadership.

The application of this theory of leadership to organizational practice was quite clear. If, for example, an organization was plagued by members who lacked focus and discipline, then the correct match of a leader would be someone who was high on initiating structure. In contrast, if the organizational situation featured a group of employees who were technically strong but lacked confidence, then the desired leader should be high on consideration.

The Ohio State Leadership Studies comprised the forefront of leadership theory until the late 1970s when it began to be challenged by the work of Burns (1978) and Bass (1985). Bass, whose work is based on the earlier work of Burns, proposed a two-factor model comprised of transactional leadership and transformational leadership. The transactional style embodies a *quid pro quo* relationship, whereby the leader provides worker-desired rewards for achieving some mutually-agreed-upon level of performance. For this leadership style to be effective, the leader must know what specific types of rewards will motivate each worker. In essence, the transactional leader is buying the worker's compliance. This purchasing of worker compliance leads Yukl (2002) to state that this leadership style is unlikely to generate worker enthusiasm or long-term commitment to task objectives.

Transformational leadership is easily contrasted with initiating structure, consideration, and transactional leadership. Unlike these alternative three styles of leadership, which some scholars label as traditional forms of leadership, transformational leadership adopts a change orientation and emphasizes emotions, values, the importance of symbolic behaviour, and the role of the leader in making events meaningful for followers (Brandt *et al.*, 2019; Busari *et al.*, 2019; Yukl, 1999). In other words, transformational leaders try to appeal to their followers' brains and hearts.

A noteworthy outcome of the transformational leader is his/her ability to inspire followers to go beyond their normal comfort zones of exertion and ambition. Through the leader's efforts to instil pride, communicate personal respect, facilitate creative thinking, and provide inspiration, followers develop strong mental and emotional attachments to the leader. The followers grow to see no leader-directed task as too large or too difficult. As an example, an Apple employee once described Steve Job's ability to hypnotize people to do the impossible because they did not realize it was impossible.

Although it is incorrect to do so, some scholars and practitioners refer to transformational leadership as visionary leadership, inspirational leadership, or charismatic leadership. The reason these three descriptions are incorrect is that each of them refers to a subpart of transformational leadership. As Bass and Avolio (1990) pointed out long ago, transformational leadership involves leadership styles that include visionary, inspirational, charismatic, individualized consideration, and intellectual stimulation.

Today's scholars and practitioners continue to draw upon the Ohio State Leadership Studies' initiating structure and consideration leadership styles (although this usually occurs under the more popularized names of autocratic leaders and participative leaders), as well as adopting the more contemporary concepts of transactional and transformational leadership. In addition to regularly employing all four of these leadership styles, current thinking (contrary to what the Ohio State researchers originally claimed) no longer views these leadership styles as being mutually exclusive. Instead, leaders can elicit one or more of these styles at any given time. In fact, scholarly research shows that leaders who combine transactional and transformational leadership styles, what researchers refer to as the augmentation hypothesis, create the highest levels of worker motivation and organizational performance.

As noted in this chapter's introduction, leadership style influences an organization's performance management system design. In particular, it was briefly discussed how autocratic leaders (i.e., initiating structure leaders) would be partial to centralized organizational structures and participative leaders (i.e., consideration leaders) would be better suited to decentralized organizational structures. We can now build on these understandings to incorporate the leadership styles of transactional and transformational. Transactional leadership is likely to be effective in both centralized and decentralized organizational settings. Transformational leadership, due to its worker-empowering characteristics, is more appropriate for decentralized settings.

Leadership style affects more than just the amount of centralization/decentralization an organization possesses. It is also connected to the complexity and formality that characterize an organization. Transactional leadership, for example, works best when there is low complexity. This need exists because the ability to enable worker compliance is a function of linking a worker's ability and effort to his/her performance. Variables outside the worker's control that impact on performance need to be excluded or controlled for. High-complexity environments, where workers have responsibility for many different tasks that might also be co-dependent on what other workers are doing, create difficulties for assigning rewards to worker performance. Low-complexity environments are much better suited to this leadership style. This compatibility with low complexity will also be true of initiating structure leadership styles, for it is much easier for leaders to prescribe rules and processes when the task features low complexity. In contrast, consideration and transformational leadership styles are amenable to work environments featuring both low and high complexity.

Formality, a further dimension of organizational structure, is additionally related to leadership. Initiation structure and transactional leaders are more compatible with high organizational formality. The emphasis on task accomplishment, which is the essence of initiating structure and transactional leadership styles, is most effective when tasks are simple and therefore amenable to the prescription of rules and procedures. Meanwhile, consideration and transformational leadership styles are better suited to informal organizational structures. These latter two leadership styles are receptive to worker diversity and eschew attempts to demand workers comply with prescribed rules and procedures.

Besides affecting the organizational structure lever of performance management, leadership is also associated with the other two levers of performance management. All four leadership styles can influence how an organization's systems, processes, and procedures are designed and operated. For example, transactional leaders will place a strong emphasis on and attach rewards to a worker's attainment of pre-specified financial and non-financial performance measures, which is entirely consistent with these leaders' quests to direct worker behaviour and reward good performance. Initiating structure leaders are also likely to place high reliance on both financial and non-financial performance measurement and attach incentives to employees' achievement of performance targets. In contrast, leaders who exhibit consideration and transformational leadership styles are likely to emphasize human resource systems over performance measurement and incentive systems. In particular, these leaders are likely to focus on ensuring their respective organizations attract the right employees, invest in their ongoing training and development, and create work settings that support and recognize the valuable contributions their employees make. The support of their employees may occur through the adoption of such organizational work practices as flextime, telecommuting, and compressed workweeks.

Leadership can also affect the organizational culture lever of performance management. As previously mentioned when discussing the leadership styles of initiating structure and consideration, the former leadership style is often used to instil discipline and focus in an organization that lacks these qualities, and the latter is used to redress problems with employee confidence and morale. In addition, an initiating structure leadership style would be best paired with a conservative organizational culture and is compatible with organizational cultures featuring low independence and low interdependence. These low-independent and low-interdependent cultures are called collective cultures.

Consideration leadership styles support an entrepreneurial culture. Furthermore, this style of leadership is consistent with the presence of either collective or collaborative cultures. The latter type of culture exhibits high independence and high interdependence.

Transactional leadership is likely to influence organizational culture by promoting an environment based on meritocracy. Although this style of leadership can support both conservative and entrepreneurial organizational cultures, its transactional focus would principally support a collective culture. Once again, transactional leadership thrives in an environment where performance is controlled by the worker and is easy to measure. Collective cultures provide this opportunity.

Transformational leadership is likely to have the greatest impact on organizational culture because of this leadership style's ability to appeal to the minds and hearts of followers. In fact, it is almost always the case that transformational leaders will feature as some of the exemplars that help define an organization's culture. Due to the inspirational element associated with this style of leadership, it is especially relevant to organizations with entrepreneurial cultures that are powered by learning and innovation (Coun *et al.*, 2019). Transformational leaders inspire workers to dream and take risks, which is the essence of entrepreneurial organizations. Additionally, its ability to inspire workers means transformational leadership will succeed for both collective and collaborative cultures.

Table 13.1 summarizes the relationships just discussed. These relationships should be viewed as being more illustrative than comprehensive. The reader should hopefully by now appreciate that the full richness of internal contingent factors and performance management levers can only ever be partially captured in an illustration like Table 13.1. In addition to showing the relationships between leadership styles and providing an abbreviated description of the three levers of performance management, this table also summarizes the compatibility that exists between the three levers of performance management and the other internal contingent factors of organizational lifecycle, organizational size, and organizational ownership, each of which will now be discussed.

Review Question 13.2: What defines a leader?

Answer: Please see the Answer section starting on page 283

Review Question 13.3: Are people born to become leaders or can they be taught to be leaders?

Answer: Please see the Answer section starting on page 283

Review Question 13.4: Identify and describe four main leadership styles. Describe how each leadership style influences performance management design.

Answer: Please see the Answer section starting on page 283

ORGANIZATIONAL LIFECYCLE

Many management scholars view organizations' existences as approximating the lifecycle of a living organism. There is a birth, which is followed by growth, maturity, decline, and eventually death. Although organizational theorists have adapted these lifecycle stages to organizations as a whole, marketing scholars have applied these principles to product and service lifecycles.

The literature typically recognizes four main organizational lifecycle stages: inception, growth, maturity, and decline (Jawahar and McLaughlin, 2001). Although all organizations are assumed to pass through these four stages, the swiftness with which they reach and the time they spend within a given stage will vary from organization to organization. In other words, some organizations may have long organizational lives and others relatively short lives.

The first organizational lifecycle stage is inception. All organizations have a beginning and a period in time when they are trying to establish themselves. This lifecycle stage demands a unique set of performance management system designs. In terms of the organizational structure, these organizations, mostly due to their associated small sizes, will feature low complexity (i.e., they are likely to have low spatial dispersion and low vertical differentiation), low formality (i.e., their smallness permits face-to-face, informal control), and high centralization (i.e., the important decisions, and practically every decision, is made by the owners).

During this inception stage, an organization will experience particular needs relating to the organizational systems, processes, and procedures it operates. The tracking of financial measures relating to its current and projected cash balances will be an essential part of its daily life. Non-financial measures are a luxury for these beginning organizations and will always play a subordinate role to survival-based measures like liquidity and leverage. Cash incentive systems are unlikely to play a significant role during the inception stage, for cash is the organization's critical limited resource. Instead, if these organizations are incorporated, they may possibly use stock incentives. During this preliminary lifecycle stage, the organization's human resource systems will receive limited attention. This relative unconcern will change as the organization enters its growth stage.

Organizational cultures characterized by entrepreneurialism and collectivism are associated with the inception stage. A start-up is by definition trying to do something better or different from others. Therefore an entrepreneurial culture should prevail. As a small, beginning organization, a collectivist culture is appropriate for this inception stage.

The second lifecycle stage is growth. This stage is associated with an organization's expansion of its customers, employees, and assets. To ensure success, an organization's strategic plans must include anticipating where the capital, either debt or equity, will come from to support this growth in resources.

As the organization grows, it will require a change in its structure. In particular, the organization will become more complex (e.g., it will have multiple operating sites and customer regions), become more decentralized (i.e., to accommodate its greater complexity), and become more formalized (i.e., to reflect its need to ensure sufficient control as it begins to decentralize) compared with its inception stage. These changes are a natural adaptation of organizational structure to the changed organizational lifecycle.

The organizational systems, processes, and procedures during an organization's growth stage will be punctuated by a high reliance on non-financial performance measures. Typical

TABLE 13.1 The compatibility of internal contingent factors and specific performance management designs

		Organizational structure						Organizational systems, processes, and procedures			Organizational culture			
		Low complexity	High complexity	Low formality	High formality	Centralized	Decentralized	High reliance on FPM and incentives	High reliance on NFPM and incentives	High reliance on human resource systems	Conservative	Entrepreneurial	Collective	Collaborative
Leadership	Initiating structure	✓	X	X	✓	✓	X	✓	✓	X	✓	X	✓	X
	Consideration	✓	✓	✓	X	X	✓	X	✓	✓	✓	✓	✓	✓
	Transactional	✓	X	X	✓	✓	✓	✓	✓	X	✓	X	✓	X
	Transformational	✓	✓	✓	X	X	✓	X	X	✓	X	✓	✓	✓
Organizational lifecycle	Inception	✓	X	✓	X	✓	X	✓	X	X	X	✓	✓	X
	Growth	X	✓	X	✓	X	✓	X	✓	✓	X	✓	✓	✓
	Maturity	X	✓	X	✓	U	U	✓	✓	✓	✓	X	X	✓
	Decline	✓	X	X	✓	✓	X	✓	X	X	✓	✓	✓	X
Organizational size	Small	✓	X	✓	X	✓	X	X	X	X	X	✓	✓	X
	Large	X	✓	✓	✓	✓	✓	✓	✓	✓	✓	X	X	✓
Organizational ownership	Tightly controlled	✓	X	✓	X	✓	X	✓	X	✓	U	U	U	U
	Dispersed	X	✓	X	✓	✓	✓	✓	✓	✓	U	U	X	✓

Key: FPM = financial performance measures, NFPM = non-financial performance measures, U = unspecified.

non-financial measures will include sales growth, market share, patents filed, and patents awarded. The organization is also likely to attach incentives, including cash bonuses, to employees' achievement of its non-financial goals and objectives. Having survived its infancy, the organization should have succeeded in generating internal or securing external sources of capital to embark on its expansion plans. Cash will therefore not be a constraining factor, or at least not during the initial expansion period. Further expansion or the undertaking of a staged expansion will likely require the organization to go back to the market (or its benefactor if it is a not-for-profit) to secure additional capital. A high emphasis on its human resource systems will also characterize organizations during this growth stage. Although it may prove challenging to keep up with the new numbers of employees needed to support its growth, ensuring the right employee will be critical to its success.

Entrepreneurial and collaborative organizational cultures will best suit this lifecycle stage. Since these organizations are still embarking on producing or providing something that is better than or different from what currently exists, they need to be innovative, creative, and possess an appetite for risk. Now that the organization is large relative to its previous lifecycle stage, the organization will find that a culture of collaboration is essential to supporting its entrepreneurialism.

Maturity represents the third lifecycle stage. This stage of an organization's life is characterized by decelerating or static growth. The organization's product/service is as well-established as it will become and its market share has peaked. The organization adopts a more measured and financially-calculating approach to any additional investment. Maintaining/defending its market share becomes its prime imperative.

The mature organization's structure displays high complexity and high formality. Although in its earlier lifecycle stage the organization exhibited decentralization as a way to meet its greater complexity, as the organization matures it develops a wide array of rules, customary processes, and standard operating procedures that erode its earlier decentralization. Depending on whether the organization is pursuing a cost leader strategy or a differentiator strategy will determine whether the organization continues being mostly decentralized or swings further towards centralization.

At this point in its life, the organization will place a high reliance on financial performance measures. It will resist sacrificing profit margins for market share. As part of its efforts to maintain its profit margins, the organization will also carefully track non-financial measures relating to efficiency. These efforts will include benchmarking its core activities against others who are considered best at the activity being measured (e.g., inventory management, throughput rates, etc.). In other words, inspiration and prescriptions for improvement can be found by looking outside one's industry. For example, in an attempt to achieve its ambitious goal of a 10-minute turnaround time for its planes, Southwest Airlines studied Formula 1 and Indianapolis 500 pit crews in an attempt to change how its ground crews operated.

Mature organizations typically provide incentives to employees who attain the financial and non-financial performance targets. The incentives are both monetary (e.g., bonuses, stock options) and non-monetary (e.g., recognition, increased autonomy). High importance is also commonly given to the operation of these organizations' human resource systems to ensure they regularly attract, train, and retain the right employees.

The organizational cultures of these mature organizations change from their earlier lifecycle stage of being entrepreneurial to now being conservative. At this point in their existence,

> *Review Question 13.5:* What are the four stages of an organizational lifecycle? Describe how each of these stages is related to performance management design.
>
> *Answer:* Please see the Answer section starting on page 283

the organizations no longer view risk as an opportunity to be seized, but instead as a threat to be avoided. Due to their relatively complex structure, and in particular their relatively large size, mature organizations will feature collaborative cultures.

The final lifecycle stage of decline also constrains/influences performance management design. During this stage, an organization will focus on maintaining its profit margins even if this means losing market share. Being in decline, the organization will be losing market share. The focus of senior managers in declining organizations – or certainly those that are for-profit – is on squeezing out all the profit they can from their dwindling pool of investments and on preparing for an orderly exit from the industry.

These organizations' structures will feature low complexity (due to their decreasing spatial dispersion and decreasing vertical differentiation), high centralization (due to their quest to reduce cost by avoiding duplication of services), and high formality (due to their desire for employees to adhere to strict policies on spending and divestment). These organizations will place a high reliance on financial performance measures. The use of incentives, however, will be limited, for these organizations will be continuously striving to cut costs. As a further cost-cutting initiative, these organizations will pull resources from their human resource systems. The cultures of these organizations will be highly conservative (based on their obsession with current profit margins) and have a collectivist orientation.

ORGANIZATIONAL SIZE

It would appear to be intuitively easy to characterize organizations as small or large. These supposedly obvious classifications are not, however, as straightforward as they at first seem. In particular, what measure of size constitutes small versus large? Is it the asset size, relative market share, employee numbers, some of these measures, all of these measures, or some other type of measure? The most common categorization method is to classify organizations with 50 or fewer employees as small.

Small organizations are commonly viewed as featuring characteristics of informality, trusting relationships, overlapping and unclear job responsibilities, ambiguous/nonstandard work processes (Gibb, 2000). They are further distinguished by being only partially correlated with the stage of an organization's lifecycle. Although organizations that are in the inception stage will invariably be small, it is only generally true that mature organizations will be large. Some organizations simply choose to remain small.

Small organizations, compared with medium or large organizations, are characterized by the following factors:

- Few people
- Few financial resources

- Limited employee skillsets
- Less access to markets
- Powerful owner personality influence.

In terms of organizational size's influence on performance management design, small organizations will feature low complexity, low formality, and high centralization. Being small implies there will be low spatial dispersion and low vertical differentiation. This exhibition of low complexity means that senior managers will be intimately familiar with the organization's activities – including its products/services, production technology, customers, and competitors – and these managers will derive no benefit from decentralizing. And because the senior managers of these small companies contribute to managing their organizations' sales, production, and/or delivery systems, these managers will have direct involvement in and oversight of their respective organizations' core processes and outcomes. As a result, formal systems would be superfluous and unnecessary.

Small organizations are likely to be paired with a low reliance on performance measures – both financial and non-financial. A former CEO of Shotover Jet, a commercial jet boating business in Queenstown, NZ, once recounted how his measure of customer satisfaction was how loudly the customers screamed as they flew past the company's Shotover River offices … the louder, the better. It has also traditionally been the case that many small organizations lack the resources to collect, compile, and examine ongoing financial and non-financial information. Often these organizations wait until the end of the year to have this information prepared by their accountants. Although today's accounting software is changing this situation, at least in terms of the real-time provision of financial information, it is still truer to describe senior managers' decision-making as a function of their direct involvement in their organization's activities and processes rather than their reactive response to being provided with financial and non-financial performance measures.

Small organizations do, however, pay significant attention to their human resource systems, especially as it relates to whom they hire. Small organizations will often speak about their family-like culture, and these organizations will report that they look for employees who can fit into their respective organizational families. Returning back to the former CEO of Shotover Jet, he recalled how 200 applications would be received whenever the company advertised for a new driver. The company almost exclusively selected from the applicants based on personality (i.e., ability to relate to customers and integrate into the Shotover Jet family). According to the CEO, applicants could easily be taught to drive a boat. The same could not be said for helping them develop good customer interaction skills or fitting into the company's high familiarity and high trust environment. These circumstances help to explain why emotions can become so raw when owners or employees of these small organizations believe they have been treated unfairly.

In addition to having a family-like feeling, a small organization's culture will be entrepreneurial and collective. Being small, these organizations are able (and generally very willing) to take advantage of and adapt to environmental change (e.g., a competitor's change in its pricing). These organizations' smallness also means that their centralized organizational structures will result in low independence and low interdependence. This outcome is indicative of a collective culture.

Large organizations will exhibit high complexity, high formality, and high decentralization. In contrast to what was stated about small organizations, large organizations will have high

---

Review Question 13.6: How does organizational size influence performance management
design?

Answer: Please see the Answer section starting on page 283

---

spatial dispersion and high vertical differentiation. The high degree of organizational complexity means senior managers will lack the breadth and depth of knowledge to make informed
decisions across the wide set of issues impacting their organizations. Accordingly, managers
of large organizations will feel obligated to decentralize. To compensate for the devolution of
decision-making, senior managers will introduce formalized systems. For example, an IBM vice
president of marketing may require each regional sales manager to submit an annual budget for
the vice president's approval prior to their undertaking any sales activities. The regional sales
managers may also be required to report monthly on their actual performance relative to the
budgeted performance.

Large organizations will place a high reliance on financial and non-financial performance
measurement systems, and generally, they will attach incentives to their employees' achievement
of the performance measures. Since senior managers of large organizations lack detailed knowledge of each day's production, customer, and employee issues, the managers will mandate regular
reporting by their subordinates on key financial and non-financial performance measures. These
reports will provide the formal control and aggregate-level understanding senior managers need
to run their organizations effectively. Human resource systems will also feature prominently
in these organizations' performance management designs. As previously mentioned, the most
popular definition of organizational size is based on employee numbers. Due to their relatively
high numbers of employees, large organizations will require comprehensive human resource
systems to manage their employees successfully.

The organizational cultures of large organizations will have a tendency towards conservatism and collaboration. Large organizations are generally the product of years of growth. Often
these companies have reached the later stages of their growth cycle or are in their mature stage.
As noted above under the section discussing organizational lifecycle, these mature organizations
have lost their appetite for risk and instead favour stability. Additionally, the complex structure
and decentralization that characterizes these large organizations mean collaborative cultures are
demanded.

ORGANIZATIONAL OWNERSHIP

The final internal contingent factor examined is organizational ownership. Two forms are discussed: tightly controlled and dispersed ownership. The former is characterized by the presence
of few owners. It might be an organization that is owned by a single family, or it might be an
organization that has just a handful of non-family-related owners. Tightly-controlled companies
are often small in size, but not always. For example, Cargill, a company that was referred to in
the previous chapter, has annual revenues of US$ 120 billion and 153,000 employees. Certainly,
this company is anything but small.

The organizational structures of tightly-controlled organizations typically exhibit low complexity, low formality, and high centralization (Helsen *et al.*, 2017; Senftlechner and Hiebl, 2015). The owners of tightly-controlled organizations are usually highly involved in their organizations' operations. Having solid understandings of their businesses, the owners will not feel the same need as other professional managers with lesser understandings of the business to hire employees with skills the managers are lacking. As a result, tightly-controlled organizations will display relatively low vertical differentiation. The low formality of tightly-controlled organizations will be a product of the owners' active involvement in and intimate understanding of the business. In other words, the owners will be able to exert control through their naturally-occurring, ongoing daily interactions with employees as opposed to any need for formalized guidelines and procedures. Due to the twin facts that the owners are well versed about and actively involved in their businesses, tightly-controlled organizations will feature high centralization.

Tightly-controlled organizations will place high reliance on financial performance measures and generally provide incentives to employees who achieve the performance measures. Since the owners are knowledgeable about and actively participate in their organizations' operations, these managers will have the grounded understandings to interpret and put into context the financial performance measures without the further need for non-financial performance measures. These organizations will place a high reliance on human resource systems. The owners will be especially interested in ensuring that employees meet the tight-knit set of beliefs and values the owners, and the organization as an extension of them, espouse.

No specific organizational cultures are encouraged by the presence of tightly-controlled ownership. Tightly-controlled organizations are as likely to be innovative and entrepreneurial in their orientation as they are to be frugally-minded and conservative. Likewise, these organizations are equally likely to feature collective orientations as they are collaborative orientations.

Organizations exhibiting dispersed ownership tend to have high complexity, high formality, and high decentralization. These organizations are generally large organizations, with all the associated issues of high vertical differentiation and high spatial complexity. Due to their complex natures, these organizations require decentralization. The use of high formalization will emerge as a means of counteracting the loss of control that occurs with decentralization.

Organizations with dispersed ownership will place a high reliance on both financial and non-financial performance measures. The managers of these firms, who are often professional managers who lack detailed industry knowledge, will require non-financial performance information to help them interpret the financial information and gauge its likely persistence. These professional managers are also likely to award incentives to employees who meet their assigned performance targets.

The organizational cultures of organizations with dispersed ownership will tend to feature collaborative orientations, which is due to these organizations' high independence and high interdependence. These organizations are not predisposed to either a conservative or entrepreneurial culture. Either organizational culture is equally likely to prevail.

Before leaving this discussion of organizational ownership and performance management, it is worth noting the literature's finding that when tightly-controlled organizations either grow large or become more professionalized (i.e., family members are replaced by professional managers), these organizations' performance management systems begin mimicking those of their larger, more dispersed ownership peers. In particular, the involvement of professional managers

> *Review Question 13.7:* How does organizational ownership influence performance management design?
>
> Answer: Please see the Answer section starting on page 283

becomes the legitimizing force for the adoption of formal performance management systems featuring the decentralization of authority and the implementation of formal financial and human resource systems (Hiebl and Mayrleitner, 2019; Marett *et al.*, 2020; Monticelli *et al.*, 2018; Pagliarussi and Leme, 2020).

CONCLUSION

This chapter identified the four internal contingent factors of leadership style, organizational lifecycle, organizational size, and organizational ownership, and discussed how each of these factors helps influence and determine an organization's performance management design. Scholars and practitioners alike must be aware of these factors. Although the matching of the right organizational structure, organizational systems, processes, and procedures, and organizational culture to a given organization's competitive strategy is a demanding and exacting task by itself, successful performance management designers will find they must go beyond this first-order level of linking performance management designs with competitive strategy. In addition, the designers must develop an appreciation of and make an accommodation for their organizations' internal contingent factors. As mentioned at the beginning of this book, far from being a simple or straightforward task, the study and practice of performance management is highly complex and challenging.

The inherent complexity and challenge associated with the field of performance management must not deter the scholar or practitioner in their/them quest to ensure employees implement the strategies of the organizations in which they work. The fact that no two organizational situations are ever likely to feature exactly the same set of facts and circumstances makes the effort to produce the most relevant and appropriate performance management design all the more rewarding.

Of course, it is not only an organization's internal contingent factors that affect performance management design. External contingent factors also influence this design. Identification and examination of these external contingent factors are the topics of the next chapter.

REFERENCES

Bass, B.M. (1985) *Leadership and Performance Beyond Expectations*, New York: Free Press.

Bass, B.M. and Avolio, B.J. (1990) The implications of transactional and transformational leadership for individual, team, and organizational development. In W. Pasmore and R. W. Woodman (Eds), *Research in Organizational Change and Development* 4, Vol. 7, Greenwich, CT: JAI Press, pp. 231–272.

Brandt, E., Andersson, A. and Kjellstrom, S. (2019) The future trip: a story of transformational change, *Journal of Organizational Change Management*, Vol. 32, No. 7, pp. 669–686.

Burns, J.M. (1978) *Leadership*, New York: Harper.

Busari, A.H., Khan, S.N., Abdullah, S.M. and Mughal, Y.H. (2019) Transformational leadership style, followership, and factors of employees' reactions towards organizational change, *Journal of Asia Business Studies*, Vol. 14, No. 2, pp. 181–209.

Coun, M.J.H., Peters, C.P. and Blomme, R.J. (2019) Let's share! The mediating role of employees' self-determination in the relationship between transformational and shared leadership and perceived knowledge sharing among peers, *European Management Journal*, Vol. 37, No. 4, pp. 481–491.

Gibb, A.A. (2000) SME policy, academic research and the growth of ignorance, mythical concepts, myths, assumptions, rituals and confusions. *International Small Business Journal: Researching Entrepreneurship*, Vol. 18, No. 3, pp. 13–35.

Helsen, Z., Lybaert, N., Steijvers, T., Orens, R. and Dekker, J. (2017) Management control systems in family firms: a review of the literature and directions for the future, *Journal of Economic Surveys*, Vol. 31, No. 2, pp. 410–435.

Hiebl, M.R.W. and Mayrleitner, B. (2019) Professionalization of management accounting in family firms: the impact of family members, *Review of Managerial Science*, Vol. 13, No. 5, pp. 1037–1068.

Jawahar, I.M. and McLaughlin, G.L. (2001) Toward a descriptive stakeholder theory: an organizational life cycle approach, *The Academy of Management Review*, Vol. 26, No. 3, pp. 397–414.

Marett, K., Niu, Z. and Barnett, T.R. (2020) Professionalizing the information security of family firms: a family essence perspective, *Journal of Small Business Management*, Vol. 58, No. 2, pp. 390–408.

Monticelli, J.M., Bernardon, R. and Trez, G. (2018) Family as an institution, *International Journal of Entrepreneurial Behaviour and Research*, Vol. 26, No. 1, pp. 54–75.

Pagliarussi, M.S. and Leme, M.A. (2020) The institutionalization of management control systems in a family firm, *Qualitative Research in Accounting & Management*, Vol. 17, No. 4, pp. 649–673.

Senftlechner, D. and Hiebl, M.R.W. (2015) Management accounting and management control in family businesses, *Journal of Accounting & Organizational Change*, Vol. 11, No. 4, pp. 573–606.

Yukl, G. (1999) An evaluation of conceptual weakness in transformational and charismatic leadership theories, *Leadership Quarterly*, Vol. 10, No. 2, pp. 285–305.

Yukl, G. (2002) *Leadership in Organizations* (5th Edition), Englewood Cliffs, NJ: Prentice Hall.

CHAPTER 14

External environment

CHAPTER OBJECTIVES

- Identify the four primary external contingent factors that constrain performance management design.
- Discuss the constraining influence of industry on performance management design.
- Discuss the constraining influence of national culture on performance management design.
- Discuss the constraining influence of government policies on performance management design.
- Discuss the constraining influence of labour markets on performance management design.

INTRODUCTION

This chapter identifies and discusses the external contingent factors that influence an organization's operation of its three levers of performance management. Similar to the previous chapter's discussion of internal contingent factors and performance management design, the current chapter examines the composition of four contingent factors that are external to an organization and discusses how each of these external factors helps determine performance management design. The four external contingent factors discussed are industry, national culture, government regulation, and labour markets.

Organizations have limited, if any, control over these external contingent factors, or at least this is the case once senior managers have chosen the industry/industries they will compete in and the countries they will operate from. As an example, if an organization elects to be a nano-medicine manufacturer, then it will become subject to all the technological and competitive forces associated with this industry. If this same company decides to locate its manufacturing and sales operations in Boston, Massachusetts, then it will become subject to the laws, labour market, and national culture of this state and the US. As this chapter will soon show, these external contingent factors determine not only how much tax an organization pays and the health and safety regimes it operates, but the external factors also help determine the organizational structures, operating systems, processes and procedures, and organizational cultures an organization will adopt.

DOI: 10.4324/9781003267195-18

Review Question 14.1: What are external contingent factors? Why are they important to performance management design?

Answer: Please see the Answer section starting on page 283

INDUSTRY

An organization's choice of the industry it competes in has a profound influence on the organization's performance management design. The focus of influence will mainly be on organizational structure. Contingency theory, which was discussed in Chapter 4, provides the rationale for this association. To fully appreciate this relationship, it is helpful to recount the scholarly and practitioner literatures that connect industry classifications with organizational structure.

Max Weber popularized the inherent superiority of bureaucratic organizational structures with the publication of his book *The Theory of Social and Economic Organization*. This book, which was posthumously published in 1947, argued that bureaucratic structures were the ideal model for management. These bureaucratic structures included the thorough specification and division of labour, high formality of rules and procedures, a clear hierarchy of workers and tasks, uniform recruitment practices, and slowly advancing, linear career paths. According to Weber, a bureaucratic structure delivered the twin benefits of high rationality and high efficiency, making it the preferred form of organizational structure. This preference transcended any other factors, including the industry in which an organization operated.

The bureaucratic form of structure was championed at about the same time that the theory of scientific management was being proposed. As discussed in Chapter 3, scientific management promoted the idea of a single best way to perform and manage work activities. Similar to and shortly after scholars and practitioners abandoned scientific management, Weber's views on the existence of a single, best organizational structure came into question. The challenge to Weber's ideas initially began with the works of Woodward (1958) and Burns and Stalker (1961). Woodward, for example, found that different production technologies (i.e., unit, mass, and continuous production processes) affected an organization's adopted structures. She found that different production technologies were associated with such structural differences as an organization's vertical differentiation, its spans of supervisory control, and the ratio of managers and supervisors to total company personnel. In fact, Woodward found that a firm's effectiveness was related to its ability to match the right organizational structure to its particular production technology, with the latter factor being highly industry-specific.

This idea that it was important, and even necessary, to choose from different organizational structures and match or fit them to the organization's environment was poignantly demonstrated by Lawrence and Lorsch (1967). These two Harvard University-based researchers undertook a set of intensive case studies of various business firms for the purpose of understanding the sources and consequences of organizational structure. They studied companies from three different industries: plastics, packaged foods, and container makers. The three industries were chosen for their differing rates of environmental change. The six firms in the plastics industry operated in a highly competitive environment, one that featured significant investments of research and development and constantly changing products. Furthermore, these firms' production processes were defined as "turbulent," whereby the inputs (in the form of scientific knowledge) and outputs (in the form of customer satisfaction) were highly uncertain.

As a point of comparison with the firms in the plastics industry, Lawrence and Lorsch studied firms from the packaged foods and container industries. The latter was intended to showcase firms that faced low levels of environmental change, while the former was meant to showcase firms with intermediate levels of environmental change. In particular, the container industry was characterized by very predictable rates of sales growth (essentially the industry's sales growth tracked the national economy's average rate of growth) and a near-total lack of new product introductions (no significant new products had been introduced in two decades). The packaged foods industry, meanwhile, featured new product introductions and sales growth rates that were more than the container industry but less than the plastics industry.

The findings of Lawrence and Lorsch were twofold. First, successful firms, as defined by market and economic indicators, were ones that matched the extent of their organizational structures' centralization/decentralization with the complexity of the environment. Generally speaking, complex environments, meaning highly competitive, unpredictable, and/or turbulent environments such as the ones faced by the plastics firms, required decentralized structures. Firms with complex environments but centralized structures were observed to be less successful than their decentralized counterparts. In contrast, firms with simple environments, such as those the container firms operated in, were most successful when they adopted centralized organizational structures. The stable and predictable environments of the container industry meant that many of the associated advantages of decentralized structures became irrelevant. Instead of improving such outcomes as decision response time, decision quality, etc., all that happened to firms using decentralized structures in the container industry was the incurrence of a higher cost structure (due to the additional management, staff, and record keeping that accompanies decentralized structures) than their centralized counterparts. As a result, the decentralized container firms were less successful than the centralized ones. Successful firms in the packaged food industry were found to have organizational structures that fell in the middle of the range between centralized and decentralized structures.

The second main finding of Lawrence and Lorsch was the recognition that the achievement of organizational effectiveness in complex environments demanded organizations do more than merely adopt decentralized structures. Decentralized structures will inevitably generate organizational conflict. This conflict is due to the decentralized units holding differing ideas about the critical imperatives facing their overall organization and how best to satisfy these imperatives. Also, it is often the case that decentralized units will come into direct competition with one another, perhaps over the formulation of a transfer price or perhaps even the recruitment of the same customer or employee. As Lawrence and Lorsch observed, far from seeking to suppress this conflict, the better performing organizations were the ones that understood this conflict was healthy for, and even essential to, the survival of their organizations. Accordingly, one of the important roles of senior managers in these decentralized firms is to manage the conflict.

It must be remembered that for firms which operate in rapidly changing and unpredictable environments, such as the plastics firms in Lawrence and Lorsch's study, the decisions are seldom easy or straightforward. Furthermore, a decision made today, due to the instability of the environment, might require altering or rescinding in the future. Added to these complications is the fact that the nature of the intra-organizational conflict in decentralized organizations, including which departments are involved in the conflict and even the origins of the conflict, is often highly dynamic. Allied departments can quickly change to competing departments, controversial issues can abruptly lose relevance, and one-time orthodox practices can suddenly fuel rebellion.

Although these descriptions of the conflict associated with decentralization may sound overwhelming to the point of being unmanageable, they clearly are not. Lawrence and Lorsch observed that if an organization can construct conflict-resolving mechanisms, or what the researchers termed integrating mechanisms, then the benefits associated with decentralization can be realized.

Lawrence and Lorsch (1967: 47) defined integration as "the quality of the state of collaboration that exists among departments that are required to achieve unity of effort by the demands of the environment." Integration is needed by decentralized organizations to ensure that the decentralized units are acting in a coherent and coordinated fashion. Lawrence and Lorsch observed that the most effective decentralized firms were the ones which anticipated conflict and established conflict-resolving departments and individuals, what they termed integrators. The role of integrators is not to demand compromise or arbitrate on conflicts, but to maintain an orderly forum in which the conflicting departments can resolve their differences. This understanding should help you appreciate why in prior chapters decentralization and formality are invariably paired.

True to contingency theory's philosophy, no single generic or best way is purported to exist for establishing integrators. Instead, its achievement can be realized in a variety of ways. Referring back to the firms studied by Lawrence and Lorsch, the decentralized firms in the plastics industry achieved conflict resolution through the efforts of integrators who resided at relatively low levels in the organization's hierarchy. It was observed that effective conflict resolution for these firms could only occur if the integrators had adequate specialized knowledge and familiarity of the situation. Invariably, this requirement meant that the integrators needed to be hierarchically close to the disputing units.

In addition to noting the generally low hierarchical levels occupied by these integrators, Lawrence and Lorsch also observed that the integrators needed to occupy an organizational space that was equidistant from the conflicting departments. This idea of equidistance was important for promoting impartiality.

In contrast to the conflicts that existed within the decentralized plastics firms, Lawrence and Lorsch observed that the conflicts in the centralized container firms were much less common and best resolved by senior managers. The stable environment and lack of specialized knowledge meant that senior managers had a strong understanding of their firm's operations and the critical factors that underpinned their firm's success. In fact, in combination with the stable environment and the lack of specialized knowledge, the typically greater years of experience of these senior managers compared with their lower-level employees meant that the senior managers were in the best position to adjudicate the conflict or even simply prescribe a solution at the outset.

From the works of Woodward (1958, 1965), Burns and Stalker (1961), and Lawrence and Lorsch (1967), the idea that there is no one single or best way to organize was developed into an organizational theory called contingency theory. In stark contrast to bureaucracy theory's one-size-fits-all approach, contingency theory argued that organizational structure will always be a function of and is contingent upon the nature of the organization's environment. Chief of these contingent factors is industry type. In a nutshell, industries characterized by low environmental uncertainty are best served by centralized organizational structures, whereas industries characterized by high environmental uncertainty are best served by decentralized organizational structures.

Before leaving the topic of industry, it is also worth noting how a further, and often overlooked, dimension of industry can influence performance management design. In particular, the degree of professionalization that characterizes an industry should factor into the organizational structures and organizational systems, processes, and procedures that are adopted.

A profession refers to a group of individuals who have achieved a common education and training experience that prepares them to apply this knowledge and exercise their skills in the interest of society. Professionals (e.g., doctors, lawyers, and accountants) profess a commitment to altruism, accountability, excellence, duty, honour and integrity, and respect for others in their chosen domain of expertise. For example, according to the International Accounting Education Standards Board, accountants are meant to share:

> a commitment to (a) technical competence and professional skills, (b) ethical behaviour (e.g., independence, objectivity, confidentiality, and integrity), (c) professional manner (e.g., due care, timeliness, courteousness, respect, responsibility, and reliability), (d) pursuit of excellence (e.g., commitment to continual improvement and lifelong learning), and (e) social responsibility (e.g., awareness and consideration of the public interest).
>
> (IAESB, 2017, IES 4, paragraph, A5, p. 59)

Organizations in industries that possess significant professional groupings (e.g., hospitals and universities) will have different performance management designs from organizations with the same or a similar set of strategic and situational characteristics, but which lack the same degree of professionalism as the former organizations. As an example, the senior managers of a hospital can typically assume that its doctors and nurses will share the hospital's prime mandate of caring for the sick. Doctors' and nurses' education and training orient them to exhibit behaviour that aligns with the goal of caring for patients. The Hippocratic Oath a doctor takes is certainly consistent with a hospital's most basic and core aim.

Since doctors and nurses display goal congruence (i.e., a situation in which the employees share the same goals as their organization), the hospital's performance management system should recognize this fact. When a substantial part of an organization's workforce possesses a professional orientation that aligns with the organization's goals and objectives, then senior managers should endeavour to leverage this orientation. In particular, the doctors' and nurses' social programming, which derives from their professional orientations, means that substantial influence already exists in the performance management lever of organizational culture. As discussed in Chapter 3, senior managers are well advised to avoid performance management designs that feature significant redundancy. Designs that include multiple forms of performance management that merely serve to duplicate one another should be eschewed. Significant redundancy not only slows employee execution of tasks, but it also runs the risk of eroding employee morale and motivation.

> *Review Question 14.2:* How does industry type influence performance management design?
> *Answer:* Please see the Answer section starting on page 283

This danger of excessive control is well captured by Kallio *et al.* (2016), who write about university academics' experiences with their institutions' ever-increasing use of procedural controls (i.e., the formulation of standard operating procedures) and outcome controls (i.e., each academic is given generic targets for publication and teaching performance based on their/them position/title). These authors show how today's academics are experiencing a serious decline in morale and motivation. The following representative quote comes from a lecturer in educational sciences. The abbreviation of PM in this quote stands for performance measurement.

> Thanks to [PM], no one sensible will pursue an academic career if (a) s/he is aware of the circumstances at work, and (b) there are other possibilities. Apparently, the system seeks to turn academia into a game of pathetic losers living in misery and competing with each other instead of being genuinely creative and protective of a good academic culture.
>
> (Kallio *et al.*, 2016: 697)

Reiterating the advice given in Chapter 3, senior managers should support and leverage professional orientations that are consistent with their organizations' missions. These managers can accomplish this task by providing a supportive environment that helps the professional orientations to flourish unhampered by additional forms of performance management, which are likely to prove less supportive than antagonistic.

NATIONAL CULTURE

National culture refers to the shared mental programming that a nation's people display. The presence of these shared conceptions means that business activities that are successful in one particular country do not necessarily translate across to another country. As a case in point, when Walmart in 1997 decided to expand its operation into Germany, it found that several of its quintessential features flopped when brought to Germany. For example, the Walmart greeter, who was stationed at the front door to make customers feel welcome, was instead found off-putting. Additionally, Walmart's policy of spreading out popular products throughout the store only served to annoy German shoppers, who wanted to shop quickly and efficiently. An even worse translation of practices involved Walmart's mandatory policy requiring employees to report co-workers who violate company rules. Germany's WWII history of Gestapo informants and neighbourhood spies led to employee suspicion and disgust with such a company policy. These and other failures by Walmart to understand the cultural clashes contained in its set of everyday organizational practices resulted in an inglorious exit from and significant loss of money from its botched German expansion.

In contrast with Walmart's failure in Germany, McDonald's has been successful in India due to its willingness to adapt. In particular, starting at an early point after its arrival in India, McDonald's accepted the need to adjust its practices to align with India's informal work culture and specific food tastes. For example, workers in India expect their organizations to be hierarchically structured and highly centralized. Furthermore, workers value friendly, relaxed relationships with their peers. The idea of worker competition was alien. Meanwhile, the significant number of vegetarians in India meant McDonald's needed to change its meat-heavy menu for one that included a greater number of vegetarian options.

Geert Hofstede's pioneering work, which he began in the late 1970s, remains the most influential source for practitioners and scholars working in this field of enquiry. Hofstede's (1980) foundational work is based on one very large multinational organization, with employees working in 40 countries and 20 separate languages. The organization was IBM. From surveying 117,000 IBM employees, Hofstede initially proposed four intercountry norm values: individualism, power distance, masculinity, and uncertainty avoidance. In subsequent research studies, he uncovered two additional dimensions of national culture: long-term orientation and indulgence (Hofstede, 1991).

Individualism represents the extent to which the goals of the individual are emphasized over the goals of the greater society. New Zealand scores high on individualism, whereas a country like South Korea scores low. A practical manifestation of this national culture dimension can be shown when a New Zealand worker and a South Korean worker are asked to describe themselves. The New Zealand worker is likely to use words/phrases like outgoing, enjoy sports, interested in music, etc. In contrast, the South Korean worker is likely to use such words/phrases as father, eldest son, and employee of Samsung. The New Zealand worker's description highlights the individualist New Zealand national culture, whereas the South Korean worker's description underlines the collectivist national culture of South Korea.

Power distance refers to the different ways in which nations address the issue of inequality among their members. High power distance cultures are accepting of high inter-member inequality. South Korea displays a relatively high power distance. Low power distance cultures expect a more equal sharing of power. New Zealand is an example of a low power distance country. The old adage that "Jack is as good as his master" epitomizes New Zealand's power distance.

The two dimensions of individualism and power distance have practical implications for performance management system design. A country like South Korea, which exhibits low individualism and high power distance, is better suited to a centralized organizational structure. In contrast, a country like New Zealand, which displays high individualism and low power distance, is better matched with a decentralized organizational structure.

Hofstede's third dimension of national culture is masculinity. High masculinity national cultures are characterized by members' belief in gender-specific work roles (e.g., males are doctors and females are nurses) and where the pursuit of money is widespread. Low masculinity cultures, which are sometimes called feminine cultures, view work as gender-neutral, place a high value on quality of life, and emphasize the importance of congenial relationships among societal members. New Zealand scores high on masculinity, and South Korea scores low on this cultural dimension.

When studying this dimension of national culture, it is important to avoid becoming bogged down with the terminology Hofstede has chosen. The word masculinity is likely to conjure up thoughts of brawn, power, and risk-taking, whereas the word femininity is likely to suggest being caring, protective, and affectionate. These traditional meanings must be avoided. Instead one must accept the definitions applied by Hofstede.

Masculinity's influence on performance management design is principally linked to the organizational systems, processes, and procedures an organization operates. When measuring and rewarding employee performance, masculine national cultures are likely to adopt extrinsic rewards. These rewards will include bonuses, pay rises, and promotions. Meanwhile, feminine cultures are likely to rely on intrinsic rewards, which involve initiatives to enrich the job and make it more satisfying for the worker.

Uncertainty avoidance refers to a society's appetite for risk. High uncertainty avoidance means a low appetite for risk, whereas low uncertainty avoidance implies the opposite. New Zealand scores low on uncertainty avoidance, and South Korea scores high on uncertainty avoidance.

The most common way high uncertainty avoidance cultures try to reduce their exposure to risk is by adopting a large number of highly-specific rules and regulations. Since employees are themselves members of the society that values predictability and dislikes uncertainty, the workers will benefit from and be averse to breaking their organization's rules. Based on this assumption, high uncertainty avoidance cultures will crave formality and centralization. In contrast, low uncertainty avoidance cultures will be more receptive to fewer rules and greater employee involvement in decision-making.

Long-term orientation is a function of the extent to which a society stands for tradition and steadfastness or adaptation and pragmatic problem-solving. South Korea exemplifies the former type of national culture. Even the most casual observer of South Korean culture will quickly perceive the profound influence tradition plays in these people's lives. Status, age, and gender punctuate a myriad of personal interactions ranging from everyday encounters to infrequent rituals and rites of passage. New Zealand is an example of a country with a low long-term orientation. Although part of the reason for its orientation derives from its fairly recent history, western cultures in general are known to display relatively low long-term orientations.

Long-term orientation will influence the organizational structures organizations adopt. Organizations located in countries with high long-term orientations will be likely to use formal organizational structures. Organizations situated in countries with low long-term orientations will tend to use informal organizational structures.

Indulgence is Hofstede's final national culture dimension. This dimension refers to people's ability/inability to control their desires and impulses. In high indulgent cultures, such as New Zealand, people seek immediate gratification. Meanwhile, in low indulgent countries, like South Korea, people exhibit a greater willingness to delay their present cravings and invest in the future.

A nation's propensity for indulgence will likely influence the organizational systems, processes, and procedures performance management lever. Organizations located in indulgent countries will employ performance measurement systems that have an annual or even quarterly focus. In contrast, organizations situated in countries with low indulgence will construct performance measurement systems featuring long planning periods and extended evaluation periods.

Before ending this discussion on national culture, it is important to recognize that Hofstede's national culture taxonomy is not the only framework that exists. In addition to the scholarly contributions of Hall (1976) and Hampden-Turner and Trompenaars (1996), Jonathan

> *Review Question 14.3:* How does national culture influence performance management design?
> *Answer:* Please see the Answer section starting on page 283

Haidt, in his book *The Righteous Mind* (2012), offers the idea that national culture can be defined by the collective morality of a nation's citizens. Haidt identifies six dimensions of morality: care/harm, liberty/oppression, fairness/cheating, loyalty/betrayal, authority/subversion, and sanctity/degradation.

The taxonomies of Hofstede and Haidt share a commonality. For example, Hofstede's power distance dimension appears to be equivalent to Haidt's authority/subversion. And just as it is possible to connect Hofstede's dimensions of national culture to performance management design, so too can this mapping be accomplished with Haidt's dimensions. As one example, the dimension fairness/cheating would have a strong association with organizations' use of formal organizational structures. Organizations located in national cultures known for cheating will want to place a strong emphasis on formal systems as a way to reduce their organizations' exposure to this cheating behaviour and the harm it can cause.

As a final thought before leaving this topic of national culture and performance management design, it must be understood that national culture represents an average member's propensity to behave in a particular way. Although most people will behave in an average way, or otherwise there would be no such construct as national culture, this does not mean that everyone behaves this way. For whatever reason, whether it is due to someone's newness to a culture or a significant event that changed a person's outlook from that of other societal members, cultural diversity can and does occur. The presence of intra-country cultural diversity means that a company like Kyocera – which relies upon finding employees who are willing to work long hours, accept paternalistic management styles, and identify with a wider group of employees than just their immediate department – can find the right type of employee irrespective of its various organizational units' very different national settings.

GOVERNMENT REGULATION

National governments have the ability to influence organizations on everything from the strategies they pursue to the organizational systems, processes, and procedures they use. Governments operate commerce commissions, federal trade commissions, or other offices with similar names that have the authority to sanction or prohibit various organizational mergers. The main reason a government would prohibit a merger is if it believed the merger would not be in the best interests of the public (i.e., there would be a significant erosion in competition). A recent example of when this occurred was Vodafone NZ's attempt to merge with Sky TV. The New Zealand Commerce Commission refused this billion-dollar merger, stating it would have a detrimental effect on competition in the telecommunications industry. Thus, no matter whether it is the case of a firm that is pursuing a single-industry strategy and wants to improve its economies of scale by purchasing a competitor or a firm that wants to pursue a related-diversified strategy or even an unrelated-diversified strategy, the government can constrain these organizational aspirations.

An approach frequently used by governmental bodies responsible for reviewing planned corporate mergers is to apply the Herfindahl-Hirschman Index (HHI). The HHI is computed by summing the squares of the market shares of the firms within an industry. The purpose of squaring the market shares is to ascribe greater weight to the market shares of the largest firms in the industry based on the belief that it is these market shares that are most significant in determining the level of competition in a market.

The index can range from 0, which would require a very large number of firms that each control an infinitesimal share of the market, to 1, which would mean there is only a single producer/supplier. As an example, if an industry is comprised of 16 firms, where 6 each hold a 15% market share and the remaining 10 firms have 1% each, then the HHI is 13.6%. This can be calculated as:

$$0.15^2 + 0.15^2 + 0.15^2 + 0.15^2 + 0.15^2 + 0.15^2 + 0.01^2 + 0.01^2 + 0.01^2 + 0.01^2 + 0.01^2 + 0.01^2 + 0.01^2 + 0.01^2 + 0.01^2 + 0.01^2$$

Which can be simplified to:
$$(0.15^2 \star 6 \text{ firms}) + (0.01^2 \star 10 \text{ firms}) = 13.6\%$$

By contrast, in an industry where there are again 16 firms, but in this second case the top firm controls 80% of the market, 5 firms control 2% each, and the final 10 firms control 1% each, the HHI is 64.3%. Although the number of firms comprising the industry has remained the same, a higher HHI is to be expected now that one firm has a very large share of the market. The calculation of the HHI is as follows:

$$0.80^2 + (0.02^2 \star 5 \text{ firms}) + (0.01^2 \star 10 \text{ firms}) = 64.3\%$$

In the US, the Department of Justice (DOJ) and the Federal Trade Commission (FTC) use the HHI. The Antitrust Division of the DOJ views HHIs between 15% and 25% as indicative of "moderately concentrated" industries and HHIs above 25% as representing "highly concentrated" markets. Irrespective of these bands, proposed mergers that produce an HHI increase of 2% or more (e.g., HHI changes from 12% to 14%) will generally result in enhanced scrutiny.

Beyond constraining what mergers an organization can undertake, governments can also dictate the employee rights an organization is obligated to offer its employees. For example, EU Articles 5, 114, 115, 151, and 153 of the Treaty on the Functioning of the European Union (TFEU) state that employees have a right to information, consultation, and participation in such matters as restructurings, work-life balance, working hours, and occupational health and safety. In other words, EU legislation mandates a measure of organizational decentralization which may constrain what an organization might otherwise have implemented.

In addition to influencing an organization's strategy and structure, government legislation can impact the employee benefits an organization offers. These benefits, which would be captured in the performance management lever relating to human resource systems (which is itself a subset of organizational systems, processes, and procedures), are often used to support an organization's competitive strategy. For example, an organization that is pursuing a cost leader strategy would generally make sparse use of employee benefits. The cost leader would usually see employee benefits as an extravagance. Furthermore, since the cost leader typically sticks to tried-and-tested products/services and process technologies, it would not feel it is in the same race for the best employees as its competitors who pursue a differentiation strategy, especially those that differentiate on their products/services' innovation. However, an industry's innovators, or what Miles and Snow (1978) would term prospectors, would likely place quite a high value on attracting employees with above-average skill sets. To help attract these employees, prospectors would probably offer relatively generous employee benefits.

Some countries, however, have national legislation that mandates the minimum levels of employee benefits organizations can offer. Generally speaking, European countries have relatively high thresholds on the minimum standards organizations must give their employees. In Denmark, for example, workers who are made redundant receive 90% of their earnings for the previous 104 weeks. In the US, redundant workers receive just 40–50% of their previous weekly earnings for every week (up to a maximum of 26 weeks) that they remain redundant. Table 14.1 shows a variety of employee benefits and the different entitlements employees in various European countries and the US are entitled to.

Based on Table 14.1, European countries have very generous employee benefits compared with the US. Although any given European employer can exceed their nation's minimum entitlements in an attempt to attract better-qualified employees, in the US, which starts from a very low base, it is relatively easier for organizations to differentiate themselves from their competitors. Google is one such company that tries to use its employee benefit programmes to stand out from its competitors.

Google's very generous set of employee entitlements include running a free bus between areas all around the Bay Area and its Googleplex in Mountain View, California. Similar to Facebook, the company offers bikes to commute around its Googleplex and a fleet of electric cars to drive for off-campus business. In addition to the bikes and electric cars, the Googleplex has on-site fitness centres, as well as doctors, chiropractors, physiotherapists, and masseurs/masseuses. Not only does the company offer advice to employees on managing their finances for retirement, but if an employee dies, his/her spouse/partner receives 50% of the deceased employee's salary for the next decade. On top of this, the surviving children receive $1,000 a month until they reach 19 (or 23 if they are studying full-time). Google further offers free on-site smoking cessation programmes, cooking classes, and more. The company supports its employees' higher

TABLE 14.1 Employee benefit entitlements for various European countries and the US

Employee benefit	European country	US
Redundancy	In Denmark, 90% of employee's previous earnings for 104 weeks	40–50% of employee's previous earnings for up to 26 weeks
Sick leave	In the Netherlands, 104 weeks at 70% of salary	An average of five days, although 50% of employees receive nothing
Maternity leave	In the UK, 52 weeks (first six weeks at 90%, next 33 at£140/week, and final 13 unpaid)	12 weeks all unpaid
Paternity leave	In Finland, 45 working days	12 weeks all unpaid
Annual/vacation leave	In Sweden, France, and Denmark, 25 days paid leave is the minimum	An average of two weeks, although 25% of workers receive nothing

> *Review Question 14.4:* How do government policies influence performance management design?
>
> *Answer:* Please see the Answer section starting on page 283

degree studies, and even funds something as tangentially related to work as guitar lessons. Based on this plentiful array of employee benefits, it is easy to see how Google can differentiate itself from other organizations competing for similar employees.

LABOUR MARKETS

In the earlier discussion on industry's effect on performance management design, the presence of employees' professional orientations was examined. Although professionalism is certainly an employee characteristic associated with various labour markets, it was viewed as a defining dimension of industry and therefore included in this topic's discussion. Unlike employee characteristics that can be associated with particular industries, this section of the chapter discusses employee characteristics and other factors that are more generally associated with labour markets.

The level of unemployment in a labour market exerts a key constraint on an organization's performance management design. If unemployment is low, then organizations will need to compete for what are scarce, due to the low unemployment, human resources. As part of their competition, organizations are likely to make more liberal use of employee benefits. In contrast, in times of high unemployment, organizations will have less need to be so generous with their employee benefits.

Besides unemployment, labour markets can be characterized by the general abilities and personalities of the employees. For example, an often overlooked characteristic is the attitude employees have for challenge. Hackman and Oldham (1980) have argued that employees can be distinguished by their growth need strength (GNS). GNS, which is generally assessed by administering a questionnaire (in other words, it could be part of a battery of psychometric tests), measures an individual's propensity for challenge. Low-GNS workers do not like challenge, whereas high-GNS workers do.

The application of GNS to work settings is quite simple but profound. Attempts to enrich work environments through such programmes as worker empowerment and participative decision-making are likely to fail if the workers possess low GNS. These workers simply do not want the challenge associated with these enriched working environments. As a consultant at Stanley Tools, I observed this predisposition firsthand. The company had called me in to help implement a job enrichment programme in one of its production departments. After interviewing several employees, it became apparent that these employees were not interested in, and in fact were keen to do anything they could to avoid, becoming part of an enriched work environment. They saw their work as solely a vehicle for purchasing life's necessities and whatever luxuries the leftover component of their pay cheques could buy. Because these workers had so

> *Review Question 14.5:* How do labour markets influence performance management design?
> *Answer:* Please see the Answer section starting on page 283
> *Review Question 14.6:* What is growth need strength? Provide examples of organizational
>   settings where it is likely to differ. How is its presence associated with performance
>   management design?
> *Answer:* Please see the Answer section starting on page 283

little desire for challenge, the idea of creating higher satisfaction and motivation by providing them with more control and responsibility for aspects of their job was never going to be realized. As one worker explained, "Managers are responsible for the decisions here and should not be ducking this responsibility by telling me to make the decisions for them. I am here just for the pay cheque."

Understanding employees' GNS is fundamental to and must be understood prior to making any decisions about organizational structure, especially decisions about the amount of centralization/decentralization to operate. Employees with low GNS are better matched with centralized organizational structures, and high-GNS employees are compatible with decentralized organizational structures.

CONCLUSION

This chapter identified the four external contingent factors of industry, national culture, government regulation, and labour markets and discussed how each factor serves to influence performance management design. External contingent factors are seldom discussed in the performance management literature; and on the rare occasions they are discussed, only the most nondescript, passing remarks are made.

As was the case when discussing the effect of internal contingent factors in Chapter 13, scholars and practitioners must be aware of the set of external contingent factors that can influence an organization's performance management design. Without these understandings, scholars may produce specious findings and practitioners may develop performance management designs that are not fit for purpose.

REFERENCES

Burns, T. and Stalker, G.M. (1961) *The Management of Innovation*, London: Tavistock.
Hackman, J. and Oldham, G. (1980) *Work Redesign*, Reading, MA: Addison-Wesley.
Haidt, J. (2012) *The Righteous Mind*, New York: Random House.
Hall, E.T. (1976) *Beyond Culture*, New York: Doubleday.
Hampden-Turner, C.M. and Trompenaars, F. (1996) A world turned upside down: doing business in Asia. In P. Joynt and M. Waner (Eds), *Managing Across Cultures: Issues and Perspectives*, London: Thomson, pp. 275–305.

Hofstede, G.H. (1980) *Culture's Consequences: International Differences in Work-Related Values*, Beverly Hills, CA: Sage.

Hofstede, G.H. (1991) *Cultures and Organizations*, London: McGraw-Hill.

International Accounting Education Standards Board. (2017) *International Education Standard 4: Initial Professional Development – Professional Values, Ethics, and Attitudes 2015*, New York: International Federation of Accountants.

Kallio, K., Kallio, T.J., Tienari, J. and Hyvönen, T. (2016) Ethos at stake: performance management and academic work in universities, *Human Relations*, Vol. 69, No. 3, pp. 685–709.

Lawrence, P.R. and Lorsch, J. (1967) *Organization and Environment*, Boston, MA: Harvard Business School, Division of Research.

Miles, R.E. and Snow, C.C. (1978) *Organizational Strategy, Structure, and Process*, New York: McGraw-Hill.

Weber, M. (1947) *The Theory of Social and Economic Organization*, Glencoe, IL: Free Press.

Woodward, J. (1958) *Management and Technology*, London: Her Majesty's Stationery Office.

Woodward, J. (1965) *Industrial Organisations: Theory and Practice*, London: Oxford University Press.

Conclusion

INTRODUCTION

This chapter extends and concludes the book's previous discussions on the interconnected nature of the elements of performance management. Throughout the book, the idea that performance management represents an integrated package of influence of and control on employee behaviour has been promoted. Further and final comments on the interconnectivity of an organization's performance management system are provided.

The chapter ends with a discussion of the research opportunities that exist in the field of performance management. This discussion covers examinable research propositions, issues associated with construct specification, and research method choice.

PERFORMANCE MANAGEMENT AS A HOLISTIC PACKAGE

The thesis of this book is that one of the most critical tasks of any group of senior managers is ensuring employees implement their organization's strategy. Although strategy formulation is undoubtedly a critical senior management responsibility, unless employees are continuously working to implement their respective organizations' strategies, their organizations will suffer. Performance management is the process that senior managers use to ensure employees' effective and efficient implementation of organizational strategy.

Performance management relies on three primary levers of influence to promote the type of employee behaviour that will best support the organization's implementation of its strategy, as well as the ultimate attainment of the organization's long-term goals and objectives. As this

DOI: 10.4324/9781003267195-19

book has shown, far from operating in isolation, these three performance management levers are interconnected. It is for this reason that Figure 3.1 represents the performance management process as jigsaw pieces that interlock with each other and the organizational strategy they are trying to enable. Significant discussion was devoted to describing how organizational strategy (see Chapters 7 and 8) illuminates and gives purpose to the decisions an organization makes about the organizational structure (see Chapter 10), organizational systems, processes, and procedures (see Chapter 11), and organizational culture (see Chapter 12) it will adopt.

Unlike the singular prescriptions of agency theory, the approach taken in this book emphasizes the more holistic performance management designs that contingency theory promotes. This theory recognizes that although general relationships exist between competitive strategies (e.g., cost leadership, differentiation, and confrontation) and performance management system designs, these relationships are only ever provisional. In particular, the final specification of an organization's performance management design must await the further specification of an organization's internal contingent factors (i.e., leadership style, organizational lifecycle, organizational size, and organizational ownership) and external contingent factors (industry, national culture, government regulation, and labour markets). These contingent factors were extensively examined in Chapters 13 and 14.

The book's visualization of performance management as a combination of interlocking levers of employee influence that fuse together to support employees' implementations of their respective organizations' strategies is consistent with previous literature's claims about the superiority of conceptualizing performance management from a holistic perspective, or what is called a package or system approach (see Demartini and Otley, 2020), rather than a reductionist perspective that views performance management elements in isolation of one another. For example, Malmi and Brown (2008) have forcefully argued for viewing performance management as a unified package of interconnected organizational systems that serve to direct employee behaviour. Malmi and Brown proceed to list five types of controls that comprise their particular performance management framework: planning, cybernetic, rewards and compensation, administrative, and cultural controls. Figure 15.1 presents an adapted version of the Malmi and Brown model.

The perceptive reader will see significant similarities between this book's Figure 3.1 and Malmi and Brown's framework. For example, Malmi and Brown's cybernetic controls – most notably the parts they label as budgets, financial performance measurement systems, non-inancial performance measurement systems, and hybrid performance measurement systems – are similar to and form part of this book's organizational systems, processes, and procedures performance management lever. Malmi and Brown's planning control can also be mapped to this book's organizational systems, processes, and procedures lever of performance management. The planning control these authors refer to is part of the budgeting process described in this book (see Chapter 11). A key part of budgeting does after all involve planning.

Malmi and Brown's reward and compensation control parallel this book's employee incentive systems. Moreover, the components of what Malmi and Brown refer to as administrative control would map across two of this book's main levers of performance management. There is an obvious one-to-one correspondence between what Malmi and Brown and this book call organizational structure. The only real distinction between Malmi and Brown and this book is that organizational structure assumes greater prominence in this book, by virtue of it being one of the three main levers of performance management. Policies and procedures, which is the

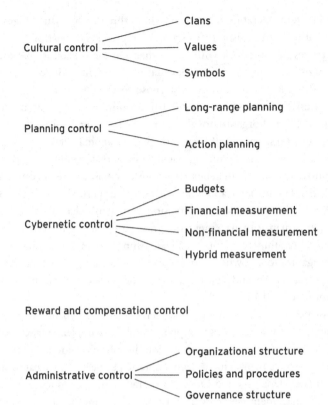

Cultural control —— Clans
—— Values
—— Symbols

Planning control —— Long-range planning
—— Action planning

Cybernetic control —— Budgets
—— Financial measurement
—— Non-financial measurement
—— Hybrid measurement

Reward and compensation control

Administrative control —— Organizational structure
—— Policies and procedures
—— Governance structure

FIGURE 15.1 Malmi and Brown's model of performance management as a package of control.

Source: Adapted from Malmi and Brown (2008: 281).

second component of Malmi and Brown's administrative control, feature as part of this book's organizational systems, processes, and procedures lever of performance management.

There are, however, two elements of Malmi and Brown's model that fail to match well with this book's performance management framework. The first is their governance structure, which they describe as "the company's board structure and composition, as well as its various management and project teams" (2008: 294). Although the second half of their description harmonizes with this book's organizational structure performance management lever, their first part (i.e., board structure and composition) would fail to be seen as relevant by the majority of performance management practitioners and scholars.

Malmi and Brown's cultural control presents the most problematic fit with this book's model. At first glance this would not seem to be the case. This book, after all, extensively discusses culture. The problem is that although this book is quite clear about the need to view organizational culture as separate from national culture, the Malmi and Brown model seems to ignore the need for such a distinction. This oversight is most unfortunate. Organizational culture serves as a powerful lever of performance management. In contrast, national culture is an external contingent factor that scholars and practitioners must be aware of when studying and designing performance management systems.

The lack of recognition and understanding awarded to organizational culture and national culture continues to handicap the study and practice of performance management. Sometimes it is due to conflating these two separate cultural constructs, and on other occasions, it occurs when scholars relegate culture to the status of a contextual variable. For example, Ferreira and Otley (2009: 267) refer to organizational culture as "a notable contextual variable." The end result of these misrepresentations of organizational and national culture is the failure by practitioners and researchers to award these two constructs the full and separate attention they deserve.

In fact, a strong case can be made for how the literature's inability to recognize and document the role organizational and national culture play in performance management can at least partly explain why the average senior manager takes insufficient interest in organizational culture. How frequently, for example, does an organization's newly appointed CEO look to revamp organizational structures and decree new organizational budgeting, planning, and employee incentive systems? The answer is almost invariably. In comparison, how often do new CEOs try to mould their organizations' cultures to better support their organizations' respective strategies? Here the answer is seldom. Although modifying an organization's culture will always be highly challenging and will always require significant commitments of time and resources, the rewards for those who are willing to make the investment are substantial. Perhaps if the literature was clearer about the separate compositions of organizational culture and national culture and this literature was able to convey the powerful contribution organizational culture makes to employees' implementation of their organizations' strategies, then maybe more CEOs would be willing to invest in their organizations' cultures to ensure they fully support the strategies being pursued.

One further commonly overlooked element of performance management is the influence of human resource management practices. Although this book does not recognize human resource systems as a separate lever of performance management, the book does present it as one of the three main pillars that comprise the performance management lever called organizational systems, processes, and procedures. A section of Chapter 11 was devoted to enunciating the components of human resource systems and explaining how they contribute to an organization's attempts to influence employees' implementation of the organization's strategy.

In contrast to the recognition human resource systems receive in this book, other performance management writers either ignore it (e.g., Anthony and Govindarajan, 2007), make vague reference to it (Ferreira and Otley, 2009), or assume it resides under various performance management elements (Malmi and Brown, 2008). The closest Ferreira and Otley (2009: 278) come to discussing human resource systems is when they write, "Targets [are] generally set centrally by the board of directors after consultation with human resources, finance, and planning and control managers." Meanwhile, Malmi and Brown claim that an organization's human resource practices and systems are subsumed under various components of their five performance management controls. They assume that employee selection is part of their cultural control, employee placement falls under their organizational control, and employee training belongs to both their administrative control and cultural control. With the exception of this book, the performance management literature's relegation of human resource systems to an insignificant or ancillary role contradicts organizational scholars' general consensus that these systems play a key role in encouraging high employee commitment, motivation, and performance.

In sum, compared with other performance management frameworks, the model presented in this book offers a strong holistic model, one that Ferreira and Otley (2009) would likely term as a tightly coupled, holistic model. These scholars view such performance management models as representative of one endpoint on a wide-ranging continuum for describing performance management models. Drawing on contingency theory, Ferreira and Otley (2009) view positions along this continuum as being more or less amenable to organizational success depending on the specific set of contingent factors an organization faces. According to Demartini and Otley (2020: 2), the loose or tight coupling of an organization's performance management system should be based on the organization's need for responsiveness and distinctiveness. Responsiveness is regarded as enabling organizational control and efficiency, while distinctiveness is seen as enabling autonomy and innovation. Organizations with high needs for both responsiveness and distinctiveness should use loosely coupled performance management systems, while organizations with low needs for both responsiveness and distinctiveness should use tightly coupled performance management systems. Organizations with intermediate needs for responsiveness and distinctiveness should use medium coupled performance management systems.

Otley and his colleagues' approach to the design of performance management system coupling requires careful scrutiny. As previously mentioned, Otley and his colleagues view organizational culture as a "notable contextual variable" (Ferreira and Otley, 2009: 267) rather than a critical performance management lever of influence. Not only do Otley and his colleagues overlook organizational culture's centrality to performance management, but their description of coupling invariably involves formal measures of control. For example, Demartini and Otley's (2020: 8) "three pairs of couplings" comprise budgeting and non-financial performance measurement, budgeting and performance appraisal, and non-financial performance measurement and performance appraisal. The idea of how formal mechanisms of budgeting, non-financial performance measurement, and performance appraisal can be combined with informal systems like organizational culture is never discussed. This book's readers will know that the three performance management levers of influence can be relied upon in varying amounts to create the desired amount and type of overall employee influence an organization requires. Using Demartini and Otley's (2020) terminology, organizations with high needs for responsiveness and distinctiveness will wish to implement flat, organically-operating organizational structures and foster organizational cultures defined by employee collaboration and empowerment. The performance management lever of organizational systems, processes, and procedures should play a subdominant role. As a point of contrast, organizations with low needs for responsiveness and distinctiveness would feature tall organizational structures, industrious, as opposed to creative, organizational cultures, and place high reliance on organizational systems, processes, and procedures as a way to ensure organizational activities are standardized and reliably repeated.

This book has consistently adopted the position that it is the combined effect of the three main levers of influence that allow an organization to achieve the right employee motivation and performance. As illustrated in Figure 3.2 in Chapter 3, successful managers will find they must use judicious combinations of the three levers of influence; otherwise, they risk creating too little or too much influence, with both states being detrimental to organizational performance. This idea of using different combinations of employee influence to achieve desired organizational outcomes, along with the idea that different combinations can substitute for one another, can be likened to Sandelin's (2008) concept of equifinality.

As noted at the book's outset, the novel performance management model presented draws upon the business disciplines of management accounting, strategic management, organizational behaviour, and organizational theory. Accordingly, beyond offering a model featuring greater holism, this book's model provides clear recognition of the formal/informal and constraining/enabling influence of performance management. No true understanding of performance management can exist without an appreciation of these different properties.

As discussed in Chapter 10, organizational structure involves the specification of the amount of formality or informality an organization operates. The extent to which an organization prescribes many rules and procedures (and therefore displays high formality) will depend upon a host of salient organizational and environmental factors, including the competitive strategy, the existence of various internal and external contingent factors, and the design and operation of the organization's other performance management levers. Some situations will call for more formal organizational structures and others for more informal structures. Although this observation seems natural and obvious, as Cardinal (2017) has shown, the performance management research has overwhelmingly studied formal control. Future research needs to redress this imbalance, and hopefully this book's model can serve as the theoretical foundation from which these research studies can be built.

Cardinal (2017) has also demonstrated that the literature focuses mostly on the employee-constraining influence of performance management. Largely overlooked is the enabling influence of performance management. As this book has discussed, it is invariably the case that performance management will serve the dual role of constraining/coercing and enabling/empowering. For example, budgets – which are represented under the performance management lever of operating systems, processes, and procedures – serve to both constrain and enable. In particular, on the one hand, budgets dictate the means within which employees and their subunits must operate. On the other hand, budgets bestow authority and resources on employees and enable them to make decisions and take action. As another example, organizational culture will support employee behaviour that is consistent with the organizational group's values, norms, and beliefs, but it will also sanction and punish employees when their behaviour falls outside the group's shared conceptions of acceptability. In other words, performance management will invariably exert a dual constraining and enabling role.

Today's organizations and the organizational environments they are operating in are becoming increasingly complex and turbulent. Furthermore, the key drivers of organizational success are more and more a function of organizational innovation and learning. Ensuring an organization's employees fully understand and are continuously working to support their organization's strategy implementation has never been so important. The margin for organizational error has decreased markedly over the past decade and continues to do so.

In my long experience of working with organizations, the differences between highperforming and poor-performing organizations are surprisingly small. I have witnessed examples of quite good, and even exemplary, management practices among some of the laggards and sometimes even among the organizations that failed. In fact, no matter how poorly performing the organization may be, it is a rarity to find an organization with performance that is deficient across the board. Instead it is usually a small subset of things, and often just a handful, that the good organizational performers do better than their underperforming counterparts.

Review Question 15.1: How does this book's model of performance management represent a strong holistic model?

Answer: Please see the Answer section starting on page 283

Review Question 15.2: How does this book's performance management model compare to Ferreira and Otley's (2009) and Malmi and Brown's models?

Answer: Please see the Answer section starting on page 283

Review Question 15.3: How does this book's performance management model feature both constraining and enabling influences on employees? Give examples of these constraining and enabling influences for each of the three performance management levers.

Answer: Please see the Answer section starting on page 283

Invariably, however, the one factor that sets apart the good and poor performers is the fitness for purpose of their performance management systems. I have yet to witness a poorly performing organization that did not also have an ill-suited performance management system. Having reached this point in the book, I trust that the meaning of ill-suited can be recognized as an organization's inability to appropriately design the three main levers of performance management in a manner that supports employees' implementation of the organization's strategy. When designing these three levers, senior managers will need to take into consideration the organization's internal and external contingent factors.

My hope in writing this book is that practitioners and managers will be better able to understand the composition of performance management and the vital role it plays in enabling organizational success. For no matter how good an organization's products/services may be, how loyal its customers are, how hard its employees work, or how much charisma its leaders exude, organizations that fail to properly design their performance management systems will themselves fail too.

RESEARCH DIRECTIONS

This book's presentation of performance management as an interconnected set of three main levers of employee influence offers numerous and immediate avenues for research. First, this book's Figure 3.1 provides the foundation for developing several research propositions. The most obvious research propositions have been referred to throughout the book. Table 7.4, for example, presents the expected relationships between corporate-level strategies and the design of the three performance management levers. Table 8.2 offers similar prescriptive advice for the relationships between competitive strategies and the design of the three performance management levers. Table 13.1 provides a further set of expected relationships between internal contingent factors and the design of the three performance management levers. And finally, Chapter 14 extends the set of researchable relationships by proposing linkages between four external contingent factors and the performance management levers.

When studying the proposed relationships, it is essential that researchers understand that the entire set of variables represented in this book's Figure 3.1 needs to be included as part of

> *Review Question 15.4:* What are some of the future performance management research opportunities awaiting today's scholars?
>
> *Answer:* Please see the Answer section starting on page 283

their research designs. To do otherwise, by perhaps omitting key internal and external contingent factors and focusing on only the relationships between competitive strategies and the design of the three levers of performance management, would contravene this book's thesis that performance management must be understood as a holistic and integrated package of employee behaviour influence and control.

Researchers will of course find that before they can even embark on studying the relationships that are inherent in Figure 3.1, they must initially provide fuller enunciation and ultimately operationalization of the constructs presented in Figure 3.1. And once they have accomplished this task of construct specification and operationalization, researchers must also be prepared to develop survey instruments capable of capturing the underlying phenomena.

Case study work is likely to be the favoured research method. Despite Otley's (1980) long-standing call for performance management research to incorporate an integrated-package approach, it has received only the faintest response in reply. Until sufficient inductively-developed theory exists, larger and cross-sectional studies must await their appointed time. In fact, it may be wiser not to rush into, or even eschew altogether, cross-sectional research. Longitudinal studies may be necessary to reveal and account for delayed or intermittent effects between the variables comprising performance management.

There will be no shortcuts to the programme of research required. Although this may frustrate some researchers, hopefully, the challenge presented will inspire others. As Mihaly Csikszentmihalyi (2008) once stated, "The best moments in our lives are not the passive, receptive, relaxing times …The best moments usually occur if a person's body or mind is stretched to its limits in a voluntary effort to accomplish something difficult and worthwhile." Or perhaps inspiration for action can be gleaned from John F. Kennedy's impassioned 1962 speech, when he announced the goal of landing an astronaut on the moon, saying, "We choose to go to the moon in this decade and do the other things, not because they are easy, but because they are hard." In a similar vein to Csikszentmihalyi and Kennedy, I challenge my peers who work in the field of performance management to refrain from undertaking research that is easy but unlikely to significantly advance our knowledge. Instead, I urge them to traverse a path that is more difficult and arduous, but ultimately more meaningful and rewarding.

REFERENCES

Anthony, R. and Govindarajan, V. (2007) *Management Control Systems* (12th Edition), New York: McGraw-Hill-Irwin.

Cardinal, L. (2017) An examination of organizational control-outcome relationships and the challenges of 21st century organizations, *Performance Measurement Association Australasia Conference*, Dunedin, New Zealand, 1–3 March.

Csikszentmihalyi, M. (2008) *Flow: The Psychology of Optimal Experience* (1st Harper Perennial Modern Classics ed.), New York: Harper Perennial.

Demartini, M.C. and Otley, D. (2020) Beyond the system vs. package dualism in performance management systems design: a loose coupling approach, *Accounting, Organizations and Society*, Vol. 86, pp. 1–16.

Ferreira, A. and Otley, D. (2009) The design and use of performance management systems: an extended framework for analysis, *Management Accounting Research*, Vol. 20, No. 4, pp. 263–282.

Malmi, T. and Brown, D.A. (2008) Management control systems as a package – opportunities, challenges and research directions, *Management Accounting Research*, Vol. 19, No. 4, pp. 287–300.

Otley, D. (1980) The contingency theory of management accounting: achievement and prognosis, *Accounting, Organizations and Society*, Vol. 5, No. 4, pp. 413–428.

Sandelin, M. (2008) Operation of management control practices as a package: a case study on control system variety in a growth firm context, *Management Accounting Research*, Vol. 19, No. 4, pp. 324–343.

Cases

AOTEAROA PURE ICE CREAM

In spite of the seasonal nature of our business, the sale of ice cream is generally easy to predict from one quarter to the next. Because of this high predictability, decision making is centralized. The New Zealand home office experiments with and decides on the introduction of any new ice cream flavours. And I, as the US-based regional manager, make decisions, in consultation with our home office, on where to locate new stores or what existing stores should be expanded or closed. Presently we have stores in five areas of California: San Diego, Los Angeles, Monterey, Carmel, and San Francisco. I also decide, again in consultation with home office, on the menu prices. The company is in an expansion mode. We presently have 45 stores throughout Australia, Asia, and Europe and are planning on opening five more stores over the next 15 months. One of the stores is planned for Portland Oregon and the other for Seattle Washington. It is a truly exciting time to be part of the company.

Ann Cotton, US Regional Manager

Ann Cotton was the US-regional manager of Aotearoa Pure. She had worked in this role for the past three years, being instrumental in the opening of Aotearoa Pure's first store, which was the Los Angles store located in Venice Beach.

Hector Rodríguez was the Los Angeles store manager. He managed the store with the help of two part-time employees. Each part-time employee worked an average of 20–25 hours per week.

Hector described the last three months of operations as "frustrating," stating:

This summer has been frustrating. There has been terrible weather as a result of the El Niño that has prevailed since May. An El Niño is a climate pattern defined by warmer-than-average Pacific Ocean water that brings wetter and colder weather to California. Some long-time residents say it was the worst summer that they can remember. Sunny southern California just didn't live up to its reputation. Instead it was cold, rainy, and at times downright nasty ... at least for southern California standards. Everyone knows ice cream sells best when the weather is sunny and hot. And furthermore, not only was the weather bad, but the road construction that took place outside the store for most of July and part of August surely didn't help matters.

Each of the five California ice cream stores was treated as an investment centre. For Hector, the three months ending 31 August were associated with sub-par performance. In fact, he had just finished reading an email from Ngaire Hapeta, the company's CFO, criticizing his performance. Exhibit 1 provides a copy of this email, and Exhibit 2 provides a copy of the budget and actual results of the store's performance referred to in Ngaire's email.

According to Ann, careful attention was paid to the construction of each store's budget. As Ann proceeded to say, "We take into consideration such factors as a store's previous performance, local competitors' strategies, the company's growth expectations for each individual store, and even historical weather data. Essentially nothing is omitted." Exhibit 3 reports key budget assumptions and weather statistics pertaining to the latest quarter's performance.

As explained by Hector, Aotearoa Pure sought to appeal to customers' love for ice cream, as well as their fascination with New Zealand. Hector noted:

We have a reputation as a shop selling premium ice cream at premium prices. Generally speaking, our menu prices are about 20–30% higher than our competitors. We also try to showcase a bit of New Zealand in our stores. Our walls display photos of bungie jumping in Queenstown, Great Walks like the Milford Track, and whales, penguins and other wildlife in New Zealand's coastal waters.

Customer service is a vital component of our strategy. We pride ourselves on the high level of customer service we offer. We match our use of the finest ice cream ingredients with ensuring our stores are immaculate, tidy and welcoming. We are proud to be the servants of our customers and will do all we can to please them. For example, while most ice cream shops only mix different flavours of ice cream if it is for full scoops, we are happy to cater to any of our customers' calls for multiple ice cream flavours. If a customer wants five different flavours, that's okay. It might mean serving half or even quarter scoops, but we'll do it.

Ann picked up on this point of customer service, stating:

We want our customers to thoroughly enjoy their experience. In fact, a key to our plans for expansion is customer service. We know, and our customers always testify to this, that we have the best ice cream. But because we charge relatively high prices, we need to have exceptional customer service. One way we encourage this is through the way my salary, travel and other expenses are allocated. Previously, we allocated these costs, which are about $100,000 per year, equally to the five stores. In other words, each store was allocated $20,000 per year. Starting in the current year, we changed the cost driver from stores to customer satisfaction.

Out of my budget, we hire an independent marketing company to measure each store's customer satisfaction every quarter. Customers choose from one of four categories: very happy with service, somewhat happy with service, somewhat unhappy with service, and very unhappy with service. For each store we add together the percent of customers who report being somewhat or very unhappy to create a store-specific dissatisfaction score. We next sum the five store's dissatisfaction scores to produce an aggregate total. A ratio comprised of the numerator showing a particular store's score and the denominator showing the five store's aggregate total is used to allocate the overhead costs associated with my regional manager's role. Exhibit 4 contains the calculated allocations of overhead costs for the past quarter.

In summing up the past three months, Hector stated:

> It has been an unusual three months. I know head office is not pleased with my store's performance, but I think my staff and I performed quite well under what were very trying conditions. It is just unfortunate that this is not being reflected in the performance measures. I know our customer satisfaction showed a significant decline, but this I feel can be largely attributed to the road construction which caused all sorts of problems with noise, dust and even parking. As a result, the annual ROI-based bonus I usually count on is shot. There is no way I will be able to make up for this past quarter.

QUESTIONS:

1   What competitive strategy is Aotearoa Pure Ice Cream pursuing?
2   What is your assessment of Hector Rodríguez's store's performance?
3   What is your assessment of Ann Cotton's method of allocating the overhead costs associated with her regional manager's role to each of the five stores?
4   What advice do you have for improving Aotearoa Pure Ice Cream's performance management system?

EXHIBIT 1: MEMO FROM HEAD OFFICE

From: Ngaire Hapeta
Sent: 5 September 2016
To: Hector Rodríguez
Subject: Store performance 1 June to 31 August 2016

Store performance was well below expectations for the summer period. This is meant to be our busiest time of year. We normally record 35% of our profits during this three-month period. I note that revenue was nearly 33% lower than budgeted and profit was over 90% lower than

Balance Sheet 31 August 2016 (in USD)	
Cash	$8,100
Inventory	$750
Prepaid insurance	$900
Leasehold improvements	$180,000
Equipment	$50,000
Total	$239,750
Accounts payable	$15,750
Debt	$140,000
Owners' equity	$84,000
Total	$239,750

budgeted. In addition, when the exchange rate is taken into consideration, your revenues and profits fare even worse. We budgeted an average cross rate of USD/NZD[1] of 1.47, but the average rate turned out to be 1.43. In other words, we expected NZD profit before taxes to be $56,124 (Exhibit 2's budgeted profit of $38,180 * the exchange rate of 1.47). Instead, the converted profit was only $5,949.

I further note that based on the capital your store employs, which is detailed in your store's balance sheet which I reproduce below, your ROI before taxes was only 1.7% for the three months ended 31 August (i.e., your store's profit of $4,160 divided by assets of $239,750). Even annualizing this rate would produce an ROI well below corporate expectations of 20%. In fact, at the ROI your store is generating, the company should probably be thinking of investing in AAA corporate bonds instead of tying its money up in your Los Angeles store.

Immediate corrective actions are required. We cannot afford another period like this past one. In fact, the very survivability of your store is at stake.

EXHIBIT 2: ACTUAL VS BUDGET FOR 1 JUNE TO 31 AUGUST 2016 (IN USD)

	Budget	Actual	Variance
Revenue	184,000	124,080	(59,920)
Variable expenses:			
Ice cream, cones, toppings, etc.	93,000	63,500	29,500
Part-time salaries (includes benefits)	12,000	9,000	3,000
Utilities (variable)	1,500	1,000	500
Total Variable expenses	106,500	73,500	33,000
Fixed expense:			
Rent	6,000	6,000	0
Store manager salary (includes benefits)	15,000	15,000	0
Utilities (fixed)	1,300	1,300	0
Depreciation	4,520	4,520	0
Interest	3,000	3,000	0
Insurance	2,000	1,700	300
Advertising	2,000	2,000	0
Cleaning supplies	500	400	100
Regional manager allocated costs	5,000	12,500	−7,500
Total fixed expenses	39,320	46,420	−7,100
Total expenses	145,820	119,920	25,900
Profit before taxes	38,180	4,160	(34,020)

NB: Bracketed numbers in the "Variance" column are unfavourable and non-bracketed numbers are favourable.

1 This ratio of United States dollars to New Zealand dollars should be interpreted as how many New Zealand dollars one United States dollar will buy. In other words, a rate of 1.47 means one United States dollar buys 1.47 New Zealand dollars.

EXHIBIT 3: BUDGET ASSUMPTIONS AND WEATHER STATISTICS FOR 1 JUNE TO 31 AUGUST 2016

	Budget assumptions	Actual
June:		
Days of bad weather (rain ≥ 1 mm and/or temp < 20°C)	3	18
Days of good weather (rain < 1 mm and temp ≥ 20°C)	27	12
Average daily number of customers	389	231
Average revenue per customer (1 June–31 August; in USD)	$5.00	$5.24
July:		
Days of bad weather (rain ≥ 1 mm and/or temp < 20°C)	1	14
Days of good weather (rain < 1 mm and temp ≥ 20°C)	30	17
Average daily number of customers	410	278
Average revenue per customer (1 June–31 August; in USD)	$5.00	$5.35
August:		
Days of bad weather (rain ≥ 1 mm and/or temp < 20°C)	2	17
Days of good weather (rain < 1 mm and temp ≥ 20°C)	29	14
Average daily number of customers	400	247
Average revenue per customer (1 June–31 August; in USD)	$5.00	$5.38

EXHIBIT 4: COST ALLOCATION PERCENTAGES AND ABSOLUTE AMOUNTS FOR CALIFORNIA STORES FOR THE PERIOD FROM 1 JUNE TO 31 AUGUST

	Percent of customers reporting dissatisfaction	Cost allocation (%)	Allocated costs of regional manager @ $25,000/quarter
Los Angeles	35	50	12,500
Carmel	6	8.5	2,143
Monterey	7	10	2,500
San Diego	13	18.5	4,643
San Francisco	9	13	3,214
Total	70	100	25,000

ELLINGTON KNITTING MILL, INC.

John Green, the President of Ellington Knitting Mill, and his brother Joe, the company's VP of Manufacturing, sat together in John's office awaiting the arrival of Jim, their brother, and the company's Chief Financial Officer. It was 8:30 am on a Monday, the appointed time for their weekly sales and production meeting. John and Joe were discussing the status of an order when

Jim strode into the office. Jim looked unusually sombre. When asked by Joe if there was any-thing wrong, Jim replied, "Plenty! For starters, just look at this." Jim thrust out a set of company financial statements (see Exhibit 1). John and Joe quickly read down the Income Statement's year-to-date column and understood the reason for Jim's concern.

JOHN: "I don't understand. I mean, I understand why we had the small profit for our first six months. Our accountant encouraged us to take high salaries to avoid the double taxation situation of our company being taxed on its profits and then we being taxed when the company's profits are distributed to us as dividends. However, I worked particularly hard during the past six months to bring in extra business and cannot understand how our sales could have decreased from the first half of the year. It just makes no sense."

JOE: "Are you sure you have these numbers right, Jim?"

JIM: "Yes, I am. I worked most of the weekend preparing these statements. At first, I too was surprised. But I double checked my work and am quite certain it is right."

JOHN: "I think getting to the bottom of these numbers has to be our top priority. Let's cancel today's scheduled meeting. Jim, I see you have copies of the financial statements. Please give one to Joe and leave the other for me. I suggest that each of us takes an independent look at the numbers and come up with some ways to improve what is an apparently sinking set of company fortunes. We will reconvene in my office at 8:30 tomorrow morning to discuss your ideas."

Company history and industry background

The three Green brothers started Ellington Knitting Mill on 1 September 1999 in their home-town of Ellington, Connecticut. In starting this business, they had taken their collective inheri-tance of their parents' estate and put it toward the establishment of the knitting mill.

John was given the role of President, Jim the role of Chief Financial Officer, and Joe the role of VP of operations. In some ways, these titles were ornamental, for the company consisted of only the Green brothers and two machine operators. As such, John was primarily responsible for sales, Jim for the accounting, and Joe for production.

Ellington Knitting Mill was a relatively small mill. It operated 15 identical knit-ting machines. These machines were purchased second hand, being surplus to a very large, Mississippi-based knitting mill. (Mississippi is a US state located in the deep south and borders on the Gulf of Mexico.) While these knitting machines were generally capable of producing any type of final design, they were better suited for less complex designs. This was primarily due to the greater time and trouble needed to set up the machines in comparison to new, more modern machines.

The knitting mill business was quite straightforward. Orders were received from the "converters." The converters then sold the fabrics to the garment producers. There were two main garment-producing centres in the US. New York City controlled the high fashion industry (i.e., women's dresses and men's suits), while Los Angeles dominated the manufacture of sports-wear. Ellington Knitting Mill supplied fabric exclusively to New York's high fashion market.

Knitting fabric was produced in rolls, the widths of which could vary considerably in size. While most rolls were sized between 56 and 60 inches, some special fabrics were produced in roll widths of less than 30 inches. These special fabrics were largely demanded by the Los Ange-les market for its production of women's sports tops. The length of a roll could be almost any amount but usually was between 50 and 100 yards.

The vast majority of the US knitting mills were located in southern California, typically Los Angeles, or the US's southeast. In recent years, Miami, Florida had become the Southeast's main centre for knitting mills. The knitting mills that once flourished in South Carolina had either migrated to Miami or closed down altogether. The major reason for this consolidation into Miami was the ever-increasing price competition exerted by overseas mills. Japan and Korea had historically supplied this competition. More recently, the Chinese had become the main competitive threat. Although the reputation of these Chinese knitting mills was for low cost and quality, their product quality had – and was continuing – to improve. In an attempt to meet this overseas threat, many of the Southeast mills had relocated to Miami, where they employed Hispanic workers for one-half to two-thirds of the salaries they had been paying.

Fabric destined for the high fashion market was divided into three broad categories. The low end consisted of fabric that fetched prices between $2.50 and $6.00 per yard. The medium market supported fabric prices between $7.00 and $15.00. The high end was characterized by fabric prices between $16.00 and $30.00. The Chinese, already a dominant player in the low end of the market, were now trying to muscle into the medium market as well.

On many occasions, and this was always the case for Ellington Knitting Mill, the convert-ers provided the knitting mills with the yarns for spinning. As a result, the knitting mill's sole responsibility was to spin the yarns according to the converters' specified designs.

Tuesday, 8:30 am

John began the meeting by tabling the financial statements and reiterating his concern about the company's deteriorating financial performance. He asked his brothers for their ideas. Jim said he felt the problem was due to the drop in sales. He noted that there had been a large unfavourable volume variance. The company had estimated production of 8,000 "standard-sized" rolls for the second six months of operation, exactly the same as was achieved during the first six months. Instead, only 6,500 rolls were produced. A standard-sized roll was 5 feet wide by 50 yards long.

JOHN: "Well, don't look at me. During the second half of the year, I went out and brought in plenty of extra business. In fact, some of the converters are now calling me daily to find out why their orders haven't been delivered. I'm starting to look pretty silly."

JOE: "Not so fast, John. And you too, Jim. I can see what you're trying to do. You're trying to put all the blame on me. Yeah, I can see that you think it's all my fault that the orders aren't getting shipped on time. But the kind of orders you keep winning for us John are the ones that require lots of machine set-up time. And furthermore, the orders seem to be for increasingly small quantities. The changeovers keep getting quicker and quicker."

JOHN: "Well, that is the nature of business these days, Joe. Either we compete with the other industry players or we're toast. We all agreed at the end of our first six month period of operations, when we discovered that we were slightly below 80% of capacity, that we needed to bring in more business. Well, I have done that for us."

JOE: "But is it the right business?"

JOHN: "Business is business. And furthermore, we get a premium price for work that is more complex and involves more time-consuming machine set-ups. Isn't that right, Jim."

JIM: "That's right. The more complex the work, the higher the price we charge. All work is meant to provide us with a 50% gross profit."

JOE: "Jim, remind me again how you achieve that."

JIM: "Sure. Our product costs are made up of a variable and a fixed charge. The variable charge consists of power, supplies and maintenance. I estimated these at $.05 per yard of fabric. This number was calculated from a pilot study I performed on one of the machines and is consistent with what the CFO from the knitting mill we bought the machines from said his firm experienced. The fixed charge consists of machine depreciation, rent expense on the factory premises, and production labour (which is your salary, Joe, and the two machine operators you employ). These annual costs are estimated at $400,000."

Before I could figure out the fixed cost per yard of material, I needed to know our expected annual production. Now we all have a pretty good idea about the amount of production we should achieve when the work is simple. We learned about this first hand when we called around to the company that sold us the machines. We watched these machines produce at a rate that equated to 111 rolls per machine per month, when operated over two eight-hour shifts per day. We even have experience with achieving this rate ourselves."

Of course, this number of 111 is achieved when the machine is operating near its ideal capacity. When setting prices, we assumed that our machines would operate at 80% of ideal capacity. Using this 80% benchmark, I calculated that each machine should produce 89 rolls per month. And this equated to just around 16,000 rolls per year. Next, it was a simple matter of dividing the annual costs of $400,000 by the 16,000 rolls. This resulted in a cost of $25.00 per standard-sized roll or $.50 per yard. As a result, the cost for a typical, simple job would be $.55 per yard, comprised of the variable cost of $.05 and the fixed cost of $.50. I then doubled this number to ensure that we achieved the 50% gross profit margin we wanted."

JOE: "Why did you double this number? And where have you made a provision, as you say we do, for a job's complexity in the price we charge? I keep trying to tell you that I find the set-up time varies considerably from one job to the next depending on the fabric design requested, and yet I don't see any reflection of this in the pricing scheme you have outlined."

JIM: "I doubled the number because that allowed us to achieve the same gross profit margin as the average company in our industry. As for all jobs receiving the same pricing, this is not true. You are forgetting that I grade each job based on its relative complexity. Simple work is graded 1 and is priced using the formula I have just outlined. Moderately complex work is graded 2 and attracts a surcharge of 5%. Highly complex work is graded 3 and attracts a surcharge of 10%."

JOHN: "I think we have a good pricing system, Joe. It certainly seems to support our ability to win orders."

JOE: "If that is so, then why aren't we still winning the less complex orders?"

JOHN: "I don't know, Joe. But I think we have to stop blaming things around us. I say we get our tails up and start working a bit harder."

QUESTIONS:

1 What generic business strategy is Ellington Knitting Mill pursuing?
2 What is your evaluation of the company's costing and pricing systems?
3 What is your opinion of the company's financial performance? What, if any, suggestions do you have for improving this performance?
4 What further advice would you have for the Green brothers?

EXHIBIT 1

Ellington Knitting Mill, Inc.
Income statement
For the six months ended 28 February 2000 and the year ended 31 August 2000

	28 February 2000	31 August 2000
	$'000	$'000
Sales	$440	$825
Cost of goods sold*	$220	$438
Gross profit	$220	$387
Selling and Administrative†	$210	$420
Net income before interest and taxes	$10	$-33
Interest expense	$8	$16
Net income before taxes	$2	$-49
Taxes	$1	$0
Net income	$1	$-49

*Cost of goods sold:	28 February 1999	31 August 2000
Joe's salary	$100	$200
Machine operators (2)	$40	$80
Machine depreciation	$45	$90
Rent expense for factory building	$15	$30
Power, supplies, and maintenance	$20	$38

† Selling and Administrative:		
John and Jim's salaries	$200	$400
Travel, phone, paper supplies	$10	$20

Ellington Knitting Mill, Inc.
Balance Sheet
As at 31 August 2000

	$'000			$'000
Assets:		Debt:		
Cash	$10	Accounts payable		$5
Accounts receivable	$100	Deferred Liabilities		$4
Inventory	$10	Long-term notes payable		$160
Machinery & fixtures	$360	Total debt		$169
		Stockholders' Equity:		
		Common Stock		$360
		Retained Earnings		$-49
		Total stockholders' equity		$311
Total Assets	$480	Total debt and stockholders" quity		$480

JELLY COMPANY

Company background

Jelly Company manufactured a wide variety of ink cartridges for use in computer printers. Jelly's ink cartridges were sold to original equipment manufacturers (OEMs) and to wholesalers. The wholesalers resold the ink cartridges to retailers who in turn sold them as replacement parts to the end customer. The latter market was called the "aftermarket" (AM). Exhibit 1 shows the company's profit and loss statement for 2014.

Responsibility centres

As shown in Exhibit 2, Jelly operated a divisionalised structure, whereby each of its two divisions was responsible for product manufacturing (i.e., the Ink Cartridge Division) or warehousing (i.e., the AM Division), as well as the marketing and distribution of its respective products. The Ink Cartridge and AM Divisions were managed by separate vice-presidents.

The Ink Cartridge Division manufactured its products at an Australian plant, a Singapore plant, and a Japanese plant. Each plant maintained its own set of finished goods inventories and shipped parts directly to OEM customers. About 60% of each plant's output was sold to OEMs, with the other 40% being sold internally to the AM Division.

The AM Division was responsible for supplying Jelly's ink cartridges to AM wholesalers. To support its mission, the division operated large, state-of-the-art distribution warehouses in Sydney, Singapore, and Tokyo.

Customer requirements

Jelly's senior management listed the Ink Cartridge Division's order-winning criteria as the ability to provide reliable, innovative, and cost-effective ink cartridges that were delivered on time to meet their customers' just-in-time manufacturing requirements. Cost control was critical because the market was very price competitive.

The primary order-winning criterion for the AM Division was the ability to ensure customers' orders could be quickly filled. All of the AM Division's customers maintained electronic inventory connections with its suppliers and expected delivery within 48 hours of ordering. Quality and price were seen as further, though secondary, order-winning criteria.

Performance measurement

Until the start of the 2014 fiscal year, Jelly had treated all its divisions and the business units under each division as profit centres. In particular, the vice-presidents of the two divisions, as well as the three plant managers and the three distribution warehouse managers, were all evaluated by comparing their respective business units' budgeted profits to their actual profits. Because each manufacturing plant and each AM distribution warehouse had completely different sets of customers (i.e., based on OEMs versus wholesalers and geographic locations), senior management felt it was only logical that each business unit should maintain its own sales team. Budgets were flexed to ensure changes in volume did not unfairly penalize or advantage a business unit or its manager.

Starting in July 2013, the company changed the performance evaluation of its business units and managers to return on investment (ROI). The CEO made this change because he felt the business unit managers were paying insufficient attention to controlling their respective business units' asset bases. The divisional vice-presidents had full autonomy over capital investment decision making in their respective divisions. While this autonomy for capital investment decision making did not formally extend to either the plant or distribution warehouse managers, the CEO felt these managers had substantial influence over such decisions, stating he had never seen a good capital investment request turned down. The CEO further chose to change to ROI because he believed it produced more accurate performance comparisons across the different business units and the business units' responsible managers.

Each business unit and its manager had an annual ROI target to meet. The ROI targets for the Ink Cartridge and AM Divisions' managers were set by the Chief Operating Officer and were based on ensuring the ROI targets she set would support Jelly's five-year strategic plan. The ROI targets for the manufacturing plant managers and the distribution warehouse managers were set by their respective divisional managers. These targets were set to ensure the overall divisional ROI targets, as established by the Chief Operating Officer, would be achieved.

The budgeted and actual ROI was calculated as profit (including allocations of corporate and divisional overheads and an allocated income tax expense) divided by average-year assets minus current liabilities. Property, plant and equipment were valued at gross book value.

Jelly's accounting system permitted the tracing of sales; cost of goods sold; accounts receivable; inventories; property, plant, and equipment; and current liabilities to each division and to each business unit within each division. Corporate overhead and income tax expenses were allocated to business units based on each unit's actual sales to the total company's actual sales. An adjustment to each business unit's asset base was made to reflect the fact that Jelly's corporate headquarters maintained one companywide cash account. Exhibit 3 presents the computation of the Melbourne plant's actual 2014 ROI.

Senior management's reason for including allocated overhead expenses and taxes in the calculation of profit was to instil market discipline by ensuring its managers were aware of the full costs of doing business. Furthermore, these allocations ensured that the sum of the business units' profits equalled Jelly's companywide profit. Meanwhile, an average of the opening and ending net asset balances was used to calculate the investment base because senior management felt this approach provided the fairest representation of the assets used to produce the year's profits.

EXHIBIT 1 PROFIT AND LOSS STATEMENT

30 June 2014	
Sales revenue	$35,010,500
Cost of goods sold	$19,255,775
Gross margin	$15,754,725
General, selling, and administrative	$11,028,308
Profit before taxes	$4,726,417
Taxes	$1,417,925
Profit	$3,308,492

EXHIBIT 2 PARTIAL ORGANISATION CHART

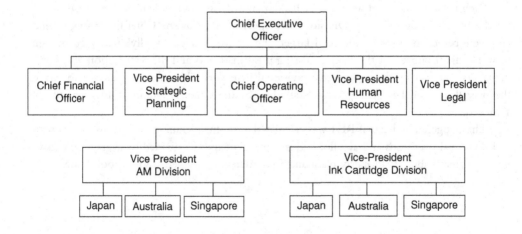

EXHIBIT 3 ACTUAL 2014 ROI CALCULATION – MELBOURNE PLANT

Profit and ROI Statement, 30 June 2014

Sales revenue (includes sales to AM Div. of $4.6 million)		$11,028,308
Cost of goods sold		$4,962,738
Gross margin		$6,065,570
R&D, selling, and other non-manufacturing expenses	$1,823,398	
Division expenses assigned	$2,084,350	
Corporate expenses assigned	$889,567	$4,797,315
Profit before taxes		$1,268,255
Taxes assigned		$380,477
Profit		$887,778

Net Assets Assigned as of 1 July 2013 and 30 June 2014

	1 July 2013	30 June 2014
Total Assets:		
Cash and receivables	$1,297,448	$1,319,138
Inventories	$620,341	$619,000
Property, plant & equipment (gross book value)	$6,310,631	$6,468,030
Total Assets	$8,228,420	$8,406,168
Less current liabilities	$563,700	$619,341
Net Assets	$7,664,720	$7,786,827
ROI (887,778/[(7,664,720 + 7,786,827)/2])		11.5%

MIRAMAR INDUSTRIES

Quinn Snyder, the VP of Miramar Industries' Earthworks and Excavation Division, located in Wellington, New Zealand, sat at his desk trying to make sense of the numbers that lay before him. Tomorrow morning he was due to make his year-end divisional report to the company's Board of Directors. Based on the numbers themselves, he could see that he would face an uphill battle trying to convince the board that he and his division had performed well.

Although his sales had increased significantly (see Exhibit 1), his division recorded a loss for the year. Since the company used ROI to evaluate performance, he realized that his performance for the year would look particularly bad. While Quinn had always been suspicious of the utility of the company's ROI system, he was especially perturbed this year.

Looking at the numbers, he could see that there had been a substantial increase in the amount of corporate service costs allocated. Part of the reason was due to the five week power outage suffered in Auckland during February 1998, which caused the shutdown of the corporate services unit for nearly a month. A significant amount of overtime was incurred getting the unit current again.

Just then the phone rang. It was Denise Green, the VP of the Landscape Design Division. She asked Quinn if he had seen the latest corporate results (see Exhibits 1 and 2). Denise went on to crow about how this year's results represented the fourth straight year that her pre-tax ROI was at or above 45%, and this was after her division had paid a massive $300,000 dividend to the parent company during 1998. Quinn groaned to himself. "Why," he asked himself, "does Denise always come out smelling so sweet?" Quinn wished his conversation with Denise would end, and the sooner the better.

Company background

Miramar Industries was formed in 1982 to provide earthmoving and excavation work throughout the North Island. The company enjoyed good growth throughout the 1980s and early 1990s. In fact, by 1994 the company's cash reserves were at such a high level that the company's founder and president, Ben Gooding, began looking for ways to productively use this cash.

Initially his goal was to acquire another earthmoving and excavation company. But his search failed to identify a suitable company. Then, by sheer chance, he met Nigel Evans. Nigel was an investment banker, who specialised in the construction industry. As it happened, Ben and Nigel were seated together on the same plane. Ben warmed to Nigel right away. As they left the airplane, Ben invited Nigel to come to his office and discuss how Nigel might assist Ben in his search for a company to buy.

Nigel visited Ben the following week. He listened patiently as Ben discussed his attempts to date. When Ben had finished, Nigel asked Ben to elaborate on how Miramar's strategy related to his choice of a firm to acquire. Ben appeared puzzled by the question, so Nigel went on to explain the three corporate strategies of single business firms, related diversified firms, and unrelated diversified firms. He noted that Ben's approach to date had been narrowly focused on pursuing the strategy of a single business firm, but wondered whether he shouldn't branch out into a related diversified firm strategy. Ben said that he was unaware of the issue and asked Nigel to elaborate further. Accordingly, Nigel told him the following:

> Companies that pursue a single business firm strategy choose to commit themselves to a single segment of a particular industry. They seek to focus and concentrate their energies in one area. Meanwhile, companies that pursue a related diversified strategy choose to participate across a range of business segments in a given industry and sometimes across industry boundaries. It is always the case, however, that a common set of core competencies and operating synergies underlies the related diversified's business nexus. Companies that adopt the related diversified strategy seek to benefit from risk diversification, economies of scale, and economies of scope.

The idea of pursuing a related diversified strategy intrigued and interested Ben. When Nigel mentioned that he knew the managing director of an Auckland-based landscape design firm, who was looking to sell his business and retire, Ben became even more intrigued and interested. He felt that an excellent opportunity presented itself for growing the firm and leveraging its core competencies. Furthermore, he could see great potential for business referrals between the two companies. Not only would there likely be a flow of business from landscape design to earthworks, but also the major task of finding and disposing of fill would likely be facilitated by the combined operation of the two businesses.

Immediately following his meeting with Nigel, Ben was on the phone with his accountant and next his lawyer. He told them of his desire to buy the landscape design firm and instructed them to research, appraise, and value the potential acquisition. Within a month, Ben had completed the purchase of the landscape business.

Following the acquisition, Miramar structured the two businesses (earthmoving & excavation and landscape design) as autonomous divisions and left them to operate from their original locations (Wellington and Auckland). While the Earthworks and Excavation Division continued to operate from an office and warehouse building that had been purchased in 1982, the Landscape Design Division rented its office space. Furthermore, since Ben knew he had much to learn about the business of landscape design, he moved himself and his support staff – consisting of human resources, law, accounting, and tax – up to Auckland. This corporate services unit rented office space that adjoined the Landscape Design Division.

The next couple of years proved to be especially challenging for Ben and his staff as they tried to come to grips with the landscape design business. Ben recalls those days as follows:

> My staff and I were terribly naïve when we first entered the landscape design business. We found ourselves on a steep part of the learning curve during the first couple of years. At times I felt we were totally out of our depth. But we devoted a lot of time and energy to understanding the landscape design business. Today we are feeling more confident and a lot better about the decision, although I would be the first to admit that we still have more learning to do.

Performance evaluation

The two divisions were evaluated using ROI. When calculating ROI, all corporate service expenses were allocated to each of the divisions. These corporate service costs were allocated based on the percentage of each division's sales to the combined divisions' sales. Top management's stated reasons for doing this were that it gave the divisional managers a clearer perspective of the true costs of doing business, it provided greater insight into each division's contribution to the corporate bottom line, and it made comparisons between outside standalone companies easier.

All assets were included as part of the investment base. As shown in the balance sheet, these assets were comprised of cash, marketable securities, and accounts receivable. Additionally, in the case of the Earthmoving and Excavation Division, the investment base also included machinery and equipment and land and buildings. A more detailed description of these assets is provided below.

Cash and marketable securities

Each Miramar division maintained a cash account in a local bank. These bank accounts were used for divisional payroll and to pay other, typically minor, local bills. The company's corporate controller monitored the two divisions' bank balances, with cash either being added to or transferred out as deemed necessary by the controller. In general, these accounts had minimal balances.

All supplier invoices were routed to the corporate controller's office and paid out of an account maintained by corporate headquarters. Likewise, as is discussed more fully below, the collection of accounts receivable was also performed by the corporate controller's office. It was believed that the central control of cash would lead to a better matching of cash inflows and outflows than if each division maintained its own separate cash balances. This in turn would minimize the amount of cash needed.

Accounts receivable

All accounts receivable were collected and managed by the corporate controller's office. The company's terms on accounts receivable were 2/10, E.O.M. (i.e., 2% discount if paid within ten days of the end of the month).

It was the responsibility of the corporate controller's office to check the credit worthiness and risk of customers. There was a firm company policy that no sales contracts could be entered into prior to the undertaking of a customer credit check and the issuance of a satisfactory credit report. Furthermore, company policy did not permit cash sales in situations of poor credit.

Around the 20th of each month, an accounts receivable report was prepared by the corporate controller's office and sent to each division. This report was titled "An Analysis of Accounts Receivable by Age." It included a grand total of each customer's accounts receivable and an aging of this total.

Machinery and equipment

Machinery and equipment were depreciated over their estimated useful lives using straight-line depreciation. The average piece of machinery and equipment had an estimated useful life of ten years. When calculating ROI, the assets' gross values were used.

Ideas for buying or selling machinery and equipment had to be approved by the corporate controller's office. The company had a standard form that accompanied all such requests. This form highlighted details about the rationale for the request, how the request would fit with the division's strategy, and the affect the request would have on the division's set of key performance indicators. The only exceptions to the above rules were if the idea involved the purchase of an asset that cost less than $10,000 or the sale of an asset with a book value of less than $10,000.

Land and buildings

The Earthworks and Excavation Division operated from an office and warehouse building that was purchased in 1982. The Landscape Design Division rented its office space. Therefore no amount was recorded for either land or buildings.

The buildings of the Earthworks and Excavation Division were depreciated on a straight-line basis using a useful life of 50 years. When calculating ROI, the gross book value for buildings was used and the market value for land was used. Company management believed that this use of gross book values and market values allowed clearer comparisons to be made between the company's divisions and outside companies by reducing the distortions that different aged assets create.

Similar to the rules pertaining to machinery and equipment, any acquisitions or dispositions of the Division's land and buildings had to have the corporate controller's prior approval. The company felt that such a safeguard was needed to prevent a manager from scrapping relatively old, but otherwise perfectly good assets.

QUESTIONS

1   How would you rate the respective performances of Quinn and Denise?
2   Do you feel that the accounting system adequately captures the managers' performance?
3   What weaknesses, if any, do you believe exist in Miramar's management control system?
4   Do you have any suggestions for improving the management control system of Miramar?

EXHIBIT 1

	Income Statement (in thousands) 1997		Income Statement (in thousands) 1998	
	Earthmoving & excavation	Landscape Design	Earthmoving & excavation	Landscape Design
Sales	6,000	4,000	7,000	3,000
Cost of sales	4,500	2,000	5,200	1,650
Gross margin	1,500	2,000	1,800	1,350
General & administration	1,200	800	2,100	900
Net Income before taxes	300	1,200	<300>	450
Taxes	100	400	<100>	150
Net Income	200	800	<200>	300

EXHIBIT 2

	Balance Sheet (in thousands) 1997		Balance Sheet (in thousands) 1998	
	Earthmoving & excavation	Landscape Design	Earthmoving & excavation	Landscape Design
Cash & S-T mrkt. securities	120	80	120	175
Accounts receivable	900	600	890	525
Machinery, equip, leasehold impr.	4,680	320	4,530	300
Land and Building	3,000	____	2,960	____
Total	8,700	1,000	8,500	1,000
Accounts payable	50	20	50	20
Debt	4,000		4,000	
Owners' equity	4,650	980	4,450	980
Total	8,700	1,000	8,500	1,000

PLAINTREE HOLDINGS AUSTRALIA

Valerie Latta, the Chief Operating Officer of Plaintree Holdings Australia, addressed her company's Board of Directors at its April 2018 meeting. The meeting was a particularly important one, for Valerie was proposing that her company enter a new industry. Addressing the board, she said:

> Our company has performed really well financially over the past five years, earning an average annual after-tax ROE of 15%. As you know, we hold strong positions in three separate industries: cruise ships, private country clubs, and five-star hotels. Although the three lines of business are quite different and demand different operational competencies, the obvious common connection is the service industry. Of course, our competitive success is built on much more than the service theme. In all three industries, we are focused on providing high quality, personalised service to customers with high disposable incomes and highly demanding expectations. For example, each of the two country clubs we operate, one in Scotland and the other in southern California, offers a world-class golf course designed by a previous World Number 1 golfer. Both country clubs also feature an assortment of clay and grass tennis courts, and each club has a restaurant headed by a Michelin-starred chef.[2] Our cruise ship business and five-star hotels similarly cater to the very rich. We employ Michelin starred-chefs at each location and ensure our staff pamper our guests in the manner they have become accustomed. In other words, we apply to all three industries our particular adeptness in knowing how to offer a differentiated, high value service for the discriminating customer, who is in turn willing to pay a price premium. Or to put it more crassly, we understand rich people, know how to pamper them well and in the process we make a good profit.

> Building on our ability to know people and leverage this into making profits, an opportunity to buy a small rest home in North Otago, New Zealand has arisen. The rest home building was the former estate of a wealthy early 20th century industrialist. In the late 1960s, the home was converted into a retirement home. In 2010, the home's 14 bedrooms, two lounges, dining room and kitchen were extensively renovated.
> The current owner of the rest home wants to retire and head to Sydney to be closer to her daughter's family. She is both the rest home's facility manager and its RN. She employs five caregivers to comply with NZ rest home regulations requiring at least one carer being present at all times. The other two employees are a chef and a cleaner.

Valerie proceeded to hand out reports on the rest home's financial statements (see Exhibits 1 and 2) and a brief background report on NZ rest homes (see Exhibit 3). She then continued her presentation, saying:

> The rest home's financial statements for the past three years have been audited. Exhibit 1 shows the income statements and Exhibit 2 shows the most recent balance sheet. As you can see, the rest home has been quite profitable. Its owner is willing to sell at a price of $1.75M. Using a free cash flow valuation model, our accountants estimate the rest home's fair value at $1.96M. The WACC used for the business valuation comes from a recent Grant Thornton report on aged residential care (see Exhibit 4). Our company has sufficient cash reserves to buy the business.

---

2 Michelin is a rating system of chefs, whereby a chef can be awarded up to three stars. A three-star chef is exceedingly rare, with there being only five in the UK and 13 in the US. Earning a single star is a notable achievement.

Purchasing the rest home would give us a foothold in NZ's growing rest home market. With the NZ population continuing to age, rest homes play an essential role. Exhibit 5 uses the GE Matrix to show the strategic profiles of our current three lines of business and our expectations for the rest home business.

Rangi Ellison, Plaintree Holdings Australia's Chairman, thanked Valerie for her presentation and asked his board members if they had any questions. Shannon Tait asked what risks would accompany the company's entry into the NZ rest home market. She mentioned that she had read the full Grant Thornton report and learned that NZ's Ministry of Health had set ambitious targets aimed at significantly cutting the per capita rate of people over 65 living in rest homes. The latest initiative was its "Home is my First Choice" campaign. Valerie responded, saying:

> Good question Shannon, but the overall numbers still work in our favour. The growth in elderly people is simply too great for any government initiative to make a dent. We'll be more than fine. Furthermore, once we introduce the rest home employees to our Service Quality Programme (SQP), the same programme we use to ensure exceptional customer service in the current industries in which we compete, I am more than confident that our customer base will grow. We will purchase and probably even get into the construction of additional rest homes. With more rest homes and more rest home residents, we will achieve economies of scale that will enable our charging lower fees and enhance the value proposition we offer residents. Furthermore, applying to the rest home the same profit sharing programme we use in our other companies will encourage the rest home workers to provide excellent customer service and in turn produce increased numbers of residents.

Scott Richards, another board member, asked why carer salaries had increased by 17% between 2016 and 2017. Valerie explained this was due to the NZ government's pay equity settlement, which sought to redress the past undervaluation of care and support work (a job that is primarily undertaken by women). Starting on 1 July 2017, the minimum hourly rate for care and support workers increased from the existing national minimum wage to $19. As noted in Exhibit 3, the government sets the fees rest homes charge. The government increased the fee by an amount equal to the increase in carer salaries, which also mostly explains the increase in the rest home's revenues between 2016 and 2017.

With no further questions forthcoming, Rangi again thanked Valerie and proposed a motion that the company enter negotiations with the rest home owner to purchase her business. The motion was unanimously passed.

QUESTIONS

1   Identify and comment on what you believe is the strategy of Plaintree Holdings Australia.
2   Calculate and comment on what you believe is the fair price/price range Plaintree Holdings Australia should pay for the North Otago rest home.
3   Would you recommend that Plaintree Holdings Australia purchase the rest home? Why or why not?

EXHIBIT 1

North Otago Rest Home
Income statement

For the years ended 31 December 2015, 2016, and 2017

	2017	2016	2015
Revenue	$667,392	$630,392	$617,784
Manager/RN salary	$40,000	$40,000	$40,000
Carer salaries	$185,900	$158,600	$153,400
Chef/cook	$37,440	$37,069	$36,702
Cleaner	$17,160	$16,990	$16,822
Food	$50,960	$49,961	$48,981
Utilities	$5,600	$5,437	$5,279
Rates	$8,000	$7,805	$7,615
Insurance	$5,500	$5,366	$5,235
Maintenance	$16,300	$21,000	$21,500
EBITDA	$300,532	$288,164	$282,250
Depreciation	$69,000	$66,930	$64,922
EBIT	$231,532	$221,234	$217,328
Interest expense	$53,300	$54,200	$55,200
Tax expense	$53,470	$50,110	$48,638
Net income	$124,762	$116,924	$113,490

EXHIBIT 2

North Otago Rest Home
Balance Sheet

31 December 2017

Cash	$3,500	Accounts payable	$15,346
Accounts receivable	$25,669	Bank Loans	$820,000
		Common stock	$50,000
Property, plant & equipment	$2,000,000	Retained earnings	$1,143,823
Total assets	$2,029,169	Total liabilities & stockholders' equity	$2,029,169

EXHIBIT 3

REST HOMES IN NZ

Rest homes in NZ are highly regulated by the NZ government's Ministry of Health. A variety of codes and regulations apply to the operation of rest homes. For example, every rest home must engage a manager who holds a current qualification or has experience relevant to both management and the health and personal care of older people. Furthermore, rest homes must pay for their residents' GP visits and prescriptions, and they must ensure that residents have a minimum of two hours contact with a registered nurse (RN) each week. On top of all this, the NZ government was the dominant buyer of rest home services, paying the full fees of about 70% of rest home residents, which meant that it ended up setting the price for all rest home residents.[3] The NZ government's reimbursement rate of $123.89/day was the same rate that every other resident paid. In sum, the regulated nature of NZ rest homes meant there was no opportunity to compete on price or any other significant service feature. Rest homes could, however, supplement the daily charge with modest fees related to providing a TV in a resident's room, providing a room with a nicer view, etc. These fees amounted to about $10/day.

EXHIBIT 4

Grant Thornton Aged Residential Care Service Report (Excerpt)
Table 11 Weighted average cost of capital (WACC)

Target capital structure		
D/V		40.0%
E/V		60.0%
t_c		28.0%
Cost of debt	**Low**	**High**
R_t	5.9%	5.9%
DRP	2.5%	3.5%
$K_d = r_t + DRP$	**8.4%**	**9.4%**
Cost of quity	**Low**	**High**
t_i	28.0%	28.0%
$T_t(1 - t_i)$	4.2%	4.2%
β_a	0.60	0.70
$\beta_\theta = \beta_a(1 + D/E)$	1.00	1.17
TAMRP	7.5%	7.5%
SCRP	3.0%	4.0%

3 The NZ government means tested rest home residents; and for those residents whose assets were less than a specified threshold, their rest home fees were fully paid by the NZ government.

Target capital structure		
$K_\theta = r_f(1 - t_i) + \beta_\theta\,(\text{TAMRP}) + \text{SCRP}$	14.8%	17.0%
$\text{WACC} = K_\theta E/V + k_d(1 - t_c)\, c/v$	11.3%	12.9%
Mid point		12.1%

EXHIBIT 5

GE Matrix - Prospect Holdings Australia

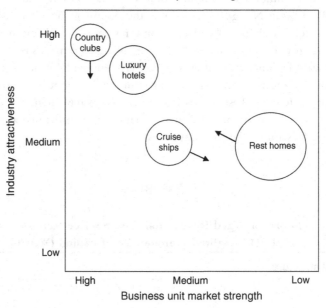

SOUTHERN PLANTATION MUSEUM

Southern Plantation was built in 1709 by the Davis family in Greenville, North Carolina. Initially, its workforce comprised European indentured servants and Native Americans. But this changed in 1719 with the arrival of the first captive Africans to the United States' colonies.

After more than 250 years of growing tobacco, the ever-decreasing demand for US-grown tobacco prompted Southern Plantation to scale back its production. By 1985, Southern Plantation completely stopped growing tobacco. The Davis family turned its attention to leasing its farmland to local pig and vegetable farmers. Due to a series of bad stock market investments and the family members' extravagant lifestyles, the family fell upon hard times in the early 2000s and its fortune dwindled. Initially, the family sold parcels of its extensive farmland to property developers. When these land sales had been exhausted, the family turned to refinancing its remaining property. Unfortunately, the Global Financial Crisis ended up being the final straw. Unable to cover its instalment loan and pay its property taxes, what remained of the plantation was repossessed.

Greenville City and the Davis family's bank were the primary creditors. Together they approached the Organization for Equality of Rights (OER) with a proposal. If OER would agree to take ownership of the remaining land and buildings and create a museum dedicated to preserving and displaying the history embodied by the Southern Plantation, the city would waive all back taxes owing and the bank would slash the debt owed down to $1 million. The actions of the city and bank were motivated by the potential for local employment and, in the case of the bank, receiving sole corporate sponsorship rights for the next ten years. On 28 September 2010, OER agreed to purchase the plantation for $1.

The mission of OER is:

> The Organization for Equality of Rights is dedicated to creating a society in which all individuals have equal political, educational, social, and economic rights, thus eliminating race-based discrimination and ensuring the health and well-being of all citizens. We will accomplish this by using democratic processes to remove any and all racial discrimination barriers, seeking the enactment and enforcement of all laws (both US-based and international) aimed at securing civil rights, educating the public about the US's history of racial discrimination and the social and economic injustices caused, and informing people on their constitutional rights and how to take lawful action to secure their exercise of these rights.

Following the purchase of the Southern Plantation, OER spent $2 million over the next three years faithfully restoring to their original conditions the plantation's slave cabins, outbuildings, the Davis mansion, a freedmen's church, and memorials built to honour the enslaved. OER's board of trustees expressed great satisfaction with the end result, with the board's chairman stating she looked forward to seeing the Southern Plantation Museum (SPM) supporting the piece of OER's mission dedicated to educating the public about racial injustice in the US by using the museum to preserve and display a particularly shameful and painful period of US history.

SPM opened its doors to the public in July 2013. Today it is recognized as one of the US's premier, not-for-profit museums dedicated to the United States' slavery period. In 2017, the SPM was included in USA Today's annual list of best museums.

SPM's popularity led OER's board of trustees to conclude a full-time CEO at SPM was needed. The ensuing CEO search led to the hiring of Scarlett Johnson. She had previously been managing a large adventure park in the US's southern state of Alabama and came highly recommended.

Scarlett began working for SPM in July 2016. Shortly after she arrived, SPM published its 30 June 2016 fiscal year ending financial statements that showed an operating deficit for the third year in a row (see Exhibit 1). After touring the museum facilities, Scarlett felt the museum did not provide an exciting enough visitor experience. She noted that the museum exhibits were largely static, consisting of tools hanging from a wall or a room that could be viewed but not entered. Often there was a placard that described a particular scene, and sometimes a visitor could use a headset to hear a narrator provide more background about what was on display.

Scarlett, wanting a more invigorating visitor experience, came up with the idea of conducting Civil War battle re-enactments on a large tract of land that once comprised the Davis family's sprawling gardens. Following years of neglect, the gardens had become completely overgrown, the sculptures broken, and the fountains inoperable. Scarlett remembers it as one of her easiest decisions when she ordered the land be cleared and replanted with grass. Nowadays, a 45-minute battle re-enactment comprised of local volunteers is conducted at 1 pm every Saturday and Sunday, an initiative that Scarlett credits with increasing SPM's visitor numbers by 70% since starting her job.

In July 2017, Scarlett introduced a second change. She converted the largest of SPM's slave quarters into a gift shop and appointed a full-time sales manager to run the shop. Beau Smith, the new shop manager, initially filled the gift shop with wall art prints, water colours, and books that invariably featured themes relating to the antebellum era (i.e., the US plantation era). Although the gift shop turned a small profit of $10,000 during its first year of operation, Scarlett felt much more could be achieved if only she could properly motivate Beau to be more entrepreneurial. This thinking led Scarlett to establish a gain-sharing programme for Beau, whereby Beau would share 50:50 in any increase in profits from one year to the next. (Profit was calculated by subtracting the controllable costs of Beau's base salary of $45,000 and the cost of the merchandise sold.) In response to Scarlett's gainsharing programme, Beau began stocking the gift shop with Civil War memorabilia (e.g., Union and Confederate[4] military uniforms and flags), fireworks, and even locally-distilled southern whisky.

By the start of the 2018 northern summer, visitor numbers had almost doubled from when Scarlett first started at SPM. In response to the higher visitor numbers, Scarlett sought and received approval from OER's board of trustees to hire a full-time manager to oversee the staffing and operations of the museum buildings and a second part-time manager to oversee the battle re-enactments. Next, wanting to empower these managers to be more business-focused, she gave both managers the responsibility for operating as investment centres. In particular, she would trace revenue to each investment centre whenever possible. For the purposes of general admission revenue, this would be evenly shared by the two investment centres. The gift shop would not receive any of the admission revenue because it was already receiving revenue from the items it sold. The two investment centres' expenses would be comprised of their share of employee payroll expense, insurance expense (i.e., the museum buildings and the antiques they housed), property tax expense, and depreciation expense (e.g., the buildings and the equipment used for the battle re-enactments). Scarlett decided the advertising expenses would be shared equally between the two investment centres, and the interest expense would be allocated based on the asset book values of the two investment centres. Finally, the profit generated by each investment centre would be compared to their respective assets (i.e., book values of land, antiques, and buildings for the museum manager and book values of land and battle equipment for the battle re-enactments manager) to create a return on assets measure.

---

4 Union is the name of the Northern warring party in the American Civil War and Confederate is the name of the Southern warring party.

Scarlett's changes prompted immediate action by the newly appointed manager overseeing the museum's buildings. He made renovations to the mansion's kitchen and ballroom and began taking bookings for large parties wanting to use SPM for weddings, anniversaries, birthdays, Christmas parties, or other types of special occasions. Meanwhile, the part-time manager overseeing the battle re-enactments partitioned the land for the battles into two pieces. One piece was retained for the battle re-enactments and the second was subleased to a North Carolina-licensed state grower of medicinal marijuana.

Following a full year of Scarlett's latest changes, the financial statements for the year ended 30 June 2019 were published (see Exhibit 1). Scarlett felt immensely satisfied by the significant surplus. She noted that 2019's surplus produced an ROA of nearly 12% and a return on total accumulated funds of nearly 14%. OER's CFO had previously told her that SPM's weighted average cost of capital was simply computed as the interest rate on its bank loan, which was 5%. Being a recognized charity, the museum paid no taxes. As she prepared for her upcoming annual performance meeting with OER's board of trustees, Scarlett felt she had good reason to be proud of her achievements and looked forward to meeting with the board to discuss her accomplishments in more detail.

QUESTIONS

1   Identify and comment on what you believe is the strategy of SPM.
2   Evaluate from a performance management perspective each of the changes made by Scarlett and Beau.
3   What advice would you have for the board of Organization for Equality of Rights?

EXHIBIT 1: FINANCIAL STATEMENTS FOR SPM FOR THE YEARS 2014–2019

Statement of Revenue and Expenses

	2019	2018	2017	2016	2015	2014
Revenue						
Admission revenue	$1,065,000	$955,000	$742,000	$530,000	$524,000	$522,000
Gift shop revenue	$155,000	$65,000				
Special functions revenue	$120,000					
Sub-lease of farmland	$75,000					
Total revenue	$1,415,000	$1,020,000	$742,000	$530,000	$524,000	$522,000
Expenses						
Employee salary expense	$320,000	$250,000	$210,000	$138,000	$133,900	$130,000
Gift shop merchandise expense	$77,500	$55,000				
Catering expenses for special functions	$78,000					

Statement of Revenue and Expenses

	2019	2018	2017	2016	2015	2014
Advertising expense	$53,250	$52,000	$37,800	$27,000	$27,000	$26,000
Insurance expense	$128,000	$124,000	$120,500	$117,000	$113,300	$110,000
Property tax expense	$149,000	$146,000	$142,000	$140,000	$137,700	$135,000
Depreciation expense	$75,000	$75,000	$75,000	$75,000	$75,000	$110,000
Interest expense (on bank loan)	$28,750	$31,250	$33,750	$36,250	$38,750	$41,250
Total expenses	$909,500	$733,250	$619,050	$533,250	$525,650	$552,250
Total Surplus/(deflcit) for the period	**$505,500**	**$286,750**	**$122,950**	**($3.250)**	**($1,650)**	**($30,250)**

Statement of Financial Position

	2019	2018	2017	2016	2015	2014
Current Assets						
Cash	$11,500	$9,900	$10,100	$9,800	$8,600	$9,250
Short term inverstments	$497,200	$55,000				
Accounts receivable	$16,900	——	——	——	——	——
Total Current Assets	$525,600	$64,900	$10,100	$9,800	$8,600	$9,250
Noncurrent Assets						
Property and chattels	$3,468,950	$3,474,150	$2,892,200	$2,819,550	$2,874,000	$2,925,000
Land	$200,000	$200,000	$200,000	$200,000	$200,000	$200,000
Total Noncurrent Assets	$3,668,950	$3,674,150	$3,092,200	$3,019,550	$3,074,000	$3,125,250
Total Assets	$4,194,550	$3,739,050	$3,102,300	$3,029,350	$3,082,600	$3,134,250
Liabilities						
Bank loan	$550,000	$600,000	$650,000	$700,000	$750,000	$800,000
Total Liabilities	$550,000	$600,000	$650,000	$700,000	$750,000	$800,000
Net Assets	$3,644,550	$3,139,050	$2,452,300	$2,329,350	$2,332,600	$2,334,250
Accumulated Funds						
Capital contributed by owners	$2,400,000	$2,400,000	$2,000,000	$2,000,000	$2,000,000	$2,000,000
Donated capital	$364,500	$364,500	$364,500	$364,500	$364,500	$364,500
Accumulated surpluses / deficits	$880,050	$374,550	$87,800	$-35,150	$-31,900	$-30,250
Total Accumulated Funds	$3,644,550	$3,139,050	$2,452,300	$2,329,350	$2,332,600	$2,334,250

BLUE SKY LIMITED

Blue Sky Limited (BSL) was a large publicly-traded company headquartered in Perth Australia. The company prided itself on identifying companies that were underperforming and turning them into market leaders. Its CEO Jing Lee stated, "Our company has a particular knack for sniffing out hidden gems, or at least companies that have the potential with a bit of work to be polished into gems."

BSL consists of six companies operating in six separate industries: rocket manufacturing, medical instruments, robotics, solar technology, pharmaceuticals, and organic farming. Exhibit 1 presents BSL's organizational chart, and Exhibit 2 presents a GE Matrix showing the strategic positions of the six companies.

Nature's Best Ltd (NBL) was the strategic business unit in charge of BSL's organic farming. NBL owns 15 free-range egg farms, 30 apple farms, and 10,000 beehives in various locations in Tasmania, Australia, and the North and South islands of New Zealand. While its customers ranged from large supermarkets to small restaurants, the common thread connecting its customers was their willingness to pay premium prices for products perceived as superior in quality and produced using sustainable and ethical farming practices.

Jack Wells became president of Happy Hen Farms (HHF), a division of Nature's Best, in January 2016. Exhibit 3 presents the company's organizational chart. Prior to working for HHF, Mr Wells was the plant manager at a large New Zealand brewery. He felt egg farms and breweries were a lot more similar than one might expect, stating:

> In my previous job, ensuring high production volumes was a key performance indicator. The same is true for egg farming. Chickens are assets in a production process in exactly the same way the plant equipment is in a brewery. The only difference in my mind is that we call the former biological assets and the latter plant and equipment. But the reality is that in both settings the key to success is ensuring you get the maximum output possible from the assets.

Anahera Potene, the new farm manager at HHF's Timaru egg farm (which is shown in Exhibit 3's organizational chart as South Island HHF 2), discussed the significant changes that preceded his arrival, stating:

> The farms used to be treated as profit centres, but that, or so I have been told, was before Mr Wells arrived. He felt it was crazy to treat a factory as anything but an expense centre. So now all the farms are engineered expense centres. We have standards assigned to every cost aspect of egg production. As Mr Wells continually reminds us, we need to decrease our cost per egg if we are going to be successful. In addition to screwing down variable costs such as feed costs, Mr Wells has also emphasised increasing production volume so we can reduce the per unit fixed costs. To help me focus my attention on costs, Mr Wells recently announced that he plans to reduce my salary by 25% and introduce a gainsharing plan that would allow me to recoup and potentially surpass my previous salary.

We used to have nearly three hectares of grassy yard between the farm's two main chicken sheds for the birds to free range in. If you can imagine three rugby fields lined up side by side, that is about the size of the old yard. The farm's previous manager built rain and wind shelters in the yard to help protect the birds during bad weather. But by the end of 2016, the shelters were removed and the two sheds were both doubled in size. Today, the yard is about the size of a single rugby field.

Mr Wells picked up on this point stating:

When I first arrived at HHF, I ran into a battle with a couple of the South Island farm managers. They were a bit set in their ways, you might say. They were understocking their farms and needlessly encouraging their flocks to be outside.

Free-range is defined by birds having "access" to outdoor spaces. All our birds certainly have this, and I would always be one of the first to insist this be the case. But building outside shelter breaks, like some of the farm managers were doing, was excessive and wasteful. After all, everyone in the free-range industry knows that one-third to one-half of free-range birds never venture outside their sheds. And why should they? The birds have everything they need inside, including the food we specially formulate for their high protein needs.

Just as a brewery, carmaker or any manufacturer for that matter wants to control each variable that influences production, so too must our farms do the same thing. Having chickens needlessly venturing outside means we can't control their nutrition, waste time trying to find where eggs are being laid and incur higher egg losses than is necessary.

Amelia Wilson, one of the two marketing employees at the Timaru egg farm, recounted the changes she had witnessed over the five years she had been in her job, stating:

Prior to Mr Wells' arrival, we were treated as a discretionary expense centre. Mr Wells told us this made no sense, and he changed us to a revenue centre.

It used to be the case that my co-worker and I were glorified order takers. We sat by the phone and waited for buyers, who were willing to pay a premium price for everything we produced. However, I have seen this situation change over the past three years. For example, the large orders we once received from restaurants from Christchurch to Dunedin aren't happening as much. While I don't know why this is occurring, I happened to be sitting next to the mother of a teammate on my son's basketball team who said her brother's restaurant in Dunedin, which used to buy from us, now buys its eggs from a local farmer. She said the restaurant's chef cited a drop in the quality of eggs as the reason for switching suppliers. I suggested to Mr Wells that we might want to conduct an investigation into what is happening, but he said that we are selling all the eggs we produce and we'd just be wasting our time.

While it is true that we still sell everything we produce, and this is no small feat seeing how our production has doubled during the past three years, I do note that our average prices are down by 19%. Mr Wells says this is to be expected, for pricing is a simple function of supply and demand. Now that we are supplying more, our prices will naturally have to come down.

I also note that my co-worker and I are working harder than ever to maintain our take-home pay at the levels we were accustomed to. To motivate us, Mr Wells reduced our salaries in two stages. There was a $2,500 decrease in 2017 and a similar decrease in 2018.

That's the bad news. The good news is that for every dollar of sales we book, we each earn a one-half of one percent sales commission. Mr Wells says his approach has something to do with goal setting theory. I don't know what that means, but what I do know is that my co-worker and I can no longer wait by the phone and take orders. Nowadays, we are much more proactive. Over the past year and a half, we have each spent on average 1–2 days a week traveling the lower east coast of the south island looking for new customers and trying to promote further consumption by existing customers. And it appears we might be doing even more travelling in the future. Mr Wells advises us that he wants to add a further 5,000 hens to our laying stock, which will mean an additional output of 1.5M eggs per year.

Chloe Martin, BSL's Chief Financial Officer, said the financial performance of the South Island HHF 2 had largely kept pace with BSL expectations, especially in relation to Happy Hen Farms' weighted average cost of capital of 8.5%. Exhibit 4 presents three years of HHF 2's income statements and Exhibit 5 presents its 2018 balance sheet. Ms Martin said the one notable change over the past three years was Mr Wells' restructuring of the HHF 2 office staff. He said that various advances in accounting software meant it was more economical to outsource HHF 2's accounting. This led to his releasing one of the office workers at the start of 2018.

QUESTIONS

1   Do you agree with Mr Wells that egg farms share similar characteristics to factories and should be treated as expense centres?
2   What is your view about the changes made to HHF 2? When considering these changes, relate them to the company's strategy.
3   What would you recommend the company should do?

EXHIBIT 1: ORGANISATIONAL CHART – BLUE SKY LTD

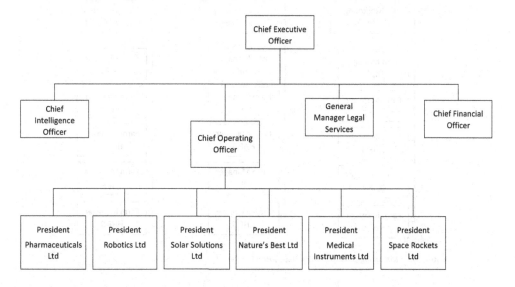

EXHIBIT 2: GE MATRIX – BLUE SKY LIMITED

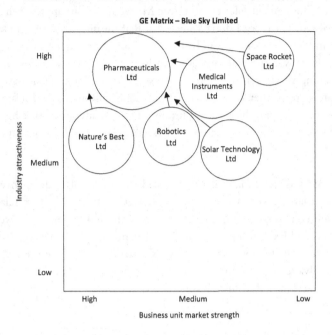

EXHIBIT 3: ORGANISATIONAL CHART HAPPY HEN FARMS

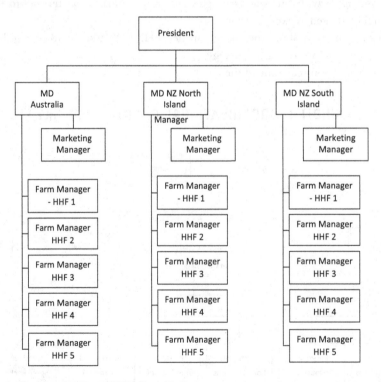

Notes: MD = Managing Director, HHF = Happy Hen Farms

EXHIBIT 4: HAPPY HEN FARMS – SOUTH ISLAND #2

Income statement
For the years ended 31 December 2016, 2017, and 2018

	2018	2017	2016
Sales	$2,835,000	$2,362,500	$1,750,000
Cost of goods sold	$2,113,000	$1,621,000	$1,101,500
Gross profit	$722,000	$741,500	$648,500
General, selling and administrative expenses:			
Sales salaries	$90,000	$92,500	$95,000
Sales commissions	$14,175	$11,813	$8,750
Sales travel	$60,000	$30,000	
Farm manager salary	$80,000	$80,000	$80,000
Office administrators	$45,000	$100,000	$100,000
Outside accounting services	$15,000		
Miscellaneous	$24,000	$35,000	$37,000
Earnings before interest and taxes	$393,825	$392,187	$327,750
Interest expense	$58,175	$58,175	$58,175
Earnings before taxes	$335,650	$334,012	$269,575
Taxes	$93,982	$93,523	$75,481
Net income	$241,668	$240,489	$194,094

EXHIBIT 5: HAPPY HEN FARMS – SOUTH ISLAND #2

Balance Sheet
For the years ended 31 December 2018

Current assets:		Current liabilities:	
Cash	$11,417	Accounts payable	$246,000
Accounts receivable	$236,250	Current portion of long-term debt	$250,000
Inventory (feed)	$97,333	Long-term liabilities:	
Biological assets (hens)	$800,000	Bank Loans	$645,000
		Stockholders' equity:	
Non-current assets:		Common stock	$200,000
Property, plant & equipment	$1,100,000	Retained earnings	$904,000
Total assets	$2,245,000	Total liabilities & stockholders' equity	$2,245,000

ZEUS INDUSTRIES

Zeus Industries began as a small, for-profit energy consulting company in 2005. Initially, it provided energy consulting services to a wide range of companies located on New Zealand's South Island. Through a rapid series of mergers, it grew from a single Dunedin office to a network of ten offices located throughout New Zealand and Australia. Each office had an average of 13 professional employees and two support staff. The latter two took turns staffing the reception desk and answering incoming phone calls. They also managed the professional staff's travel, offered some typing assistance, helped with IT/computer issues, and performed some of the more basic accounting and finance functions not performed at the corporate level (e.g., processing travel reimbursement claim forms). The company's founder, Doug Richards, took the company public in September 2015, with the idea that he would retire within the next few years. On 30 November 2015, an international investment fund, which saw great potential in Zeus, acquired 51% of its shares. Doug stepped down as CEO on 1 January 2016 and Aria Parata, a seasoned CEO with an excellent reputation for leading knowledge-intensive companies, assumed the CEO's job. She, along with her four senior executives (CFO, VP-ECD, VP-EVD, and VP HR), retained the company's Dunedin-based headquarters.

In July 2016, the company added to its business operations the retailing of new electric vehicles (EVs). Soon afterwards, the company was split into two operating divisions: Energy Consulting Division (ECD) and Electrical Vehicles Division (EVD). Exhibit 1 presents Zeus' organizational chart.

Karen Collins, the vice-president of EVD, recalled Zeus's entry into the retailing of EVs and the opportunities it offered, stating:

The establishment of EV dealerships in Dunedin and Sydney in July 2016 was a truly exciting day for us. I am confident that 20 years from now, shareholders will look back at this decision as a transformational point in our organisation's history.

We made a bold choice to enter early and get in on the ground floor of this fast-growing industry. EVs are the future of the world's car fleet. The growth in EV ownership is increasing exponentially. Two years ago, for example, there were a handful of EVs in Otago. Today, there are over 300 such cars.

Most people want an EV because its annual operating costs are about NZ$2,000 cheaper than a petrol or diesel engine car. This savings is based on driving 12,500 kilometres a year, which is what the average New Zealanders and Australians do. Such a substantial cost savings creates a compelling sales proposition. Driving an EV has the further benefit of letting owners feel like they are doing something positive for the environment.

An EV's relatively high initial purchase cost is the only thing stopping everyone from buying EVs. A new Renault Zoe EV costs about NZ$47,000, which is about NZ$20,000 more than a new petrol or diesel engine car like a Toyota Corolla. Some car owners can't see past this $20,000 higher cost. We need to help them understand that the financing costs on this extra amount is more than compensated for by the EV's annual cost savings. Ideally, for example, a buyer would extend his/her home mortgage by an amount equal to the cost of the new car. Assuming a home mortgage rate of 5%, the financing costs on the additional $20,000 would be $1,000 per year. This results in an overall annual savings of $1,000 ($2,000 annual operating cost savings - $1,000 annual additional financing costs). If we can raise the financial literacy of car buyers, EVs will own the entire market. This dominance will accelerate as the price of EVs continues to drop. We know we are riding a winner in the form of EVs, and that is why we entered the market when we did.

Dimensions of competition

ECD had a strong reputation for offering its customers unparalleled total customer solutions. In particular, ECD provided a full range of sustainable energy consulting services, spanning the provision of energy audits to the design and construction of small to medium-sized energy generation plants. The company had a proven record in designing and constructing wind, water, and solar-powered energy generation stations. When invited by prospective customers to tender a price for a project, ECD was seldom the lowest bidder. What invariably won them a customer's contract was ECD's reputation for providing complete solutions to customers' needs. Underpinning this ability was the willingness of the ten offices' employees to share their ideas and sometimes collaborate on projects. Aria expanded on this competency stating:

> It is really important for our employees to share innovative solutions. We work in a knowledge-intensive industry. To be successful, you must turn tacit knowledge (knowledge that exists in someone's head) into institutional knowledge (knowledge that is formalised and made a part of an organisation's systems and processes).

EVD competed in the competitive and highly congested new car sales market. Since the purchase of a car was a large investment for the vast majority of customers, a car's price, functionality, and quality were carefully weighed up as part of the purchase decision. As a result, no car dealership could ignore or trade-off any of the order-winning criteria. In fact, there was a constant need to improve the customer value proposition embodied by these criteria.

Divisional, manager, and employee performance evaluation

Both divisions and their subunits were evaluated on their ROI. Corporate service costs were allocated based on the percentage of each division's sales to the combined divisions' sales. Top management's reasons for doing this were: (1) it gave the divisional managers a clearer perspective of the true costs of doing business, (2) it provided greater insight into each division's contribution to the corporate bottom line, and (3) it made comparisons between outside standalone companies easier. All assets were included as part of the investment base, with accounts payable being deducted to model more accurately the investment base. Accounts payable were viewed as a free source of capital. Exhibits 2–5 present the financial statements of ECD and EVD divisions.

The divisional and regional managers of ECD and EVD were partly compensated based on their achieved ROIs versus their budgeted ROIs. For every tenth of a percent their respective ROIs were above the budgeted ROI, the manager earned an annual bonus of $1,500. Aria explained the ROI-based compensation plan saying:

> We set an ambitious companywide ROI target for our four regional managers and two divisional managers. Our CFO calculates our company's weighted average cost of capital (WACC) each year. For 2017, as well as 2018, he calculated it at 11%. I then set a companywide after-tax ROI target above this level to motivate employees to achieve beyond the WACC's minimum level of required performance. Similar to 2017, I set 2018's after-tax ROI target at 15%. If at the end of this year a manager posts an ROI of, say, 16%, this manager will receive a bonus of $15,000.

The company operated profit sharing and gain sharing plans for employees below the level of regional managers for both ECD and EVD. In terms of the former, when an office's or dealership's actual ROI exceeds the companywide ROI target, then each employee of that office receives an automatic bonus of 10% of their salary. Meanwhile, the gain sharing plan rewards employees for their cost savings ideas, whereby 50% of the derived cost savings are shared equally among an office's or dealership's employees. In 2017, for example, EVD-Sydney changed its dealership location and pocketed savings of $60,000. This meant that the EVD dealership's three employees each received a $10,000 bonus (i.e., one half of the $60,000 divided by three employees).

Aria, and her four senior executives were capable of earning stock options. Aria set goals for each senior executive at the start of the year. Depending on an executive's performance against his/her goals, it was possible to earn stock options valued up to 30% of the employee's base salary. A similar stock option performance plan was used for Aria, with the one difference that it was overseen by Zeus' Board of Directors.

Organizational culture

Aria believed workers needed to be constantly challenged. She likened her leadership approach to applying "heat," stating:

> I believe that for people to grow, they need to be put under heat. Workers need to be taken out of their comfort zones, otherwise they grow stale and stodgy. My favourite approach for creating heat is to encourage inter-employee competition. Peer rivalry weeds out complacency and ensures everyone stays sharp and focused. As an example, we compare the ROI performances of the 10 ECD offices and two EVD dealerships with one another. In times of poor economic growth, like a recession, these peer comparisons allow us to reward relative performance. For example, one of the ECD offices may discover midway through the year that due to an economic slowdown it is unlikely to meet the companywide ROI target. Rather than giving up, this office can still earn that bonus if its ROI places it among the top 25% of the combined set of ECD offices and EVD dealerships. Since there are 10 offices and two dealerships, this means a business unit must be among the top three performers.

A similar use of benchmarking is performed at the regional and divisional level. If a regional manager fails to meet the companywide ROI target, he/she can still earn a bonus if his/her unit's ROI performance is better than the ROI performance achieved by the three other regional managers. Likewise, a divisional manager who comes up short against the companywide ROI target can still earn a bonus by beating his/her peer divisional manager. In fact, this is exactly what happened in 2017 when the ECD Divisional Manager could not meet the companywide ROI target but did post an ROI better than the EVD Divisional Manager.

I think our organisational systems, processes and structures – both singly and together – do a good job supporting the competitive environment we seek to create. For example, the use of ROI-based bonuses focus managers' attention on beating budgets. They accomplish this feat by bringing in more customers and weeding out inefficiencies. I know that just as my stock options serve to motivate my behaviour, our use of bonuses does a wonderful job motivating our employees. I am confident that we know how to get, and are getting, the best out of every one of our employees.

QUESTIONS

1   What type of competitive strategy is ECD pursuing?
2   What type of competitive strategy is EVD pursuing?
3   Explain how the performance management system fits or fails to fit with each division's strategy.
4   What performance management changes or business improvements, if any, would you recommend?

EXHIBIT 1

Zeus organizational chart

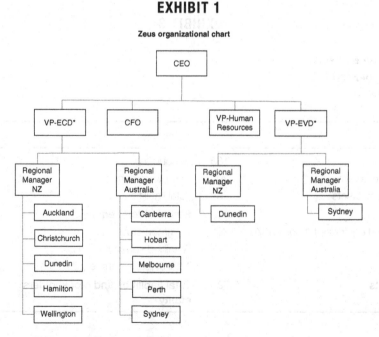

* ECD: Energy Consulting Division, and EVD: Electrical Vehicles Division

EXHIBIT 2

ECD Income Statement
For the year ended 31 December 2017
(in NZ$'000s)

Sales		**22,500**
Operating expenses:		
Salaries (including bonuses)	19,200	
Rent	1,250	
Travel and client entertainment	380	
Utilities	240	
Insurance (malpractice)	150	
Depreciation	190	
Miscellaneous	34	21,444
Net income before interest, tax and allocated corporate expense		1,056
Other expenses:		
Corporate overhead	506	
Interest expense	45	551
Net income before taxes		505
Income tax expense		152
Net income		353

EXHIBIT 3

ECD Balance Sheet
31 December 2017
(in NZ$'000s)

Assets		Liabilities	
Cash	185	Accounts payable	70
Accounts receivable	2,200	Long-term debt	450
Other current assets	58	Total liabilities	520
		Stockholders' equity	
Property and equipment (Gross $970)	350	Common stock	1,700
		Retained earnings	573
		Total stockholders' equity	2,273
Total assets	**2,793**	**Total liabilities and stockholders' equity**	**2,793**

EXHIBIT 4

EVD Income Statement
For the year ended 31 December 2017
(in NZ$'000s)

Sales (Footnote 1)		19,750
Cost of goods sold		<u>16,788</u>
Gross profit		2,962
Selling and general expenses:		
Sales commissions	98	
Salaries (including bonuses)	320	
Advertising	91	
Supplies and utilities	22	
Insurance	35	
Depreciation	19	
Rent	<u>240</u>	825
Net income before interest, tax and corporate allocated expenses		2,137
Other expenses:		
Interest on new inventory	388	
Other interest	68	
Corporate overhead	<u>444</u>	900
Net income before tax		1,237
Income tax expense		<u>371</u>
Net income		<u>866</u>

Footnote 1: Car sales	**Units**	**$000s**
Nissan Leaf	240	9,600
Renault Zoe	120	5,640
BMW i3	<u>55</u>	<u>4,510</u>
	415	19,750

EXHIBIT 5

EVD Balance Sheet
31 December 2017
(in NZ$'000s)

Assets		Liabilities	
Cash	50	Accounts payable	95
Accounts receivable	1,646	Notes Payable – vehicles	4,844

Assets			Liabilities	
Inventory:			Long-term debt	680
Nissan Leaf	2,273		Total liabilities	5,619
Renault Zoe	1,255			
BMW I3	2,470	5,998	**Stockholders' equity**	
			Common stock	1,000
			Retained earnings	1,135
Property and equipment (Gross $110)		60	Total stockholders' equity	2,135
Total assets		7,754	**Total liabilities and stockholders' equity**	7,754

PIERRE'S HAIR SALON

Pierre's Hair Salon comprises three hair salons operating in eastern Canada. Its owners, Martha and Jeff Kuhn, started the first salon in Saint-Sauveur, Canada in 2010. Saint-Sauveur is located 70 kilometres northwest of Montreal amongst Montreal's most popular ski resorts. Pierre's quickly amassed a reputation for offering cutting-edge hair design in a private, relaxing, and elegant setting, one that features sparkling crystal chandeliers, plush sofas and chairs, and elegant full-length mirrors. The pampered environment Pierre's offers, which includes offering clients pastries, cappuccinos and lattes when they arrive, underpins their charging a relatively high price. While the median price for a haircut in eastern Canada is about $25, Pierre's charges $55. Part of the premium price derives from Pierre's employment of highly experienced stylists. To attract these stylists, Pierre's pays $25/hour, which is about 25% higher than a Montreal stylist's hourly rate. Another difference between Pierre's and other hair salons is that a Pierre's stylist typically sees 5–6 clients per day, whereas a stylist elsewhere averages 10–12 clients. One additional characteristic that sets Pierre's apart from its competitors is the high emphasis it places on cross-selling, which involves stylists convincing clients to buy additional hair products, such as curl creams, spray foams, and scalp exfoliators.

Within months of its opening, the salon became exceedingly popular. Over the course of the next six months, Martha and Jeff installed three additional stylist stations and hired three new stylists. These additions, which brought the salon to full capacity, proved to be only a temporary fix. Even with everyone putting in six 6.5-hour shifts per week (i.e., 39 hours per week), they could not keep up with demand.

Noting that many of their clients travelled from Montreal to Saint-Sauveur exclusively to have their haircut, Martha and Jeff believed opening a salon in Montreal could work well. Fortunately for Martha and Jeff, a former tailor shop that was located in what is called Old Montreal became available for rent. After further enhancing the shop's elegance with elaborate and ornate furnishings and hiring a replacement for himself at the Saint-Sauveur salon, Jeff and two newly hired stylists began working at the Montreal salon. This salon too quickly became popular and two further stylists were hired, which brought the salon to full capacity.

After several years of strong financial success (see Exhibit 1's most recent income statements), Martha and Jeff were presented in early 2019 with an interesting business proposition. Jessica, one of the first employees they hired, was moving to Halifax, Canada. She proposed that Martha and Jeff establish a Pierre's salon there and make her its manager. To sweeten the deal, Jessica offered to base her entire salary on the salon's profitability. She proposed that they make her a profit centre and allow her to share 50:50 in profit before interest and taxes up to a maximum of 125% of her current salary of $50,700. In other words, her minimum salary could be zero, while her maximum salary could be $63,375. The reason for choosing profit before interest and taxes was because she felt all the items comprising it were controllable by her, or at least under her influence. After speaking with their own accountant and performing some independent research on the Halifax hair salon market, including learning that the average salary for a hair salon manager in Halifax is between $50,000 and $70,000 per year, Martha and Jeff agreed to Jessica's proposal.

Jessica spent her first month in Halifax searching for a suitable property. She identified three possible sites, and Jeff flew to Halifax to help make the final selection. Photos and detailed descriptions of each were sent to Martha. Following a further three weeks of back and forth communications, Jeff, Martha, and Jessica decided to rent a suite of rooms in a building on Beaufort Avenue that had once served as the Nova Scotia governor's residence. Over the next three months, Jeff and Jessica oversaw significant leasehold improvements, supervised the installation of $20,000 worth of hair salon equipment (i.e., salon chairs, backwash units, and hair styling stations), hired a hair stylist to work with Jessica, and outfitted the salon with the luxurious trappings Pierre's had become synonymous with (i.e., chandeliers, plush sofas and chairs, and full-length mirrors). Jeff remained on hand for the salon's 1 June opening. When he left the following day to return to Montreal, he did so with strong confidence in the Halifax salon's prospects for success.

During its first three months of operation, the Halifax salon's client numbers averaged nine per weekday and 12 per Saturday. The financial statements relating to the Halifax salon's first three months of operation are shown in Exhibit 2.

The results were disappointing. Although the reported loss was small, Jessica's self-designed compensation plan meant she was entitled to $450 in salary (i.e., her 50% sharing of the $900 profit before interest and taxes). Jeff and Martha felt uneasy about this outcome and suggested that the salon be closed. Jessica pleaded that she be given one more month to see if she could turn the situation around. With trepidation, Jeff and Martha agreed.

Jessica noted that other than the cost of the hair treatment supplies used during haircuts of about $3/client, the cost of pastries, cappuccinos, and lattes served to clients of about $4/client, and the cost of the stylist she hired at $22/hour (plus the associated payroll taxes of 7.37%), nearly all the remaining costs were fixed. Based on the high fixed cost structure, she decided the answer to her problem was getting more clients. Observing that Halifax was not as affluent as either Saint-Sauveur or Montreal, and thus the reason she could hire a highly experienced stylist for 12% less ($22/hour versus $25/hour) than Pierre's does in Saint-Sauveur or Montreal, she figured the best way to attract more clients was to lower the price of a haircut closer to eastern Canada's median price of $25. While more clients would require more stylists, the salon was presently operating at 40% of its capacity. It had always been anticipated that there would be a gradual build up from the two stylist stations currently being operated to the five stations Jessica and Jeff had installed.

Using information supplied by the Allied Beauty Association (Canada's sole beauty professional organization), Jessica estimated the three impacts of dropping the price of a haircut to $45, $35, and $29, with the assumption that these new prices would produce average daily client numbers of 14, 32, and 45 respectively. To compensate for the lower prices, Jessica planned to decrease the time of a client's haircut modestly for the $45 option, slightly more for the $35 option, and significantly for the $29 option. The anticipated changes would require no new personnel for the $45 option and two additional stylists for both the $35 and $29 options. Jessica further planned to fill any required stylist positions with junior stylists at $20/hour rather than the current $22/hour. Exhibit 3 presents pro forma income statements for each option, which shows that the highest profit before tax is associated with the $29/ haircut option. A 50:50 profit sharing of the $96,520 pre-tax income would mean she would earn about $48,260, which would bring her close to the $50,700 she used to make in the Saint-Sauveur salon.

In a rather fortuitous twist of circumstances, Jessica was then approached by the workers' union representing Dalhousie University, Saint Mary's University, and Mount Saint Vincent University. As an added benefit to its members, the union was making exclusive deals with a select set of Halifax-based businesses. In return for promoting Pierre's among its members, the union was asking that Jessica offer discounted haircuts to its members that matched the Halifax average price of $25. Representing over 5,000 employees, Jessica estimated that, of the likely group of employees such an offer would appeal to, the incremental impact on her business would be 72 extra clients per week. Since the salon was already outfitted with five stylist stations, there was capacity available to accommodate this increase in clients. A quick marginal cost calculation indicated a highly profitable outcome (see Exhibit 4). Sharing 50:50 in this additional expected profit meant Jessica would earn an annual salary close to $58,885 ($48,260 from the $29 pricing option plus another $10,625 from the workers' union offer).

With great excitement, Jessica wrote the email which is reproduced in Exhibit 5. After sending the email, she reflected on the experience that had been gained over the past few months and the positive platform she felt was now in place for going forward.

QUESTIONS

1   What type of competitive strategy is Pierre's pursuing?
2   How well suited is this strategy to the city of Halifax?
3   What is your view about the changes Jessica has made and wishes to make?
4   What overall advice would you have for Martha and Jeff?

EXHIBIT 1: INCOME STATEMENTS FOR SAINT-SAUVEUR AND MONTREAL FOR THE YEAR ENDED 31 DECEMBER 2018

Revenue:	Saint-Sauveur	% of total sales	Montreal	% of total sales
Sales – haircuts	$496,980	84.6%	$498,960	84.6%
Sales – hair products (net of cost)	$90,360	15.4%	$90,720	15.4%
Total revenue	$587,340	100.0%	$589,680	100.0%
Cost of sales:				
Salaries	$263,250	44.8%	$263,250	44.6%
Payroll taxes	$19,396	3.3%	$19,396	3.3%
Hair treatment supplies	$27,108	4.6%	$27,216	4.6%
Depreciation on equipment	$8,333	1.4%	$8,500	1.4%
Gross Profit	$269,253	45.8%	$271,318	46.0%
Expenses:				
Rent	$56,700	9.7%	$56,400	9.6%
Power and lighting	$7,320	1.2%	$7,764	1.3%
Insurance	$18,000	3.1%	$18,000	3.1%
Salon licence	$1,000	0.2%	$1,000	0.2%
Amortisation leasehold improvements	$10,000	1.7%	$10,500	1.8%
Depreciation furniture and fixtures	$20,000	3.4%	$20,500	3.5%
Maintenance	$15,072	2.6%	$14,568	2.5%
Marketing and advertising	$20,400	3.5%	$20,400	3.5%
Cleaning supplies	$7,560	1.3%	$8,136	1.4%
Pastries, cappuccinos & lattes for clients	$36,144	6.2%	$36,288	6.2%
Other (water, phone, rubbish removal)	$3,612	0.6%	$3,816	0.6%
Sub-Total Expenses	$195,808	33.3%	$197,372	33.5%
Net income before interest and taxes	$73,445	12.5%	$73,946	12.5%
Interest	$10,500	1.8%	$11,250	1.9%
Net income before taxes	$62,945	10.7%	$62,696	10.6%
Federal and provincial taxes	$9,442	1.6%	$9,404	1.6%
Net income	$53,503	9.1%	$53,292	9.0%

EXHIBIT 2: FINANCIAL STATEMENTS FOR PIERRE'S HALIFAX SALON

Income Statement for the three months ended 31 August 2019

Revenue:		% of total sales	Industry Avg.%
Sales – haircuts	$49,665	93.2%	96.3%
Sales – hair products (net of cost)	$3,612	6.8%	3.7%

Revenue:		% of total sales	Industry Avg.%
Total revenue	$53,277	100.0%	100.0%
Cost of sales:			
Salaries	$11,583	21.7%	51.2%
Payroll taxes	$853	1.6%	3.8%
Hair treatment supplies	$2,916	5.5%	11.2%
Depreciation on equipment	$2,167	4.1%	1.9%
Gross Profit	$35,758	67.1%	31.9%
Expenses:			
Rent	$12,900	24.2%	8.3%
Power and lighting	$1,320	2.5%	1.7%
Insurance	$3,600	6.8%	2.7%
Salon licence	$250	0.5%	0.2%
Amortisation leasehold improvements	$2,250	4.2%	1.2%
Depreciation furniture and fixtures	$3,750	7.0%	1.6%
Maintenance	$165	0.3%	2.3%
Marketing and advertising	$4,500	8.4%	2.6%
Cleaning supplies	$1,719	3.2%	1.7%
Pastries, cappuccinos & lattes for clients	$3,564	6.7%	—
Other (water, phone, rubbish removal)	$840	1.6%	0.9%
Sub-Total Expenses	$34,858	65.4%	23.2%
Net income before interest and taxes	$900	1.7%	8.7%
Interest	$2,813	5.3%	2.1%
Net loss before taxes	$(1,913)	–3.6%	6.7%
Federal and provincial taxes	$0	0.0%	1.0%
Net income	$(1,913)	–3.6%	5.7%

Statement of financial position as at 31 August 2019

Current Assets		Current Liabilities	
Cash	$350	Accounts payable	$1,300
Inventory (hair products)	$1,100	Wages payable	$528
Prepaids	$150	Rent payable	$378
Total Current Assets	$1,600	**Total Current Liabilities**	$2,206
Noncurrent Assets		**Noncurrent Liabilities**	
Salon equipment (net of deprec.)	$18,902	Notes payable	$150,000
Furniture and fixtures (net of deprec.)	$146,250	**Total Liabilities**	$152,206
Leasehold improvement	$87,750	**Owners' Equity**	
Total Noncurrent Assets	$252,902	Kuhn, Capital	$102,296
Total Assets	$254,502	**Total Liabilities and Owner's Equity**	$254,502

EXHIBIT 3: PRO FORMA ANNUAL INCOME STATEMENTS USING HAIRCUT PRICES OF $45, $35, AND $29

	$45	$35	$29
Revenue:			
Sales – haircuts	$204,120	$362,880	$413,424
Sales – hair products (net of cost)	$18,144	$41,472	$57,024
Total revenue	$222,264	$404,352	$470,448
Cost of sales:			
Salaries	$46,332	$130,572	$130,572
Payroll taxes	$3,414	$9,621	$9,621
Hair treatment supplies	$13,608	$31,104	$42,768
Depreciation on equipment	$8,667	$8,667	$8,667
Gross Profit	$150,243	$224,388	$278,820
Expenses:			
Rent	$51,600	$51,600	$51,600
Power and lighting	$5,280	$5,300	$5,320
Insurance	$14,400	$14,400	$14,400
Salon licence	$1,000	$1,000	$1,000
Amortisation leasehold improvements	$9,000	$9,000	$9,000
Depreciation of furniture and fixtures	$15,000	$15,000	$15,000
Maintenance	$660	$660	$660
Marketing and advertising	$18,000	$18,000	$18,000
Cleaning supplies	$6,876	$6,876	$6,876
Pastries, cappuccinos & lattes for clients	$18,144	$41,472	$57,024
Other (water, phone, rubbish removal)	$3,360	$3,390	$3,420
Sub-Total Expenses	$143,320	$166,698	$182,300
Net income before interest and taxes	$6,923	$57,690	$96,520
Interest	$11,250	$11,250	$11,250
Net income before taxes	$(4,327)	$46,440	$85,270
Federal and provincial taxes		$6,966	$12,791
Net income	$($4,327)	$39,474	$72,480

EXHIBIT 4: CONTRIBUTION MARGIN ANALYSIS FOR UNION OFFER (ASSUMES 50 WEEKS DUE TO STATUTORY HOLIDAYS)

Sales (72 clients * 50 weeks * $25)		$90,000
Variable costs		
Hair stylist	$40,560	
Payroll taxes (@ 7.37%)	$2,989	

Hair products (72 clients * 50 weeks * $3)	$10,800	
Pastries, cappuccinos, and lattes (72 clients * 50 weeks * $4)	$14,400	$68,749
Contribution margin		$21,251

EXHIBIT 5: EMAIL FROM JESSICA TO MARTHA AND JEFF

From: Jessica Edwards <Jessica.edwards@pierres.com>
Sent: Tuesday, 10 September 2019 7:41 AM
To: Jeff Kuhn <jeff.kuhn@pierre's.com>
Subject: Halifax salon's road to profitability

Hi Martha and Jeff,

I believe I have found the key to our success in Halifax. The price we now use for haircuts, which is the same as our Saint-Sauveur and Montreal salons, is just too high for Halifax. I ran three reduced-price scenarios and found that if we reduce the price of a haircut to $29, have faster workflows, and hire two more stylists to manage the added business we will get, we can make a more than $96,000 annual net profit before interest and taxes prior to calculating any profit sharing I would be entitled to (please see Exhibit 3). On top of this, I have been approached by a workers' union that represents the three main universities in Halifax. They have agreed to promote our salon if we give their members a preferential price of $25. I have calculated the financial implications of this proposal, which would require our hiring an additional stylist, and find that we would make a contribution margin of a bit over $21,000 (please see Exhibit 4). In other words, our annual net profit before interest and taxes would be approximately $117,000 before any profit sharing. And this profit is conservative, for it does not include the cross-selling sales we can expect.

I have some ideas about the type of stylists we should hire and how I will motivate them. First off, there are plenty of young hair stylists in Halifax that are looking to gain experience. I can save costs by hiring them at the average Halifax stylist rate of $20/hour. Being young, they will not come with any preconceived work ideas and will be amenable to the fast growth, fast work culture I want. We will, after all, be looking at moving from our current average of 5.5 clients per stylist per day to an average of 11–12 clients per day. I will also be looking to measure the stylists' performance, and perhaps at some point incentivise them on it, based on such objective measures as the number of clients they see per day and the variable costs used per client. I read an article about the importance of cost-effectively using hair products, which you can find at https://www.hairfinder.com/hairquestions/shampoocost.htm.

In sum, with the changes I am proposing, I am sure we will now succeed.

Kind regards,

Jessica

Review Question Answers

CHAPTER 1

1.1 What four business disciplines contribute to the study and practice of performance management?

 The four business disciplines that contribute to the study and practice of performance management are:

- Strategic Management
- Organizational Behaviour
- Organizational Theory &
- Management Accounting

1.2 What is the difference between multidisciplinary and interdisciplinary approaches?

 A multidisciplinary approach refers to the study of a particular topic from various fields of speciality, while remaining always within one's own speciality. In other words, this approach involves studying a phenomenon with a specialist lens, without referencing other disciplinary lenses or seeking to adopt a unified lens. In contrast, an interdisciplinary approach requires situating oneself at the intersection of the multiple contributing disciplines and using an integrated, singular lens.

1.3 What are some examples of the insights each of the four business disciplines provides to the study and practice of performance management?

 Strategic management involves the formulation, implementation, and control of organizational strategy. An organization's senior managers, for example, will employ principles of strategic management to grow and leverage their business units' competencies as part of their construction of and pursuit of competitive advantage. The pursuit/implementation of an organization's strategy has particular and direct relevance to performance management.

 Organizational behaviour is essentially applied social psychology in workplace settings. Its focus on employee motivation, leadership, and communication helps to facilitate the understanding and practice of performance management.

 Organizational theory involves the study of the organization as a whole and the subgroups of people and agents within the organization. A key use of organizational theory is to design and structure organizations in light of internal and external contingent factors. This process of alignment is especially relevant to performance management's goal of achieving good supporting mechanisms to support employees' implementation of an organization's strategy.

Management accounting involves the gathering, assimilating, and communication of information sets specific to an organization's internal decision making. Budgets are a classic feature of management accounting and also occupy a prominent place in performance management. For example, budgets serve to allocate resources based on strategic intentions and priorities.

1.4 Why must senior managers be capable of both energizing and directing employee behaviour?

Energizing employees is an important beginning, but it is incomplete on its own. Employees must also be given direction on expected performance outcomes and general guidelines about the activities that will be needed to sustain this performance. As described in this chapter, a past manager of the UK's Department of Social Development successfully energized his employees but failed to adequately direct them. The employees' answer to eliminating long queues of beneficiaries who were waiting outside the building was to move these same people inside the building by moving the reception area deeper into the building and constructing a labyrinth of queuing paths in the newly emptied space. In other words, the employees were energized, but due to inadequate direction they addressed the problem's symptom and not its cause.

CHAPTER 2

2.1 What is the origin of the term performance management?

The term performance management first appeared in the applied psychology/management literature in 1983, being originally coined by Dr Aubrey Daniels and Theodore Rosen in their book *Performance Management: Improving Quality and Productivity Through Positive Reinforcement*. In 1999, Professor David Otley introduced the term into the management accounting literature. Although his initial efforts were aimed at rebranding a university course featuring dwindling student enrolments, his 1999 *Management Accounting Research* article almost single-handedly changed the vernacular from management control to performance management.

2.2 How have the roles of middle-level managers changed over time and what are the reasons for this change?

In the 1950s and the 1960s, middle-level managers were a ubiquitous institutional feature. Their prominence was propelled by prevailing views about the superiority of bureaucracies and hierarchies. During this time, management control studies chiefly looked at how to control/influence middle-level managers to ensure lower-level employees were effectively and efficiently pursuing their organization's strategies. This trend continued into the 1970s and early 1980s. The introduction of JIT (just-in-time) and TQM (total quality management) upended the sacred canons that had grown up around bureaucracies and hierarchies. JIT and TQM preached the need for empowered employees who took charge of their own work responsibilities and decision making. With this emergence of self-managing teams and autonomous work groups, organizational structures became flatter, and the need for middle-level managers ended.

2.3 How does performance management compare to management control?

The two are one and the same. Management control was the term used to describe the process of influencing employees to implement their organizations' strategies prior to Professor Otley's rebranding of the field to its more modern and commonly used name of performance management.

2.4 Who is responsible for overseeing an organization's performance management system?

The design and operation of an organization's performance management system is the responsibility of an organization's senior managers. It is especially the task of those senior employees whose positions of authority put them in opportune positions to influence other members of the organization to implement and drive the strategy for the benefit of the organization.

2.5 How does the concept of performance management fit into the role of an accountant?

Accountants contribute in many ways to the practice of performance management. As one example, the budgets they help create significantly impact employee behaviour and, by extension, performance management. Accountants also contribute to the design of other performance measures. Many may be financial, some may be ratios derived from financial statements (e.g., return on assets), and still others may be non-financial (e.g., quality measures, production/ service delivery efficiency measures, etc.). Another example of how accountants can contribute to performance management is through the conduct of an organizational culture audit.

2.6 What are the differences between management accounting systems, accounting information systems, and performance management systems?

All three systems share the goal of improving organizational performance. How this goal is achieved differs substantially, especially in the approach adopted by performance management systems. In particular, performance management systems are designed to influence employee behaviour, and more specifically energize and direct employees' implementation of their particular organization's strategy. In contrast, management accounting systems and accounting information systems are decision-support systems that focus on supporting organizational decision making without necessarily impacting the behaviour of subordinate managers and employees. As an example, management accounting systems may provide cash flow information that may be used in deciding whether to invest in a new machine or launch a new line of products. Meanwhile, accounting information systems frequently provide financial and accounting data on a wide range of customer and operational matters. An example of the former is an account receivable aging report, and an example of the latter is an inventory reordering system. Unlike performance management systems, neither management accounting systems nor accounting information systems have either an inherent strategic focus or a specific aim of influencing employee behaviour.

2.7 How do strategy formulation, implementation, and control relate to performance management?

Strategy formulation is the process of strategy selection. Strategy implementation is the process of enacting an organization's chosen strategy. Strategic control is the process of collecting and measuring information relevant to determining whether an organization's chosen strategy is on track and meeting key strategic milestones. Performance management is primarily concerned with strategy implementation. In other words, it focuses on the process of ensuring an organization's strategy is being efficiently and effectively pursued by the employees.

CHAPTER 3

3.1 What is scientific management theory?

Taylor's scientific management theory is based on the concept that there is a single best way to organize, structure, and manage business activities. Proponents of scientific management view machines and humans as extensions of one another. According to the theory, the mandate of managers is to ensure the most compatible and economical fit between the two. Time and motion studies are central to the theory's implementation, for they help to standardize work into highly specialized tasks and, in the process, create optimal/most efficient workflow designs.

3.2 What theory challenged scientific management theory, and why did this occur?

The human relations school of thinking challenged and largely replaced scientific management theory. As part of applying scientific management theory, in the mid-1920s, Western Electric conducted experiments to determine the optimal configuration of its Hawthorne factory. Far from suggesting a single best way to design, the experiments' results suggested no best way. Elton Mayo, a professor at what is now called the Harvard Business School, was called in to provide an explanation for the unexpected results. He concluded that instead of being interchangeable parts of an overall production architecture, workers possessed complex social needs that required their consideration and incorporation into the design of work.

3.3 What is a taxonomy and why is it important to the study of accounting in general and performance management in particular?

A taxonomy is a process/system that provides ordering to objects, artefacts, places, concepts, or principles. Taxonomies have been used in financial accounting to classify the elements of financial statements into such categories as assets, liabilities, and equity. In management accounting, a taxonomy exists for classifying costs as fixed, variable, and mixed. In performance management, taxonomies have been used to classify the types of control/influence senior managers can exert when attempting to motivate employees' pursuit of their organization's strategy.

3.4 When comparing this book's PM taxonomy with other scholars' taxonomies, what are some of the similarities and differences?

The new taxonomy provided in this book offers a unified framework that draws together the earlier taxonomies of Anthony, Hopwood, Merchant, and Ouchi. Unlike the previous frameworks, the book's taxonomy creates three primary levers of performance management that are concretely grounded in the language of practising managers and contain mechanisms for exerting influence that can both promote and constrain employee behaviour.

3.5 Performance management is meant to constrain/coerce as well as enable/empower employee behaviour. What examples can you provide of this dual performance management influence?

One example of performance management's constraining/coercing and enabling/empowering of employee behaviour is the use of organizational budgets. On the one hand, budgets communicate, through the financial authority they bestow, the type of actions employees can take. This authority helps to energize and direct employee behaviour. On the other hand, budgets serve to constrain employee action by virtue of the limited resources expressed in a budget. This idea of limited resources means that employees must learn to operate within the means of their budget.

Another example of performance management's dual influence is the use of organizational charts. These charts communicate the devolved powers an employee possesses, as well as the reporting responsibilities they must meet. In other words, organizational charts promote the exercise of authority, while at the same time regulating and constraining how and where the delegated power can be used.

3.6 Can an organization have too much performance management? Discuss why.

The "Goldilocks" principle applies to the design of performance management systems. Neither too much, nor too little, but just the right amount of performance management is required. Too little influence will mean employees are being insufficiently energized and directed. Too much influence will lead to information overload and employees being distracted from going about their core tasks.

CHAPTER 4

4.1 What theories help to explain performance management practice?

Contingency theory, agency theory, goal-setting theory, stakeholder theory, and resource-based theory all help to explain performance management theory and practice.

4.2 Why is theory essential to the practice of business disciplines like performance management?

Theory is essential to the practice of business disciplines, for, without theory, improvement in practice would be based on methods of trial and error. This latter approach can be costly and time-consuming. Furthermore, it will make actions and decision making very slow, and inefficiencies will abound in organizational learning and practice.

4.3 Are some theories better at explaining parts of performance management? If so, which theories better explain which parts?

Certain aspects/features of performance management are better explained by different theories. Resource-based theory, for example, is best suited to explaining such performance management elements as vision and mission, success factors, strategy and plans, key performance measures, and organizational change. Goal-setting and agency theories are best suited to explaining organizational target setting, performance evaluation processes, the use of incentives/rewards, and an organization's information flows. Both stakeholder theory and contingency theory address a large proportion of the elements of performance management. Stakeholder theory helps explain the organizational goals and objectives that become enshrined in any particular organization's mission and vision statements. It also provides an understanding of the success factors and targets an organization uses, as well as the performance evaluation systems and information flows it operates. Meanwhile, with the exception of failing to address the formulation of an organization's strategy (i.e., mission and vision, success factors, and strategies and plans), contingency theory helps explain the use and design of all the major performance management elements.

4.4 What theory or theories do you believe are best suited to the field of performance management?

Contingency theory offers the greatest insight into the various elements of performance management. With the exception of strategy formulation, it helps explain all the other aspects of performance management design, including the setting of performance targets, the types of and reliance on information flows, and the choice of organizational structure. Its broad application shows why it is the most often used theory for conducting performance management research. Stakeholder theory also features extensively in performance management research. Similar to contingency theory, stakeholder theory's relevance to a broad range of performance management elements makes it a popular second choice.

4.5 What are the implications of goal-setting theory on performance management design?

Goal setting follows the SMART acronym, which is based on ensuring goals that are Specific, Measurable, Ambitious, Reasonable, and Time-targeted. Such goals create a conducive environment for managers to set appropriate motivation and for employees to attain good performance. From a performance management perspective, goal setting suggests that the creation of SMART goals with connections to an organization's strategy must be a top priority of senior managers.

CHAPTER 5

5.1 What are stakeholders?

Stakeholders constitute any party, whether it is an individual or a collection of individuals, who possesses an interest in the operations of an organization. Typical stakeholders include investors, employees, customers, clients, suppliers, and government.

5.2 Why are stakeholders important to organizations?

Stakeholders, especially when the definition is limited to those parties who contribute materially to or are impacted materially by the organization's activities, collectively determine an organization's goals and objectives. In particular, since the commitment of all stakeholders is needed by an organization to sustain its existence, the collective goals and objectives of the various stakeholders must be reflected in the organization's goals and objectives.

5.3 How are organizational goals determined?

From a stakeholder perspective, organizational goals can be seen as the product of the collective stakeholders' ambitions and values. Since any given stakeholder group's power/influence is subject to change over time, and since the ambitions and values of different stakeholder groups may be in opposition, an organization's goals can change over time. For example, a tight labour market may promote the goals of employees to a higher degree than before, or the election of a more private sector-friendly government may result in an organization prioritizing the goals of shareholders.

5.4 What are mission statements, vision statements, and company slogans? What are the essential characteristics of these statements and slogans?

A mission statement communicates the nature, scope, and focus of an organization's activities, its resources, and the key stakeholders undertaking such activities. A vision statement is meant to be a company's *raison d'être* and serves to motivate and even inspire the key stakeholders connected with the organization. While mission statements declare what an organization is about, vision statements declare what the organization wants to be. A company slogan is a further distillation of a vision statement's essence, often to the point that it is captured as a catch phrase that can fit on a T-shirt.

Mission statements are meant to be succinct (about a paragraph in length), factual, clearly described, focused on the present to the near future and reference stakeholders, market segments to compete in, and the organization's values and objectives. Vision statements are meant to be succinct (a sentence or two in length), clear, timeless in appeal, and inspirational. Company slogans tend to be highly succinct (a few words long), catchy, have a peculiarity or mystery about them and capture the attention and imagination of the reader.

5.5 Why are the goals and objectives of many for-profit firms similar?

Being for-profit, all these organizations will automatically share the goal of profitability or the need to be financially sound. Furthermore, because organizations are generally conceived with the idea of existing in the long-term, and not simply the short-term, organizations will find they need to operate as good community citizens. A major part of this undertaking will require them to be responsive to their customers/clients, fair and respectful to their employees, and faithful to their suppliers.

5.6 How is the mission statement of a not-for-profit related to its strategy?

The goals and objectives of not-for-profit organizations tend to be unique in nature. In particular, not-for-profit organizations are created to provide a service that typically no other organization is able or willing to provide. This fact (i.e., that no other organization provides the service) means the need for a competitive strategy is unnecessary. Accordingly, not-for-profit organizations will find that their mission statements substitute for a strategy.

5.7 Describe the relationships between an organization's mission statement, vision statement, strategy, and goals and objectives.

The mission statement establishes an organization's fundamental purpose. A vision statement distils the vision statement into a very succinct declaration of what an organization wants to become. An organization's strategy indicates how the organization's vision will be achieved. The pursuit of this strategy, assuming it is a viable strategy, will result in the organization's achievement of its goals and objectives.

CHAPTER 6

6.1 Define ethics. How is it related to such concepts as morality and lawfulness?

Ethics comprises how moral principles guide and proscribe individual behaviour. Although abiding by prevailing laws forms a part of ethics, the concept encompasses much more and includes striving to live a good life, being a responsible citizen, and making good moral decisions.

6.2 In what way is ethics a fundamental part of a professional such as medicine, accounting, and law? Provide an example for each of these three types of professions.

The existence of a code of ethics is one of the distinguishing characteristics of a profession. Medicine, accounting, and law each have stringent codes of ethics by which their members must abide. One of the ethical mandates of accountants is that they must maintain independence at all times, both in action and appearance. Lawyers have professional ethical standards that require them to act for their clients in a manner that is free from compromising influences or loyalties. Part of a doctor's ethical responsibilities is related to the Hippocratic Oath they swear, which includes the responsibility of ensuring they do no harm and commit to helping the sick.

6.3 What are the names of the common documents organizations and professional bodies use to convey ethical expectations and standards to their members?

Organizational codes of ethics, organizational codes of conduct, and organizational employee handbooks are the three common terms used to describe the codified ethical standards and practices professional members/employees are required to meet.

6.4 Explain how ethics is related to performance management.

Performance management comprises the practice of ensuring employees are being influenced to implement their organisation's strategy. Since the very essence of strategy is focused on the long-term, as opposed to short-lived, performance, unethical behaviour will never be congruent with strategy and the performance management practices that help guide its implementation.

6.5 What are the main cost categories associated with organizational ethical failing? Give examples for each type of cost category.

Organizational ethical failings result in both direct and indirect costs to the offending organization. Direct costs include fines and penalties, as well as lawsuit settlements and the legal fees to defend these actions. Indirect costs include employee turnover, lost employee productivity, decreased share prices, and reputational harm.

6.6 Beyond the committees and boards different professions may operate to investigate, judge, and discipline members' ethical violations, and identify the main public bodies and organizations that police organizational ethical failings.

The main public bodies that police organizations' ethical failings are respective countries' financial markets authority (e.g., the Financial Markets Authority in NZ), federal/national departments/ministries of justice (e.g., the US Department of Justice), and public-funded oversight agencies dedicated to industry-specific organizational reporting activities (e.g., the Public Company Accounting Oversight Board).

6.7 What is the 10-80-10 rule?

The 10-80-10 rule is a consulting practitioners' rule of thumb which claims that 10% of employees are always honest, 80% are honest most of the time, and 10% will commit fraud or act unethically whenever an opportunity presents.

6.8 What are the main factors associated with employees making bad ethical decisions?

The three factors associated with employees making bad decisions are opportunity, rationalization, and motivation. These factors are simultaneously represented in the model known as the fraud triangle.

6.9 Name three approaches an organization can take to minimize the likelihood that employees will behave unethically.

Three approaches to minimizing unethical behaviour include the Institute of Internal Auditors' three lines of defence, Daniel Kahneman's system 2 thinking, and the judicious design and use of employee incentives.

CHAPTER 7

7.1 What is strategy?

Strategy involves how an organization marshals its resources into coordinated activity sets that provide value for customers to ensure their continued patronage of the organization and its offerings. Organizational strategy can be classified into two elements: corporate-level strategy and business–unit-level strategy.

7.2 Why is strategy important to organizations?

Strategy serves as the vehicle an organization uses to achieve its goals and objectives. A clearly stated strategy that is fully understood and is being actively pursued by employees is a key to both successful strategic control and, by extension, organizational long-term success.

7.3 What is the difference between organizational strategy and functional strategy?

An organizational strategy is an overall strategy that governs and directs an organization's efforts in being competitive, that is, bringing value to customers and securing their ongoing patronage. Functional strategies are specific and unique to various job groupings in an organization, such as marketing or production. As such, functional strategy operates in a subordinate role to and is meant to support an organization's overall strategy.

7.4 What are the three types of corporate-level strategy? Describe and give examples of each.

The three types of corporate-level strategies are single industry, related diversified, and unrelated diversified. Single-industry strategy involves an organization being highly focused on an individual industry. Firms pursuing this strategy focus on sticking to what they do best, with examples including Google and American Express.

Related diversified strategy comprises an organization choosing to operate companies in different industries. To be an effective strategy, firms that choose this strategy must ensure the presence of synergy, which might derive from the sharing of operating/manufacturing facilities, logistics, and/or marketing systems. Examples of related diversified firms include KPMG, Avon Products, and Levi Strauss & Co.

Unrelated-diversified strategies occur when an organization chooses to operate across a swath of industries without any inherent shared advantages/synergies. The success of this strategy relies on the parent organization's ability to apply and transfer superior management expertise and/or financial resources across its network of unrelated companies. Examples of unrelated-diversified firms include Samsung, General Electric, Siemens, and 3M.

7.5 How does the GE/McKinsey Matrix link with an organization's pursuit of an unrelated-diversified strategy?

The GE/McKinsey Matrix, which was developed by McKinsey and Company in the early 1970s, is an improved extension of the BCG Growth Share Matrix. The GE/McKinsey Matrix views an unrelated-diversified company's success as being dependent on its ability to maintain a portfolio of products/services in different stages of its lifecycle. Basically, some companies in the unrelated-diversified portfolio will be in the mature or decline stages of their lifecycle and will be a source of cash that can be applied to other business units. Meanwhile, companies in the growth stage of their lifecycle will require cash. At a future point in time, these latter companies will become generators of the cash that will be applied to the newly emerging and growth-orientated sibling companies.

7.6 What are the general associations between corporate-level strategies and performance management design?

Single-industry firms will feature simple organizational structures, loose organizational systems, processes, and procedures, and singular cultures. In contrast, unrelated-diversified firms will have complex organizational structures, tight organizational systems, processes, and procedures, and pluralistic cultures. Related diversified firms will exhibit performance management designs that fall somewhere in the middle between single-industry and unrelated-diversified firms.

CHAPTER 8

8.1 What is competitive strategy?

Business-unit strategy is commonly referred to as competitive strategy. It involves the intelligent choices managers make while deciding on, constructing, and linking activities together for setting up the activities that define an organization's value proposition. A unique and working value proposition highlights the client-side engagement and gives a firm a competitive advantage. It is senior management's prerogative to establish a competitive strategy and engage the same in their strategic business units.

8.2 What are strategic business units (SBUs), and how do they relate to competitive strategy?

A strategic business unit (SBU) is an organizational subunit that has a defined set of products or services to sell to defined sets of customers/client groups. In relation to competitive strategy, SBUs are usually found in large, diversified companies, have distinct missions relative to other SBUs, compete for customers against well-known competitors, are distinct from other SBUs in the same organization, and are given high decision-making autonomy.

8.3 How do Miles and Snow, Porter, Cooper, and Kim and Mauborgne conceptualize strategy?

Miles and Snow contend that the strategy a firm develops is based on its beliefs and experiences. They present four strategic archetypes. These archetypes are known to address three fundamental strategic problems and include selecting and adjusting products/services, decisions about how to produce the products/services, and the creation of organizational structures capable of establishing roles, relationships, and organizational processes that are consistent with and support the first two problem types.

The four archetypes Miles and Snow establish are Prospectors, Defenders, Analyzers, and Reactors. Prospectors seek out change, as they look to broaden their product ranges. Defenders are believers of refinement and efficiency. Analyzers have a dual efficiency and innovation focus. Finally, reactors have non-systematic approaches to the three strategic problems, and this strategic archetype is deemed non-viable.

Porter views strategy as revolving around two distinct choices: cost leadership and differentiation. Both cost leadership and differentiation can be pursued using a generalist scope or a specialist scope. Cost leadership is based on laying claim to having the lowest prices in a given industry. In contrast, a differentiation strategy is based on the possibility of a firm offering some non-cost-based competitive uniqueness or advantage. Such superiority or market differentiation can be achieved in product/service features, service methods pre and post-sales, distribution innovation, and firm image/reputation.

Cooper believes that for some industries competition will by necessity adopt a strategy comprising the same order-winning criteria. Industries likely to feature this generic, industry-wide strategy, which he terms confrontation strategy, are ones that are characterized by significant maturity and high competition. Firms that compete with a confrontation strategy do not shy away from the competition. Rather, they compete head-to-head for customers.

Kim and Mauborgne introduce the concept of blue ocean strategies. A blue ocean strategy consists of offering so unique and appealing of a value proposition that there is no competitor in sight. This strategy demands the simultaneous pursuit of segment differentiation and the provision of low prices. It involves using hybrid strategies that deliver simplicity, ease of use, superior productivity, environmental friendliness, and fun.

8.4 What are order-winning criteria, and how do they relate to competitive strategy?

Order-winning criteria or OWC are the tangible representations of competitive strategy; that is, these criteria are the reason that customers choose to buy from one firm and not another. Porter and Miles and Snow capture the need and essence of having a single order-winning criterion. But Cooper and Kim and Mauborgne insist on promoting a multiple OWC approach.

8.5 Provide an example of at least one firm for each of the following competitive strategies: cost leader, differentiator, defender, prospector, analyzer, and blue ocean.

Cost Leader: Bank of America, HSBC, Celtic Bank

Differentiator: Apple Computers, Tesla

Defender: British Telecommunications, Four Seasons

Prospector: 3M Company, Meta/Facebook

Analyzer: IBM, Anheuser-Busch, Kyocera

Blue Ocean: Southwest Airlines, Uber Technologies

8.6 What are the general associations between the competitive strategies of Miles and Snow, Porter, Cooper, and Kim and Mauborgne, and performance management design?

As Table 9.2 shows, cost leaders and defenders are supported by performance management designs that feature formal and standardized organizational systems, processes and procedures, functional organizational structures, and conservative organizational cultures. Differentiators and prospectors are supported by performance management designs that feature informal and customized organizational systems, processes and procedures, divisional organizational structures, and collaborative and entrepreneurial organizational cultures. The performance management systems for organizations pursuing analyzer, blue ocean, and confrontation strategies will feature characteristics that borrow from both ends of Table 9.2's continua for each of the three levers of influence.

CHAPTER 9

9.1 Define each of the following terms: data, information, knowledge, digitized, digital technology, and digital business transformation (DBT).

Data are raw, unanalyzed, unorganized, unrelated, and uninterrupted facts, figures, numbers, and records. Information is the set of data that has been processed, analyzed, and structured in a meaningful way. Knowledge is the combination of information and experience that helps managers take action and make successful decisions. Digitized refers to an environment that consists wholly of binary coding (i.e., a world where 0s and 1s are used to represent characters, instructions, and literally everything). Digital technologies are electronic tools, systems, devices, and resources that generate, store, or process data. These technologies include analytical tools and applications, mobile tools and applications, platforms to build shareable digital capabilities, and social media. DBT describes an organization's journey to harness a digitized environment by leveraging the opportunities and evolving practices of digital technologies and their impact on society in an operationally optimal and strategic manner.

9.2 Describe and provide examples of some of the early manifestations of DBT.

The offshore processing of accounting data and overseas situating of call centres are some of the earliest forms of DBT. Dell Computers' late 1990s foray into selling personal computers directly to customers and Netflix's 1997 establishment as one of the world's first online DVD-rental stores are two slightly more recent, but still embryonic, examples of DBT.

9.3 Is DBT more or less relevant for certain types of organizations? Explain your belief.

DBT is as relevant to high-tech companies as it is to more ordinary, less sexy organizations. It is helpful to all organizations wishing to become more agile, efficient, people-focused, innovative, and customer-centric. As an example, Howden, a UK-based application engineering company, which provides solutions in air and gas handling, is known for its use of DBT to improve its service offerings and provide better customer support.

9.4 DBT is often described as a journey that requires the holistic integration of business practices. Discuss and provide examples of why DBT is likened to a journey and provide examples of what business practices require holistic integration.

Rather than being viewed as a large, quantum, single step, DBT is best viewed as a journey involving an organization's strategic and prioritized use of digital technologies. It requires significant changes to workplace practices, usually entailing the creation of seamless transitions between work processes and workers themselves. Organizations that implement DBT will invariably observe that success requires winning over both the hearts and minds of a wide set of stakeholders residing both inside and outside the organization. As such, this requires time and patience. Some of the required holistic integration of DBT comprises ensuring not only the integration of digital technologies like social media, internet-connecting devices, and software and apps, but also the high collaboration between customer-facing workers, IT specialists, and business specialists.

9.5 Identify and explain which elements of the book's performance management model are affected by an organization's adoption of DBT.

DBT affects all three levers of performance management: organizational structure, organizational systems, processes and procedures, and organizational culture. DBT affects an organization's strategy formulation by virtue of its ability to help the organization enhance its product lines and create additional revenue streams. In other words, DBT's connection with organizational strategy means there will be a natural association between DBT and performance management.

9.6 Explain how and provide specific examples showing the influence of DBT on performance management practice and design.

DBT's presence will influence all three levers of performance management. First, it will affect organizational structure, for the preferred type of organizational structure will be flat, decentralized, and promote the ability for networked employee groups to transcend functional silos. Second, DBT will influence an organization's design of its organizational systems, processes, and procedures. In particular, an organization's systems, processes, and procedures must be designed to enable greater agility and better customer focus. Third, DBT will affect organizational culture, by requiring the culture to feature high trust, the democratization of information, and the empowerment of people.

CHAPTER 10

10.1 What is organizational structure?

Organizational structure can be compared to the structure of a building. Just as buildings differ in design, purpose, and use, organizational structures differ from firm to firm. Organizational structure is connected to the cost structure of the organization and is a critical driver for the organization's performance. Organizational structure can influence the behaviour of people within the organization and includes the following three purposes.

1   foster organizational outputs and achievements
2   minimize the effects of employee mistakes and variations on the organization's outputs, and
3   determine and govern the flow of information through an organization

10.2 What are the three dimensions of organizational structure?

The three dimensions of organizational structure are complexity, formalization, and centralization. Complexity consists of horizontal differentiation, vertical differentiation, and spatial dispersion. Formalization is represented by the extent to which an organization is characterized by codified rules and procedures. Centralization refers to the degree to which decision making is consolidated at the top of an organization, which refers to highly centralized, or is widely distributed throughout the organization, which is highly decentralized.

10.3 How does organizational structure influence employee behaviour? Provide some examples.

Organizational structure is a tool used by senior management to influence employee behaviour. Senior managers use organizational structure to create employee groups and, in the process, establish and exert control and coordination on these groups. A bank branch, for example, will have a structure where there is a manager for each group/team (bank tellers, bank lenders, etc.). The performance and behaviour of each group/team employee will be subject to the evaluation of the group/team leader. Each team leader will in turn be accountable to a more senior manager either in the branch or at a corporate level.

Organizational structure further comprises the degree of formality an organization adopts. Greater formality requires employees to follow pre-established patterns of work practices. Finally, an organization's amount of centralization/decentralization sets limits on the amount of decision-making lower-level employees can undertake. Greater amounts of decision making at low hierarchical levels signify decentralization, while lesser amounts indicate centralization.

10.4 How are the three dimensions of organizational structure related to one another?

Centralization and formalization are closely linked. As one increases or decreases, so too does the other. Also, complexity and centralization are linked. The more complex an organization becomes, the more need there is for decentralization. This in turn sets off a need for greater formalization of systems, procedures, and processes, as senior managers may feel a loss of control over the decentralized unit(s) and seek to compensate for this fact by introducing codified rules and procedures that communicate expected standards and set boundaries on work practices and behaviour.

10.5 What is a responsibility centre?

A responsibility centre is a group of employees comprising a lead employee, usually called a manager, and the remaining group of employees. Each responsibility centre will be responsible for a given type and breadth of work activities. The creation of responsibility centres is closely related to an organization's use of centralization and decentralization and is seen as a manifestation of organizational structure.

10.6 What are the four main types of responsibility centres an organization can choose from? Describe each type and give examples of the organizational units that are likely to adopt each type.

There are four main types of responsibility centres: revenue centres, expense centres, profit centres, and investment centres.

Revenue centres are mainly used by marketing and sales units. These business units are responsible for sales. Senior managers generally provide revenue centres with a budget and sales targets to reach. Since sales volume is the only measure, efficiency cannot be measured. Revenue centres can also be responsible for expenses incurred but they are primarily in charge of revenues. A revenue centre approach is usually preferred by marketing and sales business units. This is because they usually control and navigate a product and service mix in terms of number of units but not the cost of the units.

Expense centres are responsible for managing and being accountable for costs corresponding to their respective centres. They can be of two types: discretionary expense centres or engineered expense centres. Discretionary expense centres focus on input and process alone. They are under the control of the respective managers. Typical discretionary expense centres are support departments found inside a company and include such departments as accounting, finance, research and development, human resources, customer relations, legal, and public relations. Engineered expense centres are used when there is predictable, cause-and-effect relationship between the number of inputs and the number of good/quality outputs. Factories are typically run as engineered expense centres.

Profit centres are responsible for managing both expenses and revenues. Profit centres are seen as an ideal way of aligning employee behaviour with an organization's most fundamental need to be profitable, or to at least generate an adequate surplus. Due to the delegated powers profit centres have, this type of organizational structure is associated with quicker decision making and aids a profit centre manager's professional development and future promotion prospects. Examples of a profit centre include a hotel manager who is responsible for the revenue and expenses of his/her hotel.

An investment centre is responsible for managing its profits and its assets. Whereas profit centres are helpful in aligning employee behaviour with an organization's goal of profit, investment centres extend the goal congruence a further step. This outcome is achieved by encouraging employees to invest in additional resources only if the expected return is greater than or equal to the organization's cost of capital. A regional manager of a hotel chain is a good example of an investment centre. This manager is responsible for the profits of the hotels in his/her region and these hotels' assets.

10.7 What is meant by the terms controllability and separability? How are they relevant to responsibility centre design?

Spiller (1988) introduces the twin mandate of controllability and separability. These principles make sure that the right items are measured for the right purpose. For example, if you want to measure the performance of the manager of a responsibility centre, you have to measure the factors that are under the control/influence of the manager. This is the principle of controllability, wherein an employee should view and have control over the measure being used to assess their performance. Separability refers to only assigning revenues and costs where there is a direct link to their receipt/ incurrence. This principle is used when evaluating a business unit's, as opposed to manager's, performance.

10.8 From a contingency theory perspective, what organizational structures are commonly encouraged for each of the competitive strategies discussed in Chapter 9? Explain why.

Cost leader and defender strategies are supported by centralized, functional organizational structures featuring high formalization. Differentiator and prospector strategies are supported by decentralized, divisional organizational structures featuring lower formality and higher amounts of informal control. Analyzer, blue ocean, and confrontation strategies are supported by lean organizational structures featuring equal doses of formalization and informal control.

CHAPTER 11

11.1 What are the main purposes of a performance measurement system?

The main purposes of a performance measurement system are to establish position, communicate desired organizational direction, influence behaviour, stimulate action, and facilitate organizational learning.

11.2 What are the distinguishing characteristics of a budget?

Key characteristics of a budget are:

- Relate to a future period, mainly a year
- Stated in financial/monetary terms
- Convey an implicit or stated commitment to achieving the budget's revenue and expense goals
- Are reviewed and approved by an authority higher in the organizational hierarchy than the department/manager covered by the budget
- Once approved, budgets become fixed and are only modified under special circumstances
- At regular intervals, a budget is compared against actual results, with differences being the subject of analysis and explanation.

11.3 What are tight control and loose control? Provide examples of each.

Budgets can be controlled in a tight or loose manner. Tight budget control means employees are expected to achieve the budget and no excuses are tolerated. It is also often the case that a reward is attached to achieving the budget and a penalty for non-achievement. Tight control is amenable to certain organizational settings (e.g., companies in mature stages of their organizational life cycle facing stable, predictable environments). When used in unsuitable environments (e.g., a start-up organization that is trying to disrupt its market with revolutionary technology), it can produce unwanted dysfunctional behaviour that includes introducing slack, earnings management, and even fraud.

Loose budget control means the budget serves primarily for planning and coordination purposes. The evaluation of sub-units or employees is not undertaken, and no thought is given to attaching incentives and rewards to a budget's achievement. Loose budgets can avoid some of the dysfunctional employee outcomes that tight control may encourage. However, it may be less motivating for employees who work in more predictable environments, who crave ongoing feedback on how they are performing, and who like to be rewarded when their performance meets or surpasses agreed–upon targets.

11.4 What are strategic cost drivers?

Strategic cost drivers allocate common costs based on long-term, strategic considerations. This approach can be contrasted with traditional cost drivers (e.g., machine hours, number of production set-ups, etc.) that rely on identifying and reinforcing cause-and-effect relationships or use an approach that applies common costs to the ability for a cost object (e.g., a department, product) to bear the costs.

11.5 What are the limitations of using profit as a measure of performance?

Performance is a complex phenomenon that involves a lot more than the dollar value attached to it. Thus, the use of a performance measure based on profit will be insufficiently holistic, may undermine employee achievement on other aspects of performance, and can lead to employees creating budget slack.

11.6 What is budgetary slack? Is it good or bad? How can senior managers influence its occurrence?

Budget slack occurs when employees deliberately underestimate revenues and overestimate expenses in an attempt to inflate their performance. In essence, budgetary slack involves the creation of low-hanging fruit goals that can be easily achieved. Employees, being eager to increase their likelihood of receiving organizational rewards and avoiding penalties, may try to introduce slack into their budget targets.

Too much budgetary slack is problematic for an organization. It presents a false picture of what can be reasonably expected of employees and it fails to encourage management and employees' goal alignment. Although too great an amount of budgetary slack is seen as unwanted and to be avoided, some scholars believe that small amounts of budgetary slack can be beneficial. In particular, budgetary slack gives time for employees opportunities to experience success (by meeting their performance targets) and to reflect and learn from their performance, which in turn opens up possibilities for employee innovation and creativity.

Senior managers can do two things to minimize the occurrence of budgetary slack. First, they can decouple budget evaluation from employee rewards. Second, senior managers can incentivize honesty in the budget-setting process through a budgeting technique like truth-seeking budgets.

11.7 Why might a manager submit a budget that is biased, and how should senior management respond?

Managers may submit biased budgets in an attempt to gain an advantage for themselves or their business units. Senior management can respond by either decoupling budget evaluation and employee rewards or by introducing truth-seeking budgets. The latter seeks to incentivize honesty in budget-setting. Instead of merely rewarding employees when unambitious budget targets are achieved, truth-seeking budgets incentivize employees for nominating **and** achieving highly ambitious budget targets.

11.8 What are the benefits of using EVA rather than ROI?

ROI, which is computed as net income divided by investment, produces a ratio. This ratio is often compared to a benchmark like weighted average cost of capital (WACC) to determine if a business unit and its responsible manager have been financially successful. Ratios above WACC indicate success and below WACC indicate failure. The trouble with ROI is that managers will be uninterested in pursuing projects/investments for which the ROI is below the ROI currently being achieved. Furthermore, and what serves to make ROI an unsuitable managerial performance measure, is that this disinterest will occur in spite of a project/investment being desirable (i.e., having a return above the organization's WACC). In other words, ROI produces a lack of goal congruence.

In contrast to ROI, EVA measures value creation. Its formula, which is net operating profit before taxes minus a cost of capital charge, leads to either a positive number (meaning value has been created) or a negative number (meaning value has been destroyed). Managers will always be motivated to pursue projects/investments with positive EVAs. This means that goal congruence exists between managers and their organizations.

11.9 What are non-financial performance measurement systems, and why are they used?

Contemporary organizations are complex in size and scale. Unlike past generations of organizational managers, in which the senior managers had long tenures in the industry and the companies they led, today's senior managers typically lack the same degree of company and industry familiarity. Unlike their predecessors who could appreciate what caused the financial performance measures, present-day leaders require the additional help non-financial performance measurement systems offer. In addition, non-financial performance measures offer broader and early signal insights into financial performance measures.

Although lacking financial measures, non-financial performance measurement systems include information that invariably contributes to the financial performance measures observed at a future date. Common non-financial performance measures are shipment rates, defect rates, machine capacity, lead times to the introduction of new product lines, etc. According to Hall et al. (1991), the four main non-financial performance measurement groupings are quality, lead time, resource use, and people development.

11.10 What are hybrid performance measurement systems, and why are they used?

Hybrid performance measurement systems rely on a combination of financial and non-financial performance measures. Kaplan and Norton's balanced scorecard and Cross and Lynch's performance measurement hierarchy are two examples of hybrid systems. These hybrid measures are used to portray a holistic view of performance in organizations. In particular, it enables the viewing of the whole picture rather than just the financial aspects. Hybrid measures are based on the premise that performance is a complex phenomenon and cannot be viewed with one lens only. The balanced scorecard, for example, assesses enterprise performance from four broad perspectives: financial, internal business, customer, and organizational capacity. The financial perspective relates to how the organization answers shareholder needs, while the other three perspectives relate to client management, improving the delivery of products and services, and assembling and marshalling resources that will enable the required employee foundational behaviour.

11.11 What types of employee incentives can an organization use?

Employee incentives can be financial or non-financial. Non-financial incentives can be recognition, promotion, increased job responsibilities, and increased autonomy. Non-financial incentives are more closely associated with the use of intrinsic factors to motivate workers. Financial incentives can take the form of salary increases, bonuses, enhanced benefit packages, and perquisites. Financial incentives can be time dependent and goal dependent. These incentives are aimed at directing motivation for better performance, such as using a bonus to increase sales.

11.12 How do scholars and practitioners generally perceive the value of employee incentive systems?

Employee incentive systems play a key role in both agency theory and goal-setting theory. Agency theory views workers as self-interested and lazy. This theory contends that incentives are needed to overcome employees' inherent selfishness. Goal-setting theory argues that the use of SMART goals (Specific, Measurable, Ambitious, Reasonable, and Time-bounded) motivates workers. HR and compensation practitioners like to extend this acronym to SMARTER by including the additional elements of Evaluate and Reward.

The literature on incentives shows that the relationship between the use of incentives and such outcomes as greater worker productivity, less absenteeism, and higher organizational commitment is often ephemeral and can have the perverse effect of diminishing employees' intrinsic motivation. Organizations that insist on using pay-for-performance plans should proceed with a high level of caution.

11.13 Describe how organizations use human resource management systems to attract, train, and retain employees.

Human resource management (HRM) is primarily concerned with the relationship between the management of an organization's human resources and the organization's performance. It therefore seeks strategic alignment between an organization's employee hiring, training, and retaining cycle and the organization's strategic vision, performance, and culture.

HRM promotes the use of pre-hiring tests and analysis of prospective employees to analyze their suitability to the firm. Pre-hiring tests measure cognitive abilities, personality, learning styles, reasoning, and decision-making styles. Training at both the beginning of employment and conducted during employees' time with their employers is critical to the employees' and their respective organizations' success. It is important to ensure that training programmes are strategy-aligned, adequately resourced, rigorously evaluated, and utilize the best delivery methods. Retention of the right employees with the right knowledge, right skills, and right attitudes depends on such factors as an organization's culture and the leadership styles enacted by its senior managers.

CHAPTER 12

12.1 What is organizational culture?

Organizational culture comprises a set of broad and tacitly understood rules by which organizational members agree to be governed (Camerer and Vepsalainen, 1988: 115). These rules become the organization's guiding principles, helping to determine which behaviours are deemed acceptable and which are view as unacceptable behaviour. Peer pressure will be exerted to conform to the prevailing culture. Those employees who do not will find themselves ostracized or exiled.

12.2 What six dimensions comprise organizational culture?

The six dimensions of organizational culture are:
- Shared beliefs
- Shared values
- Shared experiences
- Symbols
- Exemplars
- Power structures.

12.3 What is a cultural audit?

An organizational culture audit comprises the formal process of measuring and documenting an organization's culture. More specifically, it involves collecting information about an organization's six dimensions of culture: shared beliefs, shared values, shared experiences, symbols, exemplars, and power structures. Following this collection of information, the employee(s) conducting the organizational culture audit will create a profile of the organization's culture as it actually exists. This profile will then be compared against the ideal organizational culture, which is the type of culture that would best support and promote employees' implementation of their organization's strategy. Any observed gap between the actual and the ideal organizational cultures will require intervention either in the form of an organization's leaders enacting culture change through modelling behaviour and/or by reconfiguring an organization's human resource systems.

12.4 How can a cultural audit be used to create a better performance management system?

An organizational culture audit is used to determine if gaps exist between an organization's existing culture and its ideal culture. The ideal culture is the type of culture that best supports employees' implementation of their organization's strategy. Should gaps exist between the current culture and the ideal culture, closing the gaps will enhance employees' pursuit of the organization's OWC and ultimately its strategy.

12.5 Explain the need for organizational cultures to support organizational strategy and align with an organization's structure and the systems, processes, and procedures it operates.

A strong alignment between the three levers helps avoid employee confusion, enables smooth organizational operations, and improves the likelihood of achieving strategic vision and mission.

12.6 If a cultural audit identifies a mismatch between the organization's culture and the desired culture, what are the two main ways senior managers can create organizational culture change?

An observed mismatch between an organization's current culture and its desired culture can be resolved in one of two ways. First, the senior managers can act as exemplars and model the behaviour they expect. Second, human resource systems can be used to not only energize and direct employees but also to attract and retain the most qualified employees. Research shows that superior human resource practices are associated with employee recruiting advantages and higher employee retention rates.

CHAPTER 13

13.1 What are internal contingent factors? Why are they important to performance management design?

Internal contingent factors are salient organizational properties situated within an organization's boundaries. They can be contrasted with external contingent factors which sit outside the organization's boundaries. Similar to external contingent factors, internal contingent factors may either reinforce or constrain an existing or planned performance management design. In situations where the contingent factors undermine the design that is required, such as an autocratic leader heading up an organization that is pursuing a prospector strategy and therefore would benefit from a decentralized organizational structure, the performance management designer must compensate for this misalignment. Prominent internal contingent factors include leadership style, organizational size, organizational life cycle, and ownership type.

13.2 What defines a leader?

In most basic terms, leaders are individuals that followers get behind. Leaders are responsible for energizing and giving direction to followers' actions. A leader's motivation of his/her followers can produce good or bad outcomes. John F. Kennedy inspired a nation to travel to the moon. In contrast, Adolf Hitler led his country into a world war and oversaw mass genocide.

13.3 Are people born to become leaders or can they be taught to be leaders?

Two opposing views predominate. Some believe that leaders are predisposed to assume their positions of authority. Studies, for example, have correlated the presence of a gene, MAOA-L, with leadership. This gene is often found in entrepreneurs. Other studies have observed links between the amount of testosterone a fetus is exposed to during critical prenatal periods and later leadership roles. In contrast to the view that leaders are born, other scholars believe that leadership is a function of leadership skills that can be learned, in the event they are missing or insufficient. An entire industry of leadership training has emerged over the past three decades.

13.4 Identify and describe four main leadership styles. Describe how each leadership style influences performance management design.

The four main leadership styles are initiating structure, consideration, transactional, and transformational. Initiating structure leadership involves a leader being task oriented. Such a leader exhibits a keen interest in determining the set of tasks that should be accomplished and by whom. Consideration leadership style is characterized by a leader who is people-focused. This leader consults with his/her staff, keeps them apprised of changes that could affect their working conditions, and is willing to be flexible to help the worker balance the demands of work and life more generally. Transactional leadership embodies a *quid pro quo* relationship, whereby the leader provides worker-desired rewards for achieving some mutually agreed-upon level of performance. Transformational leadership adopts a change orientation and emphasizes emotions, values, the importance of symbolic behaviour, and the role of the leader in making events meaningful for followers. This final leadership style includes subdimensions of visionary, inspirational, charismatic, individualized consideration, and intellectual stimulation.

Table 13.1 summarizes the compatibility between the four leadership styles and performance management characteristics. Initiating structure leadership styles best supports organizational structures featuring low complexity, high formality, and centralization; organizational systems, processes, and procedures that place high reliance on both financial and non-financial performance measures and incentives; and conservative and collectivist organizational cultures. Consideration leadership best supports organizational structures that are decentralized, exhibit low formality, and have either low or high complexity; organizational systems, processes, and procedures that place high reliance on non-financial performance measures, incentives, and human resource systems; and organizational cultures spanning a wide range from conservative to entrepreneurial and collectivist to collaborative. Transactional leadership best suits organizational structures with low complexity, high formality, and are either centralized or decentralized; organizational systems, processes, and procedures that place high reliance on both financial and non-financial performance measures and incentives; and organizational cultures that are conservative and collectivist. Finally, transformational leadership best suits organizational structures that are decentralized, exhibit low formality, and have either low or high complexity; organizational systems, processes, and procedures that place high reliance on non-financial performance measures, incentives, and human resource systems; and organizational cultures that are entrepreneurial and collectivist or collaborative.

When an organization's strategy is supported by the type of performance management system that its leader(s) display(s), then the desired employee influence is reinforced. When incompatibility is present, then the performance management designer needs to compensate for the lack of compatibility.

13.5 What are the four stages of an organizational lifecycle? Describe how each of these stages is related to performance management design.

The four stages of an organizational lifecycle are inception, growth, maturity, and decline. Again, Table 13.1 summarizes the compatibility between these four lifecycle stages and performance management characteristics. These relationships include inception being associated with low complexity, high formality, high centralization, high reliance on financial performance measures, and entrepreneurial and collectivist cultures. The growth lifecycle stage is associated with high complexity, high formality, high decentralization, high reliance on non-financial performance measures and incentives, high reliance on human resource systems, and entrepreneurial organizational cultures punctuated by collectivism or collaboration. Maturity is associated with high complexity, high formality, high reliance on a wide range of formalized organizational systems processes and procedures, and conservative and collaborative organizational cultures. The decline lifecycle stage is associated with low complexity, high formality, high centralization, high reliance on financial performance measures and human resource systems, and conservative and collectivist organizational cultures. When an organization's strategy is supported by the particular lifecycle stage in which the organization finds itself, then the desired employee influence is reinforced. When incompatibility is present, then the performance management designer needs to compensate for the lack of compatibility.

13.6 How does organizational size influence performance management design?

Table 13.1 summarizes the relationships. Small organizations are associated with low complexity, low formality, and centralization. Furthermore, these organizations show a high reliance on human resource systems and entrepreneurial and collectivist organizational cultures. Large organizations are associated with high complexity, high formality, and decentralization. These organizations also display a high reliance on financial performance measures, non-financial performance measures, and human resource systems, and are conservative and have high collaboration. When an organization's strategy is supported by the performance management characteristics related to its size, then the desired employee influence is reinforced. When incompatibility is present, then the performance management designer needs to compensate for the lack of compatibility.

13.7 How does organizational ownership influence performance management design?

Table 13.1 summarizes the relationships. Tightly controlled organizations are associated with low complexity, low formality, and centralization. Furthermore, these organizations show a high reliance on financial performance measures, incentives, and human resource systems. Organizations with dispersed ownership are associated with high complexity, high formality, and decentralization. These organizations also display a high reliance on financial performance measures, non-financial performance measures, and human resource systems, and feature organizational cultures with high employee collaboration. When an organization's strategy is supported by the performance management characteristics related to its ownership, then the desired employee influence is reinforced. When incompatibility is present, then the performance management designer needs to compensate for the lack of compatibility.

CHAPTER 14

14.1 What are external contingent factors? Why are they important to performance management design?

External contingent factors are salient properties situated outside an organization's boundaries that must be accounted for when designing an organization's performance management system. They can be contrasted with internal contingent factors which sit inside the organization's boundaries. Similar to internal contingent factors, external contingent factors may either reinforce or constrain an existing or planned performance management design. In situations where the contingent factors undermine the design that is required, such as government regulation that may prevent an organization's pursuit of concentric diversification, the performance management designer must compensate for this misalignment. Prominent external contingent factors include industry, national culture, government regulation, and labour market.

14.2   How does industry type influence performance management design?

As shown by organizational theorists, complex environments (i.e., those that are characterized by significant and rapid change in market growth, competition, product/service offerings, product/service technology, and customer preferences) require complex organizational cultures. The latter manifest as decentralized organizational structures. In contrast, simple environments are best served by centralized organizational structures. Decentralized firms will also find they need integrating systems to manage the inter-unit conflict that decentralization invariably brings. All these ideas are captured as part of contingency theory.

14.3   How does national culture influence performance management design?

Hofstede argues that national culture is comprised of six subdimensions: power distance, individualism/collectivism, uncertainty avoidance, masculinity/femininity, long-term orientation, and indulgence. Each of these subdimensions exerts an influence on performance management design. For example, national cultures with high power distance are better aligned with centralized and highly formalized organizational structures. Meanwhile, national cultures with high individualism are better aligned with individual-based incentives based on objectively determined performance measures. And as one further example, national cultures with high uncertainty avoidance may struggle to support organizational cultures that require entrepreneurialism.

14.4   How do government policies influence performance management design?

Government rules and regulations can influence performance management design in two main ways. First, it can restrict an organization's attempt to enact strategy. Governments invariably have departments responsible for guarding against anti-competitive behaviour. These departments may restrict an organization's attempt to merge or acquire other organizations. In other words, an organization's ability to enact its organizational-level strategy, whether this strategy is based on an expansion in its single industry or a desire to become related diversified or unrelated diversified, may be constrained. Government regulation may also constrain the ability to adopt competitive strategies. For example, the government may regulate an industry to such a high level that anything other than a confrontation strategy is not possible.

Government rules and regulations may also mandate specific thresholds for employee rights and benefits. Accordingly, to the extent a government sets employee benefits (sick leave, maternity, leave, paternity leave, holiday/annual leave, etc.) at a high level, then the ability for organizations to use generous employee benefit packages to attract and retain employees may not be possible, for all organizations are offering a similar set of benefits. In other words, an organization may not be able to use human resource systems to help implement its strategy and may need to rely upon other performance management techniques to influence employee behaviour.

14.5   How do labour markets influence performance management design?

Labour markets may offer tailwinds or headwinds to an organization's implementation of its performance management system. For example, tight labour markets will result in greater inter-firm competition for employees and will likely require organizations to be more generous in the employee benefits their human resource systems provide. Because labour markets are based around specific employee skill sets (IT, accounting, HR, medicine, law, etc.), labour market shortages and surpluses refer to particular employee groupings. Knowing the overall unemployment rate is not nearly as important as knowing what is happening in the relevant labour market.

14.6 What is growth need strength? Provide examples of organizational settings where it is likely to differ. How is its presence associated with performance management design?

Growth need strength (GNS) is defined as an individual's desire for challenge. Employees with high GNS crave challenge, and those with low GNS are creatures of habit who actively avoid change and challenge. Work settings that are characterized by low innovation are likely not to need workers with high GNS. An example of such a setting would be the industrial laundry services industry. In contrast, a company that prides itself on innovation, for example, Apple, would want workers with high GNS. When workers have low GNS, performance management designs should not include attempts to decentralize or encourage employee participation, for workers will resist these efforts. Conversely, high GNS workers will expect, and even demand, decision-making responsibility around the design and execution of their work. In other words, organizations will want to ensure high levels of decentralization for their high GNS employees.

CHAPTER 15

15.1 How does this book's model of performance management represent a strong-holistic model?

The book's model is holistic in its attempt to bring together four main fields of study, each of which offers insights into the theory and practice of performance management. These four fields are management accounting, strategic management, organizational behaviour, and organizational theory. The model is strongly holistic in its fuller inclusion of the performance management influences that each of these fields discusses. For example, organizational culture is often marginalized or neglected in other performance management models, whereas in the present model it is shown as one of the three main levers of employee influence.

15.2 How does this book's performance management model compare to Ferreira and Otley's (2009) and Malmi and Brown's models?

In contrast to the Ferreira and Otley (2009) model, this book's model gives explicit recognition to human resource systems and specifically designates organizational culture as its own, direct lever of employee influence. The closest Ferreira and Otley (2009: 278) come to discussing human resource systems is when they write, "Targets [are] generally set centrally by the board of directors after consultation with human resources, finance, and planning and control managers." Meanwhile, Ferreira and Otley (2009: 267) essentially ignore organizational culture, referring to it as "… a notable contextual variable."

Unlike Malmi and Brown's model, this book's model divides organizational culture from national culture. As noted in the book, organizational culture serves as a powerful lever of performance management. In contrast, national culture is an external contingent factor that scholars and practitioners must be aware of when studying and designing performance management systems. As a further contrast to the Malmi and Brown model, this book's model eschews relegating human resource systems to an insignificant or ancillary role. Heeding the call of organizational scholars, who argue that human resource systems play a key role in encouraging high employee commitment, motivation, and performance, this book's model offers prominent coverage of human resource systems under its organizational systems processes, and procedures lever of influence.

15.3 How does this book's performance management model feature both constraining and enabling influences on employees? Give examples of these constraining and enabling influences for each of the three performance management levers.

This book's three levers of influence are capable of both encouraging and constraining employee behaviour. Budgets, a component of the organizational systems processes, and procedures lever of influence, offers employees authority for undertaking certain activities. For example, the budget may contain a line item relating to overtime work. Budgets will also serve to constrain behaviour, for employees are constrained by the budget in terms of what they can incur expenses on. In particular, a common refrain is: if it is not in the budget, then you are not allowed to do it. Organizational structures also exert an encouraging and constraining role. As an example, organizational charts indicate what functional area the employee is meant to operate in and has responsibility over. The employee may be a supervisor in a production department and is responsible for managing 50 production employees. This supervisor is not, however, authorized to act on behalf of the organization on matters outside their jurisdiction. For example, legal decisions lie with the legal department, HR decisions with the HR department, and so forth. Organizational culture comprises the broad set of tacitly understood rules by which organizational members agree to be governed. These tacit rules will encourage certain behaviour (perhaps working long hours) and constrain/discourage other behaviour (perhaps taking on high-risk projects).

15.4 What are some of the future performance management research opportunities awaiting today's scholars?

Future research is needed in two main areas. First, most of the research to date has focused on formal control systems. Much less study has been directed at informal control systems. Future research needs to redress this imbalance, and hopefully, this book's model can serve as the theoretical foundation from which these research studies can be built.

A second area in which more research is needed is on the encouragement of action, and not simply the discouragement of action, that performance management provides. Performance management systems certainly have controlling/constraining elements to them. But they also comprise systems that encourage and even inspire action. Not only should good/supportive organizational cultures be capable of doing both, but so too should good/supportive organizational structures and organizational systems, processes, and procedures.

Company index

Subject index

Printed in the United States
by Baker & Taylor Publisher Services

Printed in the United States
by Baker & Taylor Publisher Services